**WRITING
IN PUBLIC RELATIONS
PRACTICE**

FORM & STYLE

**WRITING
IN PUBLIC RELATIONS
PRACTICE**

FORM & STYLE

Doug Newsom
Texas Christian University

Tom Siegfried
Texas Christian University

Wadsworth Publishing Company
Belmont, California
A Division of Wadsworth, Inc.

Senior Editor: Rebecca Hayden
Production Editor: Carolyn Tanner
Designer: Joe di Chiarro
Copy Editor: Carol Dondrea
Technical Illustrator: Larry Jansen

© 1981 by Wadsworth, Inc. All rights reserved. No part of this book may be reproduced, stored in a retrieval system, or transcribed, in any form or by any means, electronic, mechanical, photocopying, recording, or otherwise, without the prior written permission of the publisher, Wadsworth Publishing Company, Belmont, California 94002, a division of Wadsworth, Inc.

Credits: p. 364

Cover photograph by George Fry III

Printed in the United States of America

2   3   4   5   6   7   8   9   10—85   84   83   82

Library of Congress Cataloging in Publication Data

Newsom, Doug.
  Writing in public relations practice.

  Includes index.
  1. Public relations. 2. Persuasion (Psychology)
3. Public relations—Authorship. I. Siegfried, Tom, joint author. II. Title.
HM263.N493   659.2   80-21260
ISBN 0-534-00884-4

Dedicated to
our students' employers,
who have implored us:
"Please, teach them to write!"

PREFACE

Students taught that PR is a management function sometimes find that the realities of PR practice are dismaying. PR practitioners are expected to have a ready command of communication skills, and are expected to write, not just a little, but a lot—and do so effectively. As if this were not enough, they are also expected to fathom easily the mysteries of all media.

Entry-level positions in PR ask a great deal of the beginner, particularly in writing. This book will introduce you as PR students to the variety of writing tasks expected of you and help you develop PR writing skills.

Our introductory chapter examines the role of writing in PR practice and the importance of communicating successfully to all audiences. Chapter 2 discusses the use of persuasion in the communication process. It considers how opinion is formed and changed and sets forth the steps in persuasion. The chapter also points out the ethical considerations in persuasion.

Underscoring the ethics discussion is research, the subject of Chapter 3. A good PR practitioner *knows all* the available facts in the situation, not just those favorable to one side. Doing research—fact finding—is a primary task. It is the cornerstone for communication in any PR situation.

The second section of the text—Part Two—deals first with problems all writers have, and then with problems specific to PR writers. PR writers work with all kinds of people. They often work with people who have something to say, and know they need to communicate with audiences, but don't know how to present the information. They work with others who have something to say but don't know they need to communicate or how to present their information. Some think they have something to say, but don't. Still others think they know how to present their information, but don't. Mix and match these any way you wish and you'll arrive at some of the typical PR situations a practitioner can face. An essential part of communicating is simplifying the complex and presenting information in a form that both respects the language and takes advantage of its flexibility. We deal with these aspects of PR writing in Chapters 4, 5, and 6.

In considering the audiences for PR writing, the practitioner makes an initial division between general audiences and specialized ones. General audiences are what we sometimes call "the public." To communicate with them, we use news releases for print media, writing of many different types for broadcast media, and advertising copy as well as speeches and scripts for slide presentations and films. Chapters 7 through 10 cover these topics (Part Three).

Writing for internal audiences—those who share the institutional image and other special audiences—involves preparing copy for specialized media such as annual reports, institutional magazines and employee publications, newsletters and brochures, backgrounders, and position papers plus memos and letters. We talk about this kind of PR writing in Chapters 11 through 15 (Part Four).

The final section—Part Five—consists of a project we hope will stimulate you to try all types of PR writing to see how all of it fits together.

We are grateful to reviewers of our early material for the guidance they gave us for this book: Stephen H. Baer at the University of Southern California, Bill L. Baxter at the University of Oklahoma, Norman R. Nager of California State University at Fullerton, Harold C. Shaver from Kansas State University, and Nancy M. Somerick at the University of Akron.

For patience and help in reviewing the completed manuscript we are indebted to: Randall L. Murray at California Polytechnic State University at San Luis Obispo, Dennis L. Wilcox at San Jose State University, and, again, to Dr. Baxter and Dr. Somerick.

Our special appreciation needs to be expressed to senior editor Rebecca Hayden whose creative suggestions we incorporated, to developmental editor Autumn Stanley whose insistence that we clarify kept us practicing what we preach, and to Chris Beckelhymer Siegfried, who proofed, typed, and criticized the effort through to production.

DN & TS

CONTENTS

PREFACE **vi**

LIST OF EXAMPLES, FIGURES AND TABLES **xiv**

PART ONE WRITING AND PR 1

CHAPTER 1 PUBLIC RELATIONS AND THE WRITER **2**

   Defining Public Relations **3**
   Publics, Channels and the Role of the Writer **5**
   Conclusion **10**
   Selected Bibliography **11**

CHAPTER 2 PERSUASION **12**

   Opinion Formation and Change **13**
   The Nature of Persuasion **15**
   Persuasion and Communication **19**
   Conclusion **26**
   Selected Bibliography **27**

CHAPTER 3 RESEARCH **28**

   Research in PR **28**
   Sources for PR Writers and Researchers **30**
   Skepticism—A Requisite for All Research **35**
   Conclusion **40**
   Selected Bibliography **40**

PART ONE EXERCISES **41**

PART TWO   WRITING PRINCIPLES   45

CHAPTER 4   WRITING FOR CLARITY AND INTEREST   **46**

  Message, Audience, Medium   **46**
  Clarity and Interest: Elements of Style   **48**
  Conclusion   **55**
  Selected Bibliography   **56**

CHAPTER 5   SIMPLIFYING THE COMPLEX   **57**

  Know Your Subject   **58**
  Plain English   **60**
  One Step at a Time   **63**
  Make the Central Points Clear   **64**
  Explain the Unfamiliar with the Familiar   **65**
  Conclusion   **67**
  Selected Bibliography   **68**

CHAPTER 6   GRAMMAR, SPELLING, PUNCTUATION   **69**

  Ambiguity and Grammar   **70**
  Myths of Grammar   **72**
  Using Usage Manuals   **73**
  Spelling   **76**
  Punctuation   **78**
  Conclusion   **80**
  Selected Bibliography   **81**

PART TWO EXERCISES   **82**

PART THREE   WRITING FOR GENERAL AUDIENCES   87

CHAPTER 7   NEWS RELEASES FOR PRINT MEDIA   **88**

  News   **88**
  Writing News Releases   **91**
  Preparing and Delivering News Releases   **112**
  Conclusion   **118**
  Selected Bibliography   **119**

CHAPTER 8   BROADCAST WRITING: NEWS AND FEATURES   **120**

  Facts, Sights and Sounds   **120**
  News Releases   **127**
  Talk Shows   **128**
  Mini-Docs   **128**
  Broadcast Writing Style   **135**
  Conclusion   **150**
  Selected Bibliography   **150**

CHAPTER 9   ADVERTISING COPY   **151**

   Advertising As a Persuasive Force   **151**
   Broadcast Advertising   **154**
   Advertising in the Print Media   **179**
   Conclusion   **189**
   Selected Bibliography   **199**

CHAPTER 10   SPEECHES AND SCRIPTS   **200**

   Speeches   **201**
   Scripts   **204**
   Conclusion   **207**
   Selected Bibliography   **207**

PART THREE EXERCISES   **218**

PART FOUR   WRITING FOR SPECIAL AUDIENCES   **221**

CHAPTER 11   ANNUAL REPORTS   **222**

   Clarity Versus Accuracy   **222**
   Planning the Annual Report   **225**
   Writing the Report   **227**
   Conclusion   **238**
   Selected Bibliography   **238**

CHAPTER 12   MAGAZINES AND EMPLOYEE PUBLICATIONS   **240**

   Topics   **240**
   Research   **242**
   Writing   **244**
   Employee Publications   **248**
   Conclusion   **250**
   Selected Bibliography   **250**

CHAPTER 13   NEWSLETTERS AND BROCHURES   **251**

   Newsletters   **251**
   Brochures   **258**
   Designing Layouts and Writing Copy to Fit   **262**
   Conclusion   **264**

CHAPTER 14   BACKGROUNDERS AND POSITION PAPERS   **265**

   Backgrounders   **266**
   Position Papers   **275**
   Format   **277**
   Conclusion   **278**
   Selected Bibliography   **278**

CHAPTER 15   MEMOS AND LETTERS/REPORTS AND PROPOSALS   **281**

   Similarities   **281**
   Differences   **282**
   Memos   **283**
   Letters   **285**
   Reports and Proposals   **299**
   Conclusion   **302**

PART FOUR EXERCISES   **303**

PART FIVE   WRITING FOR PR—A PROJECT   305

   Project Tasks 1–13   **306–309**
   Project Background Information 1–3   **309–325**

APPENDICES   333

APPENDIX A   READABILITY FORMULAS   **334**

   Flesch   **334**
   Gunning   **335**
   Dale-Chall   **335**
   Other Readability Tests   **336**

APPENDIX B   FINANCIAL REPORTING REQUIREMENTS   **338**

APPENDIX C   COPYFITTING   **353**

   Sizing Copy   **353**
   Sample Copyfitting Problems   **354**

APPENDIX D   AP STYLE GUIDELINES   **356**

   Abbreviations   **356**
   Capitalization   **356**
   Numbers   **357**
   Punctuation   **357**
   Spelling   **357**

INDEX   **358**

CREDITS   **364**

LIST OF EXAMPLES, FIGURES, & TABLES

1-1 (figure): A Person—A Member of Many Publics Simultaneously   6
1-2 (figure): Internal and External PR   8
2-1 (figure): The Basic Process of Attitude Formation   14
2-2 (figure): Maslow's Hierarchy of Needs   17
3-1 (table): Checklist for Interviewing   33
3-2 (example): Questionnaires   36
4-1 (table): Writing Checklist   55
5-1 (example): Tomatoes Are Easier to Understand   66
5-2 (table): Simplifying the Complex—Checklist   67
6-1 (table): Commonly Confused Words   74
7-1 (example): News Releases   92
7-2 (example): DFW Airport Release   97
7-3 (example): DHR Release   102
7-4 (example): A Response Release   108
7-5 (example): Arlington C of C Release   110
7-6 (example): Unusual Opportunities   113
7-7 (example): Computerized News Releases   116
7-8 (table): News Release Checklist   118
8-1 (example): Fact Sheet and News Release   122
8-2 (example): TV and Radio and Print Releases   129
8-3 (example): Mini-Doc Outline   134
8-4 (example): Media Kit Sample   137
8-5 (example): Wire Stories: Broadcast and Newspaper Versions   146
8-6 (example): First Lead on the Breaking Story in Example 8-5   148
8-7 (example): Print Media Versions: Abbreviated and Expanded   149
9-1 (example): Set-up of Commercial Scripts   158
9-2 (example): The Beginnings of a Storyboard   166
9-3 (example): Television Commercial   168
9-4 (example): Writing Radio Scripts with Special Effects   169

9-5 (example): PSA Spot Announcements **173**
9-6 (example): Creativity Lures Customers **180**
9-7 (example): Billboard Advertising **186**
9-8 (example): Identity and Advocacy Advertising **190**
10-1 (example): Excerpt from Slide Show Script **208**
10-2 (example): Excerpt from Film Script **210**
11-1 (example): Chief Executive's Letter, Exxon Corporation 1974 Annual Report **230**
11-2 (example): The 1979 Annual Report of Armstrong World Industries, Inc. **232**
11-3 (table): Annual Report Questionnaire for Executives **236**
11-4 (table): Annual Report Timetable **237**
12-1 (table): Magazine Article Writing Checklist **249**
13-1 (example): Cub Scout Newsletter **253**
13-2 (example): PR Agency Newsletter **254**
13-3 (example): Bank Newsletter **255**
13-4 (example): A Congressman's Newsletter **256**
13-5 (example): Informational Brochure **260**
14-1 (example): Position Paper on the Licensing of Lay Midwives **268**
14-2 (example): Backgrounder Formats **279**
15-1 (example): An Action Memo: PR Planning Memo **286**
15-2 (example): Thank You Letter **295**
15-3 (example): Proclamation **296**

**WRITING
IN PUBLIC RELATIONS
PRACTICE**

FORM & STYLE

P A R T

O N E

WRITING AND PR

Most public relations jobs, particularly entry-level positions, require a great deal of writing—for all media. PR writers need to be skilled in fact finding and knowledgeable in the art of persuasion.

1

PUBLIC RELATIONS AND THE WRITER

What is public relations? Some people think public relations is mostly writing, in the form of news releases or advertising. Others think it is smiling at your customers and asking how the family is doing. Some business executives assume all you need for good PR is a good product and a money-back guarantee. Others think the goal of PR is getting the company name in the papers (or keeping it out of the papers) as much as possible.

Unfortunately, all of these conceptions of public relations are misconceptions. Much of the confusion arises because the term *public relations* has two senses—a literal sense and a professional sense. In the literal sense of "relating to the public," good public relations is just getting along with people. It involves the ways an organization's operations and policies affect people—the face-to-face interaction of employees with customers or clients and the organization's participation in the affairs of the community.

Good public relations in the literal sense is essential to the overall public relations effort for any organization. But it is not enough. Good policies and good performance are worth little if people don't understand the policies and don't know about the performance. Achieving this understanding and knowledge is the task of public relations in the professional sense.

Public relations in the professional sense involves communication skills, expertise in dealing with the media, and knowledge of mass communications, the dynamics of public opinion, and the principles of persuasion. At the heart of professional public relations is communication—in particular, writing.

Yet professional public relations is more than writing. It is not simply preparing publicity releases or writing advertising copy. Professional public relations is an art and a science that involves analysis and judgment, and counseling and planning—in addition to writing. In this chapter we'll try to clarify the nature of PR (in the professional sense) and examine the writer's role in it.

CHAPTER 1
PUBLIC RELATIONS
AND THE WRITER

DEFINING PUBLIC RELATIONS

Even people who practice public relations don't all agree on just what PR is. Each practitioner probably has a slightly different definition, depending on his or her particular PR experience. Definitions have been composed, though, that express the meaning of PR to the satisfaction of most professionals. One of the latest definitions was adopted in 1978 at Mexico City during the First World Assembly of Public Relations Associations and the First World Forum of Public Relations:

> Public relations practice is the art and science of analyzing trends, predicting their consequences, counseling organization leaders, and implementing planned programs of action which will serve both the organization's and the public interest.

It's a broad definition, but it's a useful one. By examining it more closely we can get a better understanding of what PR is and where the writer fits in.

Analyzing, Predicting, Counseling

The central part of this definition of PR outlines the main roles of the professional public relations person: "analyzing trends, predicting their consequences, counseling organization leaders."

Doing this job well requires a broad educational background, expertise in many areas, and most of all, good judgment. Unlike the corporate attorney or accountant, the PR practitioner has no body of laws or procedures that prescribes behavior under given circumstances. Instead, the public relations person must know human behavior and combine that knowledge with specific information about people within the institution and people the institution deals with. For example, the PR director for a bank must consider the views of bank officers and bank employees, as well as the views of customers, the community, legislators and government regulatory agencies. The PR person for the local school district must be aware of the feelings of students, parents, voters and the regional accrediting agency. Any institution has many audiences, and the PR director must be able to advise management about the possible impact on those audiences of various policies and actions.

In addition to analyzing audiences and counseling management on the effects of policy, the PR person must be alert for signs of change. The right policy today will not necessarily be the right policy tomorrow. People's attitudes and opinions evolve, and the composition of the audience changes. The capable PR person notes trends in public opinion and predicts the consequences of such trends for the institution.

The PR director usually also serves as spokesperson for the organization and oversees the entire public relations program. The mature

PR person at the top of the department spends little time on basic PR techniques like writing. The basics are handled by entry-level people, the staff writers.

Frank Wylie, a former president of the Public Relations Society of America, describes the division of PR labor this way. Mature public relations people are likely to spend 10 percent of their time with techniques, 40 percent with administration and 50 percent with analysis and judgment. At entry level it's 50 percent techniques, 5 percent judgment, and 45 percent "running like hell."[1]

Advertising, Publicity and PR

Much of the "running like hell" is done to carry out those "planned programs" of action mentioned in the definition of PR. These programs are the most visible part of public relations practice. Since they include publicity, and sometimes advertising, many people confuse public relations with publicity or advertising.

For that matter, advertising and publicity are themselves often confused. *Advertising* is media time or space purchased to display a message prepared (or approved) by the purchaser. The content of an ad is controlled by the buyer of the time or space. *Publicity* is information supplied to a news medium without cost. The decision to use that information and its final form are controlled by the medium.

People hired for public relations jobs often help design and write copy for ads, but advertising is usually a separate program, either a complement to the public relations program or subordinate to it. Ads for products and services (marketing-type advertising) are almost always handled exclusively by advertising copywriters. Another type of advertising—image, identity or institutional advertising—may be written by someone in a PR department. Such ads are usually message-oriented rather than sales-oriented. They are used either to build an organization's image or communicate views on some public issue.

Most business executives understand the difference between advertising and publicity, but many still think publicity is synonymous with public relations. It's true that publicity is usually handled by PR people, but public relations involves a much wider spectrum of responsibility, including policy making. A publicist merely disseminates information. A public relations person, as we discussed, is involved in the analysis, counseling and planning that precede the dissemination of information. Or, as PR authority Edward L. Bernays says, "Publicity is a one-way street; public relations is a two-way street."[2]

The Two-Way Street

The last part of the Mexico City definition of PR speaks of serving "both the organization's and the public interest." Publicists who simply transmit their organization's views to the media are not likely to serve the public interest. As Bernays says:[3]

> Public relations is not a one-way street in which leadership manipulates the public and public opinion. It is a two-way street in which leadership and the public find integration with each other and in which objectives and goals are predicated on a coincidence of public and private interest.

This means that the task of PR people is not simply communicating management's view to the public. The task also involves communicating the views of the public to management. The objectives of an institution and its PR program must be designed with the needs and desires of the public clearly in mind.

Going one way, the PR person analyzes public opinion and the needs of the community, and opens channels of communication that allow such information to flow into the institution. Using this information, the PR person advises management on the policies that are likely to be of mutual benefit to the institution and the public—or at least acceptable to the public, if not beneficial.

Then—going the other way down the PR street—the PR person opens channels of communication that reach out from the institution to the public. These channels are used to interpret the institution's policies and actions to its various audiences. Communication in this direction is largely the responsibility of the PR writer.

PUBLICS, CHANNELS AND THE ROLE OF THE WRITER

It is a simple thing to say that the task of PR writers is communicating with the public. But in practice there is nothing simple about it. It's not as though there is one single "public" to write for. Rarely is a PR message important to everybody in the "public."

If an oil company wants to say it's not withholding gasoline, it will likely aim its message at car owners, government agencies and Congress; it won't be concerned with middle-school students. Those students might be a very important audience, though, for the amusement park advertising its new roller coaster ride. A welfare agency announcing new food stamp rules is most interested in getting the message to low-income families. A mayor raising money to help a downtown renovation project is likely to appeal to the city's business leaders.

Car owners, legislators, students, business leaders—all are examples of publics. A *public* is any group of people tied together by some common factor. And as public relations writers soon discover, there are many, many such groups. As some PR people say, the "public" in public relations really should be "publics."

The Public in Public Relations

In his book *The Mass Media,* Stanford professor Bill Rivers describes the endless variety of publics in this way:[4]

> There are as many publics as there are groups with varying levels of income, education, taste, and civic awareness; as many as there are groups with different political allegiances, different religious loyalties, and so on. What concerns and convinces one public may seem trivial to another.
>
> Furthermore, the definition of each public is never static; it changes as the issues change. For example, when California is voting for a governor, a Los Angeles college student becomes one member of a large and diverse public that includes a San Francisco stevedore and excludes a college professor at the University of Maine. But, when higher education in the United States is at issue, the college student is one member of a public that includes the professor but excludes the stevedore—except that the stevedore's working partner may have a daughter who attends the University of Idaho . . . and so on in bewildering variety.

1-1 A PERSON—A MEMBER OF MANY PUBLICS SIMULTANEOUSLY

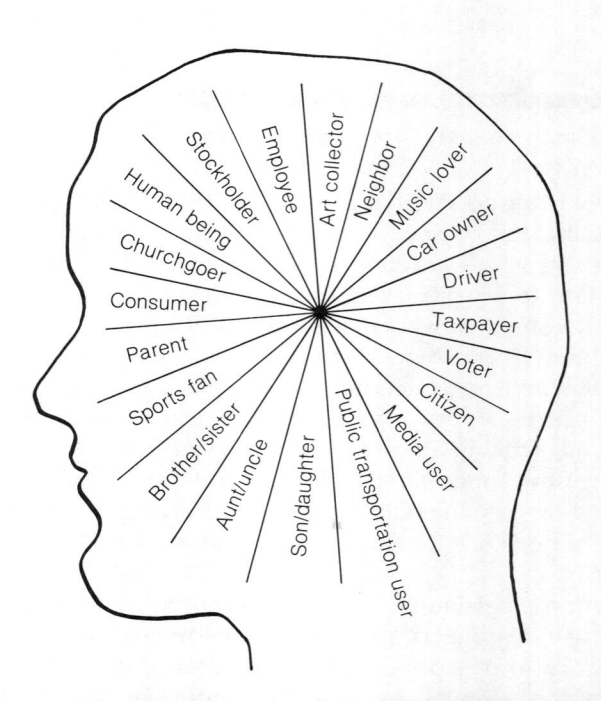

Obviously, each one of us belongs to many different publics (see Figure 1-1). If you're a student, you're naturally a member of a public important to the university or college you attend. If you're about to graduate, you belong to a public important to prospective employers in the community. If you've just been married, you're part of a public important to real estate firms eager to sell you a house. If you belong to the local chapter of the Sierra Club, you're part of a public important to politicians and energy companies.

Just as each individual belongs to many publics, each institution must communicate with many publics—from customers and suppliers to employees and stockholders. A PR writer for a university must write for faculty, students, administrators, alumni, financial benefactors, community leaders, legislators and football fans. The PR writer for a political candidate tailors messages to fund raisers, voters, reporters and precinct workers.

The variety of publics is so vast that PR people often find it useful to divide the publics they deal with into two broad classes: internal and external. *Internal* publics are groups within the organization (like employees or the board of directors). *External* publics are groups outside the organization (like the media, your company's customers, or the state legislature). The distinction between the two is not always clearcut; stockholders, for example, though essentially an external public, can have close ties to the institution. (Publics and the media used to reach them are suggested in Example 1-2.)

Target Audiences

On any one project it is impossible to direct attention equally to all publics. Therefore, PR people must select audiences that are most important for the communication effort. They may include the group that a new policy will affect the most, or the groups whose opinions are especially important. In any event, the groups considered most important for a communication effort are called the *target audiences*.

How do PR people select target audiences? Only by knowing the characteristics of the members of the various publics. They discover these characteristics through advance research, which is essential. PR people must, for example, collect certain statistical data about members of their publics—facts like their age and sex, where they live, how they make a living, the amount of money they earn, their educational level and such. Such statistics about groups are called *demographics*. Almost any survey form you fill out has places for such information.

But demographic information alone does not tell writers all they need to know about a public. Statistics like age, sex and income are not useful in predicting whether a person would be likely to subscribe to the magazine *Dog World*, for example. Dog lovers come in all ages, both sexes, and most income groups, groups that may seem totally unrelated if judged by demographics alone.

1-2 INTERNAL AND EXTERNAL PR

	INTERNAL	EXTERNAL	
		Direct	Indirect
PUBLICS	Management (top and middle) Staff and employees (union and employee organizations—non-union) Stockholders Directors	(Marketing communications) Customers Sales representatives Traders and distributors Suppliers Competitors	(Institutional communications) Potential customers Potential investors (stockholders) Financial community Special community of institution Government (local, state, federal) Community (environmental)
MEDIA	Personal (person to person/person to group) Audio/visual (specialized media: films, slides, videotape, closed circuit TV) Publications (specialized media: books, magazines, newspapers, newsletters) Direct mail Exhibits (including posters and bulletin board materials internally displayed as well as personalized items such as pins, awards, etc.)	Personal (person to person/person to group) Audio/visual (films, slides, videotape, mass media, specialized media available to external audiences such as externally distributed slide presentations, etc.) Publications (mass and specialized, including controlled and uncontrolled publicity as well as institutional and commercial advertising) Direct mail (personalized, institutional and sales promotion) Exhibits (mass and specialized externally displayed and product packaging, graphics, including point of sale promotions)	

In fact, what PR people call *psychographics* is frequently more important to the PR writer than demographics. Psychographics classifies people by what they think, how they behave, and what they think, as well as by what their interests are, such as in dogs. Psychographic information is not merely helpful to the PR writer—it is often necessary. Consider the public relations director for a university's alumni association who was responsible for the magazine distributed to all members. In editing the magazine she had a feeling she didn't know who was "out there." With some dismay she said, "How can I possibly appeal to an 80-year-old graduate of the engineering school and a 22-year-old sociologist?" So she had a research study done that revealed a psychographic pattern identifying the common elements that bound all the alumni to the institution. This information showed what sort of articles would interest alumni. The editor was then able to make much more informed decisions—and she felt a great deal more comfortable in doing so.

Channels

To reach different publics, the PR writer must choose channels of communication carefully. To get the message across, the channel must be one that the target audience will receive and believe. For example, the amusement park that wants middle-school students to try its new ride would be foolish to run an ad in *Harper's* magazine. Few middle-school students even know that *Harper's* exists. They would not receive a message placed in that medium. But they do listen to radio and watch TV, so those are the channels the amusement park would probably use.

The channel must also be appropriate for the message. Radio is not a good channel for conveying messages on complex subjects like a university's endowment. Such subjects are better suited to a magazine, a channel that readers can spend time with. Radio, though poorly suited for discussing endowments, works just fine for telling students the dates for fall registration.

Channels through which PR people reach their publics are called "media." Each medium has characteristics that make it suitable to send a particular message to a particular audience at a particular time.

When communication media are mentioned, you are likely to think of publications and audiovisuals. Publications may be books, magazines, newspapers, newsletters or reports. Audiovisuals may be films, videotape, slides or television—mass or closed circuit. But publications and audiovisuals aren't the only channels of communication. People may be channels, as in person-to-person contact or person-to-group communication such as speeches or meetings. Another channel is direct mail of personalized letters or institutional or promotional pieces. Exhibits are another channel. They encompass anything from a tradeshow display to a campaign button.

Specialized Media Media designed for a particular audience are called *specialized*, to distinguish them from media for general audiences. Specialized media include the internal publications that institutions produce to communicate with employees, staff, management and others close to the institution, like directors and stockholders. Also included in specialized media are audiovisuals intended for internal use only, such as closed-circuit television and training films. Specialized media are usually controlled by the institution using them.

Mass Media The mass media include magazines, books, newspapers, radio and television. Since the circulation or audience of these media is not controlled by the institution, mass media are usually used for communication with external publics. PR writers using mass media to reach general audiences must remember, however, that such media are seen by internal publics as well. For example, some women airline employees complained about an advertising campaign they said not only projected the female flight crew as sex objects but also sounded sexually suggestive. French police did not like billboards portraying them as "helpful" rather than as crime fighters facing danger.

Role of the Writer

PR writers must be knowledgeable not only about publics and channels, but about all aspects of their institution as well. The PR writer for a social work agency must understand welfare eligibility rules and federal funding guidelines. A writer for the highway department must know about everything from road-building materials to traffic laws. PR writers must know enough about the financial aspects of a business to prepare the right message for security analysts and to develop an annual report that the stockholders can read and the auditors will approve.

In addition to a broad knowledge of their company's business, PR writers must have the ability to research specific subjects to determine what's important and what isn't. They must be able to borrow ideas from other fields—psychology, social psychology, sociology and political science, for example—to help put that research in perspective. PR writers must be alert to changing patterns of thought and behavior in society and must fully comprehend the issues of the day.

Finally, and most important of all, the PR writer must be an expert in communication. If you want to be a PR writer, you must know how to write well and write persuasively. You must know the principles of good writing and be familiar with the vast body of scientific research on communication and persuasion. Your goal is to be an efficient, effective communicator. No matter what messages you communicate, what audiences you communicate with, or what media you use to reach those audiences, you have to know what words will work and why. You are critical to the PR function.

Preparing you to do these things is what this book is all about.

CONCLUSION

Professional public relations people must be good communicators in all media. Fundamental to this skill is the ability to express ideas simply, clearly and directly. Entry-level PR positions are mostly writing—writing in a variety of styles for many different media, with many different audiences in mind. This book is devoted to helping you master those skills.

NOTES

[1] Frank Wylie, "The New Professionals," speech to the First National Student Conference, Public Relations Student Society of America, Dayton, Ohio, 24 October 1976. Published by Chrysler Corporation, p. 5.

[2] Edward L. Bernays, *Public Relations* (Norman: University of Oklahoma Press, 1952), p. 5.

[3] Ibid., p. 83.

[4] William L. Rivers, *The Mass Media* (New York: Harper and Row, 1975), p. 22.

SELECTED BIBLIOGRAPHY

Edward L. Bernays, *Public Relations* (Norman: University of Oklahoma Press, 1952).

Allen H. Center, "Canvassing the Calling," *Public Relations Journal* 33 (November 1977): 41.

Commission on Public Relations Education, "A Design for Public Relations Education," pamphlet distributed in 1975, published by the Public Relations Society of America and the Public Relations Division of the Association for Education in Journalism through the Foundation for Public Relations Research and Education.

D. Newsom and A. Scott, *This Is PR* (Belmont, Calif.: Wadsworth, 1976).

Frank W. Wylie, "Public Relations: A Frontier Profession," reprint of speech by Wylie, Public Relations Director U.S. Automotive Sales, Chrysler Corporation, to the First National Student Conference, Public Relations Student Society of America, Dayton, Ohio, October 24, 1976; published by Chrysler Corporation.

2

PERSUASION

A nuclear engineer especially good at explaining technical matters once gave a talk to a civic club in a small Texas town. He used dozens of slides and charts and graphs to describe the operation of nuclear power plants and explain how safe they were.

At the end of his talk an elderly lady thanked the engineer for his presentation. "I didn't understand anything you said," she told him, "but I agree with you a hundred percent."

In other words, people don't always form their opinions on the basis of information and logic. Sometimes, as in this example, information and logic play almost no part at all. At most other times, people do rely on information and logic in forming their opinions, but only to a degree. Other elements always come into play. Persuading people to a certain point of view has emotional as well as rational aspects.

Much of the writing you will do as a PR person is aimed at persuading a given audience to a given viewpoint. To be most effective, you need to have some idea of what arguments—factual and emotional—will work best with your audience. Common sense can give you some clues, but you'll do a much better job if you know something about the science of persuasion. Common sense is no substitute for what decades of research have discovered about how and why people form their opinions. As PR pioneer Edward L. Bernays puts it, "Like Columbus, you can sail west and reach new land by accident. But if you have charts, you can do better; you can arrive at a destination decided upon in advance."[1]

When engineers design bridges or buildings, Bernays points out, they apply a knowledge of physics and chemistry and other sciences. Doctors treat patients using a knowledge of the laboratory findings of biochemists and medical researchers. In the same way, PR people should apply the relevant findings of social sciences like psychology, sociology and communication when they embark on a persuasion effort.

Knowledge of these disciplines will help the PR writer answer some of the many questions that come up time and again in persuasive writing. Should you give both sides of the story or only your side? If you give both, which side should you give first? Should you draw an explicit conclusion or is it better to let the audience figure it out for themselves? Which should you give first, the good news or the bad news?

Other questions come up again and again, too. How effective are fear techniques? Should you make a point once or repeat it several times to make sure it sinks in? Which work better: emotional arguments or rational arguments? These are the sorts of questions that social scientific research can help you answer.

Of course, research findings can only *help* to answer these questions. Research results can be valuable guides in planning persuasive communication, but they are not laws of nature. In many cases, the findings collected so far are not conclusive. At times, you have to rely on personal experience and knowledge of the audience.

Nevertheless, social science has found out a lot about the nature of persuasion, and it would be foolish not to put that knowledge to use. Research data is better than top-of-the-head speculation about the how and why of opinion formation.

OPINION FORMATION AND CHANGE

The first thing you need to know as a persuasive writer is that you are not likely to change many minds. The reason for this is simple. The few minutes a person gives to read your prose is not likely to change attitudes built up over a lifetime. However, if you're going to make any headway at all, you need to know something about what attitudes and opinions are and how they form.

Attitudes and Opinions

Some authorities see no need to distinguish between attitudes and opinions. But to understand persuasion it is useful to define an "opinion" as a specific (usually verbal) *application* of an attitude to a given object or issue. For example, people who have a general attitude against change are likely to express a negative opinion about replacing their local mayor with a city manager. Attitudes and opinions are closely linked, however, so we can discuss their formation together.

Models of Attitude Formation

Many different models have been devised to illustrate how attitudes form. But all these models have many elements in common. Thus, if we concentrate on the main points, it will be enough for us to look at just one of them. M. Brewster Smith's "map" of attitude formation was designed as a tool for studying political attitudes, but its main parts apply to attitude formation in general. Figure 2–1 is an adaptation of Smith's more elaborate diagram. It's easy to see that attitude formation is a complex process.

2-1 THE BASIC PROCESS OF ATTITUDE FORMATION

```
HISTORICAL SETTING                                          →IMMEDIATE SITUATION
  Historical, economic, political
  and societal determinants
  of issue characteristics,
  social norms, personality
         ↓
SOCIAL ENVIRONMENT      →  PERSONALITY PROCESSES          ENGAGED     POLITICAL
  Issue characteristics     AND PREDISPOSITIONS           ATTITUDES   BEHAVIOR
  Norms of important social   Bases of attitudes    Attitudes
  groups                      Issue appraisal       Attitudes toward
COMMUNICATION--→Socially available information    Mediation of        the issue:
  Life situations and           relationships        Stereotypes
  socialization experiences   Ego defense            Dispositions
                              Traits                 Action or policy
                                Cognitive              orientations
                                Temperamental        Other attitudes
                                Behavioral             engaged
                                                     Other attitudes
                                                       disengaged
```

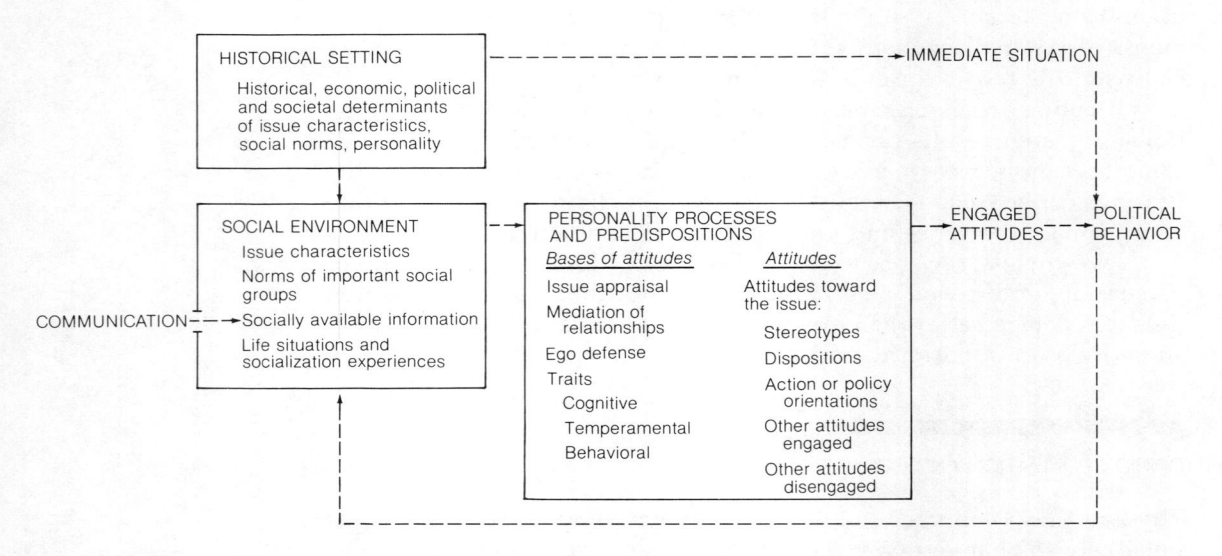

Adapted from "A Map for the Analysis of Personality and Politics," M. Brewster Smith (1968). Used by permission.

To begin with, an individual's historical setting plays an important role. Where was the person born, where did he or she grow up? What were the social and economic conditions of the day? These factors help to shape personality. Historical factors also shape the issues that persuasive writers deal with.

All of these historical considerations are part of the social environment in which communication and persuasion take place. Individuals belong to groups with social norms that affect their opinions. A person's life situation and life experiences also play a large part in attitude formation. And, naturally, the characteristics of the issue at hand are important.

One other major element of the social environment influences attitude—available information. Here is the one door open to the persuasive writer. The writer has no power to change a person's history or the norms of social groups. And rarely can a persuader expect to change someone's life situation or provide a significant new experience. But a writer can hope to add to the amount of information available for forming attitudes.

On the one hand, the limits of this situation are not very encouraging. On the other hand, the information door does let you have some effect on how an individual will appraise an issue. To use this door most effectively, though, you need to understand the nature of persuasion.

THE NATURE OF PERSUASION

Persuasion can be seen as a learning process, or a "power" process (where one forces new views on another), or simply as an emotional process. No single view of persuasion is likely to be adequate since, as we've seen, the formation of attitudes is a complex process. But we can outline some aspects of the persuasion process that, taken as a whole, provide a fairly useful model.

Aspects of Persuasion

One of the best such outlines appears in Otto Lerbinger's *Designs for Persuasive Communication*. Lerbinger describes five different "designs" of persuasion: (1) stimulus-response; (2) cognitive; (3) motivational; (4) social; and (5) personality.[2]

Stimulus-Response The stimulus-response design is the simplest approach to persuasion. It's based on the idea of association. If two things are seen together many times, people will think of one of them when they think of the other. Stimulus-response persuasion clearly doesn't involve any intricate thought on the part of the audience. Stimulus conditioning works as well with dogs and cats as it does with people. The classic illustration is Pavlov's dog experiments, where a bell was rung every time the dogs were to be fed. Soon any ringing bell caused the dogs to start drooling in anticipation. One cat owner (a nonscientist) discovered she could call her cats out from any hiding place simply by starting up the electric can opener. The cats had learned to associate the sound of the can opener with open cans of cat food and thus with dinner.

Obviously the stimulus-response design is not a very good way to persuade someone on a complex issue. But if you want to persuade people that Kentucky Fried Chicken is "finger lickin' good," the stimulus-response design can be effective.

Cognitive Writers dealing with complex issues must consider the fact that people can think and reason about what they read. The cognitive design of persuasion is based on the idea that people will reach the right conclusions if given the right information in a logical, understandable way.

The cognitive approach can be effective with some things. If a person has no personal stake in an issue, and no preconceived notions about it, the simple presentation of information may be effective. People like to think of themselves as fair and reasonable, and if you provide reasonable arguments, they will be likely to agree with you—other things being equal.

Of course, other things are seldom equal. You can't expect to dump your message (whether stimulus-response or cognitive) into people's heads without considering what is already in them. To persuade someone to take a certain position, you have to know what will motivate the person to take that position. This idea is the basis of the motivational design of persuasion.

Motivational Generally, motivational persuasion tries to show a person how changing an opinion will fulfill some need. In essence, the persuader offers the members of the audience some kind of emotional reward for accepting the communication.

What are some needs that motivate people? A convenient outline of human needs was devised by the psychologist Abraham Maslow, who grouped human needs into a hierarchy ranging from the most basic (at the bottom) to the most intangible (see Figure 2–2). At the bottom of this hierarchy are physical needs like food, water, air and sleep. One step up is the general need for safety, or the need to be free from fear of harm. Then come the social needs: the need to belong to groups, to associate with people, the need for love. Next come personal needs, like the desire for self-respect, the desire to feel important, the need for status. At the top of the scale are the self-actualizing needs: the need to fulfill potential, be creative, have a rewarding life.

Whether or not these needs are being fulfilled can play a major role in an individual's reaction to persuasion attempts. Persuasion that ignores these needs in order to concentrate on reason and logic is not likely to get very far. It's important also for the writer to identify the relevant needs of audience members. Persuasion attempts that don't meet the right needs will fail, too.

Social Closely related to the motivational approach is the social design for persuasion. This design takes into account an individual's background, social class and group norms. Often, group membership is the most important element in determining opinions. On issues where opinions are closely tied to social conditions, persuasion must be designed to address the social factors that influence the individual.

Personality Finally, a persuader cannot ignore the fact that each individual is unique. Personality characteristics can determine what arguments will work best with a given person. Of course, a persuasive message is frequently directed to a large group containing a number of different personality types, so the personality design cannot be used effectively. But writers should still be aware of how personality characteristics affect persuasibility.[3]

2-2 MASLOW'S HIERARCHY OF NEEDS

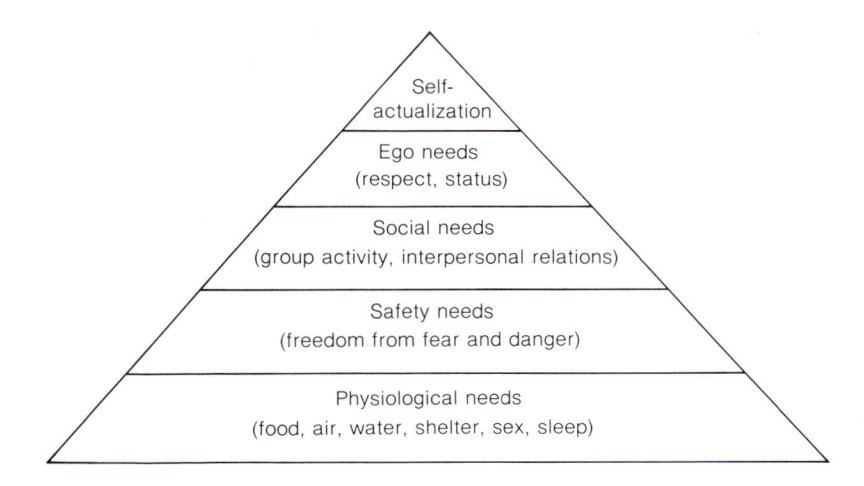

```
                    Self-
                 actualization
                Ego needs
             (respect, status)
           Social needs
    (group activity, interpersonal relations)
          Safety needs
     (freedom from fear and danger)
        Physiological needs
   (food, air, water, shelter, sex, sleep)
```

People have different kinds of needs, ranging from the most basic, physical needs (like food, water and sleep) to sophisticated needs for self-actualization, such as achieving personal fulfillment.

Steps in the Persuasion Process

Obviously there are a number of different approaches to the act of persuasion, although most successful persuasion uses a combination of these. But once you've considered all the different approaches, how do you actually go about persuading someone?

To answer that, we must first identify the steps in the persuasion process. Social psychologist William McGuire lists six such steps: presentation, attending, comprehending, yielding, retaining the new position, and acting.[4]

Presentation To begin with, you can't persuade anyone of anything unless he or she is at the right place at the right time to perceive a message. A person who doesn't own a TV set will probably not see your TV commercial. So no matter how well written the ad is, it won't persuade that person at all.

Attending The person next door probably has a TV set, however, and he might see your commercial. But he may not pay the least attention to it. He may be looking straight at the screen but thinking about who's going to win the upcoming football game—he's not getting your message. He must *attend* to the message—that is, pay attention—if you're to have any hope of persuading him.

Comprehending Suppose this guy's wife does pay attention. She watches the screen and listens intently to the sounds. But she's a Mexican-American and in a South Texas town and she doesn't speak a word of English. She likes to watch football games even though she can't understand the announcers. But she can't understand the commercials either, so there isn't much chance that you'll persuade her.

Yielding If we go to the next house we may find a person who does have a TV set, does pay attention to your commercial, and does understand English. She fully comprehends the message: You want her to buy a new kind of toothpaste because it is much better than other kinds of toothpaste. She watches your "whiter teeth" demonstration very closely. As the commercial ends she says, "Nonsense. No toothpaste can do that." The viewer has been presented with the message, she attended, she comprehended. But she did not yield. No persuasion occurred.

Retaining the New Position Let's assume this woman's husband saw the same commercial and was impressed. "That looks like great toothpaste," he says. "I'll have to buy some of that." But it's a month before his supply of toothpaste runs out. By that time, he has forgotten the name of the toothpaste he saw on your commercial. The persuasion succeeded up to the point of getting the viewer to accept the arguments. But he didn't retain his new opinion, so for all practical purposes this persuasion attempt, too, failed.

Acting Now let's assume instead that the viewer didn't forget. Maybe he saw the same commercial again and once more expressed a desire to buy the product. He may go to the store, look straight at the new brand, remark to himself that he should try that brand, and then reach for the old brand, plop it into the shopping cart, and leave the new brand on the shelf. Your commercial, then, did persuade the viewer to a new opinion, but the persuasion was not successful enough to get him to act on that new opinion.

To be successful, persuasion must accomplish all six of these steps. You must get your message to the audience. More important, you must get someone to pay attention to it. And the message must be understandable—people are more likely to read things that are easy to understand. In any event, they aren't likely to come over to your side if they don't understand what your side is. But understanding isn't enough. Your arguments must be convincing. The audience must be willing to give in, or yield. Then they must remember that they gave in, and act on their new opinions.

All these steps must be considered when designing persuasive communication. Techniques that work well to achieve some steps might be useless for other steps. Some persuasive writing gets people to pay attention, but is not understandable. Messages designed only to produce yielding might not get the audience to act. For example, one study tried to decide which persuasive methods were best to get new mothers to come to the maternity ward for an examination. As it turned out, the best method depended on how the results were measured. One method got the most mothers to say they would come back a month later, but another method produced the most mothers who actually did come back in a month.[5] Obviously one method was good at inducing yielding, but the other was better for retention and action.

PERSUASION AND COMMUNICATION

Persuasion is a special type of communication. To understand the persuasion process fully, then, we must first understand something about communication. Like persuasion, the communication process can be broken down into a number of elements.*

Harold Lasswell, a pioneer in communication research, said the process of communication can be described by answering this series of questions: Who, says what, through what channel, to whom, with what effect?[6] Using this analysis, we can say communication involves a source, a message, a medium, an audience, and an effect. Changes in the characteristics of any of these elements can cause differences in the communication's persuasiveness.

Source

At first glance it doesn't seem likely that you can change the "who"—the source of the communication. You're stuck with who you are. But then again, it is sometimes possible to change some of your characteristics (or some of the characteristics of your institution). At the very least you should design your communications to take advantage of any helpful qualities that the source does possess.

What qualities of the source of a communication influence the effectiveness of persuasion? Certainly one of the most important is credibility. A more credible source is usually a more persuasive source.[7] Your institution or organization, therefore, must strive to remain believable if your persuasive writing is to be effective. And the best way to remain believable is to always tell the truth, the whole truth, and nothing but the truth. Persuasive public relations writing must be honest and accurate. What you write must correspond to your company's actions. As Lerbinger puts it, "The communicator realizes that what he says must correspond to the realities of a given situation. The management he represents cannot be doing one thing while he is saying something else."[8]

---

*McGuire calls the relationship between the steps in the persuasion process to those in communication the "matrix of persuasive communication."

Credibility can be broken down into two distinct elements: expertise and objectivity. The audience is more likely to believe you if they think you know what you're talking about. But to believe you completely, they also must assume that you are motivated to tell the truth. If you have a vested interest in an issue, your objectivity will be suspect. McGuire says, "For maximum believability, the source must be perceived as not only knowing the truth but being objective enough to be motivated to tell it as he sees it."[9] Several studies have confirmed that disinterestedness makes a source more persuasive. In fact, a source is most persuasive of all when arguing *against* his or her own best interests.

Credibility isn't the only source characteristic that can aid persuasion. Your audience is likely to be persuaded, too, by sources they like. Of course, it isn't always clear whether people are persuaded by a source because they like it or whether they like the source because they agree with it. In any event, being liked helps make persuasion more successful. So does being similar to the audience members in some way, especially when the similarity is ideological and not merely physical or social. Your persuasion, then, is more likely to be effective if you can establish some ideological similarities between yourself and your audience.

A third source characteristic that leads to more effective persuasion is perceived power. Put simply, this means your boss is more likely to persuade you than your neighbor is. Your boss has power over you; your neighbor doesn't.

Because many different source qualities affect persuasive success, it isn't always possible to predict what changing one of those qualities will do. For example, if you work hard to appear to be an expert, your audience may very well perceive your expertise but might not agree with you as much as they would otherwise. By becoming more of an expert, you have become less similar to your nonexpert audience. The increase in agreement produced by higher expertise can be more than offset by the loss of agreement caused by the decrease in similarity. In many cases, then, some intermediate level of expertise is probably best. Audiences tend to believe people who know more than they do, but not too much more.

Message

The "what" of Lasswell's five questions—the message—is perhaps the most important element in the success of persuasion. It is, at least, the element of communication that a writer is most concerned with. The writer must decide what things to say and how to arrange them. In doing so, a writer will be faced with any number of difficult decisions on fundamental questions. Here is what research has to say about some of them.

Should you give one side or both sides?

In general, studies have shown that it's better to give both sides of the story. One-sided arguments are frequently dismissed, especially if an audience is highly educated or tends to oppose your viewpoint at the beginning. If the audience doesn't like you, or if the audience doesn't already agree with you on the issue at hand, it's best to give both sides. It's also better to give both sides if the audience is likely to hear the other side of the story at some later date.

Is there any time when it's good to stress your side of the story only? Possibly, if circumstances present all three of these conditions: the audience is not well educated; the audience is friendly to you; the audience probably will not hear any arguments from the other side. Only rarely, however, are all these requirements met.

A related question is occasionally faced by PR people: Should an issue be raised at all? Sometimes people (especially corporate executives) feel it's a good idea to "let sleeping dogs lie" and not bring up a potentially controversial subject until somebody else does first. This is almost always a mistake. If there's any chance at all that someone will bring up an issue in the future, you should strike first with your side. In fact, research indicates that the first communicator has a significant advantage in winning public opinion to his side because of the "inoculation" effect. That is, the audience can be "inoculated" against the opponent's views, just as a person is inoculated against a disease by an injection of a weakened form of the same disease. Thus, it is more effective to raise the opponent's issues yourself, before the opponent does.

A smart persuader will supply a weakened form of the opposition arguments, and then refute these arguments before the opposition can present its case. The audience will resist persuasion by the opposition at a later date. This strategy, studies show, works better than providing the audience with large amounts of propaganda designed merely to provide the persuader's views while ignoring the existence of conflicting opinions.

Which side should you give first?

If, as in most cases, you use both sides of the story, whose side should you give first? Unfortunately, the evidence on this question is not clear. Giving the opposition arguments first is apparently better when dealing with controversial issues, but not when dealing with noncontroversial issues.

Which should come first, the good news or the bad news?

In general, give the good news first. This approach will probably get you the most overall agreement with your message.

Should you make conclusions explicit or let the audience draw its own conclusions?

In essence, this question asks whether it's better to tell people what to think or offer the facts and let them figure it out. It's true that a person drawing his or her own conclusion is likely to hold the new opinion more strongly. The problem is, the conclusion might not be the conclusion you wanted. Generally, then, it is safer to make the conclusion explicit, especially when the issue under consideration is complex.

There are exceptions to this general rule, however. A highly intelligent audience can probably be trusted to form its own conclusions, and in fact might consider the statement of an obvious conclusion to be insulting. Sometimes an initially hostile audience reacts negatively to explicit conclusions. And when the issues are very personal, and members of the audience have a high ego involvement with your conclusions, it's definitely wiser not to make the conclusions explicit.

Do fear techniques work?

The research on this point seems to indicate that fear appeals do enhance persuasion. But only up to a point. Mild fear appeals appear to be more effective than strong fear appeals.

McGuire offers an explanation for this. Fear may be effective in passing the yielding step of persuasion. But high fear levels may work against other steps in the process, like comprehension or remembering. If you scare people too much, they either won't get the substance of the message or will put it out of their minds and forget the matter. Thus, as with expertise, some medium level of fear is probably the best approach. Keep in mind, though, McGuire's observation that the more complex the message, the less fear arousal is desirable.[10]

Is it better to use emotional or factual arguments?

The evidence on this question is simply not conclusive. Sometimes emotional appeals are the most persuasive, and sometimes factual ones are. It all depends on the issues involved and the composition of the audience. There are no good general rules to follow.

It is probably safe to say, however, that the best persuasive writing employs both factual and emotional arguments. Since information by itself seldom changes opinions, some writers tend to rely on emotional presentations. But information is also important to persuasion, if only to provide people with intellectual justification for opinions they have formed for emotional reasons. Information can strengthen or weaken attitudes. It can blunt the enthusiasm of an audience opposed to your position. It can strengthen the opinions of those already on your side. Furthermore, providing information to supporters of your view gives them a way to verbalize their feelings—and defend them. This reduces the chances that subsequent persuasion from the opposition will undo what your communication has accomplished.

Medium

Marshall McLuhan's well-known contention that "the medium is the message" may be a bit of an exaggeration, but there's no doubt that the medium—the "channel" in Lasswell's terms—has some bearing on persuasive power.

The medium, or channel, is obviously important for the presentation and attention steps of persuasion. You must use a medium that will get your message to your audience, and it should be a medium that the audience will pay attention to. But research findings indicate that the medium is important for other steps of persuasion as well.

One interesting finding is that spoken communication is usually more likely to bring about yielding than written communication.[11] This doesn't mean you should spend all your time writing speeches and ignore the print media. But it is useful to keep in mind that speech has more power to change minds than writing. The pen may be mightier than the sword, but the tongue may be able to outduel both.

This is not an endorsement of "fiery oration," either. In fact, studies have been unable to show much difference between the persuasive effects of intense, enthusiastic speeches and those of more subdued ones. In either case the spoken word wins out over the written word in persuasive power.

However, studies have shown that the written word achieves better comprehension. This might seem strange since comprehension is one of the steps in the persuasion process. But complete understanding is not always needed for successful persuasion. (Remember the woman at the nuclear engineer's talk.) The spoken word diminishes understanding a little, but it increases yielding a lot.

These findings would seem to recommend TV and radio as media for carrying your message. But while the evidence shows that verbal persuasion is more effective than written persuasion, it also shows that face-to-face encounters are more persuasive than mass media messages, especially in attempts to influence voting behavior.[12] Perhaps, this evidence suggests, spending a lot of money on media time and space isn't worth the expense. But if mass media messages aren't effective, then the nation's businesses are wasting billions of dollars annually trying to sell their products via the media. And there are reasons to believe that the media can play a role in persuasion, though perhaps an indirect one. It may just be that the effects of the media are difficult to isolate and measure.

Studies have shown that the mass media can successfully convey information to people (though not in all cases, and not always to the extent that the communicator would like). And though information alone is usually not enough to get people to change their opinions, it does, as we noted, play a part. Even if most people are not persuaded much by the media, opinion leaders—that is, those who influence others in face-to-face contacts—do pay attention to the media and base their opinions at least in part on media messages.

The hypothesis that opinion leaders transmit media messages to others has been described as the "two-step flow" theory of mass communications. Recent research has cast doubt on some of the details of the original hypothesis, however. For example, many people do receive input from the media, but they turn to opinion leaders for interpretations of facts more than for the facts themselves. Furthermore, the opinion leaders may receive information from sources other than the mass media.[13] Nevertheless, opinion leaders do provide a possible avenue for mass media to influence public opinion.

Another important influence of the media has been described as "agenda setting." Research has shown that issues considered important by the population often are also issues that the media devote much time and space to. Thus, it has been suggested that even if the media don't tell people what to think, they tell people what to think about. Of course, it is possible that the situation is the other way around—that people decide what's important first, and then the media begin to run stories on those subjects. Much recent work has established, though, that media coverage often comes first. So if your intent is merely to raise an issue, to bring it into the public consciousness, the mass media can be an effective channel.

Given that the mass media can be used as a channel for your persuasive messages, which media are best to use? That's a difficult question to answer. Since the media's measurable effects on opinion are small, it isn't easy to tell if one medium is more effective than another. Looking at credibility alone, the evidence suggests that people are more likely to believe TV than newspapers, and more likely to believe newspapers than radio. But, although TV is generally given the highest believability ratings, members of higher socioeconomic groups usually rate newspapers higher for accuracy and truthfulness.[14]

Audience

The greatest lesson of social scientific research on the question of persuasion is a lesson that all good writers have already learned: Know your audience. Techniques that will work wonders persuading a football team will flop on a group of music students. Most of the guidelines for preparing a message or choosing a channel depend on the characteristics of the audience.

The audience (the "whom" of Lasswell's questions) is made up of individuals. And all individuals, as receivers of messages, possess a common characteristic—they tend to forget things. This fact usually works to the persuader's disadvantage. Opinions built up from long-term experience are hard to forget, but opinions arrived at as a result of a one-shot persuasive effort are easy to forget. The "retention" step in persuasion is a difficult one.

But the human tendency to forget can also be helpful, especially to communicators with low credibility. If you are not a very credible source (perhaps because your audience thinks you are biased), your message may not induce any immediate opinion change. But several months later, the audience may show some agreement with your view. It is possible that they will remember the message, but forget where the message came from. The message, no longer associated with the low-credibility source, is now believed.

The exact nature of this "sleeper" effect, and even whether it truly exists, is a matter of some controversy. Nevertheless, it's useful to know that even a low-credibility source can be effective in persuasion under some circumstances.

Loss of memory probably carries no such benefits for high-credibility sources, who want the audience to remember everything. These communicators often repeat their message many times to make sure the point will be retained. Research on this question indicates that repetition (as with an advertisement presented many times) may indeed achieve greater effects, but only because it increases the chances that more people will see the ad.

Effect

The last of Lasswell's questions on the communication process is "with what effect?" This ties in closely with the "acting" stage in persuasion. What do you wish to persuade the audience to do? Do they do it?

From the viewpoint of the communicator, we can label this aspect of persuasive communication the "intended effect," or simply "intent," because you can't know ahead of time what the actual effect of your message will be. Nevertheless, you must ask how what you intend to communicate influences your success in persuasion.

The most obvious intention of any persuasive writer or speaker is to persuade. If the receivers know they are being persuaded, their resistance might increase. If they merely overhear a persuasive conversation, without knowing that the message is intended for their ears, they might be more susceptible to the arguments.

It might be helpful to disguise the persuasive intent of communication for maximum results. Some evidence supports this view, but some does not. At times the opposite effect can be seen. While there is little doubt that disguising the intent to persuade enhances yielding, it might hinder presentation, attention and comprehension. The benefits of making sure your audience gets the message may outweigh the disadvantages of letting your intent to persuade be clearly seen.[15]

Another question regarding intent is the matter of how extreme to make your appeal. Should you try to persuade people to change their minds only a little bit, or will you be more successful if you try to change opinions a lot? This question of "discrepancy effects" has been studied by several researchers. Generally it seems that increasing the amount of requested opinion change helps increase the persuasion, but only up to a point. If the persuader asks for too much opinion change, effectiveness decreases.[16]

CONCLUSION

The outlines in this chapter showing the steps in the persuasion and the communication processes are just that—outlines. It would take volumes to fill in the details of the many studies done on these subjects.

Furthermore, studies on such questions continue to be done—sometimes with results that contradict past findings. As time passes and circumstances change, techniques that once worked well may become worthless in persuading a given audience. Conclusions based on studies of college sophomores may turn out to be completely erroneous when the group under consideration is business executives.

For these reasons the PR writer must be tuned in to continuing research in the communication field. If you're working on a special project, general guidelines are no substitute for going straight to the research literature and finding out the details of the latest studies.

Be aware, however, that research findings are not blueprints for persuasive campaigns. All PR communications must be ethical and honest. Research may show that engendering fear will aid persuasion—but that doesn't mean you should "make up" some false fear to enhance the chance of your persuasion's success. There is nothing wrong with using scientific knowledge of human behavior to achieve your goals—providing, of course, that your goals are moral, legal, and in line with the general public well-being.

NOTES

[1] Edward L. Bernays, *Public Relations* (Norman: University of Oklahoma Press, 1952), p. 130.

[2] Otto Lerbinger, *Designs for Persuasive Communication* (Englewood Cliffs, N.J.: Prentice-Hall, 1972).

[3] See, for example, Irving L. Janis, "Personality as a Factor in Susceptibility to Persuasion," in *The Science of Human Communication*, ed. Wilbur Schramm (New York: Basic Books, 1963), pp. 54–64.

[4] William J. McGuire, "Persuasion, Resistance, and Attitude Change," in *Handbook of Communication*, ed. Ithiel de Sola Pool et al. (Chicago: Rand-McNally, 1973), p. 221.

[5] Stanley Lehmann, "Personality and Compliance: A Study of Anxiety and Self-esteem in Opinion and Behavior Change," *Journal of Personality and Social Psychology* 15 (1970): 76–86. Cited in McGuire, "Persuasion," p. 223.

[6] Wilbur Schramm, "The Challenge of Communication Research," in *Introduction to Mass Communications Research*, ed. Ralph O. Nafziger and David M. White (Baton Rouge: Louisiana State University Press, 1963), p. 29.

[7] This is not always true, however. See B. Sternthal, L. Phillips, and R. Dholakia, "The Persuasive Effect of Source Credibility: A Situational Analysis," *Public Opinion Quarterly* 42 (Fall 1978): 285–314.

[8] Lerbinger, *Designs*, p. 25.

[9] McGuire, "Persuasion," p. 231.

[10]Ibid., p. 234.

[11]William J. McGuire, "Nature of Attitudes and Attitude Change," in *Handbook of Social Psychology*, ed. Gardner Lindzey and Elliot Aronson (Reading, Mass: Addison-Wesley, 1969), p. 225.

[12]Ibid., pp. 228-229.

[13]Everett M. Rogers, "Mass Media and Interpersonal Communication," in *Handbook of Communication*, ed. Ithiel de Sola Pool et al. (Chicago: Rand-McNally, 1973), pp. 292-298.

[14]McGuire, "Nature," pp. 230-231.

[15]McGuire, "Persuasion," p. 231.

[16]Elliot Aronson, Judith Turner and J. M. Carlsmith, "Communicator Credibility and Communication Discrepancy as Determinants of Opinion Change," *Journal of Abnormal and Social Psychology* 67 (1963): 31-36.

SELECTED BIBLIOGRAPHY

Elliot Aronson, Judith Turner and J. Merrill Carlsmith, "Communicator Credibility and Communication Discrepancy as Determinants of Opinion Change," *Journal of Abnormal and Social Psychology* 67 (1963): 31-36.

Edward L. Bernays, *Public Relations* (Norman: University of Oklahoma Press, 1952).

Bernard C. Hennessy, *Public Opinion*, 3d ed. (Belmont, Calif.: Wadsworth, 1975).

Carl I. Hovland et al., *The Order of Presentation in Persuasion* (New Haven, Conn.: Yale University Press, 1957).

Otto Lerbinger, *Designs for Persuasive Communication* (Englewood Cliffs, N.J.: Prentice-Hall, 1972).

M. E. McCombs and D. L. Shaw, "The Agenda Setting Function of the Media," *Public Opinion Quarterly* 36 (1972): 176-187.

William J. McGuire, "Nature of Attitudes and Attitude Change," in *Handbook of Social Psychology*, 2d ed., vol. 3, ed. Gardner Lindzey and Elliot Aronson (Reading, Mass.: Addison-Wesley, 1969), pp. 136-314.

William J. McGuire, "Persuasion, Resistance, and Attitude Change," in *Handbook of Communication*, ed. Ithiel de Sola Pool et al. (Chicago: Rand-McNally, 1973), pp. 216-252.

Ithiel de Sola Pool et al., *Handbook of Communication* (Chicago: Rand-McNally, 1973).

Ithiel de Sola Pool et al., "Public Opinion," in *Handbook of Communication*, ed. Pool et al. (Chicago: Rand-McNally, 1973), pp. 779-835.

Everett M. Rogers, "Mass Media and Interpersonal Communication," in *Handbook of Communication*, ed. Ithiel de Sola Pool et al. (Chicago: Rand-McNally, 1973), pp. 290-310.

Wilbur Schramm, "The Challenge to Communication Research," in *Introduction to Mass Communications Research*, ed. Ralph O. Nafziger and David M. White (Baton Rouge: Louisiana State University Press, 1963), pp. 3-31.

Wilbur Schramm, ed. *The Science of Human Communication* (New York: Basic Books, 1963).

David O. Sears and Richard E. Whitney, "Political Persuasion," in *Handbook of Communication*, ed. Ithiel de Sola Pool et al. (Chicago: Rand-McNally, 1973), pp. 253-289.

M. Brewster Smith, "A Map for the Analysis of Personality and Politics," *Journal of Social Issues* 24 (1968): 15-28.

Brian Sternthal, Lynn Phillips, and Ruby Dholakia, "The Persuasive Effect of Source Credibility: A Situational Analysis," *Public Opinion Quarterly* 42 (Fall 1978): 285-314.

3

RESEARCH

As pointed out in Chapter 1, public relations writing requires information. And getting information requires research. Research is done by PR practitioners at all stages of their careers.

RESEARCH IN PR

The most important activity for any public relations person, entry-level or senior counselor, is fact finding. That statement can be made unequivocally, without reservation. Information is essential for PR practice, and information comes only through carefully, often tediously searching for, stockpiling, and then applying facts to the solution of public relations problems. Problem solutions can also be found by applying ideas borrowed from others. This is why public relations includes the collection and examination of case studies in the field.

PR Research Components

Research for public relations involves collecting facts and ideas, reviewing their applications, and evaluating their use and usefulness. The scope of PR research covers three significant areas. It covers material to use in decision making—in planning and acting. It also covers the choice and use of media. And third, it covers the messages themselves. That is, research helps determine what to say to which publics, taking into consideration what other research has indicated those publics know, think they know, and want to know or believe.

Material Public relations planning and decision making depend on the accumulation of facts and ideas. In building a public relations program, you need to gather background on the situation, and you need to know the base you'll be starting from. You also need to know what possible goals you can set, and you need some ideas on how to reach them. All of this involves research, whether the PR situation is troubleshooting or just directing a special event like a Mayfest or Aqua Carnival. Starting with the reporter's basic questions—who, what, when, where and why—you build an elaborate, sophisticated system that accommodates situations as simple as planning, promoting and conducting a symposium to those as complex as reacting to a crisis at a chemical plant or an airport. You gather facts and you glean ideas from ways others have handled similar situations.

Media   In working your way through any public relations situation, you will be using channels of communication. Which ones you choose depend on which ones research shows will be most effective for the particular problem or situation. Before you can choose, however, you need to know the characteristics of the various media—their technical qualities, what they can and can't do, and their emotive qualities, how people react to them, use them. You'll be making some serious choices about whether to use general or specialized media. It's not an easy decision, and since it involves investments of time and money, you need to know, not guess. How you know is through research.

Once you have chosen the media you'll need to know—both while you are using them and afterwards too—whether they were indeed effective and efficient in this particular PR problem. Did you reach the target audiences with a message that was heard and accepted and, most importantly, acted on?

Messages   What you said in the media has a great deal to do with your success. This is where research into the different types of publics is critical. Who are they? What type of message provides them with information that will persuade them to respond to the PR situation? Research should tell you not only what you need to say to each audience, but how you need to say it.

Research for Storage and Retrieval

PR practitioners would have more serious communication problems than they do if intensive spadework in material, media and messages had to be fresh with each PR situation. However, as part of the PR operation, PR people accumulate research, instigate research for later use, and plan for research needs.

Much of public relations research is borrowed from the social sciences, especially from behavioral research. Useful research studies are accumulated and indexed for future application. Also, research about publics and about media is continuously accumulated and stored by the PR practitioner. Much of the research about publics comes from comprehensive studies done by the commercial media about their audiences. Other studies come from product and service institutions concerned about their own publics.

A particular PR situation may require some original fact finding. In conducting original research or in hiring a research firm to gather the data, the public relations practitioner must know clearly what is needed, or the resulting information will be imposing but inadequate.

Organizing Since public relations information comes from such a variety of sources—it can be borrowed, accumulated, commissioned or conducted—organizing it can be a problem. One common organizational pattern follows the lines of our previous discussion. Information is categorized according to material (substantive facts bearing on the PR situation), media (facts about media use and ideas from similar situations) and messages (facts about publics).

Presenting The organization of the research should consider how it will be presented and used. In presenting the information, it is important to explain the implications of the findings when these are not obvious, and suggest what bearing the research has on the situation. The information should also indicate what other research might be useful in completing the picture.

Updating Organization of the research should allow for easy updating, especially where ongoing research, such as periodic opinion measurement (as in an election campaign) is critical. Most research now is stored in a computer, and the PR practitioner must know enough about the method of storage to use the system efficiently. What works best for the information systems people is not always what will work best for the PR person trying to use the data.

Reusing Adding to or reusing research is difficult if it is not readily accessible. The retrieval process, therefore, is critical. PR practitioners must work with information systems people to tell them how the information will be applied—what will be needed, under what kinds of conditions, and within what time periods. For PR research needs, the system must be designed so the data is organized, presented in a meaningful way, and easily updated as well as reused. Anticipation is the key to success in this endeavor.

SOURCES FOR PR WRITERS AND RESEARCHERS

Writers and researchers of all types, not just PR practitioners, depend on research from two basic sources: paper and people. Of course, "paper" doesn't always mean books. It may be computer programming tape, or it may even be some form of electronic storage. The important point to remember is that sources are secondary (paper, or stored) and primary (people).

Secondary Sources for Research

The library is usually the place to initiate secondary research projects. However, you can do a great deal with some basic reference guides before you go to the library. For example, you must know the types of sources you need to tap, and there are books to guide you to reference works you may want to look for in the library. One important one is Jacques Barzun and Henry F. Graff's *The Modern Researcher,* third edition. Another is William L. Rivers' *Finding Facts.* Both describe reference works so you will know what to expect from them. Another help is a good reference librarian, who can cut many corners if you can state succinctly the information you want. Some reference librarians will answer simple direct questions by phone.

Library Most metropolitan areas have a library with adequate resources for basic research. Also, they usually have cooperative agreements with other libraries to get information on loan. Colleges and universities usually have libraries with some of the scholarly materials you might need. Some churches have substantial holdings of religious works, and most cities have law libraries. Some libraries have special collections—such as the Lyndon Baines Johnson Library in Austin, Texas—that they will open for honest research projects.

Reference Works Primary tools of the reference librarian and researcher in the library are collections of information and reference works. These are maps to where the treasures of information you seek might be found. Standard reference works are encyclopedias, biographical dictionaries, dictionaries of quotations and concordances of the Bible and famous authors, atlases and gazetteers, chronologies or other books of dates, handbooks and source books—including dictionaries of all kinds.

Bibliographies One reference source that is especially important is the bibliography. Authors who have accumulated and categorized bibliographies have provided you with paths through labyrinths of footnotes. Bibliographies usually identify reliable sources of information and, generally, give descriptions of sources you might want to tap. Many libraries now offer electronic access to stored bibliographies so you can call up on a screen all the most likely sources. You often get sources you cannot use because the subject tag used for identification calls up related materials not central to your inquiry. These you have to sift through, but at least you know the search is exhaustive, and one that would normally take several hours is accomplished in a matter of minutes. Hard copies (printed) are also available from material in the data bank.

Periodicals One resource accessible in electronic systems is the *New York Times Index.* Stories that have appeared through the years in the

New York Times can be tracked, called up and read. Since the *New York Times* makes a significant effort to be a newspaper of record, it is possible to do a great deal of research through its index. For commercial publications the most useful magazine index is the *Readers' Guide to Periodical Literature*. You can also find indexes for most scholarly publications and even for a few newsletters that belong to national institutions or organizations.

Other good references for events and issues of the day are *Facts on File* and the encyclopedia yearbooks. These too are indexed to make your search easier.

Public Records Government records at all levels—local, state and federal—are available to you unless they are classified. Some government agencies offer research assistance. The Library of Congress is extremely helpful in locating information and often offers advice to put you on the right trail. Remember, you pay taxes supporting these services, so why not use them?

Government Offices Most government offices are storehouses of information for public use. Many government offices distribute their own materials. The federal government has its materials published by the U.S. Government Printing Office (GPO) and a central store in Washington, D.C., has information on every imaginable subject as do the regional outlets in cities with federal centers. Ask to be put on the GPO's mailing list. Each month you'll get a list of materials available at a very nominal cost. One source of information that is essential for PR people is the *Statistical Abstract of the United States*, published by the U.S. Census Bureau.

Files and Public Access The Freedom of Information Act has opened files of both public and private institutions to examination. This means that normally you now have access to any document—titles on property, budgets of state institutions, court proceedings and such—that has been filed in a public place. A wealth of information exists in these documents. I. W. Stone, muckraking editor and publisher of the newspaper *The Iconoclast,* claimed he never found it necessary to "steal" a government document. All he did to research and develop the stories he published was sit in his office and read the public documents available to anyone.

Primary Sources — People

Interviewing After you have done some fundamental research, you are ready to begin asking questions of people who might be knowledgeable in your subject. In any interview ask open-ended questions that will develop information through discussion—not yes-and-no type questions. Find authorities through your research, develop questions for them, and then follow up any leads they may give you.

3-1 CHECKLIST FOR INTERVIEWING

1. Research your subject before the interview.
2. Know something about the person you are interviewing.
3. Prepare a list of questions in advance.
4. Let the interviewee know in advance the kinds of questions you will be asking.
5. Whenever possible use a tape recorder *and* take notes. Never put complete trust in a machine, or your memory.
6. Ask for explanations if you don't understand something.
7. Ask specific questions. Vague questions elicit vague answers.
8. Ask one question at a time. Don't throw several questions into the same sentence and expect the interviewee to answer—or even remember—all of them.

Although some people seem to have a natural talent for getting information from others, interviewing skills should be developed and practiced. Like people who play musical instruments by ear, natural interviewers—and all others—are still better with practice.

Go to an interview prepared. Have questions on paper and keep in mind information gained from your research. Then you can follow a different line of questioning if the opportunity arises. Take notes and also use a tape recorder. Try not to rely completely on either, however. Listen to what the person is telling you and try to *remember* the information by putting it into the frame of reference your research has prepared. Encourage responses by asking relevant questions and by participating in the conversation. Avoid being judgmental. You are asking, not telling. (See 3–1 for an interviewing checklist.)

Some of the information you get from an interview will be from observations. Watch for nonverbal communication cues, and note physical characteristics, as well as environmental factors, that could be telling. Note particularly the significant details such as gestures that seem to be personality characteristics and remember emotional emphases. These latter are particularly evident in the way something is said: the inflection of the voice, the expression on the face. Be cautious, however, about reading more into a situation than is there. Be aware of your own bias and involvement with the subject so you don't misinterpret what you experience.

Questionnaires Another way to elicit information from people is through the questionnaire. This source of information is the research workhorse. Drafting a questionnaire is difficult, however. For example, it sometimes takes three or four simple questions to get an answer to a question you are concerned with. This breaking down of questions is one reason why developing a questionnaire is so difficult.

A second problem is asking the question in such a way that the respondent knows what you mean. For example, a national survey asked a question about "consumer movement leaders." Another researcher, attempting to replicate part of the study, used that expression with different audiences and was asked by one respondent for a definition of "consumer leader." Did the researcher want to know about movement activists, government appointees or civil servants involved in consumer information, or corporate employees charged with responding to consumers? The question was invalid because it was being interpreted in different ways. Usually pretesting will identify problem questions, but not always.

To develop a questionnaire, begin by stating simply all the information you want to know. Or use simple questions instead. Next, consider the respondents. Who is going to be asked these questions and under what circumstances? People get impatient with long telephone questionnaires. But one that can be answered and returned by mail can be more detailed because a respondent can choose when to answer. The age and educational level of the respondents are also factors in how the questions are phrased. Familiarity with the material is another factor—the unfamiliar requires more explanation. Questions should be arranged in logical sequence so the thought develops naturally in the mind of the respondent. Proper development and sequential ordering make the questionnaire easier to answer.

It's also important in writing the questions to consider how the questionnaire will be administered and scored. If a questionnaire is used in a busy shopping mall, for example, or in a spot phone call, the respondent will not want to take time to answer long or involved questions. Open-ended response questions are difficult to score. How you ask the questions affects the response and that, of course, determines whether or not the information you get from the questionnaire is valid. (See 3–2.)

Verifying

When you start putting information from all of your sources together to make some sense of your findings, you will want to cross-check your sources. Check primary sources against each other. If you find areas of conflict, look for other primary sources.

Also, check primary sources against secondary sources. People, you will discover, have fallible memories. The John Deans of this world are not numerous, and where he was able to recall whole weeks in great detail for Watergate prosecutors, more common is the experience of a young reporter sent to do an anniversary story. It was the anniversary of a famous World War II battle, and the reporter found a highly decorated veteran known in the community for his tales of World War II experiences. After getting the story, the reporter returned to the paper and went to the reference room because some of the veteran's information didn't coincide with what she remembered learning of that historic event. Research revealed so many discrepancies that she convinced the city editor that more checking was needed. What eventually emerged was rather a sad story. The man had been in military service no longer than three weeks. He had been excused as emotionally unfit. The story—all of his stories—were fabrications. The paper did without an "anniversary" story that day and learned not to use the man as a source.

In attempting to check out stories, you'll often find conflicts among secondary sources. Historians sometimes spend years tracking an elusive date for an event. Most PR researchers don't do that type of research, but it pays to be that careful, especially now when much information is highly technical and specialized. If authorities disagree, you need to know it and have some explanation of why. Check, and keep checking, until some pattern appears.

The sleuthing and unraveling you do will give you confidence in your research and let you identify trouble areas—when authorities disagree, potential controversies arise. Test your information against experience and other information as it becomes available. In PR, the research role is an ongoing process.

SKEPTICISM—A REQUISITE FOR ALL RESEARCH

Research involves digging and thinking, verifying, then expressing and sharing. In discriminating between what is probable or improbable, true or false, likely or doubtful, you will be making decisions—decisions about information from primary and secondary sources. Barzun and Graff say these decisions are based on a combination of knowledge, skepticism, faith, common sense and intelligent guessing.[1]

Questions to Ask

Fundamental to the success of a PR researcher is an attitude of "show me" skepticism, even when it's your side of the story—maybe especially when it's your side of the story. Writers are now legally accountable for false information in publicity stories, in advertising copy claims and in many other areas of public relations writing. You can't afford to take the word of any one person that information you have been given is "the truth." You need documentation and some unbiased authority.

Probe, for your own protection, with questions like: Who says this is true? What documentation is available? Where is the evidence? Is there outside authority to substantiate? Can I test it myself? What is the experience within the industry? What does other research suggest might be the case? What is my instinctive reaction to the credibility of all sources?

3-2 QUESTIONNAIRES

```
Exercise:

                        First Version
     Do you jog, run, play ball or take some exercise outside
of PE classes?

     What type of exercise do you take and how often?

     Do you use tobacco now?  Do you think you will?

     Do your friends use tobacco?



                       Second Version
DIRECTIONS:  PLEASE CIRCLE THE NUMBER CORRESPONDING TO YOUR
             ANSWER IN THE SPACE PROVIDED.  ANSWER EACH
             QUESTION AS IT IS READ TO YOU BY THE MODERATOR.

1a.  On a weekly basis, excluding your P.E. class, how
     often do you do physical exercises?
                         Daily, 7 days a week-----1
                         5 to 6 days a week-------2
                         3 to 4 days a week-------3
                         1 to 2 days a week-------4
                         None--------------------5

1b.  How often in the past year have you participated in the
     following:

          ACTIVITY              Never    1-5    6-10   11 or more
        1 Jogging or running      1       2      3        4
        2 Jump rope               1       2      3        4
        3 Roller skating          1       2      3        4
        4 Skateboard              1       2      3        4
        5 Frisbees                1       2      3        4
        6 Bicycle riding          1       2      3        4
        7 Organized sports        1       2      3        4
           (football, volleyball,
            baseball, basketball)
        8 Dancing                 1       2      3        4

1c.  Which activity do you enjoy the most?

4e.  Do you currently smoke cigarettes or chew tobacco?
                         Smoke cigarettes-----------1
                         Chew tobacco---------------2
                         No, neither---------------3
```

The American Heart Association is working to inform youths about cardiovascular disease. The association's Texas affiliate decided to develop a questionnaire to find out what middle school youngsters knew about heart disease, and also to find out what their

4f. (IF NO) Do you intend to start smoking cigarettes or chewing tobacco?

    Yes, smoke cigarettes-----1
    Yes, chew tobacco---------2
    No, neither---------------3

4g. Do any of your friends smoke cigarettes or chew tobacco?

    Yes, most of my friends---1
    Yes, some of my friends---2
    No, none of my friends----3

Third Version

DIRECTIONS: PLEASE <u>CIRCLE</u> THE NUMBER CORRESPONDING TO YOUR ANSWER, OR WRITE YOUR ANSWER IN THE SPACE PROVIDED. ANSWER EACH QUESTION AS IT IS READ TO YOU BY THE MODERATOR.

1a. On a weekly basis, excluding your P.E. class, how often do you do physical exercises?

    Daily, 7 days a week-----1
    5 to 6 days a week-------2
    3 to 4 days a week-------3
    1 to 2 days a week-------4
    None---------------------5

1b. In the past 12 months, how often have you participated in the following activities:

	Activity	Never	1-5	6-10	11 or more
1	Jogging or running	1	2	3	4
2	Jumping rope	1	2	3	4
3	Roller skating	1	2	3	4
4	Skateboard	1	2	3	4
5	Frisbees	1	2	3	4
6	Bicycle riding	1	2	3	4
7	Football	1	2	3	4
8	Basketball	1	2	3	4
9	Baseball	1	2	3	4
10	Softball	1	2	3	4
11	Volleyball	1	2	3	4
12	Swimming	1	2	3	4
13	Tennis	1	2	3	4
14	Bowling	1	2	3	4
15	Golf	1	2	3	4
16	Dancing	1	2	3	4

1c. Of all activities listed, which one do you enjoy most? _____

habits were in order to determine which areas to stress in messages—diet, exercise, and so on. This example shows how one set of questions evolved from inception to finished questionnaire.

4e. Do you currently smoke cigarettes, chew tobacco or dip snuff?

   Smoke cigarettes----------1
   Chew tobacco--------------2
   Dip snuff-----------------3
   No------------------------4

4f. (IF NO) Do you intend to start smoking cigarettes, chewing tobacco or dipping snuff?

   Yes, smoke cigarettes-----1
   Yes, chew tobacco---------2
   Yes, dip snuff------------3
   No------------------------4

4g. Do any of your friends smoke cigarettes, chew tobacco, or dip snuff?

   Yes, most of my friends---1
   Yes, some of my friends---2
   No, none of my friends----3

Fourth Version

How often do you exercise each week, not counting your P.E. class?

   Daily--7 days a week   5
   5 to 6 days a week   4
   3 to 4 days a week   3
   1 to 2 days a week   2
   None   1

During last year (1979) how often did you exercise in the following ways:

Activity	Never	Sometimes	Often	Regularly
Jogging or running	4	3	2	1
Jumping rope	4	3	2	1
Roller skating	4	3	2	1
Skateboard riding	4	3	2	1
Frisbee throwing	4	3	2	1
Bicycle riding	4	3	2	1
Dancing	4	3	2	1
Swimming	4	3	2	1
Team sports like football, volleyball, soccer, baseball, basketball	4	3	2	1

```
The activity I enjoy most is (circle only one)

        Jogging or running     1
        Jumping rope           1
        Roller skating         1
        Skateboard riding      1
        Frisbee throwing       1
        Bicycle riding         1
        Swimming               1
        Dancing                1
        Team sports            1

Do you smoke cigarettes, chew tobacco or dip snuff now?

        Smoke cigarettes       1
        Chew tobacco           2
        Dip snuff              3
        No, none of these      4

Do you think you will smoke in the future?   Yes--1   No--2

Would you chew tobacco?                      Yes--1   No--2

Do you think you will dip snuff?             Yes--1   No--2

Do you have a close friend who smokes cigarettes, chews
tobacco or dips snuff now?                   Yes--1   No--2

Do any of your friends smoke cigarettes, chew tobacco, or
dip snuff?
      Yes, most of my friends---1
      Yes, some of my friends---2
      No, none of my friends----3
```

Answers to Questions

Answers to questions also offer opportunities for research. Each answer needs to be examined for agreement with established findings in the field. The credibility and reliability (track record) of the source must also be checked. Examine too any supporting evidence, the language of the response (was it emotional? less likely to be substantiated?), the testability of the response and the overall pattern the responses make in the documented research.

CONCLUSION

There is no way to be sure you will always be right since you are relying on many different sources for your information. But you can increase your own credibility with your publics by doing enough thorough research to be confident yourself. A public relations person needs to be an accomplished researcher, since so many rely on that PR counsel to help them decide on significant action.

NOTES

[1] Jacques Barzun and Henry F. Graff, *The Modern Researcher,* 3d ed. (New York: Harcourt Brace Jovanovich, 1977), p. 99.

SELECTED BIBLIOGRAPHY

Jacques Barzun and Henry F. Graff, *The Modern Researcher,* 3d ed. (New York: Harcourt Brace Jovanovich, 1977).

William L. Rivers, *Finding Facts* (Englewood Cliffs, N.J.: Prentice-Hall, 1975).

Bill Porterfield / The sinister shape of today's news

THERE WAS a time in the city rooms of America when almost any journeyman reporter could tell the difference between a real news event and a staged one.

Only cub reporters had a problem with that kind of thing, cub reporters and columnists. The latter were not expected to care one way or the other where their material came from, or why. After the who, what, where and why of journalism school, theory was transformed into practiced habit to meet the demands of daily deadlines. It was not something you sat around talking about. You went out and looked for it, and once you found it you knew what it was. Once in a while the subject might come up on a slow night around the desk, and likely as not someone would tell the old story about the cub reporter who went to cover a political speech and came back without a story.

"Well, what happened?" his editor wanted to know.

"Oh," the cub replied, "the candidate got up to make his speech, but before he could get a word out he fell dead on the podium. So I turned around and came back to the office."

We used to elaborate on that story (there are many versions) and conclude that every one of our editors had been that kind of reporter.

No, but seriously, this thing about actual news events and staged happenings is no longer a laughing matter. There has always been press agentry, and there have always been journalists who were sucked in by it, but in the past no serious reporter felt threatened by it.

Today, I think, there is not an earnest journalist who isn't disturbed over the shape of today's news. I'm not talking about how it appears in the paper, but how it looks when the reporter first gets to it. Often he finds that he is not the first there, that some PR man has planted himself firmly at the gate, and there's no question that he has portfolio. You're lucky if you can talk to the actual people involved in the event. Usually you have to deal with the go-between.

Nolan Estes was almost a phantom as the Dallas school superintendent. You could get to Howard Hughes easier than Estes. He surrounded himself with PR men who carried sweet incense and tar buckets to obscure the real superintendent. The only time you saw Estes was when he wanted to be seen, when he was firmly in control of the situation. Now we know how. Surely the balance is shifting. Once upon a time, the reporter and his editors decided what was news and what wasn't. Now we have to grapple with newsmakers and image-makers who have taken it upon themselves, at great commercial call, to get out the word.

Once, events worth recording seemed to come across our desks with a drama and spontaniety that made every press run a bold banner of exclamation.

Today, it seems, the editor and his reporters stand before an assembly line of news items neatly packaged and labeled by people who stand to profit from the publicity. It is hell separating the wheat from the chaff.

I don't know what the breakdown is, but I'd be willing to guess that there are more PR men and press aides running around with releases in their briefcases than there are reporters with legitimate, dug-up stories in their hip pockets. I don't mean that the new crop of reporters are a comedown. They are better than they have ever been by almost every standard. They are better educated and much more versatile than we were. I hate to say it but so are the editors, give or take an old grouch here and there. It isn't that the working press is dogging it. You can see the results in every edition. It is simply that we are outnumbered by people who pretend to be of help but are really a hindrance, whose very reason for being is anathama to our code.

The business of making news, of manufacturing it, is bigger than the profession of gathering it in the raw and reporting it directly from the source.

There are more trained liars, people who major in advertising and public relations, graduating from journalism schools than there are more-or-less trained truthtellers who major in reporting. The journalism schools dump these disciplines together because they need the enrollment and money that the new glamour media courses generate. What distresses me is that kids finish school not knowing the difference between being a hack for special interests and being a reporter on special assignment. Because they've seen wornout, soldout reporters go back and forth between these fields, they assume that it is all the same thing, really, and that PR is more attractive because it pays more.

It bothers me that they feel they can move from being paid to varnish the truth to being paid to bare the truth without the slightest disorientation. It is the same thing to them. They are bionic technocrats with a part missing. Eventually they fill up the press clubs and drive all the real reporters away.

Ask some child today what is the shape of milk, and he will say it comes in the shape of a glass or, if he has opened the icebox door or been to the store with Mommy, he will say it comes in the shape of plastic or cardboard containers.

Ask that same child, or even his parents, what is the shape of the news, and he would probably say it comes in the shape of a Cronkite on TV or in the shape of a newspaper. Ask Walter himself, or some editor, and he would probably say, wearily, that it comes in the shape of press conferences and briefings, speeches and demonstrations and planned happenings which have been set up to draw reporters and cameramen.

Ask any child who can read what milk is and they might well look at the label and say that milk is: a grade A, pasturized, homogenized, fortified drink with 2000 U.S.P units of Vitamin D added per quart with not more than 2 per cent butterfat and only 1 and a half per cent nonfat milk solids added.

What ever happened to the cow?

The same thing can be asked of the shape and taste of real events. They are buried beneath the cosmetics and costumes of image-making.

If Coke is the real thing, what is its equivalent in news? I'd say, hastily, that it is something of interest that happens in the natural sequence of human life that it is something that happens in and of itself, regardless of whether an image-maker is there to alter it to suit a client.

These interlopers, these skillful makeup artists, have painted the face of human events to the point where the last two presidential campaigns were nothing more than costume parties, masquerades for poseurs to become president.

The great question of '72 was not would Richard Nixon win again, but was he alive and well in the White House? For all we saw of him in the flesh the question was not all that outlandish. We saw and heard him on film and tape, and in that remove we saw and heard him read the speeches of his writers, but could we be sure it was the real man and not some old footage cleverly edited and reconstructed? Richard could have been some wax cadaver with a Moog synthesizer mouth. When we finally found him trying to cower in a non-existent corner of the oval office it was too late. The damage had been done.

The Jimmy Carter we thought we knew in the race of '76 was not the real Jimmy Carter. That is incredible, after all that news coverage. It is more than that. It is chilling. The image-makers won again. But what is even more chilling is that there was not really another alternative. Jerry Ford was just as much a product of the mortician's art as Jimmy was.

There is no reason to believe that it will change come 1980.

1. a. Defend the use and usefulness of PR writing in a letter to columnist Porterfield.

   b. Define the words *hack* and *flack*. Do these apply to PR writing? Explain.

   c. Columnist Porterfield calls PR people "hired liars." Is this true? Explain.

2. Much of persuasive writing depends on using words for their connotative (the attitude or emotion they evoke) rather than denotative meaning.

   a. In the following list of words, fill in the blanks with an appropriate word:*

Complimentary	Derogatory	Neutral
investigator	spy	( )
captive	( )	prisoner
( )	bureaucrat	government employee

---

*For example, complimentary: public servant; derogatory: jailbird; neutral: detective.

b. Add ten more sets of words to the examples in this list.

c. Language often indicates attitude, and the following passages each indicate a specific attitude. Define the attitude and rewrite the passage to suggest a different point of view.

   (1) "From the averted faces and cold shoulders of the poll readers in Washington, the President escaped by steamboat to the smiles and welcome of Middle America." ("Cruisin' Down the River," *Time*, September 3, 1979, p. 18).

   (2) "Some Jewish organizations and intellectuals who were previously identified with the aspirations of black Americans become apologists for the racial status quo." ("'With Sorrow and Anger,'" *Time*, September 3, 1979, p. 16).

   (3) These criminal defendants have a clear interest in making false and sensational charges in an effort to bargain for leniency.

3. You are given responsibility for promoting the university's blood drive. Where would you go to look for information about blood banks, blood drives, blood donors—the material for your releases? Who are your publics? How would you find out what they know, and what their attitudes are about donating blood? How would you find the most effective media for reaching these publics? What kinds of questions do you need to be asking in your research effort?

4. Design a questionnaire to give to students (a) before the blood drive and (b) after the blood drive. The questionnaire should try to determine why students do or do not give blood and what promotional methods might be most effective in getting them to do so.

P A R T

TWO

WRITING PRINCIPLES

PR writers must have a basic understanding of writing principles. But simply knowing how to construct sentences and paragraphs is not enough. Chapters 4–6 discuss some of the finer points of writing to communicate.

4

WRITING FOR CLARITY AND INTEREST

"Every successful piece of nonfiction," says writer William Zinsser, "should leave the reader with one provocative thought that he didn't have before. Not two thoughts, or five—just one."[1]

Zinsser's book *On Writing Well* is full of excellent advice on how to produce good writing. It's worth reading. But all the advice in all the books about writing is worthless if you don't learn the most important point first: *Write so people will understand what you mean.* That is the one provocative thought you should take with you from this chapter.

Unfortunately, thousands of students and beginning writers never learn this lesson. They are taught all sorts of grammar rules and innumerable terms for tenses and cases, figures of speech and other rhetorical devices. Somehow all these details obscure the purpose for writing—communication. Good writing is writing that succeeds in communicating. Bad writing is writing that fails to communicate.

You won't be very successful in communicating if you just pour words onto paper without giving them much thought beforehand, or with more concern for displaying your vocabulary than for communicating with your readers. You can't expect to flip on the typewriter and rattle off page after page of high-quality prose. Writing well is harder than that.

For some, the ability to arrange words and express meanings clearly is a skill that comes naturally, a gift. For most of us, though, writing well is hard work. It is a craft that must be learned.

How do you produce prose that succeeds in communicating? There is no magic formula, but there are a few basic guidelines. This chapter discusses some of those guidelines.

MESSAGE, AUDIENCE, MEDIUM

An important part of good writing is being properly prepared before you sit down at the typewriter. You must do the necessary research on the subject matter so you will understand the material, understand what is important, and know just what you want to communicate. You must know who will receive your communication, and you must know something about them. You must know how to reach the people you want to get your message, and you must know how different ways of reaching people affect the manner in which you prepare your material. In short, you must know your message, your audience, and your medium.

Message

Most writing, whether for public relations purposes or otherwise, has one goal: to convey a message. The goal of any writer is to transfer his or her thoughts to the minds of other people, via a piece of paper or some other visual, verbal or electronic medium. Step one, then, is deciding just what you want to say. If you don't understand what you're trying to say, neither will your audience.

This means you must know *exactly* what you are trying to say. Don't express your message in hazy, abstract terms. A psychologist points out that communication attempts often fail simply because the message is not "spelled out."[2] For example, an executive wrote a memo asking for "more loyalty" in his department. What he really wanted was somebody around "to answer the telephone when he called at 7:30 a.m." And then there is the woman who tells her husband that "she wants to be 'really cared for.' What she means is that she wants to go out to dinner."

Make sure you understand your message before you begin to write. If you can't write a short, simple sentence that summarizes the point you want to make, you probably need to do a little more thinking.

Audience

It's not enough, however, for you to understand your message. You must phrase it so the audience will also understand. You must know who your readers (or listeners) are (see target audience, p. 7), and you must know something of their characteristics, values and beliefs (see demographics and psychographics, pp. 7–8). Otherwise, you won't be able to communicate effectively. In short, you must tailor your message to the audience.

Medium

Part of tailoring your message to an audience is choosing the right media to reach that audience. In the same way, different media are appropriate for different types of messages. Choosing the right media is an important aspect of successful communication (see pp. 8–10).

The choice of medium in turn affects the way you should frame the message. Articles written for magazines are done in an entirely different style from public service announcements on radio. You must use the style appropriate for the medium, being aware of the medium's technological advantages and limitations.

These three rules—know your message, know your audience, know your medium—will take you a long way toward successful writing. Both the substance and the style of what you write depend on them.

These rules, however, apply only to the planning stages of writing. Even if you know your message, your audience, and your medium, your writing may fail. The execution is just as important as the preparation. So add two rules for successful execution: Write clearly so your readers will understand, and make what you write interesting so your readers will want to read it.

CLARITY AND INTEREST: ELEMENTS OF STYLE

Clarity, of course, is the number one aim of writing style. If your audience doesn't understand what you've written, your efforts have been wasted. But even if your writing is clear, a dull style can put your readers to sleep, and they won't get the message in that case, either.

Fortunately, the ability to write clear prose is not mysterious. It can be learned. Thanks to scientific research in the field of readability, the principles of clear writing are well known. You simply must learn them and practice them.

Readability

"If a person's motive is strong enough," writes readability expert Robert Gunning, "he will plow through any complexity of words, signs or hieroglyphs."[3] Sometimes the audience of a PR writer is intensely interested in the subject and will read through the worst writing to try to glean the slightest bit of new information. Usually, though, interest is not that great. And readers, bombarded from all sides with innumerable PR messages from different communicators, are likely to toss aside any messages that demand too much time or effort. Remember, the easier something is to read, the more likely it is that someone will read it.

What qualities make writing "easy to read"? This question has been the subject of a vast amount of research. And, especially as interpreted by writing consultants like Gunning and Rudolf Flesch, it has revealed a number of elements that make writing readable. As early as 1935 researchers had identified more than 60 qualities affecting readability, and more have been found since. However, many are related to the two qualities usually considered the most important: sentence length and word length.

Sentence Length The first principle of readable writing is to keep most sentences short. For the meaning to be clear, the reader must be able to grasp at once the relationship among the words in a sentence. Long, tangled sentences tend to obscure those relationships.

Of course, not *every* sentence should be short. An endless stream of short sentences makes for dull reading. And it is possible to write a long sentence that is also clear—just make sure that the sentence is properly constructed.

The key to readability, then, is *average* sentence length. An occasional long sentence is no problem. It is the never-ending series of long sentences that leaves readers dizzy. According to Gunning, modern prose read by the public has an average sentence length of about 16 words.[4] If your sentences are, on the average, much longer than that, your prose probably isn't as readable as it should be.

There are two major reasons why sentences are too long. One is the tendency of writers to connect independent clauses with coordinating conjunctions or to add details that could be left to later sentences. The other is simply the presence of a lot of words that don't need to be there. The cures are easy: Use more periods and fewer words.

Some long sentences, for example, can simply be cut in two with a period at the right spot. Take the following sentence-paragraph, for example:

> That may have worked out just dandy for the cigarette companies where advertising's influence on brand switching is the lowest of any major product category, but what about a company, or an industry, under fierce attack from many sides, including a press which itself has the opportunity to use time on radio and television to present the side of the story they wish to take?

The sentence is fairly clear. But it would be easy enough to put a period after "category" and give the reader a chance to breathe.

Other sentences need a little more work than just a period, especially sentences that are long because they don't stick to the point. Consider this example from a bank's PR magazine (the names have been changed to protect the guilty):

> The goal of the campaign, developed and implemented by the ABC Agency of Metropolis, is to communicate through all major media—radio, television, outdoor and newspaper—that Smallville National is the best bank to serve the people of Smallville because it is the largest.

This 44-word sentence is just longer than it needs to be to say what it has to say. It starts out well enough, promising to tell what the goal of the new ad campaign is. But along the way the sentence gets sidetracked into details about who designed the campaign and what media will be used. Stripped of the unneeded details, the sentence might read:

> The campaign will tell people that Smallville National is the best bank for them because it is the largest.
>
> Details could come in the following sentences.
>
> Ads will appear in all major media—radio, TV, newspapers and billboards. The ABC Agency of Metropolis developed the campaign.

Now, instead of one 44-word sentence, we have three sentences averaging just 13 words in length.

Sometimes sentences are too long simply because of extra words, not extra ideas. Writers frequently use three or four or five words where one will do. And often words are tossed in that aren't needed at all. Take this sentence, for example:

> Students educated in the concept that PR is a management function once on the job sometimes find the realities of PR practice demand a dismaying command of communication skills.

The phrase "educated in the concept" can be replaced with "taught"; "once on the job" can be deleted completely. The sentence is shorter and the message is clearer.

Keeping sentences short is just the starting place in writing clearly, though. Short sentences won't make reading easy if the words within those sentences don't make any sense. You can't write clear sentences if you don't use clear words.

Word Length A student with an exceptional vocabulary once turned in what he thought was an especially well-written paper. The professor's comment scribbled across the paper was simply: "Avoid sesquipedalianism." Since the student's vocabulary wasn't *that* large, he scurried to a dictionary to look up "sesquipedalianism." He found it means the excessive use of long words.

The professor could easily have written "Don't use so many long words" and the student would have understood immediately. The point for PR writers is twofold. First, if you use long words, some readers won't understand them. Second, even if you use long words with well-known meanings, you make reading more difficult.

There is no need to say "precipitation" when you mean "rain." There is nothing wrong with saying "use" instead of "employ" or "utilize." "Fair" is just as good a word as "equitable."

Some writers can't resist filling their prose with important sounding phrases like "integrated conceptual analysis" or similar verbose nonsense. At least twice in every sentence they use words ending in -ment, -ancy, -ial, and -ation. Avoid such words when you can. They make reading more difficult and diminish the forcefulness of your statement. As PR writer Alden S. Wood points out, who would have responded to these words?

> Retain your earth! Abstain from engagement in interpersonal ballistic relationships unless these relationships are initiated by the power incumbents. If, however, it becomes apparent that overt hostile interaction is to commence, let this commencement have its genesis in this geopolitical region.

The average sentence length in this paragraph is less than 14 words. But the words are so foggy that the meaning is completely lost. Fortunately, Captain John Parker didn't talk like that. Instead he uttered the famous command, "Stand your ground. Don't fire unless fired upon. But if they mean to have a war, let it begin here."

Why do long words make reading more difficult? One reason is that long words tend to be abstract. Readers comprehend more quickly if words are concrete—that is, if they evoke visual images. If an oil company says it's spending money on "petroleum exploration facilities," for example, the average reader won't have a very clear notion of what the company is buying. They will, however, if the company says "drilling rigs."

Also, long words are often unfamiliar to readers. Common words, which readers recognize immediately, are usually short. Why say "remuneration" when "pay" will do?

Readability Formulas Short sentences and short words are the prime ingredients of clear writing. These ideas have been incorporated into various formulas to gauge the "readability" of a piece of writing (see Appendix A). These formulas—notably those devised by Gunning and Flesch—can be very useful to writers who want to check the clarity of their prose. Keep in mind, though, that a good readability score doesn't guarantee good writing. Readability formulas are actually nothing more than measures of structural simplicity, and, as Gunning points out, "nonsense written simply is still nonsense."[5]

Besides, clarity may be the first goal of writing, but it's not the only goal. Clear writing can be stilted and unnatural. Writing can be so simple that it's just plain boring. Clarity is worthless if the writing isn't also interesting, for writing that isn't interesting usually isn't read.

What makes writing interesting? Primarily, the subject matter. Some subjects are interesting to some people but not to others (which is why you should know your audience).

Here, though, we're concerned with style. The basic goals of style are, in addition to clarity, the logical development of ideas and a smooth transition from one idea to the next. Of course, style must also help maintain the reader's interest. Writing must be lively, with generous use of active verbs and vivid phrases. Interesting writing sounds natural, is not monotonous, and, in general, is "pleasing to the ear." Interesting writing uses personal words like *you* and *people* to enhance human interest. Thus, along with the fundamental goal of clarity, good writers strive for naturalness, variety, euphony, and human interest.

Naturalness

Reading is easiest if the style is conversational. Readability experts agree that one of the basic rules of readable writing is "write like you talk." Of course, you can't write exactly like you talk. There is a difference between the written and the spoken language. Spoken sentences are not carefully structured, and there is a great amount of repetition. In speaking, meaning can be shaded by intonation, inflection, facial expressions and gestures. You can't duplicate such features of the spoken language in your writing. But you can write prose that sounds natural, as though someone *could* have spoken it.

The following sentence, for example, is clear, but it sounds like it was written and not spoken:

> Smith was not disturbed that Johnson had submitted his resignation. He said that the position held by Johnson was not of high significance.

The same thing could have been written in a more natural, conversational manner:

> Johnson's resignation didn't really bother Smith. He said Johnson's job wasn't very important, anyway.

A good test of naturalness is to read aloud what you've written. If you stumble over phrases and your tongue gets twisted, the sentence is not easy enough to read. Try again. If you still have trouble writing sentences that sound natural, try this approach. Write what you want to say as you would say it in conversation. Then go back and rewrite the sentence with proper syntax, making sure the pronouns are in the right place and the meaning is clear.

Another guide to natural writing can be found in radio and TV newscasts. The style is conversational, but the words would make perfect sense if written on paper.

A device that helps writing sound natural is the contraction. Use contractions freely. Everybody uses contractions in speech, and no matter what your old grammar school teacher used to tell you, there is absolutely nothing wrong with using them in writing. You suffer no loss of meaning when you use *don't*, *won't*, or *can't* instead of *do not*, *will not*, or *cannot*. Avoiding contractions does nothing but slow the reader down, and readers don't like to be slowed down.

Variety

Monotony can poison an otherwise good style. It's not enough to string a number of clear and natural sounding sentences together if their structure is so similar that readers get bored. The style must push the readers along and keep them going. Readers shouldn't feel they have to force themselves through sentence after sentence.

Variety means following the rules wisely. For example, we already mentioned that not all sentences must be short. True, a series of long sentences makes it hard for a reader to follow the flow. And it's easy to get lost in a maze of adverbial prepositional phrases. But an occasional long sentence, if constructed properly, can improve the flow of the narrative. A compound sentence can take the reader from one idea to the next. An occasional inversion of subject and verb reduces monotony and can emphasize the action in the sentence.

Use of the passive voice can also aid variety. The passive voice can be appropriate if the object of the action is the most important thing in the sentence. But keep passive sentences few and far between. Nothing is more boring than an endless stream of passive sentences.

Notice the improvement when we substitute the active voice for the passive in the following sentences:

Passive: Everything possible was done by company engineers to restore service.

Active: Company engineers did everything they could to restore service.

Passive: It was requested by the company president that the exhibit be kept open by the museum officials.

Active: The company president asked museum officials to keep the exhibit open.

Many writers aware of the need for variety in sentence structure go out of their way to achieve variety in word choice. This leads to sentences where three or four words are used to describe the same thing, as in:

When my books arrived, I took the hardbound texts from the package and placed the treasured volumes on my bookcase next to my other bound publications.

Usage experts call this "elegant variation." "There are few literary faults so widely prevalent," says one expert.[6] No doubt the problem stems from the widespread belief that you should never use the same word twice in one sentence. But no such prohibition exists in any rule book, and a single repetition is seldom as terrible as some writers think. Of course, repeating the same word several times can get boring. But you don't have to thumb through a thesaurus to find a synonym. Usually a pronoun works well enough: "I took the books out of the box and put them on the shelf with my others."

In other cases, there's no need to repeat the word at all: "Jones, Smith and Brown all won races; it was Jones' first win, Smith's third victory, and Brown's fourth triumph." But the vocabulary lesson is unnecessary. It's just as clear to say it was Jones' first win, Smith's third and Brown's fourth.

If there's no way to get around repetition, go ahead and use the same word again. It won't hurt you. And the reader won't have to figure out if you used different words because of some real difference or because you were trying to display your vast vocabulary.

As for the thesaurus, don't throw it away. But use it only when you are looking for a specific word, the exactly right word, which you know but just can't think of at the moment. It is rarely wise to pick a word you've never heard of or used before.

Euphony

The main reason so many writers worry about sentence variety and word repetition is their desire for euphony. Indeed, there is nothing wrong with writing that is pleasing to the ear. Writing that is rhythmic, that makes appropriate use of figures of speech, is usually more enjoyable to read than straightforward stilted prose.

The only way to achieve euphony is to read good writing and develop an ear for it. If you discover a good style that is used successfully by someone else, don't worry about copying it. Just don't get carried away. As one observer puts it, a "concatenation of mellifluous phrases may indicate more polish than insight."[7] First make sure your thoughts are clear and your message is pleasing to the mind. Then worry about pleasing the ear.

Human Interest

If you are writing about people, your writing will naturally have elements of human interest. But if your subject is something mechanical, impersonal, or abstract, your task is more difficult. How can you achieve human interest when writing about inanimate objects? The trick is to remember that you're writing *to* people even when you're not writing about them. When appropriate, address the reader as "you." Use the pronoun "we" to refer to people in general when discussing common knowledge, as in, "We know today that the world is round." Rhetorical questions and direct quotations also help make the writing sound personal.

Rudolf Flesch has used these ideas to construct a "human interest" test for prose. The formula is described fully in Appendix A. Basically, Flesch's test merely checks that the writer has used an adequate number of personal words and personal sentences. If you don't want to be bothered with the formula, just look over your writing. If you don't find any rhetorical questions or direct quotations, if you never use "we" or "you," then you're prose isn't likely to be very interesting.

**CHAPTER 4
WRITING FOR CLARITY
AND INTEREST**

4-1 WRITING CHECKLIST

1. Is the message clear? Have you said exactly what you want to say?
2. Have you identified important audiences? Does your writing speak to those audiences?
3. Is the style of writing appropriate for the intended medium?
4. Are your sentences instantly clear? Free from confusing constructions?
5. Are sentences, on average, fairly short? Have you avoided stringing long sentences together?
6. Is your writing concise, free from needless words?
7. Have you used common, concrete words? Words that evoke visual images?
8. Is your language natural? Can your writing be easily read aloud?
9. Is there variety in the sentence structure?
10. Are most sentences in the active voice?
11. Have you made sufficient use of personal words and sentences?

CONCLUSION

Most rules of writing are not ends in themselves, but means to an end. The end—the goal—is clear communication.

Only by carefully observing the principles of clear writing can you be confident of getting your message across (see Table 4–1).

The three first rules—know your message, know your audience, know the medium—are basic but only the beginning. You must also make your prose interesting, and that means it must appeal to people, sound natural, and not be monotonous. Above all, however, you must strive for clarity. Write so your readers will understand what you mean.

NOTES

[1] William Zinsser, *On Writing Well* (New York: Harper and Row, 1980), pp. 56–57.

[2] Kay Holmquist, "Feelings Poorly Defined, Says Psychologist," Fort Worth *Star-Telegram*, August 19, 1979, p. 19f.

[3] Robert Gunning, *The Technique of Clear Writing* (New York: McGraw-Hill, 1968), p. 13.

[4] Ibid., p. 51.

[5] Ibid., p. 44.

[6] H. W. Fowler, *Modern English Usage* (New York: Oxford University Press, 1965), p. 148.

[7] Kenneth E. Andersen, *Persuasion Theory and Practice* (Boston: Allyn and Bacon, 1971), p. 126.

SELECTED BIBLIOGRAPHY

Jacques Barzun and Henry F. Graff, *The Modern Researcher*, 3d ed. (New York: Harcourt Brace Jovanovich, 1977).

Rudolf Flesch, *The Art of Readable Writing*, 25th anniversary ed. (New York: Harper and Row, 1974).

Robert Gunning, *The Technique of Clear Writing*, rev. ed. (New York: McGraw-Hill, 1968).

William L. Rivers, *Writing: Craft and Art* (Englewood Cliffs, N.J.: Prentice-Hall, 1975).

William Zinsser, *On Writing Well*, 2d ed. (New York: Harper and Row, 1980).

5

SIMPLIFYING THE COMPLEX

In his first paper on the theory of relativity, written in 1905, Albert Einstein penned one of the simplest sentences you'll ever find in a scientific paper. In describing a point about time and simultaneity, Einstein wrote (in English translation):

> If, for instance, I say, "That train arrives here at 7 o'clock," I mean something like this: "The pointing of the small hand of my watch to 7 and the arrival of the train are simultaneous events."[1]

You can't get much simpler than that.

Einstein treasured simplicity in writing, and while his scientific papers did get technical in places, his writings for the general public were always clear and readable. Einstein could write simply on subjects like relativity because he understood them so completely himself. He could write clearly, without too many technical terms, because he knew his subject thoroughly enough to be able to express the ideas in plain language and still express them accurately.

PR writers are not likely to be as knowledgeable about any subject as Einstein was about physics. Yet they are still called on to translate complex subjects into language the general public can understand. There is nothing simple about nuclear power or pollution chemistry or petroleum economics. Medicine, urban affairs and social services can be as complex as advanced calculus. Yet such issues are becoming more and more important to the average citizen. PR people must be able to explain the implications of government and corporate actions in these areas, as well as interpret the latest research findings.

Millions of diet soft drink consumers, for example, are intensely interested in scientific research on the health effects of artificial sweeteners. Beverage companies, government agencies, universities and other institutions must be able to explain what's going on. Doing so is far more difficult than preparing a news release about the appointment of a new vice president. It takes special writing skills to simplify the complex without at the same time explaining it inaccurately.

Some authorities think it's impossible to explain complex things like scientific research to the general public. Even Rudolf Flesch, the ultimate advocate of simplifying the complex, advises writers not to try to give complete scientific explanations. You can describe the meaning of a discovery, he says, and indicate its importance. But a complete scientific explanation? Flesch wouldn't even try that with his own readability formula:[2]

> Here I would have to get into statistical regression formulas and multiple correlation and whatnot, and nobody who hasn't had a course in statistics would know what I am talking about.... There is only one bit of advice I can offer in this business of giving laymen an exact scientific explanation: don't try.

Not everybody agrees with this attitude. William Zinsser says "a complex subject can be made as accessible to the layman as a simple subject. It's just a question of putting one sentence after another."[3]

In practice, it isn't often much use explaining deep scientific principles to nonscientists—not because they couldn't understand, but because most people aren't really interested. If a reader is interested in a subject, however, a good writer can explain it. You can even explain statistics to people who haven't had statistics courses, *if* they are interested enough to follow what might be a fairly lengthy explanation.

Today, in many cases, people aren't "merely" interested in scientific explanations. They demand them. If your company is building a nuclear power plant near a town, you'd better be able to explain to the people who live there what that plant does and how its safety systems work. You can't get by with saying "Don't worry—it's safe."

And if the public doesn't ask technical questions directly, newspaper reporters and electronic journalists will. Today, the mass media deal with more technical subjects in greater detail than ever before. When reporters working on such stories don't understand something themselves, they often go to PR people for explanations. PR writers, frequently trained only in journalism or English and not in the technical fields they must try to interpret, often find themselves at a loss. When an activist group accuses your company of cheating on taxes, how do you explain the complexities of accelerated depreciation and the investment tax credit? How does the PR person for a factory suspected of polluting the air explain the difference between primary ambient air standards and secondary emission limits? How does the spokesperson for a nuclear plant explain the meaning of "10 picocuries of radioactivity"?

It isn't easy. These things can be explained, though. You can simplify the complex, and you can simplify it accurately. But only if, like Einstein, you know your subject.

KNOW YOUR SUBJECT

There is an old saying popular among newspaper city editors to the effect that a good reporter can cover any story. If the reporter doesn't know much about the subject, he or she can simply call up an expert, ask a few questions, and then explain it all to readers in words they'll understand. Or so the theory goes.

If this was ever true, it isn't any more. And it's no truer for PR writers than for reporters. Nevertheless, pamphlets on complex subjects are often written this way. An engineer produces a technical description of some process or machine or whatever in the peculiar twisted English characteristic of the profession. The copy is handed to the PR person, who edits and rewrites to simplify the language but keep the facts as the engineer wrote them. In theory the PR person need know nothing about the subject—the engineer provides the facts. The PR writer just needs to know how to write clearly.

The problem with this theory is that you can't simplify complex writing unless you know what it means. You must understand it thoroughly yourself before you can explain it to somebody else. You must know more about the subject than you'll ever put in print. If you don't, you won't be able to tell when a statement as simplified can stand alone or should be qualified. And you won't know the difference between a correct statement and a false one.

Consider this example from a writer trying to describe the dangers of cigarettes in simple terms:

> Opening another front in its war on smoking, the federal government plans to publicize a new peril—carbon monoxide—to prod the cigarette industry to reduce its use of that substance in cigarettes as it has reduced tar and nicotine.

Simple enough, this sentence, but also sheer nonsense. Carbon monoxide is not a substance that exists inside tobacco, waiting to be unleashed. It is a gas created when carbon (in the tobacco) combines with oxygen (from the air) as tobacco burns. The writer simply didn't know much about the subject.

The same is true of the reporter who attempted to describe nuclear fast breeder reactors:

> The fast breeder gets its name... because the chain reaction is so much faster than in conventional... reactors.

Again, this is a readable simplification of a complex idea. It's also an incorrect simplification. The "fast" in fast breeder doesn't refer to the rate of the chain reaction (which would be measured by the number of atoms splitting per second) but to the speed of neutrons, small subatomic particles that fly around inside reactors and split atoms. In ordinary nuclear power plants atoms are split mostly by slow neutrons; in fast breeders, speedy neutrons do most of the splitting.

How can you avoid such mistakes? You simply must research your subject before you begin writing, and research it thoroughly. Get help from experts on points you don't understand. Recheck any passage containing statements you're not absolutely sure of.

Finally, don't try to tell readers everything you know. That always takes you to fringe areas, where your knowledge gets a little shaky and errors begin to creep in. Statements perfectly consistent with what you know might be inconsistent with what you *don't* know. Besides, if you tell the readers everything *you* know, you're probably telling them a lot more than *they* want or need to know. Give readers just what they need to get the message.

For example, if you wished to continue the story of carbon monoxide in cigarette smoke, you might be tempted to write something like this:

> Carbon monoxide, a molecule of which consists of a carbon atom bonded to an oxygen atom, is dangerous because of its chemical affinity to hemoglobin. Hemoglobin, a complex chemical substance containing iron, serves as a transport mechanism for oxygen in the blood stream. Since the affinity of carbon monoxide to hemoglobin is greater than the affinity of oxygen to hemoglobin, carbon monoxide impairs the ability of hemoglobin to carry oxygen.

This explanation, while essentially accurate, is too much. Unless you're writing for medical students or biochemists, just say that carbon monoxide impairs the ability of the blood to carry oxygen through the body. *You* should know all about hemoglobin and oxygen transport. But you don't need to tell everybody about it. The more you know about a subject, the easier it will be to simplify, and the less likely you are to make mistakes.

There is one danger, though, in knowing a lot about a subject. When you have written on the subject for a while, you may find yourself using the jargon of the discipline. This is the fatal flaw in most writing on technical subject matter. If you want the audience to understand what you write, avoid using technical terms. Instead, follow the golden rule of simplifying the complex: Use Plain English.

PLAIN ENGLISH

Most people know plain English when they hear it. It is everyday language, free from the long words and technical terms that plague the prose of scientists, engineers, economists, doctors, lawyers, or writers in other specialized disciplines. All professions and trades have special vocabularies that members use when they communicate among themselves. Unfortunately, some members use the same words—the jargon of the field—when they try to communicate with people *outside* the discipline. It doesn't work. To write plain English, you must avoid jargon.

Avoid Jargon

Within any profession, jargon has its uses. A jargon term may stand for a complicated concept that would take paragraphs to describe in full.

Once members of a profession agree on such a term, they can use it freely since everyone within the discipline knows what it means. What communicators must realize is that people not trained in the field *don't* know what it or similar terms mean.

Writers must also recognize two other types of jargon that cause problems. One type consists of common words that have special meanings to the members of a given group. Printers, for example, use words like *flat* and *signature* in an entirely different way from most people. Writers must make sure that readers understand when a common word is used with a special meaning.

The other type consists of fancy words used for common concepts, as when members of a given group use long or obscure words instead of short familiar ones that mean the same thing. Engineers, for example, often use technical terms to sound impressive. Consider the following sentence, written by an engineer who was explaining some of the drawbacks of solar-electric power plants:

> All solar-thermal systems must accept diurnal transients and rapid transients from cloud passage during daily operation.

He was trying to say that it gets dark at night and that clouds sometimes block out the sun. The idea wasn't any more complicated than that, and there's no reason to make it sound any more complicated than that.

Or take, for example, this passage from an article on a new polymer adhesive (glue, to use plain English) used to restore some old statues and buildings:

> The degradation of polymers by ambient ultraviolet radiation is slow. The epoxies that degrade fastest take about six months to show the first signs of degradation.... One early symptom of degradation due to the absorption of ultraviolet light is discoloration of the polymer. The material begins to look yellow, and it also becomes chalky. Eventually it peels away from the stone.

This passage isn't really that bad, but it can be improved. After explaining that the ultraviolet rays are just a part of sunshine, the author could have written:

> Ultraviolet light breaks up the glues slowly. Even the weakest glues take about six months to show the first signs of breaking up.... An early sign that ultraviolet light has attacked the glue is a change in color. The glue turns yellow and becomes chalky. Eventually it peels away from the stone.

Good writers never use fancy jargon words when common words will do the job as well. Sometimes, though, common words won't do the job as well. If a word has no "plain English" equivalent, and if it's essential to your subject, you have no choice but to use it. But make sure you explain to the readers what this new term means.

Often all you need to do is supply a simple definition when you introduce the word. But usually there's more to simplifying the complex than defining technical terms; in fact, dictionary definitions are frequently as confusing as the terms themselves. Remember that your purpose is not to build the readers' vocabularies but to convey an idea. Usually you can get the idea across more clearly if you *describe* the new term instead of defining it.

Describe, Don't Define

Assume you're writing about the use of the chemical element lithium as an agent for treating psychological depression. It seems a good idea to first define lithium. So you turn to the dictionary and find: "lithium: a soft silver-white element of the alkali metal group. Atomic number 3, atomic weight 6.941." This is not a very useful definition. If this is all you tell your readers, they won't really know much more than they did before.

Instead, you could write: "Lithium is a silvery-white metal that is very light—in fact, it's the lightest metal known. It's also very soft and can be cut with a knife. Its name comes from the Greek word *lithos*, meaning 'stone.'" Now your readers will have a picture of lithium in their heads. You've removed some of the mystery behind the name and can go on to discuss the uses of lithium.

For the same reason, it does little good to define *kilowatt-hour* as "the amount of energy consumed when an electrical demand of one kilowatt is maintained for one hour." You're much better off if you describe a kilowatt-hour as the amount of electricity it takes to run a hand hair dryer for an hour, or as the energy needed to toast three loaves of bread. These are not good scientific definitions of a kilowatt-hour, but they are good descriptions—and they're much more likely to be understood.

Whether you use definitions or descriptions, though, you shouldn't introduce too many new terms. Using technical terms is a luxury to be indulged in sparingly. Don't expect a reader to assimilate several new terms at once. Of course, some writers operate on the "define and proceed" principle. This is a favorite method of textbook writers. They come to a new term—or five new terms, or however many they need—define them, and go on with the story, using the new terms freely. The unfortunate students find they must check back to the original definitions every ten seconds or so to keep track of what they're reading.

Textbook writers don't have much choice, however, since their purpose is often to teach a student the vocabulary of a new field. And this goal requires definitions. But PR writers have a different aim—to communicate a single message. You can't do that if you introduce new terms just to educate the audience. You have to convey the main part of your message in words the audience already understands. In other words, use plain English as much as possible.

If you're writing a medical brochure about interferon, a protein substance in the body that helps to fight disease, you must use the term *interferon*. But you don't need to give your readers a complete lesson in biochemistry. Avoid the temptation to use words like *fibroblasts* or *lipopolysaccharides*. Even if you define these terms, using them will obscure what you're trying to say about interferon.

What if such terms are essential to the discussion? The point is they're probably not. At least the terms themselves aren't. Fibroblasts might be important, but you can just as easily say "connective tissue cells." Simply describe such things without naming them. It will be easier for you and the readers.

Of course, you can't describe technical terms without knowing what they mean. So whenever you're writing on a specific technical subject, keep a specialized dictionary on hand. If you're writing about geology, for example, you should have a dictionary of earth science or some comparable reference work at your fingertips.

What if you replace jargon with common words where possible and do a good job of describing any necessary technical terms, and the message is *still* too complex for the average reader? In that case, you simply must provide readers with enough background so they *will* understand. But you have to be careful not to give too much background at once. Take one step at a time.

ONE STEP AT A TIME

You can confuse readers by telling them too much at once. A reader can accept one new fact if you use understandable words, but don't expect to transfer several new thoughts at the same time. The reader's mind will flash "overload" and stop taking in anything. It's like blowing a fuse when you plug too many appliances into the same outlet. The brain, like an electrical circuit, can stand only so much flow.

You have to introduce one new idea at a time. And you must do so in logical order. The first idea should help explain the second, the second, the third, and so on.

If you start with the simplest idea and proceed one step at a time, you can eventually take the reader to a high degree of sophistication. This is Isaac Asimov's description of how he wrote a book on mathematics:[4]

> It was about elementary arithmetic, to begin with, and it was not until the second chapter that I as much as got to Arabic numerals, and not until the fourth chapter that I got to fractions. However, by the end of the book I was talking about imaginary numbers, hyperimaginary numbers, and transfinite numbers—and that was the real purpose of the book. In going from counting to transfinites, I followed such a careful and gradual plan that it never stopped seeming easy.

Using the one-step-at-a-time approach, you can eventually explain almost anything. The important thing is to make sure the first step is in the right place. After you've identified the main points and put them in order, look at the first point. Will your audience know what you're talking about? Naturally, that depends on the audience. If you're explaining how a nuclear power plant works, your first point might be "splitting atoms gives off energy" or more technically "fissioning of atomic nuclei gives off energy." If your audience consists of high school science teachers, it is probably safe to assume they know about atoms, and you can start with a description of how a nucleus can be split to release energy. But suppose you're explaining nuclear power to a group of people who never went to high school but live near the new nuclear power plant. In this case you'll have to start by describing atoms.

The key to success in using this method lies in identifying the steps. You must determine at the outset what the central points are. Many writers do this well enough, but somewhere between the start and the finish the central ideas get lost. Communicating the complex is bound to fail if only the writer knows what the central ideas are. Make the central points clear to the reader.

MAKE THE CENTRAL POINTS CLEAR

Whether you're writing on a complex subject or a simple one, the objective is still the same—to convey a message. Messages must be supported with facts and figures, descriptions and explanations. You can't leave out important details. Too often, though, writers let details and descriptions obscure the message. The central point is buried in a paragraph of statistics or turns up at the end of a series of equivocal qualifying phrases. Don't lose track of your purpose. Make sure the main idea stands out.

Usually you do this by stating your main point clearly and forcefully at the outset, leaving the details to come later. It is much easier for readers to follow a chain of explanations if they know ahead of time what the point of the story is.

If you don't make the main point clear, your audience not only won't get the message, they also won't attach much importance to what you have to say. Take the case of an electric utility organization whose spokesman was asked to respond to a ruling by the Federal Power Commission. The utilities wanted the FPC to allow them to charge customers for the interest on money borrowed to build power plants, while the plants were being built. Except for a few specific expenses, the FPC said no.

When wire service reporters asked the Edison Electric Institute for a comment, the organization's president responded with this:

> We are disappointed that the Federal Power Commission, after long deliberation, has tentatively adopted such a restricted approach to construction work in progress. Inclusion of CWIP in the rate base with a commensurate rate of return is an important method of reducing the need for outside financing.

If the reporters understood what he said, they certainly didn't care. They called up an environmentalist group for its reaction to the FPC decision. That group's spokesperson said the decision was "a stunning victory for consumers" and then offered a dollar estimate of what the savings for consumers would be.

It isn't hard to guess which comment was in the lead paragraph of the UPI story that resulted. UPI led with the "stunning victory" quote and the utility statement didn't make it into the first five paragraphs, which is all that some papers carried. The Associated Press led with the environmental group's estimate of savings. The utility group showed up in paragraph nine.

Why? The environmentalists' statement is a dramatic, well-put reaction that has impact, clarity and simplicity. Their statement was written by somebody who knew how to write. They knew the point they wanted to make, and they made it. The utility statement sounds like it was written by a committee. Succeeding paragraphs continue in the same way, mixing important points with needless qualifications and elaborations. Because the main point was not identified and stated clearly, few people got the message.

Of course, failure to make the point clear was not the only problem with the utility's statement. It simply contained too many unfamiliar ideas. "CWIP," "rate base," and "rate of return" are not part of the working vocabularies of most readers. These are unfamiliar terms, and people don't grasp messages filled with words they don't understand. The solution is to explain the unfamiliar with things that *are* familiar.

EXPLAIN THE UNFAMILIAR WITH THE FAMILIAR

Reader's don't easily understand complicated explanations of things they know nothing about. But if you can tie your subject to something within the reader's experience, you can skip several steps of definition and description and get right to the explanation.

Simple analogies can work wonders in getting people to understand why things are the way they are. An electric utility often faces criticism because its large industrial users pay a lower cost for electricity (in cents per kilowatt-hour) than residential customers do. Utility rate setting is very complicated, but a writer for one company hit on an idea to explain the price difference using an analogy with tomatoes. When tomatoes, delivery trucks and catsup replace generators, transmission lines and transformers, readers can concentrate on the message instead of trying to understand unfamiliar terminology (see Example 5–1).

Scientific subjects especially call for explanations in familiar words. It is possible, of course, to explain how a mass spectrometer measures the weight of various molecules by describing electromagnetic acceleration of molecule beams and mass-charge ratios. But most people have

5-1 "TOMATOES ARE EASIER TO UNDERSTAND"

A PR writer for an electric utility company attempted to explain an unfamiliar subject—the setting of electric rates—by discussing a similar process using something familiar to most readers—tomatoes. This article appeared in a newsletter alongside a more detailed article that discussed electricity rate setting in more specific (though also readable) terms.

TOMATOES ARE EASIER TO UNDERSTAND

To put cost-of-service principles into more familiar terms, let's forget about the electric utility business for a moment. Let's talk about tomatoes.

Acme Tomato Company sells and delivers tomatoes. The company charges 10 cents for each tomato. It also charges a 50 cent fee for deliveries to cover the expenses of the delivery truck and driver.

Acme has two customers. On one side of town is Harriet, a homemaker. She buys two tomatoes each day for husband Harvey's sandwiches. On the other side of town is Craig's Catsup Company. Craig buys 50 tomatoes each day to make catsup.

Acme delivers Harriet two tomatoes and charges her 70 cents. That's two tomatoes at 10 cents each plus the 50 cent delivery fee. That figures out to be 35 cents a tomato.

$$\frac{(2 \times 10¢) + 50¢}{2} = 35¢ \text{ per tomato}$$

Acme delivers Craig's Catsup Company 50 tomatoes each day and charges him $5.50. That's 50 tomatoes at 10 cents each plus the 50 cent delivery fee. That figures out to be 11 cents a tomato.

$$\frac{(50 \times 10¢) + 50¢}{50} = 11¢ \text{ per tomato}$$

That's quite a difference in the price of tomatoes — 35 cents compared to 11 cents. Just looking at the average price per tomato it would seem that poor Harriet is being overcharged.

That's clearly not the case. The cost of delivering tomatoes remains the same and must be paid, whether it's two tomatoes or 50 being delivered. If it's 50, the delivery cost is spread out thinly over the price of the tomatoes. If it's only two being delivered, it must still be lumped on.

But no one is overcharged, and no one subsidizes anyone else. Everyone pays for the cost of service.

It is the same way in the electric utility business as it is with Acme Tomato Company. A major part of the cost is "delivering" electricity to your house.

And that's why large industrial customers pay a lower average cost per kilowatt-hour. They simply have more kilowatt-hours to spread the delivery cost over. It's just easier to understand it if you're buying tomatoes.

---

never seen a mass spectrometer and have only a hazy idea of what a molecule is. A *New York Times* writer solved this particular problem by describing the process with familiar ideas, beginning with a description of a cannon shooting iron balls of different sizes past a giant magnet.[5]

As the flying balls pass the magnet they are pulled toward it, and this causes their trajectories to curve in the direction of the magnet as they move past it. But since the balls are of differing weights, their trajectories are influenced differently by the magnet. The path of the lightest ball is most strongly curved by the magnet while that of the heaviest ball is least strongly curved.

The effect of this is to sort out the balls in order according to weight, and when they strike a target their distribution along a line exactly corresponds to their relative masses. The magnet has thus broken down a batch of assorted balls into the spectrum of their masses.

Molecules can be made to behave like such balls.

The writer then described the process with molecules, having provided the reader with a basis for understanding.

CONCLUSION

Simplifying complex subjects is one of the toughest tasks PR writers face. But in modern-day society it must be done. Complex subjects *can* be simplified and made understandable, but doing so while maintaining accuracy is not easy. It's not enough just to write short sentences and define technical terms. You must follow a number of important principles (see Table 5-2).

If you must interpret technical subjects, follow the rules of simplifying the complex. Use plain English, not the jargon of the discipline. When you must use technical terms, don't define them and proceed—*describe* them, so readers will have a clear notion of what you're writing about. Know your subject thoroughly, and be aware of what your readers don't know. Start at the beginning and proceed one step at a time.

5-2 SIMPLIFYING THE COMPLEX—CHECKLIST

1. Have you researched your subject thoroughly? Do you understand its complexities and the precise meanings of the terms you use?
2. Does your writing stay within the range of your knowledge?
3. Have you told readers only as much as they need to know to understand the point?
4. Have you used plain English as much as possible? Avoided unnecessary jargon? Have you been sure to use common words whenever they can be substituted for technical terms?
5. Have you fully described all technical terms that you can't avoid?
6. Have you made sure all technical terms used are really necessary to communicate the message?
7. Have you taken the readers one step at a time? Have you started with a point your readers will understand?
8. Have you identified the central points you want to make? Are they made clearly and not obscured by explanation and detail?
9. Have you used familiar ideas to explain unfamiliar concepts?

Know what message you want to convey. Identify the most important point and state it clearly—don't obscure the main idea with clouds of detail. If your important point is about something unfamiliar, use familiar ideas to explain it.

If you follow these rules, along with the general principles of good writing, you should be able to explain anything important enough to deserve explaining.

NOTES

[1] Albert Einstein, "On the Electrodynamics of Moving Bodies," *Annalen der Physik* 17 (1905): 891–929, reprinted in *The Principle of Relativity*, trans. W. Perrett and G. B. Jeffrey (New York: Dover, 1952), p. 39.

[2] Rudolf Flesch, *The Art of Plain Talk* (New York: Collier Books, 1962), pp. 158, 162.

[3] William Zinsser, *On Writing Well*, 2d ed. (New York: Harper and Row, 1980), p. 114.

[4] Isaac Asimov, *Opus 100* (Boston: Houghton Mifflin, 1969), pp. 89–90.

[5] *New York Times*, August 28, 1979.

SELECTED BIBLIOGRAPHY

Rudolf Flesch, *The Art of Plain Talk* (New York: Collier Books, 1962).

Rudolf Flesch, *The Art of Readable Writing*, 25th anniversary ed. (New York: Harper and Row, 1974).

Robert Gunning, *The Technique of Clear Writing*, rev. ed. (New York: McGraw-Hill, 1968).

William Zinsser, *On Writing Well*, 2d ed. (New York: Harper and Row, 1980).

6

GRAMMAR, SPELLING, PUNCTUATION

In the days when cigarette companies were allowed to advertise on TV, Winston produced a commercial that raised the hackles of grammarians across the country. The offending sentence: "Winston tastes good like a cigarette should."

English teachers howled. "Like" is a preposition, not a conjunction, they proclaimed. The correct way to express the thought is "Winston tastes good as a cigarette should."

Later, Winston came out with a series of ads that took advantage of the grammarians' criticism. "What do you want," the new ads asked, "good grammar or good taste?"

PR writers might ask a similar question: "What do you want, good grammar or good writing?" The two are not the same. And despite what the grammar experts might say, you can't always have both.

"Language is for communicating," writes direct-mail expert Luther Brock. "Words are simply a means of expressing oneself and, in our business, of convincing people to do business with us."[1] Grammatically correct writing, he points out, isn't always the best way to communicate.

"Unfortunately," writes Brock, "traditionally correct language is dishwater-dull. Why? Because it is not a reflection of the way most people talk. And talk-language just about always outsells grammar-book language."[2] As Brock indicates, the purpose of writing is to get a message across to a reader. In many respects the rules of grammar help achieve that end. But sometimes they get in the way. When they do, the good writer ignores them.

That doesn't mean you shouldn't bother to learn the rules, or that you shouldn't obey them most of the time. But you should keep the need to follow rules in perspective. "Rules," says Robert Gunning, "are substitutes for thought."[3] That's true, but they still can be useful. In many cases it's easier to follow a rule than to waste a lot of time thinking. However, when it comes to making decisions about writing readable prose, rules are *no* substitute for thought.

Take the "like" versus "as" case. One of the main principles of good writing, says Gunning, is to "write like you talk." A lot of English teachers part company with Gunning here, if for no other reason than

69

that the rules of grammar dictate "write *as* you talk" as the proper way to state the principle. But Gunning responds with three good reasons why *like* should be used instead of *as*.[4] First, good writers have always used *like* as a conjunction (Norman Mailer, for a modern example, or John Keats if you prefer the old-timers). Second, "write as you talk" breaks the rule as it states it. When speaking, people say "write like you talk"—and everybody knows what they mean. That brings us to the third point, which is that "write as you talk" has two possible meanings. It can mean "write the same way you talk" or "write while you are talking." But this is ambiguous, and ambiguity, of course, is one of the worst of all possible writing sins.

AMBIGUITY AND GRAMMAR

Avoiding ambiguity is the main reason grammar exists. Many grammar rules help us keep the meaning clear. Dangling participles, for example, are condemned by grammarians, and they should be—they can obscure the meaning of the sentence. (Sometimes a dangling participle sounds so silly that the true meaning is obvious, but in those cases the sentence is awkward and should be rewritten for that reason.)

That Versus Which

The common misuse of *that* and *which* is an example of how bad grammar can tangle meaning. Using *that* and *which* correctly is important, for it involves questions of both ambiguity and naturalness. In speaking, *that* comes more naturally: "I picked up the books *that* were on the table; where are the keys *that* I left on the shelf?" In writing, for some mysterious reason, people feel compelled to use *which*. "Attached are the copies *which* I promised to send you."

Rudolf Flesch, in *The Art of Readable Writing*, explains at great length why *that* is better in such cases.[5] His discussion is worth looking up and reading. Not only is *that* the more natural word, Flesch points out, but it avoids confusion about the meaning of the sentence. In the above examples the clauses beginning with *that* are restrictive; *which* should not be used to introduce a restrictive clause. When you say, "Bring me the books *that* are on the table," you want *only* the books on the table, none of the other books nearby. The clause is restrictive. When you say "Bring the books, *which* are on the table," you're not restricting the books, you're simply telling where they are. The comma is the clue (see pp. 79–80). If the sentence reads correctly without the comma, you should use *that* instead of *which*. (In fact, try to avoid *which* clauses altogether. Clauses with commas slow readers down.)

Subject-Verb Agreement

Another rule that aids clarity is subject-verb agreement. Subject and verb agreement helps us avoid confusion over who's doing what. There is a difference, for example, between "Growing vegetables is interesting" and "Growing vegetables are interesting."

Furthermore, it is no excuse to break the rule simply because you have misidentified the subject. A headline in a major newspaper once said, "Workings of the FAA no longer is so mysterious." The subject is *workings*, not *FAA*; the verb should be *are* and not *is*. There is no excuse for making the mistake in less obvious cases either, as in "The general, along with his men, are marching tomorrow." The subject here is singular; the additional phrase does not make it plural. The corrected sentence reads "The general, along with his men, is marching tomorrow." If that sounds awkward, simply say "The general and his men are marching tomorrow."

Like any other rule, this one is no substitute for thought. When you write, "The data you need are on page 17," you are going out of the way to show that you know there is such a thing as a "datum." Most people would say, "The data *is* on page 17," and there's no good reason not to. Your meaning will still be clear.*

Another awkward case of subject-verb agreement is the ubiquitous "none is," which grates on the eardrums like a squeaky piece of chalk. "None of the boats is going out to sea today" sounds silly. Always using a singular verb after *none*—no matter what the rest of the sentence says—is nonsense. Furthermore, any legitimate dictionary or usage manual says so. More often than not, the sense of "none" is plural. Theodore Bernstein, in *The Careful Writer*, says the rule to follow is "Consider *none* to be plural unless there is a definite reason to regard it as a singular."[6] For example, when *none* is followed by a prepositional phrase with a singular object, the singular verb sounds better. "None of the cake has been eaten" is OK. But "None of the cakes has been eaten" is terrible.

---

*There is considerable difference of opinion on the propriety of using *data* with a singular verb. Wilson Follett's usage manual (published in 1966) says there's no reason not to use the plural verb with *data*. H. W. Fowler's *Modern English Usage* says *data* is often treated as a singular in the United States. Theodore Bernstein calls the use of *data* as a singular a "solecism," and points out that nobody tries to make it plural by way of "datas." *The Harper Dictionary of Contemporary Usage*'s panel of experts, however, splits nearly 50-50 on the question of *data* as a singular.

The plain fact is that in modern American usage *data* can be construed either as a singular collective noun or as a plural. The *UPI Stylebook* points out that in a sentence like "The data is sound," *data* clearly refers to a collective unit, and not to the individual bits of information that collectively make up the "data." If you want to emphasize the individual entities in a collection of data, of course, it is correct (grammatically) to write "data are."

MYTHS OF GRAMMAR

Why does everybody think *none* is singular and should always be followed by *is* or some other equally out-of-place singular verb? Even the *Oxford English Dictionary* says *none* is usually plural. Well, at some time in the ancient past a grammar teacher decided that *none* means "not one" and should always be singular. That teacher passed it on to a student who became a teacher who passed it on to another student and so on. And all of these teachers were steadfastly devoted to the cause of rules as substitutes for thought. These are the teachers who, as Rudolf Flesch puts it, "tell students from grade school through college that they'd better learn not to write 'it's me' and never split an infinitive or they'll get shunned by society in later life and never get a decent job."[7]

Some of these grammar "pitfalls" are important; others are merely grammar myths. The old "it's me" or "it's I" question, for example, isn't worth the time it takes to quibble. Almost everybody uses "it's me" these days, and most experts accept it, even though a predicate nominative is supposed to use the subject form of the pronoun. Don't worry about it.

However, very few good writers would say "between you and I." This is not only grammatically wrong, but worse, it is stilted and unnatural. In this case the correct form is also the most common and natural one: "between you and me." The same is true for the common misuse of *myself* when *me* is the right word. "He sent a message to John and myself" is a self-conscious and awkward way of avoiding the use of *me*. *Myself* should be reserved for intensive or reflexive use, as in "I hurt myself" or "I myself will do it."

Split Infinitives

As for split infinitives, every good writer knows that infinitives should sometimes be split. Let the situation be your guide. If avoiding a split infinitive makes a sentence awkward, go ahead and chop the infinitive in two and get on with writing the story. Consider E. B. White's observation in *The Elements of Style:*[8]

> The split infinitive is another trick of rhetoric in which the ear must be quicker than the handbook. Some infinitives seem to improve on being split, just as a stick of round stovewood does. "I cannot bring myself to really like the fellow." The sentence is relaxed, the meaning is clear, the violation is harmless and scarcely perceptible. Put the other way, the sentence becomes stiff, needlessly formal. A matter of ear.

Keep in mind, though, that split infinitives sometimes cause confusion, especially if the split becomes a gorge by the insertion of several words. "He wanted to quickly, skillfully, and perhaps even artistically complete the project" is widening the split a bit too far. Remember, clarity is the goal.

Sentence-ending Prepositions

The split infinitive taboo originated with the fact that Latin infinitives are single words and thus can't be split. The same archaic logic led to the myth that you should never end a sentence with a preposition. Some people who remember nothing else at all from their grammar school days remember this "rule." But, in fact, it's just another example of somebody learning grammar from Latin in the Middle Ages and passing it down through the centuries until everybody says it's so but nobody knows why. In Latin it's very difficult to end a sentence with a preposition. Why allow English to do something denied Latin?

Fortunately, some noteworthy language experts have ridiculed this rule to the point where few people still follow it. To writers, Winston Churchill's most famous line was not about blood and tears and sweat but about the rule against sentence-ending prepositions being nonsense "up with which I will not put." Almost all usage manuals repudiate the "rule."

USING USAGE MANUALS

Once writers realize they are free from the chains imposed by grammar rules, some go off the deep end. If rules are made to be broken, why follow any of them? Well, all rules shouldn't be broken. Rules should be broken only when, by doing so, you can make the writing clearer, more natural, and easier to understand. Feel free to dismiss the pedantry of critics who rank split infinitives on the same plane with arson or manslaughter. But do strive to use the language carefully and accurately.

It is not pedantry, for example, to insist that words be used with their proper meanings. "Allusion" is not the same thing as "illusion," for example, and "imply" and "infer" are not interchangeable. "Parameters" are not "perimeters," either. Countless other words are misused simply because they sound like some other word (see Table 6–1).

Many writers scoff at such criticism, saying, "The reader will know what I mean. Lots of people use the word that way." If you adopt this philosophy, you put yourself in the position of confusing the members of your audience who *do* know the correct meanings of words. The intelligent reader is left to wonder if the writer is using this word correctly, in which case it means one thing, or is following a common mistake, in which case it means something else. Using words imprecisely can lead to such ambiguity. Choose words carefully.

6-1 COMMONLY CONFUSED WORDS

Here is a list of words commonly confused for each other. If you don't understand the differences between the members of each pair, consult a usage manual, the AP stylebook, or *Words Into Type* (See the bibliography on p. 81).

absorb, adsorb
adapt, adopt
adhesion, cohesion
affect, effect
all ready, already
allusion, illusion
apparently, obviously
appraise, apprise
arbitrate, mediate
baited, bated
canvas, canvass
cement, concrete
comprise, compose
continual, continuous
discreet, discrete
disinterested, uninterested
dual, duel
flaunt, flout
fortuitous, fortunate
imply, infer
principal, principle
compliment, complement
induction, deduction
naval, navel
pastor, minister
peddle, pedal
pore, pour
rebut, refute
rein, reign
stationary, stationery

Even some grammar "rules" deserve a little thought before they are rejected or accepted. Any given rule can be good for some situations—possibly even most situations—though bad for others. How can you decide when to follow a rule and when not to? You must decide, of course, but it never hurts to get some advice. You could, for example, call the Writer's Hotline, a grammar advice service offered by the English Department at the University of Arkansas.[9] If your long-distance budget is limited, check a few basic reference books. Besides a dictionary and standard grammar handbook, you should have at least two usage manuals that discuss points of grammar and usage in depth. Such manuals analyze many of the tricky usage questions that writers stumble across.

Fowler's *Modern English Usage* is regarded by some as the ultimate authority and is perhaps the most respected of all usage manuals. But it is oriented more to English (as in England) than American English. Margaret Nicholson has "Americanized" Fowler and her *Dictionary of American-English Usage* is available in paperback.* Another "American" manual is Wilson Follett's *Modern American Usage*. Bernstein's *The Careful Writer* is useful, and the AP and UPI stylebooks are valuable if you're writing news releases for newspapers.

Except for the wire service stylebooks, though, these are all more than a decade old and sometimes don't reflect the latest trends in usage. So you might want to consult a more recent manual, like the *Harper Dictionary of Contemporary Usage*. Another recent manual is the third edition (1979) of Strunk and White's *Elements of Style*. It is less comprehensive than other manuals but is highly respected.

When you read over some of these manuals you'll find that usage rules aren't as restrictive as you've been taught. You'll be surprised to see what some language "purists" like Fowler and Follett have to say about split infinitives, for example. You'll also, no doubt, run across subtle but important usage matters that have escaped your attention until now.

Perhaps the most important lesson you'll learn from reading usage manuals is that there is considerable disagreement among the "experts" over what should or should not be allowed. The *Harper Dictionary* is especially instructive in this respect, for it made extensive use of a panel of 136 usage authorities, including many famous writers, editors and broadcasters.[10] The editors of the manual asked the panel to vote on various usage questions. The results are given in the manual along with selected comments from the panel members. For example, 80 percent of the panel members said they had no objection to using a preposition at the end of a sentence. (The surprising thing is that 20 percent did object.) As for *data*, the panel split down the middle—49 percent saw nothing wrong with "data is," while 51 percent opposed that usage.

So don't let anybody tell you there is always a right and a wrong where grammar and usage are concerned. Gather some opinions, think about it, and then make up your own mind. Just be sure that when you break a rule, you break it for a reason, and not because you didn't know it.

---

*It is based on the first edition of Fowler (1926), however, and is somewhat dated.

SPELLING

Rules of usage and grammar are largely a matter of sense and style. The important thing is expressing a thought clearly. The rules should serve that end.

Spelling, on the other hand, is largely a matter of convention. Sometimes a slight misspelling actually changes a word from one thing to another, and meaning can become confused. So it's a good idea to have a standard English dictionary around and follow the spellings it gives. If it gives two spellings, establish a rule and use it consistently—such as always using the first spelling given.*

Who cares about spelling? Well, the people who hire PR writers for one, so if you want a job, you'll take spelling seriously. There's no excuse for *not* spelling correctly. Just keep a dictionary within arm's length whenever you're writing. If you're not *absolutely certain* that a word is spelled correctly, look it up.

Face it. If your prose is riddled with spelling errors, your readers just might conclude that you aren't too bright. Therefore, why should they believe what you've written or even read it at all? It's little consolation to say that most readers won't catch the spelling errors. Then only the intelligent people will think you're wrong.

Spelling errors do crop up now and again, even in prestigious publications. You can make every effort to eradicate mistakes, and some day a spelling error will appear in one of your finished products anyway. That is not a reason to be less diligent in your efforts. If you operate with the attitude that "just one error" isn't so bad, you'll end up with many. The old saying about "to err is human" should be applied as consolation only after the fact, not as a license ahead of time to make mistakes.

Sometimes mistakes occur not because of lack of diligence, but because of overconfidence. Some people spell well, and spell so well that they're sure they can spot any spelling mistakes. Thus, they don't look up words that they should. To avoid such overconfidence, good writers and editors should occasionally test themselves on lists of commonly misspelled words. Even good spellers will find some surprises. The list that follows contains several misspelled words. Test yourself by counting the number of words that are spelled *correctly*.

---

*The first spelling given is not necessarily always the preferred spelling. *Webster's New Collegiate*, for example, connects equal spelling variants with *or*, as in "peddler *or* pedlar." In these cases neither spelling is preferred; you must choose one and stick to it. If the spellings are connected by *also*, the second spelling is considered less common. Sometimes words connected by *or* are given in reverse alphabetical order; this indicates that the first spelling is slightly more common, though the second is equally correct. When writing news releases, be sure to follow the AP or UPI spelling rules. See pages 104–105 and Appendix D.

CHAPTER 6
GRAMMAR, SPELLING,
PUNCTUATION

badmitton
sacreligious
chaufeur
diarhea
embarass
Farenheit
flourescent
barbiturates
limosine
corollary
wierd
cemetary
mispelling
innoculate
pantomine
inocuous
perogative
excell
preceed
procede
comittee
comission
priviledge
knowledgable
sieze
satelite

If you counted two correct, you're right. Only *barbiturates* and *corollary* are spelled correctly. The rest are wrong.

If you knew that without the help of a dictionary, you're a pretty good speller and should have no trouble with the following test. Read the passage and circle the words that are spelled *incorrectly*. Assume this story is to appear in a newspaper and follow AP or UPI stylebook spelling rules.

The scientists could not reach a concensus. One physicist argued that his experiments superceded earlier findings.

Beseiged by numerous complaints, the director of the labratory devised a stratagy to accomodate the workers. He alotted each one 15 minutes to speak. One said everyone had benefitted from the experiments on liquefaction of nitrogen, but he saw no corellation between those results and the experiments on parafin.

"It would take a whole battallion of scientists to solve this dilemna," another scientist said. "We do high calibre work, but when you liquefy a miniscule amount of gas, there's no way to avoid all possible arguements about the results."

Another suggested that a questionaire should be drawn up and sent out. "If we could get them all filled out, that would be quite an achievment," he said.

"That's an inovative idea," said the physicist. "I'd like to save my copy of the form as a momento of this occassion."

You should have circled twenty words. The number of misspelled words, by sentence, is: 1, 1, 4, 1, 3, 2, 3, 1, 1, 1, 2. If you didn't find them all, a trip to the dictionary is in order (or perhaps the AP stylebook. Some dictionaries accept "benefitted," but AP allows "benefited" only.)

PUNCTUATION

While grammar is mostly a matter of making meanings clear, and spelling is basically a matter of convention, punctuation is a little of both. True, proper punctuation is usually just a matter of following the rules. But the underlying purpose of punctuation is to help make the meaning clear, and subtle changes in punctuation *can* change the meaning of a sentence. For example, the sentence "Woman without her man is an animal" can be punctuated "Woman—without her, man is an animal." Liz Carpenter, former press secretary to Lady Bird Johnson, likes to have people punctuate this sentence as a test for sexism.

Most reputable publications follow a fairly rigorous set of punctuation rules and apply them consistently. The virtue of consistency is simply that readers can pay attention to the message without being bothered by changes in the manner of punctuation. Sentences, for example, usually end with periods. Readers know this, and they don't have to think about it. They also know that if a writer ends a sentence with some other mark, it is an intentional act to tell the reader something—as when a question mark is used to indicate a question.

Inconsistent punctuation calls attention to itself. Anything that calls attention to itself takes attention away from the message, and that hinders communication. When you're trying to communicate, there's no excuse for anything that will distract the reader, however slightly.

Sometimes punctuation conventions defy logic, but these conventions are so entrenched that violators expose themselves immediately as amateurs. The prime example involves the use of periods and commas with quotation marks. Whenever a period or comma follows a quotation, it is placed *inside* the closing quotation marks. Always. Without exception (at least in the United States). It doesn't matter whether the quote is a complete sentence or a title or a single word. For example:

John's article, called "The Hands of Time," is well written.
I didn't know he wrote an article called "The Hands of Time."

The rule still applies if single quotes are used inside double quotes:

He said he "wrote an article called 'The Hands of Time.'"

Other punctuation, like question marks or exclamation points, are placed according to the sense of the sentence:

Did he write an article called "The Hands of Time"?
He asked John, "What is the title of your article?"

If this seems trivial, it is. But many PR writers are their own editors. If you want your material punctuated correctly, you need to know the rules. And in the case of this particular rule, there is nothing to be gained by breaking it. It is followed uniformly (in the United States), and departures from the convention call attention to themselves.

There are many other punctuation rules where convention is not as binding. Often standard "rules" should be broken to make the reading easier or to make the meaning clear. People are taught in school, for example, to precede direct quotations with commas, as in:

John said, "What's going on here?"

Sometimes the comma is an intrusion, however, and can be dropped with no confusion:

"What did he say?" He said "Let's go!"

Not all rules should be so casually violated. Some are important for keeping the meaning clear; most rules of this type involve the comma.

There are dozens of rules regarding commas, and it doesn't hurt to know them. Most help keep sentences clear and prevent readers from stumbling over tricky passages or linking clauses to wrong elements. In general, comma rules are helpful.

Some writers overdo their use of commas, though, and stick one in wherever they can. Too many commas clog up the works, and make for slow reading. It's a better practice to use commas only when they are necessary to avoid confusion.

Avoiding confusion is the main reason for careful use of commas with nonrestrictive clauses, for example. Restrictive clauses, which are necessary to make the meaning of a sentence clear, are not set off by commas. Consider these examples:

Restrictive clauses, which are needed for clarity, are not set off by commas.

(All restrictive clauses are needed for clarity. Thus the "which are needed" clause is merely explanatory and is not essential for the meaning of the sentence. It is a *nonrestrictive* clause and is set off by commas.)

Clauses that are needed for clarity are not set off by commas.

(Not all clauses are needed for clarity. But the "that are needed" clause is essential to the meaning of the sentence—it *restricts* the types of clauses under consideration. It is therefore a *restrictive* clause and is not set off by commas.)

Restrictive and nonrestrictive clauses are also called essential and nonessential clauses. They don't always use *that* and *which*. *Who* can be restrictive or nonrestrictive, and that makes proper punctuation all the more important. Consider these examples from the AP Stylebook:

Reporters, who do not read the stylebook, should not criticize their editors.
    Reporters who do not read the stylebook should not criticize their editors.

The first sentence says that reporters—all reporters—do not read the stylebook. Therefore, they shouldn't criticize editors. The second sentence says that some reporters—those who don't read the stylebook—shouldn't criticize their editors. There's a big difference.

Another comma error that can make sentences unclear involves appositives. An appositive is a phrase that stands for a noun and bears the same relationship to the rest of the sentence as the noun does. Example: "Joe Smith, the captain of the football team, signed a new contract today." The appositive following "Joe Smith" is set off by commas. Note that the comma after *team* is essential. "Joe Smith, the captain of the football team signed a new contract today" reads as though someone was telling Joe Smith (whoever he is) that the captain of the football team signed a contract.

Don't set off short titles with commas, however. "Team captain Joe Smith signed a new contract" is perfectly correct. "Team captain, Joe Smith, signed a new contract" is not. A similar problem sometimes comes up with restrictive appositives, when a descriptive phrase is needed for full meaning. "The American League baseball players, Rick Manning, Jim Rice, and Carl Yastrzemski, are outfielders" is not properly punctuated. This sentence makes them the only players in the American League. Omit the commas after *players* and Yastrzemski and the sentence is correct. Avoid too any related mistakes, such as the one made by a textbook author who wrote: "In his novel, *The Deer Park*, Norman Mailer describes. . . " There should be no comma after *novel*—Mailer has written more than one.

Many other punctuation rules are equally important, and it's impossible to cover all of them in a single chapter. Any serious writer takes punctuation seriously, though, and consults books like *Words Into Type* for help on the fine points.

Of course, experts sometimes disagree about proper punctuation. Don't think that every rule should be followed in every instance. But make sure you know the rules. And when you break one, know why.

CONCLUSION

Grammar, spelling and punctuation are important—not as ends in themselves, but as aids to clear communication. The PR writer's chief aim is to communicate, and following the rules of grammar and usage usually facilitates that task. Correct grammar and punctuation help to eliminate ambiguity. Consistent punctuation and spelling help direct the readers' full attention to the message, not the mechanics.

Occasionally strict interpretation of grammar rules might result in awkward or confusing writing. In those cases, PR writers should ensure clarity even at the expense of traditional grammar rules. But such a step should never be taken lightly. You should know why the rule exists and why it should be broken in a particular situation.

NOTES

[1] Luther Brock, "In Direct Mail, Ignore Friends—Pay Attention to What Pays," *Southwest Advertising and Marketing*, December 1975, p. 20.

[2] Luther Brock, "Two Professionals Disagree on the Need for Purity in Language," *Southwest Advertising and Marketing*, March 1977, p. 11.

[3] Robert Gunning, *The Technique of Clear Writing* (New York: McGraw-Hill, 1968), p. 265.

[4] Ibid., p. 121.

[5] Rudolf Flesch, *The Art of Readable Writing*, 25th anniversary ed. (New York: Harper and Row, 1974), p. 163.

[6] Theodore Bernstein, *The Careful Writer* (New York: Atheneum, 1965), p. 288.

[7] Flesch, *Art of Readable Writing*, pp. 9–10.

[8] William Strunk and E. B. White, *The Elements of Style*, 3d ed. (New York: Macmillan, 1979), p. 78.

[9] Fort Worth *Morning Star-Telegram*, 25 December 1978, p. 3h.

[10] William Morris and Mary Morris, *Harper Dictionary of Contemporary Usage* (New York: Harper and Row, 1975), p. 166.

SELECTED BIBLIOGRAPHY

Howard Angione, ed., *The Associated Press Stylebook and Libel Manual* (New York: The Associated Press, 1977).

Theodore M. Bernstein, *The Careful Writer* (New York: Atheneum, 1965).

Rudolf Flesch, *The Art of Readable Writing*, 25th anniversary ed. (New York: Harper and Row, 1974).

Wilson Follett, *Modern American Usage* (New York: Grosset and Dunlap, 1966).

H. W. Fowler, *A Dictionary of Modern English Usage*, 2d ed. (New York: Oxford University Press, 1965).

Robert Gunning, *The Technique of Clear Writing*, rev. ed. (New York: McGraw-Hill, 1968).

Bobby Ray Miller, *The UPI Stylebook* (New York: United Press International, 1977).

William Morris and Mary Morris, *Harper Dictionary of Contemporary Usage* (New York: Harper and Row, 1975).

Margaret Nicholson, *A Dictionary of American-English Usage* (New York: New American Library, 1957).

Harry Shaw, *Punctuate It Right* (New York: Barnes and Noble, 1963).

Marjorie E. Skillin and Robert M. Gay, *Words Into Type*, 3d ed. (Englewood Cliffs, N.J.: Prentice-Hall, 1974).

William Strunk, Jr. and E. B. White, *The Elements of Style*, 3d ed. (New York: Macmillan, 1979).

PART TWO EXERCISES

1. Select a passage from Chapter 4 of this book and test it for readability using the Gunning formula given in Appendix A. Choose at least three samples from different pages. Then test the readability of passages from a chapter in a science textbook. If the Gunning score of the samples from the science text is higher than for this text, rewrite the scientific passage until it has a lower readability score than the passages from Chapter 4. Has the science passage been improved? Discuss some advantages and disadvantages of using readability formulas.

2. Apply any of the readability formulas in Appendix A to a story in today's newspaper. Then apply the same formula to a passage from a modern novel. Which is more readable? What are the implications of this result?

3. Select two of the usage manuals mentioned in Chapter 6 and compare them. Examine at least five entries in one and then read the same five entries in the other. Which manual do you think gives better advice for PR writing? Why?

4. Test your understanding of some basic punctuation principles by choosing the correct sentences from the list below. You might want to consult a handbook like *Words Into Type* or the *AP Stylebook* on some of these. Answers follow.

   1. a. Buy a case of Dr Pepper today.
      b. Buy a case of Dr. Pepper today.

   2. a. I wondered why he asked me, "Where have you been?".
      b. I wondered why he asked me, "Where have you been?"

   3. a. Have you ever asked "What should I do?"?
      b. Have you ever asked "What should I do?"
      c. Have you ever asked "What should I do"?

   4. a. She said, "Who played the lead role in *Hello, Dolly!*?".
      b. She said, "Who played the lead role in *Hello, Dolly!*?"
      c. She said, "Who played the lead role in *Hello, Dolly!*"

   5. a. She said, "Who wrote the words to 'The Star-Spangled Banner'?"
      b. She said, "Who wrote the words to 'The Star-Spangled Banner'"?

   6. a. Have you ever exclaimed "My God!"?
      b. Have you ever exclaimed "My, God!"
      c. Have you ever exclaimed "My God!?"

7. **a.** First, call your doctor. (If you don't have a family doctor, call the local health clinic.)
   b. First, call your doctor. (If you don't have a family doctor, call the local health clinic).
8. **a.** First, call your doctor (if you have one.)
   b. First, call your doctor (if you have one).
9. **a.** What should I do? he asked himself.
   b. What should I do, he asked himself.
   c. What should I do, he asked himself?
10. **a.** "Will you come into my office?" he demanded.
    b. "Will you come into my office," he demanded.
11. **a.** "Did you see that catch!?," I asked.
    b. "Did you see that catch!," I asked.
    c. "Did you see that catch!" I asked.
    d. None of the above.
12. **a.** John Smith, author of "What's in a Name?," will arrive soon.
    b. John Smith, author of "What's in a Name?", will arrive soon.
    c. John Smith, author of "What's in a Name?" will arrive soon.
13. **a.** John Smith, state representative from Fort Worth, resigned.
    b. John Smith, state representative from Fort Worth resigned.
14. **a.** State representative, John Smith, resigned from his job today.
    b. State representative John Smith, resigned from his job today.
    c. State representative John Smith resigned from his job today.
15. **a.** He didn't shout "Halt, thief!"; I did.
    b. He didn't shout "Halt, thief!;" I did.
16. **a.** Have you ever said, "Let's go for a walk."?
    b. Have you ever said, "Let's go for a walk"?
17. **a.** We can go to the beach, if it doesn't rain.
    b. We can go to the beach if it doesn't rain.
18. **a.** The spinning turbine is attached to a generator, which turns conductors in a magnetic field to generate current.
    b. The spinning turbine is attached to a generator which turns conductors in a magnetic field to generate current.

Answers

1. The correct answer is (a). This is a trick question—Dr Pepper is a registered trademark and has no period after the Dr.

2. (b) is correct. The period is not needed; furthermore, periods should never fall outside quotation marks.

3. No easy answer. Logic would seem to dictate the punctuation as in example (a), but in practice three punctuation marks in a row are seldom seen. Experts would say choose which of the questions you most want to emphasize. In this case (b) is probably the best choice.

4. (b) is correct. This is one of those rare cases where three punctuation marks do follow one another. The exclamation mark is part of the title and should not be dropped.

5. (a) is correct. The quotation is the question, so the question mark falls inside the quotation marks.

6. Another tricky one. (c) is wrong, (a) seems logical, but (b) is probably the correct choice to avoid an awkward appearance. The exclamation is more important than the interrogative.

7. (a) is correct. When a complete sentence is enclosed in parentheses, so is the period.

8. (b) is correct. When only part of a sentence is enclosed in parentheses, the period falls outside.

9. (a) is correct.

10. (b) is correct. While the sentence is phrased as an interrogative, there is no question—it is more a command than a request.

11. (c) is probably the best way to punctuate this. (a) and (b) are clearly wrong—the comma is not needed. Some might use exclamation and quotation together, but most would pick one.

12. (c) is correct. Commas are not needed in this construction.

13. (a) is correct.

14. (c) is correct.

15. (a) is correct. Semicolons always go outside of quotation marks.

16. (b) is correct.

17. (b) is correct. The "if" clause is essential to the meaning of the main clause. It is therefore a restrictive "if" clause and should not be set off by a comma.

18. (a) is correct. The "which" clause is descriptive, not defining. It merely gives more information about a generator; it does not make a distinction between generators in general and the generator under discussion.

5. Rewrite the following sentences eliminating jargon and needless words to make the resulting sentence clear and concise. Suggested revisions follow.

a. Johnson supported his side of the issue by saying that contemporary revenue athletics, also known as big money sports, forces athletes to cheat in school because they have no time to study.

b. As is the case with so many of the wars over the course of time, this war was largely a result of previous wars.

c. If methods of communication had been comparable to those of the present century, there is little doubt that this war would never have begun.

d. The interaction of petroleum liquid in aqueous media produces a heterogeneous, layered liquid mixture.

e. Extent of labor and its propensity to fill time is peculiarly elastic; that is, the more time available for the completion of an assigned task, the longer it takes for the assigned task to be completed.

f. We have encountered our military adversaries and successfully engaged them, taking control of their nautical vehicles.

g. Whatever there is that needs to be done, this machine is able to accomplish it.

h. Financial statements indicate that the company's financial situation was negatively impacted during the preceding twelve months.

Suggested Revisions

These revisions are only suggestions. Many other revisions are possible.

a. Johnson said big money sports forces athletes to cheat in school because they have no time to study.

b. As with so many wars, this war was largely a result of previous wars.

c. If today's communication methods had been available, the war would never have started.

d. Oil and water don't mix.

e. Work takes up however much time is available.

f. We have met the enemy, and they are ours.

g. This machine can do whatever needs doing.

h. The company lost money last year.

P A R T

THREE

WRITING FOR GENERAL AUDIENCES

Writing for general audiences requires an understanding of the audiences. It also requires that you know the strengths and weaknesses of the media that may be used to reach them.

7

NEWS RELEASES FOR PRINT MEDIA

The news release is probably the most frequently used tool for getting publicity. It is also frequently *misused* by PR people and *not* used by the media. As one PR professor observed, "An editor's most valuable possession is his wastebasket. It's where most of his mail ends up."[1]

One editor estimated that 90 percent of the releases received were "dumped with a quick glance." Another checked the morning mail and found 61 releases. Nine survived.[2] A business editor for a Texas daily once remarked that burning unused news releases as fuel could solve the energy crisis.

Why do most news releases end up in the circular file? One survey of editors listed the three biggest reasons as: little local interest, no reader interest at all, and poor writing in the news release. An industrial editor states that most releases are "pure unadulterated garbage."[3] In some cases, of course, a paper simply doesn't have the space to print all the releases it receives. But basically, it gets down to this: Most releases don't get used because the PR people preparing them don't know what they're doing.

Some editors keep files of releases demonstrating glaring PR incompetence. One file contains a very nice piece of news release stationery that came to the editor saying "For Immediate Release." That's all it said; the rest of the sheet was blank. One release said "Do not use after Sept. 23." It arrived in the editor's mail on September 25. Another spelled the name of the firm one way on the letterhead and a different way in the body of the release. Of course, these examples are a little extreme. Many releases come to newsrooms correctly spelled and punctuated. The names and dates are all where they should be. But they still get thrown away. Why? Because they contain no news.

NEWS

The first responsibility of the PR people preparing news releases is to know what news is. If a release doesn't contain news, it won't get printed. And if it contains valuable news, editors are quite likely to overlook poor writing, typographical errors and other blunders to get the story in the paper. It's essential to know what news is.

What Is News?

Different people have different definitions for news. Textbooks on beginning reporting and articles about the mass media in society construct elaborate definitions of what news is or should be. But for PR people no esoteric or philosophical definition is necessary. A practical one will do: News is what newspapers print and what radio and TV stations broadcast on their news shows. News is *not* what *you* think it is or what the company president thinks it is. Realizing this will take you a long way toward writing more effective news releases.

In the words of the well-known PR consultant Philip Lesly:[4]

> The medium decides absolutely, in most cases, what it will use, when, and in what form. The editorial judgment or attitudes of the editors, however they may differ from those of the publicist and his organization, are the only determinants.

This is not a new idea. The best PR people have said the same for decades. Ivy Lee, one of the pioneers of public relations, once described how corporation executives would call on him to get their ideas printed in the newspaper.[5] "They say you can get a thing on the front page of the newspapers," an executive would tell Lee. He would reply: "I cannot do anything of the kind. If you want a subject to get on the first page of the newspapers, you must have the news in your statement sufficient to warrant it getting the first page."

Furthermore, Lee would point out, what good would it do if the paper *did* print something just because you wanted it to? If it has no news value, people probably won't read it. And if people are likely to read it, it *does* have news value, and an editor will be happy to print it without coercion or tricks.

Finding News

A PR person, then, need not be concerned with thinking up ways to convince an editor to use a release. If the release is newsworthy, it will be used. As a PR person, your job is to find news and put it in a form that will make the editor's job as easy as possible. To accomplish this, you must do two things. First, become familiar with the newspaper (or TV, radio station or other medium) where you're going to send releases. In other words, if you want to know what news is, you have to read the papers. You have to watch TV newscasts. You should listen to radio news shows. You'll soon develop a sense for what is accepted as news and what isn't.

The second step is to become familiar with your own company or institution, so you'll be able to find the news within it. Presumably you will work for an organization that does something worthwhile, or does things the public might find some value in knowing about. If you look around, you'll find things going on in the company that are similar to what the newspapers report about other companies. You'll find people who know things the public would like to know. You'll find research on topics that affect people's lives. You'll find unusual things that are simply interesting in themselves.

Of course, a PR writer's job is to get things into the paper that will benefit the organization. Just looking for things editors consider news, therefore, may not achieve your goals. But there is a broad area where public benefit and private benefit overlap. Generating a greater public understanding of your company and its activities is almost always beneficial, and if in the process the public is entertained and informed, then everyone benefits.

Getting News into Print

Once you find the news within your organization, your next step is to get it to the public through some medium—newspaper, TV, radio, or possibly magazine. The news release is the tool most often used to do so.

How do you get your news into the paper? First, here's the wrong way. You *don't* go down to the editor with a sheet of paper and say "This is news and if you don't print it I'll cancel my subscription and cancel my advertising and everything else." You *do* make sure that what you have is newsworthy. You prepare the information in proper form so that it looks and sounds like news, and you give it to the editor to do with as he or she pleases. If you're right and it is news, the editor will print it. Probably not exactly as you prepared it, but it will be used, in some way or another. Example 7–1 shows that releases change form in the hands of an editor.

In writing a release, the first concern is newsworthiness. Make sure you're writing about something that is genuine news, not disguised advertising. If your news release is designed only to increase your company's sales without any concern for its value to the public, you're making a mistake. Buy an ad instead. As newspaperman Horace Greeley once said, "When you want an article inserted to subserve some purpose other than the public good, you should offer to pay for it."[6] Example 7–2 is more promotion than news.

Occasionally you'll get an editor to run something as news when an ad is called for. PR counsel Edward L. Bernays observes that "you may often crowd an article in, through an editor's complacency, that you ought to pay for; but he sets you down as a sponge and a sneak forthwith."[7] In the long run, it doesn't pay. Trying to pass off advertising as news simply makes editors angry, and they won't be inclined to treat your news releases favorably in the future. One PR agency even made the horrendous mistake of buying an ad in the city's largest paper while sending the same material as a news release to a competing daily. Needless to say, the release wound up in the wastebasket—and so did the next dozen releases from that agency.

How do you know if the release you want to send is newsworthy? There are several easy tests. Is the information of general interest to readers not connected with your business? Is it about something that affects the lives of the newspapers' readers in some way (especially economically)? Is the substance of your release something unusual, out of the ordinary, or even bizarre? If you can answer yes to any of these questions, your release probably contains legitimate news, even if it also serves your own purposes.

WRITING NEWS RELEASES

How do you write up legitimate news? The answer is simple—prepare the material as you would if you were a reporter working for a paper. A news release should be written in the same form and style, following the same punctuation and spelling rules, as the publication you want it to appear in.

If you've ever been a reporter, writing a news release should be as easy as writing a straight news story. If you haven't, you need to know something about the methods of writing news.

Approach

Every reporter has a personal method for approaching a story. But all methods should have the first step in common—identifying the most important thing about the story. In writing a news release the first step is the same. You must answer the question: What's the most important thing I have to say? The answer determines what you should say in the lead.

Lead The lead—the first paragraph or perhaps the first two—is the most important part of the release. You can't write a good release without a good lead, and you can't write a good lead until you've answered the question about what's important.

Deciding what is important sometimes takes a little judgment. "Important" must be construed broadly. What you really want to isolate is the most significant *and* most interesting aspect of your subject. And you have to keep in mind that *news* is what is happening *now*.

For example, if the release is about the opening of a new plant, the most important thing is the fact that the plant is *opening*. The action is the news. But is there something especially interesting about it? Is it the largest plant of its kind? The first? Will it provide a lot of new jobs for the local economy? Once you've decided what's important and also what's interesting, you can go ahead and write a lead.

PART THREE
WRITING FOR
GENERAL AUDIENCES

7-1 NEWS RELEASES

This is what two news releases looked like when they arrived at the office of an entertainment newspaper, and what they looked like when they ultimately appeared in the paper. Notice that the printed versions are much shorter and have undergone

country dinner Playhouse

11829 Abrams Road
Dallas, Texas 75243
(214) 231-9457

PETER LUPUS PRESS RELEASE

Peter Lupus the handsome, brawny star of the television series MISSION: IMPOSSIBLE will be starring in the romantic comedy SAVING GRACE, at The Country Dinner Playhouse October 30th through November 25th. Lupus starred in seven seasons as the character Willy Armitage in the Paramount TV series, MISSION: IMPOSSIBLE, now being seen in 88 countries around the world.

Lupus was born in Indianapolis of Greek-Lebanese-French and Irish ancestry. He attended local schools and Butler University in Indianapolis, where he studied dramatics before transferring to the Jordon College of Radio, Television and Drama. He made his professional debut in the stage production of WILL SUCCESS SPOIL ROCK HUNTER? opposite Ann Corio. He appeared in the Indianapolis Starlight Musical series for two seasons and played summer stock in Milwaukee, Detroit and Bristol, Pennsylvania.

Lupus then moved to Hollywood, where he studied under actress Lurene Tuttle and Jeff Corey, while earning expenses between acting jobs as the manager of a local gymnasium. A body building enthusiast of classic Greek proportions, he is a former MR. INDIANA, MR. INDIANAPOLIS, MR. HERCULES and MR. INTERNATIONAL HEALTH.

He made his television debut in the I'M DICKENS, HE'S FENSTER series, and made subsequent appearances on numerous television shows to name a few: THE RED SKELTON SHOW, JACK BENNY SHOW, MIKE DOUGLAS SHOW, JOHNNY CARSON SHOW, MERV GRIFFIN SHOW and DINAH SHORE SHOW. He co-starred in the Hollywood feature, MUSCLE BEACH PARTY and starred in five European-made films.

CHAPTER 7
NEWS RELEASES
FOR PRINT MEDIA

extensive editing. Capitalization and punctuation has been corrected to conform to newspaper style.

country Dinner Playhouse

11829 Abrams Road
Dallas, Texas 75243
(214) 231-9457

-2-

Lupus is a member of the USO National Council, past Honorary Mayor of Studio City, Ca., past National Chairman of Cystic Fibrosis SALUTE TO YOUTH program, past "King Pin" for National "Bowl Down Cancer" campaign sponsored by the American Cancer Society, past member of the L.A. Mayor's Citizens Narcotics Commission. Lupus was voted Man of the Year by PLAYGIRL MAGAZINE, and also has been voted Best Built Actor by the World Body Building Guild.

Lupus has just finished taping 130 half-hour TV shows called PETER LUPUS' BODY SHOP. Four Star International is the syndicator. The show deals with all aspects of health and beauty. His first book, PETER LUPUS GUIDE TO RADIANT HEALTH AND BEAUTY was released this year by Parker Publishing. He has just signed to do a second book, which will deal mainly with health, beauty, exercise, nutrition, and career tips from famous male and female stars.

The production that Peter Lupus has chosen to do, SAVING GRACE, was written by Jack Sharkey. This comedy has been referred to as "Light as a feather", and "Dialogue witty and entertainment unquestionable". SAVING GRACE, will play at The Country Dinner Playhouse for four weeks beginning October 30th.

For reservations please call 231-9457...
For additional Press Information contact Margie August 231-9113...

7-1, CONTINUED

Fairmont Hotel, Dallas

(214) 748-5454 • DALLAS, TEXAS 75201

BETTY HOLLOWAY, *Director of Public Relations*

LETTERMEN TO APPEAR IN THE
VENETIAN ROOM   Oct. 29–Nov. 10

Lettermen return to the Fairmont's Venetian Room, Oct. 29 to Nov. 10, bringing their unique chemistry of sound and songs. It is a combination that has insured their survival longer than any other group among those coming out of colleges in the early 60's.

Today's trio, Tony Butala, Gary and Donny Pike, has expanded their repertoire to include such hits as "Evergreen", "You Light Up My Life", "Can You Read My Mind?" theme from Superman, as well as several disco hits.

But their devoted fans remember that these romantic and harmonic sounds were first heard on their hit "The Way You Look Tonight" and their record breaking coupling of "Going Out of My Head" and "Can't Take My Eyes Off You." Since Lettermen first put two tunes together to make a monster hit, others have followed suit and many hits today are medleys.

Gary and Tony are two of the original trio. Donny, Gary's younger brother joined them in 1974, when a third Pike brother retired from the group. The venerable Lettermen have appeared more than 2000 times in campus concerts, sung on many national variety shows, played the

--more

Lettermen -- page 2

major hotels in the country and performed before 400,000,000 viewers when the Miss Universe Pageant was shown around the world.

Lettermen have received four gold albums in the US, three in Japan and the Philippines. All 38 of their albums have made the top 100 LP charts and their popularity is actually cosmic--the Astronauts requested some Lettermen music piped into their space capsule for the trip to the Moon!

Unlike most vocal groups, Lettermen all have the same range, and can easily interchange parts. All three are accomplished soloists in their own right. This unity has created the unique Lettermen sound.

They will perform two shows nightly except Sunday at the Fairmont. For reservations, call 748-5454.

-30-

7-1, CONTINUED

Peter Lupus

TV star coming to Country Dinner

Peter Lupus, former star of the television series "Mission Impossible," will star in the romantic comedy "Saving Grace" at the Country Dinner Playouse Oct. 30 through Nov. 25.

Lupus, who appeared as muscleman Willy Armitage in the long-running "Mission Impossible" series, is a former "Mr. Indiana," "Mr. Indianapolis," "Mr. Hercules"

and "Mr. International Health."

He made his professional debut in the stage production of "Will Success Spoil Rock Hunter?" His first television appearance was on "I'm Dickens, He's Fenster," and he's been a guest on shows hosted by Red Skelton, Jack Benny, Mike Douglas, Johnny Carson, Merv Griffin and Dinah Shore. He was a co-star in the film "Muscle Beach Party."

"Saving Grace," a light comedy, was written by Jack Sharkey. For reservations call 231-9457. ☆

Lettermen

Lettermen perform next at Venetian

The Lettermen, a group whose music has been heard around the world and around the moon, will perform in The Fairmont's Venetian Room Oct. 29 through Nov. 10.

The trio, known for its early hits "The Way You Look Tonight" and the medley "Going Out of My Head"—"Can't Take My Eyes Off of You," has expanded its repertoire to include recent songs like "Evergreen," "You Light Up My Life," and "Can You Read My Mind" from the movie "Superman."

Group members Tony Butala and Gary Pike remain from the original Lettermen. They were joined by Pike's brother Donny in 1974 when a third Pike brother retired from the group.

The Lettermen have appeared at more than 2,000 campus concerts and performed before an estimated 400 million viewers at the Miss Universe Pageant televised around the world.

Their music reached into space on an Apollo moon mission when the astronauts requested piped-in Lettermen music.

The Lettermen have received four gold albums in the United States, and three in Japan and the Philippines. They have cut 38 albums, all making the Top 100 LP charts.

They will perform two shows nightly except Sunday at The Fairmont. Call 748-5454 for reservations. ☆

7-2 DFW AIRPORT RELEASE

CHAPTER 7
NEWS RELEASES
FOR PRINT MEDIA

Immediate release

DFW NEWS 239-040678

GATEWAY RECEPTIONIST PROGRAM
BEGINS MONDAY AT DFW AIRPORT

DALLAS/FORT WORTH AIRPORT, Texas, April 6, 1978 -- The Dallas/Fort Worth Airport has arrived !

With new TransAtlantic service just started last month and a general increase in international traffic to Mexico and Canada, the DFW Airport is fast becoming the international air hub it was destined to be.

A program that starts Monday will not increase the numbers of people who use the Airport for international trips per se, but it will mean official government recognition of the Airport as an international "gateway" Airport and make things easier for those who do travel here from foreign lands.

The Gateway Receptionist Program, sponsored jointly by the U. S. Department of Health, Education and Welfare and the U. S. Travel Service of the U. S. Department of Commerce, begins officially at 2 p.m. Monday.

All five receptionists involved in the initial pilot project of the program will be available for pictures and interviews at that time.

From then on, at least one official receptionist, dressed in an official uniform, will greet international flights from 11 a.m. to 7 p.m. daily.

"The obvious advantage to the Metroplex is that our Airport is being recognized by the U. S. Travel Service as a 'gateway' Airport," said John Marshall, vice president of the Fort Worth Convention and Visitors Bureau.

MORE

DALLAS/FORT WORTH AIRPORT • P. O. DRAWER DFW • DALLAS/FORT WORTH AIRPORT, TEXAS 75261

This release is more a promotional piece than a news story. The lead says nothing. The little "news" the release does contain doesn't show up until the third and fourth paragraphs. The second paragraph is mostly editorial comment that doesn't pertain to the topic of the release—a new program for welcoming foreign visitors to the airport. The release gave $2\frac{1}{2}$ pages to a story that deserved no more than a few paragraphs.

GATEWAY RECEPTIONIST PROGRAM

BEGINS MONDAY AT DFW AIRPORT

Page 2

    The Convention Bureaus and Dallas, Fort Worth, Arlington and Irving were primarily responsible for the successful application for the program.

    "As a result of this program, all their (USTS) worldwide offices and all their worldwide literature will list Dallas/Fort Worth as a gateway Airport," Marshall said. "Eventually, they will produce and distribute a four-color brochure on the Metroplex. This is just another way that internationally we will be recognized."

    The receptionists in the pilot program are all students working under a work-study program through HEW and all speak English, Spanish and at least one other language.

    "The idea is to make foreign visitors to this Airport feel more welcome and to smooth over any difficulties, particularly those that result from language problems," said DFW Executive Director Ernest E. Dean. "The receptionists will be on duty in Federal Inspection Stations primarily where the new arrival is faced with plenty of officialdom."

    Initially, the program will be installed in the FIS in the Braniff International Terminal but will be expanded to the American/Eastern Terminal later.

    "These people are not employees of the Airport, though we provide the supervision," Dean said. "Applicants for this position should contact the coordinator of student employment at their college or university."

                                 MORE

GATEWAY RECEPTIONIST PROGRAM

BEGINS MONDAY AT DFW AIRPORT

Page 3

    If the pilot program proves successful, however, the Airport could qualify for a permanent program which would not limit employment to students under work-study programs.

    "Then we could hire full-time professional people and not worry about losing them when a school year ends," Dean said.

    "Many of the students could qualify to continue under a permanent program should this happen, but we would not be limited to them in recruiting potential receptionists," he said.

##

The most important thing—in this case the action—should form the main part of the lead: "The plant is opening." The interesting thing about the story provides an "angle" for the lead: "The first plant of its kind is opening."

Note in Example 7-3 that the release writer didn't try to find what the most important part of the story was, or the lead would have been written differently. The appearance of a congressional leader is clearly the most important item in this release, and also the most interesting. It should be the angle in the lead.

Of course, emphasizing an interesting angle in the first sentence may make it difficult to write a traditional newspaper lead, with *who-what-when-where* and *why* crammed into the first paragraph of the story. Such traditional leads are frequently still the rule in wire service copy since local papers may want to use no more than the first sentence or two of a wire story. But the first sentence can get pretty long if you try to get all that information across at once. More and more, the first sentence contains only two or three of the journalistic W's, with the rest coming in the next sentence or two (as in the rewrite of the lead in Example 7-3).

If you're writing a release for the wire services, try to get who-what-when-where-why into the first paragraph, or, at most, the first two. When writing for your local daily, study the paper's style. Are all these questions always answered in the first paragraph? Or do the paper's staff writers tend more toward the grabby, interest-catching lead with the details of time and place following in the next few paragraphs? The style of the paper you write for should determine your style.

Naturally, if your lead sentence contains the most important and interesting things about your story, it most likely will also say something about who and what. You can sneak in the when, where and why a little later—but not too much later. If you haven't answered the five W's by the fourth paragraph, you'd better try again.

Once you've written a lead, read it over to make sure it does two things: states clearly what the release is about, and grabs the reader's interest. In other words, the lead must give a quick indication of what the story is about and why it is important. And it must be interesting—both to catch the eye of the editor and to get the attention of the newspaper reader.

A local angle is essential in getting the attention of the editor. Most newspapers rely on the wire services for nonlocal news, and a release without a local angle is usually dumped. In fact, some editors say lack of a local angle is the single most important reason why releases aren't used. Be sure to identify the local angle. Make it clear and get it high in the story, preferably in the lead. If you have no local angle to interest a given newspaper, don't bother mailing the release.

Amplifying the Lead Once you have a lead that meets all these tests, writing the rest of the release should be easy. Simply amplify on the points raised in the lead, giving all the details. Anticipate the questions that an interested individual might ask about your subject, and answer them in the body of the release.

Write in the style of the news writer. Use short, concise sentences, short paragraphs, and common, concrete words. Avoid the jargon of your profession. If you must use a technical term, make sure it is fully explained. Above all, avoid editorial comment. Don't try to "sell" something in a news release. A release is not an ad. If comment is necessary, be sure to enclose it in quotation marks and attribute it to a company executive.

Quotations When using direct quotations, news release writers have a great advantage over reporters—they can make up quotes. A reporter using quotation marks must report exactly what was said. You, however, can take what you've written to the executive you're supposed to be quoting and ask for approval of the words you've used.

Sometimes you won't know what to make up and must go directly to the executive to find out what he or she wants to say. The executive may scribble out a sentence or tell you to quote from the official memo already prepared on the subject. Such quotes are almost always bad. Inserted into a news release in the guise of quoted conversation, such comments sound sterile and awkward. The words must be recast so they sound like somebody said them in conversation. For example, in writing a release about your company's reaction to a new government report, you shouldn't write:

> Company President J. T. Person said, "We have not had time to adequately review the contents of the document in its entirety, nor have we ascertained the ultimate position we are likely to take on it, though, at this point in time, it seems not unlikely that we will find the conclusions, and the evidence supporting them, acceptable."

That doesn't sound a bit like spoken English. Instead, write something like this:

> "We haven't read the whole report yet," company executive J. T. Person said, "so we can't take a position now. But from what we've read so far, we think we'll like it."

As you write the release, keep in mind that you know much more about the subject than an editor or reader will. You cannot assume any previous knowledge on the reader's part—even things you are "sure" that "everybody knows." A good rule of thumb, to quote James Marlow, is "Always write for the fellow who *hasn't* read yesterday's paper."[8]

That doesn't mean you write "down" to the reader. You may assume that your readers are intelligent and capable of understanding something if explained in common English. You may not assume that they know anything to begin with.

7-3 DHR RELEASE

TEXAS DEPARTMENT OF HUMAN RESOURCES
714 North Watson Road
Post Office Box 5128
Arlington, Texas   76011

                    Contact: Bill Buchanan/Gary Blevins
                                    261-3376

    Social workers from throughout the Southwest will gather in Dallas next week for the annual regional meeting of the American Public Welfare Association (APWA).

    Theme of this year's conference, scheduled for April 9 through 12 at the Baker Hotel, is "The Give and Take of Human Services."

    Keynote speaker will be U.S. Congressman Jim Wright of Fort Worth. His topic will be the "Current Political Climate of Welfare Reform." Wright is majority leader of the U. S. House of Representatives.

    Other prominent speakers and moderators scheduled are David Broder, syndicated political columnist for the <u>Washington Post</u>, and John Henry Faulk, a Texas humorist-philosopher-entertainer. Broder will evaluate the future for social welfare programs from his media perspective, and Faulk will poke fun at welfare's foibles.

This release does many things right—it is brief, readable, people are identified properly and a phone number is given with names of people to contact for more information. On the other hand, there is no date or release date, and the lead doesn't indicate the importance of the event. A meeting of social workers is hardly interesting, but the appearance of a prominent politician and well-known writers should attract some attention. The lead should go something like this:

The subjects to be discussed in the work sessions include a range of human services agency management techniques, personnel dynamics and emerging trends in various welfare programs.

The Southwest Region of APWA is composed of Texas, Louisiana, New Mexico, Arkansas and Oklahoma.

# # #

U.S. House Majority Leader Jim Wright of Fort Worth will address a regional meeting of social workers in Dallas next week.
Wright will discuss the politics of welfare reform at the annual meeting of the American Public Welfare Association, scheduled for April 9-12 at the Baker Hotel.
Other speakers include political columnist David Broder.

The exact day and time of Wright's talk should be given, but that information isn't provided in the release. Furthermore, the release does not conform to AP or UPI style.

Length Knowing how to write a release is important. But knowing when to stop writing a release is equally important. If a release is too long, an editor may decide there isn't time to read it, and into the file it goes.

The essential points can usually be covered in one page. Sometimes an important event will call for two or three pages, and if you need that much space to cover the subject, use it. But even then write the release so an editor can chop a few paragraphs off the bottom without damaging the story. (That's especially important for releases given to the wire services.)

Long releases with pages of generally irrelevant material are especially annoying. A common example of this is the release concerning the promotion of an executive, a subject that deserves a release of perhaps two or three paragraphs. Frequently, however, such releases give pages of company history and information on the company's chief executive, who did nothing more than announce the promotion. It's a waste of paper.

Keep the releases brief, at least in most cases. If you really think more information might be needed—statistics or background, for example—attach a fact sheet to the release.

Form and Style

The most important thing to worry about in a news release is not length, of course, but making sure your message gets across to the reader. If a subject deserves lengthy treatment, use the necessary space. And if the editor—and the readers of the newspaper—are to understand what you say, you must write in a clear, understandable way. It does no good to get your release printed if nobody understands what it means.

Unfortunately, most releases are written at a more complex level than the news stories of a typical daily paper. Readability expert Robert Gunning notes that the writing in most local papers is about on the level of *Reader's Digest*, while releases from business and industry are closer to the level of *Harper's*.[9] Even when people writing the releases are ex-reporters, Gunning observes, the writing is too complex—perhaps because the writers are writing now for bosses who are business executives instead of city editors. But that's what you must learn not to do if you write news releases. *Don't* write them for your boss. Write them for a city editor, just as you would write any news story if you were a reporter.

That doesn't mean you give the facts in such a context that it makes your company look bad (as a real reporter might do). But it does mean that you *don't* leave out pertinent facts, however embarrassing they might be.

When you write a story, it's not enough to conform to newspaper style in the writing level and basic structure of the story. You must follow newspaper style to the finest detail, with every comma and period in its proper place.

For newspapers, this generally means adhering to the Associated Press or United Press International stylebook (the two are virtually identical). Most newspapers follow AP-UPI style, but many have special style rules that you should know. It's a good practice to ask local editors for a copy of their stylebook. You can get a copy of the AP or UPI stylebook at a college bookstore or by writing directly to AP or UPI.

The stylebook will tell you things such as when to capitalize, how to abbreviate, what titles to use with people. The AP-UPI book also describes certain punctuation rules that may be different from common usage. AP-UPI style, for example, does not use a comma between a name and Jr. or Sr., as in "Joe Zilch Jr." (For a summary of AP-UPI style, see Appendix D.)

As for spelling, AP and UPI have adopted *Webster's New World Dictionary of the American Language* as the standard guide for spelling (second college edition). Use the first spelling listed, or the spelling given with a complete definition if a word has more than one entry (like T-shirt and tee shirt). Exceptions to the dictionary spelling are given in the stylebook. If a word isn't in *Webster's New World,* check in *Webster's Third New International* (and think again about whether you should be using such a word).

Since anything you give to a newspaper will be edited at the copy desk anyway, you might wonder if it's necessary to pay strict attention to the details of newspaper style. Of course it's not absolutely necessary. But it's still a good idea. Even if your release is rewritten completely, the rewriter will notice a correct style—and will especially notice an incorrect style. It's a matter of making a good impression. If your style is correct, an editor will know the release was prepared carefully, by someone who knew what he or she was doing. Correct spelling is even more important. If you don't bother to spell words correctly, an editor is likely to assume that you aren't very careful with the facts, either. If an editor can't trust your information, the release is worthless.

What about grammar? Some writers worry about grammar above all else, combing every line for a possible split infinitive or a *who* that should be a *whom.* Certainly good grammar is important, and awkward, obvious errors like subject-verb disagreements should not be tolerated. But don't worry more about grammar than about communication. The first concern must be the clarity of the message. If your sentences are clear and understandable, the grammar will take care of itself (see Chapter 6).

One more word about style. If you plan to send releases to papers other than local dailies (releases about financial news, for example, might go to the *Wall Street Journal*), you should know that these papers sometimes have completely different style rules. Some PR people send the same release to all papers, using the style applicable to the majority.

You can get away with it, but it never hurts to tailor releases to individual publications. Remember that some papers—like the *Wall Street Journal* and the *New York Times*—have styles all their own.

Types of Releases

Once you know how to write a release, the next questions are why should you write one, and when? The reason for writing releases depends on the type of company or institution you write for and what its goals are. Frequently releases are just one of many tools a company uses to get publicity. Sometimes releases are an important communications tool for explaining the company's position on major public issues. But remember also that PR people, as Boston University PR professor Otto Lerbinger puts it, "have an obligation to satisfy people's 'right to know' about the operation of government units and the activities of corporations and nonprofit organizations that affect the public interest."[10] News releases are often necessary to meet that obligation.

Another reason for issuing releases is simply to keep the record straight. Tight-lipped corporations that maintain a low profile and seldom issue releases are frequently headed by executives who complain privately about the "unfair" treatment they get in the media, or who note the media's many mistakes in covering their company. But they have no business complaining about a paper getting the facts wrong if they haven't provided that paper with the correct information. News releases are one way of helping papers get the facts right when they report about your business.

It's not only a matter of information. A good news release program helps build good media relations, as well as getting publicity for your company. Reporters get paid to find news and write stories, and if you help them find news—real news—the reporters will be grateful.

When do you write releases? It's simple: When you have news, release it. Certain things call for news releases. Generally these correspond to a few basic types of releases.

Announcement Release   This can be an announcement of a new product, the opening of a new plant, the company's latest financial results, or a new company policy. Generally these are routine items that don't require long releases. Just be sure the news is legitimate. In most cases the announcement of a new line of a familiar product is material for an ad, not a news release. It has to be a completely new kind of product, or something unique, to deserve a news story.

One editor of an industrial publication was exasperated by a PR person who sent him a release about the company's new line of screws. The editor kindly explained that the release was not newsworthy and wouldn't be used. Two weeks later, the same PR man tried to pass off as news a new line of nuts. Which is why one editor said, "I'm convinced that a good many PR men working today are idiots."[11]

"Created News" Release A mere announcement often isn't enough to attract much media attention. So a company may try to "dress up" the news release by making sure something newsworthy is going on. The company may bring a well-known speaker to a company function, or stage a formal ceremony or other event like a concert or rally. This gives the news release writer something more interesting or newsworthy to say.

Remember one thing, though. There should never be any confusion about what's really going on, and who is responsible. If the company is behind an event, make that fact clear. Deception of any kind is always reprehensible, but it's twice as reprehensible in a news release.

Spot News Release Announcement releases can usually be planned in advance. But sometimes things happen without notice. An electric utility's main power plant can break down, threatening power shortages or higher costs for replacement power. An explosion can occur in a munitions factory; an airplane can be hijacked. Such occurrences are spot news, and when they happen, a news release is in order.

In these cases the PR person must function like a reporter working on deadline, gathering the information quickly and writing the release without delay. If media people aren't provided with a release immediately, they will write their stories from whatever scraps of information they can find. And frequently the reporting is inaccurate.

A spot news release often has to be followed up the next day with a second release, explaining how the initial events were resolved.*

Response Release Often news about a company reaches the media from sources other than the PR department. A consumer group may issue a report critical of the company. The government may announce an investigation into company hiring practices. A research group may publish a major study on your company's industry.

When these things happen reporters will call for a response. Companies with good PR organizations anticipate these calls and have a response release ready. The response may be a brief statement, or it may be a full-fledged news release giving the company's position in detail.

Even if you are not asked for a response, you can offer one anyway as a way of communicating your company's views. For example, when President Carter announced a national energy policy, many energy-related corporations prepared releases immediately giving their opinions of the new policy. Newspapers ran these releases, or parts of them, in stories about "local reaction" to the energy plan. (See Example 7–4.)

---

*In emergency situations, news releases aren't enough. PR people must sometimes use the telephone to transmit the latest developments to the media.

7-4 A RESPONSE RELEASE

Texas Electric Service Company
News Release

For release: Thursday, April 21, 1977   For further information:
                                            Contact: Bob Martin
                                            Phone: 336-9411

Increasing the use of coal and nuclear fuel is the "essential part" of President Carter's energy plan, Texas Electric Service Co. President W. G. Marquardt said today.

Marquardt's statements came in response to Carter's energy message delivered to Congress Wednesday night.

"The most important thing about President Carter's energy plan is the recognition that the United States faces a serious energy problem and something must be done about it," Marquardt said.

The thing to do, he said, is switch from oil and gas to coal and nuclear fuel. Texas Electric began such a program 10 years ago.

"We . . . are already producing nearly a third of our electricity with lignite coal," he said.

Marquardt warned that changing fuels is a very expensive process, requiring hundreds of millions of dollars to build new power plants.

"We can't raise these tremendous sums unless we get rate increases when they are needed, in the amount needed," he said. "Without rate increases, the fuel changing process will come to a halt."

He also stressed the need for increased conservation, and said the company plans to expand its efforts to help people to properly insulate their homes.

He cited some specifics in the Carter proposal that deserve close study because they might not be feasible or economic at this time. Among those proposals were the suggested tax on use of natural gas as a boiler fuel, conversion of existing gas plants to burn coal, and time-of-day electric rates.

-30-

When PR writers for this electric utility company heard that President Carter would give a nationwide address on national energy policy, they immediately began to prepare a news release for the following day. Advance news stories provided information about what the President would say. A writer prepared a statement that was approved by the company president and then prepared a release about the company president's statement.

Notice that the release is used to give the company's viewpoint on energy, as well as comment on President Carter's policies.

Feature Release Not every story in a newspaper involves events that happened today or yesterday. Feature stories about topics of special interest are taking up a greater share of newspaper space these days. All PR people can find feature material somewhere in their organizations—something going on in research and development, for example, like a new production process that has improved efficiency or helped reduce pollution. Such feature stories can be prepared for newspapers just as ordinary news releases.

Feature releases create a problem, however, if more than one newspaper in the same city covers your company. Newspapers don't expect special treatment when it comes to regular news—they know you give ordinary news releases to all news media. But features are different. An editor is not likely to use a feature if he or she knows some other paper might be running the same story. It's best to offer different features to different papers, or at least develop a different angle of the story for each paper in the area.

Newspaper features have many of the same qualities as magazine articles, which are discussed in detail in Chapter 12.

Bad-News Release Sometimes events occur that a company would like to keep quiet. The natural tendency in such cases is to issue no news release and hope that the problem will go unnoticed. But more often than not, attempts to keep bad news out of the media will backfire. For example, when the Oregon Department of Energy inspected a utility company's nuclear power plant, they found several rule violations. The inspectors told utility officials that a report of the violations would be filed as a public document, and suggested that the utility issue its own news release first. But utility officials didn't bother with a release. They decided instead to do nothing and hope that nobody would read the report. But within days news of the violations had leaked to the press, and the papers played the story in a rather sensational fashion.[12]

Had the company made its own announcement, the story would still have been in the papers. But it almost certainly would have been treated in a less sensational manner. If you hand over the facts to a reporter, the result is usually a straight report. But if the reporter has to dig the story out, the article will be written more dramatically. This has always been true, and since the Watergate scandals, more people have begun to realize that covering up a crime can be a worse offense than the crime itself.

Column Notes, Letters, Guest Columns Sometimes the information you'd like to see in the paper doesn't fit the form of an ordinary news story (see Example 7–5). That doesn't mean you should forget about it. Most papers have special columns or sections that print unusual items.

Figure 7–6 is an ad from a metropolitan newspaper giving readers (including PR people) an idea of the different ways to get their views into print. The most obvious way—a letter to the editor—is only one of

7-5   ARLINGTON C OF C RELEASE

THINGS ARE HAPPENING

ARLINGTON CHAMBER OF COMMERCE
P. O. BOX 607, ARLINGTON, TEXAS 76010
CONTACT WARREN GREEN (275-2613)

April 6, 1978
For Release April 9, 1978

Preparations for the "On To Victory" luncheon, boosting the Texas Rangers Baseball Club, and mailing the April issue of "Arlington" magazine demanded the greater part of time and effort at the Chamber office this week.

A "Meet the Candidates" session was conducted by the Government Liaison Task Force at the Chamber on April 4. Twenty Candidates seeking their parties' nomination for State and County offices were present to speak to local voters and to answer their questions.

Charles Starnes conducted a meeting of the Transportation Task Force on April 5 at which time the members reviewed reports of city activities in street and related construction from the 1970 bond program.

The Communications Task Force met with Jim DeShong on April 5. They continued their work on revision of an Arlington Information Booklet that has been very popular over the past two years. They hope to have reprints available by the early part of May.

The coming week will be launched with the Chamber-sponsored "On To Victory" luncheon, feteing the Texas Rangers. Tom Vandergriff will be the Master of Ceremonies. The Business Community will host the players, Manager, coaches and administrative staff of the Ball Club in showing appreciation and backing for their efforts on the field to bring the American

-2-

League Pennant and World Championship to Arlington.

The Environmental Improvement Task Force will meet at 8:30 a.m. on April 11 to critique their many recent activities and to complete plans for savings bonds presentations to the winners of this year's essay contest in Junior High Schools. The awards will be presented at the Chamber office at 4 p.m. on April 12.

Persis Forster will conduct a meeting of the Cultural Activities Task Force at 8:30 a.m. on April 13 at the Chamber office. They will continue their planning for a visual presentation about Arlington, its attractions and fine arts.

This release is dated properly and has a name to contact and a phone number, but it is not a news release. It is not written as a news story and it contains no news. Mailing the city magazine and preparing a luncheon are not the sorts of things that editors are looking for in the lead of a release.
    The material in this "release" is perhaps appropriate for a newsletter or calendar of events that might be sent to editors or reporters interested in the Chamber of Commerce. But it should not be sent in the form of a news release. The "upcoming" events on the second page might be sent as a news release to a "community events" columnist, but such a release would warrant no more than one or two paragraphs.

several methods described. Individual columnists might make use of readers' information. Or readers might want to write a "guest column." (You might want to write one under the by-line of your company's chief executive.)

These items don't always follow the same form as an ordinary news release, but they can accomplish much the same thing. Study the newspapers your organization deals with so you'll know what outlets are available.

PREPARING AND DELIVERING NEWS RELEASES

With news releases, as with most things, substance is more important than form. But that doesn't mean form is unimportant. You should know some things about form that will help you prepare releases in the most convenient way for the people who use them.

Technical Considerations

Leave space at the top of the first page. If the release is to be set in type, the editor will need some space to write instructions.

Double or even triple space your typing. This allows room for editing. (Do *not* try to outsmart an editor into using a release as you wrote it by single spacing and thus leaving no room for changes. The editor will have trouble reading it—and so will the typesetter. Consequently, it will probably be thrown away.)

Make sure the name, address and phone number of the company or organization is on the news release form. The name of a person to contact for further information should also be included, with both office and home phone numbers. A morning paper may be working on a story at midnight, and if a question comes up, someone will need a number to call.

The release should have two dates: the actual date the release was sent to the media, and the date when the release is cleared for use. If the release can be used at any time, "for immediate release" is sufficient to indicate release date. When necessary, specify "a.m. papers" or "p.m. papers" (specify, for example, if it's OK for a release to appear in the day's afternoon, but not morning, papers). Remember, some morning papers have an early edition that may appear the evening before the stated publication day. Afternoon papers often issue a street edition that appears well before noon. If it matters, specify what edition the release can be used in.

7-6 UNUSUAL OPPORTUNITIES

WAYS TO TELL IT YOUR WAY IN THE STAR-TELEGRAM

Got a gripe? Or a problem? An idea to share? Or a funny story? Don't keep them to yourself. Share them with the Star-Telegram readers. Morning, Evening, Saturday and Sunday, each edition of the paper has a place where you can express your views or share information with other readers. And we love to receive your contributions.

So, here in an easy-to-use guide are all the various ways you can get your particular interest in print.

LETTERS TO THE EDITOR
Voices of the People runs in each edition of the Star-Telegram and includes letters on every imaginable topic, from comments on political candidates to reflections on the beauty of a sunset. And reader surveys show that Voices is one of the best read sections of the paper.

voices of the people

To have your thoughts on a subject included, send a letter—250 words or less—to Voices of the People. Be sure to include your name and address. We will publish your name and city, unless there is a pertinent reason for withholding that information.

GUEST COLUMNS
Sometimes a letter simply isn't long enough to fully express your ideas. That's why we have our

expressions

Guest Column feature on the Expressions page of the morning Star-Telegram and Reflections in the evening edition. Length should

reflections

be between 500 and 800 words. Be sure to include your name and address and send to Guest Column. Not all of these submissions are published, but if you have a knack for expressing your ideas, you may well see your name and your column in print.

ED BRICE
Need some help tracking down a lost mail order or some information on a favorite rock group? Having trouble cutting through governmental red tape?

Ed Brice answers questions and solves problems in his popular morning and evening Star-Telegram feature.

Write Ed Brice

Star-Telegram and, once again, be sure to include your name, address, zip and telephone number. Ed doesn't print them, but he may need them for follow-up information from you.

READER EXCHANGE
If you have something to swap or give away, or you're looking for something rare and hard to find,

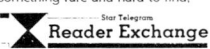

Reader Exchange

Reader Exchange is for you. Readers share goods, services and information in the Monday, Wednesday and Friday evening editions and in the Sunday features section. Sorry, we can't accept lost and found entries or items for sale.

CONTRIBUTIONS TO COLUMNISTS
Many of our Star-Telegram columnists welcome your information and anecdotes. The funny story you share with George Dolan may brighten the day of all our morning readers, or perhaps

george dolan

Jim Trinkle's SKYLINE

you have some human interest to add to Jim Trinkle's Skyline. Send your fashion anecdotes and social news to Cissy

'CISSY' STEWART

(Stewart) for the enjoyment of our Sunday readers. Also on Sunday, help Tony Slaughter tell all about Metroplex people and the things they are doing. Write each

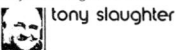

tony slaughter

columnist by name and, once again, it helps to have your name, address and phone number in case there is something a columnist

needs to clarify.

SWAPPING RECIPES
Good cooks in the area have learned never to miss Jacqueline Jones' Cooking Up a Storm column in the Thursday evening food section. Readers share their best, and sometimes most exotic, recipes. If you've been looking for a particular recipe, write Jacqueline and let a reader help you out. And, by reading the column, you may have the chance to help others find just the blend of ingredients they are seeking. To participate, write Cooking Up a Storm, Star-Telegram, 400 W. 7th St., Fort Worth 76102.

GUEST GAZER
During football season you can test your predictions against the pros as a Guest Gazer in our Star Gazers column. Each week in both a morning and evening edition, sports experts forecast the winner

the star gazers

(and the point spread) of important upcoming football matches. Submit your predictions and you may be selected as our reader expert of the week. Send in care of Guest Gazer, Sports Department, and then check your accuracy by reading the complete sports coverage in each edition of the Star-Telegram.

MAKE A CONTRIBUTION
The more people who contribute ideas and information to our paper, the better and more varied our coverage and content will be. So get involved. Take a stand. Share your thoughts and information. All you have to do is write the section of your choice c/o the Star-Telegram, PO Box 1870, Fort Worth 76101. We're waiting to hear from you.

Nobody delivers reader ideas and information like the Star-Telegram.
To subscribe, dial: DEL-IVER.

There are many ways other than news releases to get information in a newspaper. Sometimes a letter to the editor, a guest column or a note to a columnist is the best approach. The Fort Worth *Star-Telegram* offers readers a number of ways to get their views into print—and it advertises to let them know.

When the release is typed and ready to be sent, go back and check, one more time, every fact, name, place, time and date. You can't afford mistakes. Nothing is more important than absolute accuracy. If you give an editor a release with just one false sentence, one misspelled name, one wrong date—and it gets into the paper—that editor is going to have to apologize to somebody for your mistake. And the next time a release comes from you, that editor will have to take extra time to check over the facts in your story. If the editor doesn't have the time—and editors usually don't—he or she will probably throw the release away rather than risk more mistakes. It might not happen this way every time with every editor, but there's only one sure way to make sure it won't happen to you: Get everything right, every time.

Dealing with the Media

Once a release is written and checked for errors, a few important questions remain. Where should the release be sent, and to whom? When should you send the release? And, aside from preparing it properly, what can you do to make sure the release is used?

Ordinarily, you send releases to the local daily newspaper. If your company serves an entire region, your release should be of interest to several daily papers. Nationwide firms may want to send releases to every city where the company's plants or offices are located. News releases from the military are sent to the hometowns of individuals involved. Such releases are sometimes prepared by computers (see Example 7-7).

While most news release publicity begins with daily newspapers, it is a mistake to stop there. Wire services should not be overlooked if the release is of interest over a wide area. With wire services, though, the release will not go to a paper in the form you prepared it—the wire editors will rewrite it. If you want to get the release to the paper as you wrote it, you can use one of several publicity wire services.[13]

Another important place to send releases is the weekly paper that serves small towns or rural areas. Weeklies may have a low circulation, but they are well read by those who receive them. If you're trying to reach small town audiences, weeklies can be much more effective than dailies.

Most releases should also be sent to the electronic media. But remember that broadcast style is different from print style. A release prepared for a newspaper must be completely rewritten for TV or radio (see Chapter 8 on broadcast writing). Since the electronic version will normally be much shorter than the print version, you should attach the print version to the release you send to radio and TV. This makes the details available to the electronic journalists if they need them.

It's helpful to know the right person to send a release to. Most TV and radio stations have a news director, and all releases should go to that individual. Newspapers are more complicated, however. Various section editors may be interested in the news you have to offer, but sometimes their responsibilities overlap and it's hard to know the right recipient.

A few simple guidelines may be helpful in such a situation. Releases specifically aimed at a single topic (like food or sports) should go to the section editor. If a release contains strictly business or financial news, for example, it should go to the editor of the business section. If the news is of general local interest, the city editor is usually the right person for the release. (When you're in doubt about who should get the release, the city editor is probably the best bet.) If one reporter covers your company or organization all the time, send the release directly to him or her.

Sometimes it's appropriate to send a release to more than one person at the same paper—a reporter and an editor, for example. Some companies regularly send copies of releases to editorial writers, especially if the release addresses a controversial topic. Make sure, though, that if you send more than one copy of the release to a given paper, you indicate it on the release. To avoid duplicated story assignments, you must let an editor know that a reporter already has your release.

When should you send the release? On breaking news stories, as soon as possible—and you should hand deliver the release if at all feasible. For announcements of upcoming events, mailing three to four days in advance is usually sufficient. For major stories that should be released at a specific time, have the release arrive at the newspaper the day before the desired date.

Keep in mind that weekly papers have different deadline schedules from dailies, and you must know the deadlines in order to get the release delivered on time. A weekly published on Thursdays might have a deadline as early as Monday.

As for getting the papers to use your release, there is no substitute for a well-written release with genuine news value. All other considerations are secondary. But assuming the release is properly prepared, there are things you can do to enhance its chances of getting printed. One thing is proper choice of release date. Setting the release time for Sunday helps your chances, since Sunday papers are large and have more space to fill. Including a good picture with the release is also helpful, since editors are always interested in good art for page design purposes. Perhaps the best way to get a release used, however, is to get it used by wire services. Newspapers use wire stories in preference to releases to save time in editing and typesetting (if the paper uses computer punch-tape typesetting).

One thing that won't help the release get used is printing it on colored paper stock. According to one survey, an overwhelming majority of editors disliked colored news release paper—although most seemed to think that colored ink for the name on the letterhead was OK.

PART THREE
WRITING FOR
GENERAL AUDIENCES

7-7 COMPUTERIZED NEWS RELEASES

```
HQ AIR FORCE SERVICE INFORMATION AND NEWS CENTER    PAGE  1
HOME TOWN NEWS DIRECTORATE
KELLY AFB, TX       78241                                  1




        NEWS EDITOR                                   451295114
        THE OBSERVER                                  76101W07
        PO BOX 2268
        FORT WORTH TX 76101



        WICHITA FALLS, Texas--Airman Billy B. Suggs, son of
retired Air Force Chief Master Sergeant and Mrs. R.L.
Isinghood of 908 Darnell, Benbrook, Texas, has graduated
from the U.S. Air Force computer operator course at Sheppard
Air Force Base, here.
        Graduates of the course earn credits toward an
associate degree in applied science through the Community
College of the Air Force.
        Airman Suggs learned how to operate and maintain
electronic data processing equipment. He is being assigned
to Sheppard Air Force Base, Texas.
        The airman is a 1977 graduate of Romulus High School,
Romulus, Mich.
                           -30-                             (E)
```

Large organizations that send out a lot of releases on essentially the same subject sometimes let a computer do the work. The information office at one Air Force base has programmed a computer to write news releases about new personnel placements. Note that the same general information is given in both releases.

**CHAPTER 7
NEWS RELEASES
FOR PRINT MEDIA**

```
HQ AIR FORCE SERVICE INFORMATION AND NEWS CENTER    PAGE  1
HOME TOWN NEWS DIRECTORATE
KELLY AFB, TX     78241                               2


      NEWS EDITOR                                  462292257
      THE OBSERVER                                  76101W07
      PO BOX 2268
      FORT WORTH TX 76101


      RANTOUL, Ill.--Airman Jesus D. Santillan, son of Luz
Nieto of 3307 N. Pecan, Fort Worth, Texas, has graduated
from the U.S. Air Force aircraft ground equipment course at
Chanute Air Force Base, here.
      Graduates of the course earn credits toward an
associate degree in applied science through the Community
College of the Air Force.
      Airman Santillan learned how to repair generators, gas
turbines, and hydraulic pumping equipment.  He is being
assigned to Reese Air Force Base, Texas.
      He is a 1979 graduate of Trimble Technical High School,
Fort Worth.
                          -30-                          (G)
```

7-8 NEWS RELEASE CHECKLIST

1. Is the lead direct and to the point? Does it contain the most important and most interesting aspects of the story?
2. Has the local angle been emphasized?
3. Have who, what, when, where and why been answered in the first few paragraphs?
4. Are sentences short, concise? Paragraphs short? Words common and concrete?
5. Has editorial comment been placed in quotation marks and attributed to the appropriate person?
6. Are quotations natural, that is, do they sound as though they could have been spoken?
7. Has newspaper style (AP or UPI) been followed faithfully throughout the release?
8. Is spelling and punctuation correct?
9. Have all statements of fact been double-checked for accuracy?
10. Has the release been properly prepared, typed and double-spaced?
11. Is the release dated? Is release time indicated?
12. Are names and phone numbers for further information included?

CONCLUSION

News releases can be one of a PR person's most valuable communications tools—but only if they are prepared properly (see Table 7-8). If they contain genuine news, are written in the proper form and style, and if they are truthful, complete and accurate, they can help communicate PR messages and build good media relations as well.

NOTES

[1] Gerald Powers, "For Immediate Release: View from the Editor's Desk," *Public Relations Journal* 27 (September 1971): 18.

[2] Chuck Honaker, "Why Your News Releases Aren't Working," *Public Relations Journal* 34 (March 1978): 16–19.

[3] Powers, "For Immediate Release," p. 12.

[4] Philip Lesly, "Relations with Publicity Media," in *Lesly's Public Relations Handbook* (Englewood Cliffs, N.J.: Prentice-Hall, 1971), p. 348.

[5] Ivy Lee, *Publicity: Some Things It Is and Is Not* (New York: Industries Publishing Co., 1925).

[6] Edward L. Bernays, *Public Relations* (Norman: University of Oklahoma Press, 1952), p. 47.

[7] Ibid.

[8]Rudolf Flesch, *The Art of Readable Writing*, 25th anniversary ed. (New York: Harper and Row, 1974), p. 25.

[9]Robert Gunning, *The Technique of Clear Writing* (New York: McGraw-Hill, 1968), p. 225.

[10]Otto Lerbinger, *Designs for Persuasive Communication* (Englewood Cliffs, N.J.: Prentice-Hall, 1972), p. 69.

[11]Powers, "For Immediate Release," p. 12.

[12]Jane Garrick, "Oregon Utility Gets Burned by Not Revealing Nuclear Safety Errors," *The Energy Daily*, September 27, 1976.

[13]For a description of publicity wire services, see D. Newsom and A. Scott, *This Is PR*, 2d ed. (Belmont, Calif.: Wadsworth, 1981), Chapter 10.

SELECTED BIBLIOGRAPHY

Edward L. Bernays, *Public Relations* (Norman: University of Oklahoma Press, 1952).

Rudolf Flesch, *The Art of Readable Writing*, 25th anniversary ed. (New York: Harper and Row, 1974).

Robert Gunning, *The Technique of Clear Writing*, rev. ed. (New York: McGraw-Hill, 1968).

Chuck Honaker, "Why Your News Releases Aren't Working," *Public Relations Journal* 34 (March 1978): 16–19.

Ivy Lee, *Publicity: Some Things It Is and Is Not* (New York: Industries Publishing Co., 1925).

Otto Lerbinger, *Designs for Persuasive Communication* (Englewood Cliffs, N.J.: Prentice-Hall, 1972).

Philip Lesly, "Relations with Publicity Media," in *Lesly's Public Relations Handbook* (Englewood Cliffs, N.J.: Prentice-Hall, 1971).

D. Newsom and A. Scott, *This Is PR*, 2d ed.(Belmont, Calif.: Wadsworth, 1981).

C. A. Oliphant, "Is That News Release Really Necessary?" *Public Relations Journal* 27 (September 1971): 13.

Gerald Powers, "For Immediate Release: View from the Editor's Desk," *Public Relations Journal* 27 (September 1971): 12.

William Zinsser, *On Writing Well*, 2d ed. (New York: Harper and Row, 1980).

8

BROADCAST WRITING: NEWS AND FEATURES

"If it wiggles," the saying goes, "it's TV news." And the remark is only half facetious. With broadcast media, all that matter are sight and sound.

Radio stations, for example, are interested in the sounds of an event. The voice of the mayor reading a proclamation, the president of the electric company explaining a power outage, the hospital director telling about caring for tornado victims—all these are far more likely to be used than a news release telling what happened and what was said. For TV news, one 30-second film clip is worth a thousand news releases.

FACTS, SIGHTS AND SOUNDS

Facts are the vital elements of any news story, whether for print or broadcast media. Sometimes a formal news release isn't really necessary—the PR writer can provide the media with a fact sheet and the reporters can write the story. But with the electronic media, facts alone are not enough. Whether you're planning a special event, holding a news conference, or dealing with a crisis situation, you must also be aware of sights and sounds, or, more technically, visuals and audio.

Special Events

A special event is one of the most common activities PR people get involved with. Such events are held for various purposes—to raise money, perhaps, or just to draw media attention (the so-called media event). Whatever its purpose, the first thing to do when you're faced with a special event is prepare a fact sheet. It will help preserve your sanity.

The fact sheet should include a description of all activities, plus the day, date, time (and duration) of the activities, followed by the name of the person responsible. The person's title (in relation to the event) should also be given. Once the timetable is drafted, add all of the background of the event: where it will be, dates and times, charges (if any), sponsors, and your name—with all the places and phone numbers where you can be reached. Your fact sheet is then essentially complete. (See the fact sheet in Example 8-1.)

You might want to add, on a separate page, a brief history of the event, giving dates and milestones. For example, to a fact sheet on this year's pro-am benefit, you might add a single sheet describing past benefits, naming participants, and stating who won, scores, dollars raised, who benefited, sponsors, and past locations (if it changes).

For the wiggle that makes it news for TV, you'll have to stage some activity if it is a first time for this special event. After the first one, you can use film shot during the event (16mm movie and 35mm stills) as visuals for next year. One word of caution. When you use last year's pictures as an advance story, be sure you have the appropriate labels on the pictures. Sometimes editors get too busy to realize you couldn't have a picture of something that hasn't yet happened—and last year's pictures get labeled as this year's. Protect yourself and label the pictures.

You should have 16mm film, 35mm color slides and, just for safety, black and white 8-×-10-inch photos with a matte finish (glossies glow in TV lighting). It is also a good idea to have some charts and graphs on 35mm slides showing attendance figures and such from the previous year. Another slide can show dates for the upcoming event.

When you stage an activity to photograph, don't *simulate* the event. You wouldn't want to perpetrate a hoax and don't want to be innocently accused of it, either. Use preparations of the event; they qualify as legitimate news. For audio you can use the people involved, usually dignitaries, to make the announcements. These announcements should be recorded by technically qualified people so they will be of broadcast quality. As the event gets closer, use interviews with some of the participants. Your audio cassettes or tape can be supplied to both radio and television.

So much for the advance. For actual coverage by the news media find out at least three to six weeks in advance what mechanical equipment you will need to supply. You'll have to check out lighting and sound systems and prepare a list of what will be available for coverage. When the news media arrive, you should be able to offer (again) all of the materials previously mentioned, plus an update of what is happening that day and the next. Mention any changes or corrections in materials sent previously. Also, give the reporters a copy of a brief story in broadcast style. Attach it to a copy of the longer release prepared for the print media. In reworking the story or in writing their own to fit the coverage, broadcasters will find the longer release helpful.

It's important at special events to have someone at a central location to answer the telephone and respond intelligently to queries from the news media. Give that person sets of all materials and your itinerary so you can be located. (Check in every hour or so anyway.)

8-1 FACT SHEET AND NEWS RELEASE

THE TEXAS ASSOCIATION FOR MENTAL HEALTH

EXECUTIVE COMMITTEE
President
Carroll B. Bryant
Vice President—Organization & Development
Vangie Ford
Vice President—Program
Shirley Switzer
Vice President—Fund Raising
Betty Lou Nance
Vice President—Public Policy & Information
Shirley Camfield
Recording Secretary
Minette Urbach
Treasurer
John Trimble
Members at Large
Caroline Duile
Richard Fredrick
Harry Garwood
Sam Ogletree
Barbara Watkins
Immediate Past President
Tom J. Caldwell, Jr.
Executive Director
William W. Kuehn

FACTS ABOUT THE GALAXY BALL

WHEN AND WHERE: Saturday, May 29, 1976 9 p.m. to 1 a.m.
Ridglea Country Club, Fort Worth, Texas.

WHAT: A benefit ball sponsored by the Texas Association for Mental Health in alternating major Texas cities. It is the only annual statewide benefit ball of its kind in the United States.

This will be the 13th anniversary for the event first held in Fort Worth in 1963 with Mrs. John B. Connally as honorary chairwoman.

WHO: Honorary chairwoman for 1976 is Mrs. Lyndon B. Johnson and statewide chairwoman for the ball is Mrs. Katherine Buck McDermott of Fort Worth. Honorary head of the advisory group is Mrs. John B. Connally.

The ball is planned, organized and conducted by volunteers from all over Texas who give time and talent to raise funds to support the work and programs of the Texas Association for Mental Health.

HOW: The Texas Association of Mental Health is itself a voluntary citizens organization, operating at the national, state and local levels. The association relies entirely on private contributions.

BALL TICKETS: Patron table, ten persons, $1,000
           ($875 tax deductible)
Table for ten $500 ($375 tax deductible)
Table for six $300 ($225 tax deductible)
Couple $100 ($75 tax deductible)
Single $50 ($37.50 tax deductible)

Above and following are the print and broadcast versions of a release and the special events fact sheet that accompanied each release. Broadcast news releases must be written to fill a tight time spot. For that reason, details appearing in the print media release must be left out of the broadcast release. It's a good idea, however, to attach a

THE TEXAS ASSOCIATION FOR MENTAL HEALTH
103 LANTERN LANE • AUSTIN, TEXAS 78731 • (512) 159-6534

FOR IMMEDIATE RELEASE: CONTACT: NEWS 12-76
                                         Doug Newsom
                                         817-732-2901
                                         817-926-2461
                                              Ext. 288

TELEVISION NEWS PERSONALITY TO EMCEE GALAXY BALL

CBS News White House Correspondent Bob Schieffer will be master of ceremonies at the Bicentennial Galaxy Ball in Fort Worth, Texas, May 29. The Galaxy Ball which raises funds for mental health is the only statewide fund raising benefit in the nation. This is the thirteenth anniversary of the event which was first held in Fort Worth in 1963 with Mrs. John B. Connally as statewide honorary chairwoman. This year's statewide honorary chairwoman is Mrs. Lyndon B. Johnson.

- 30 -

copy of the print release as well as the fact sheet to a broadcast release so broadcast newspeople will have the additional information if they need it.

8-1, CONTINUED

THE TEXAS ASSOCIATION FOR MENTAL HEALTH
103 LANTERN LANE • AUSTIN, TEXAS 78731 • (512) 459-6584

FOR IMMEDIATE RELEASE: CONTACT: NEWS 10-76
Ms. Doug Newsom
817-732-2901
817-926-2461
Ext. 288

BOB SCHIEFFER TO BE EMCEE AT
BICENTENNIAL GALAXY BALL

CBS News White House Correspondent Bob Schieffer will be Master of Ceremonies at the Bicentennial Galaxy Ball, announced Mrs. Katherine Buck McDermott, ball chairwoman.

Benefitting the Texas Association for Mental Health, the thirteenth annual Galaxy Ball will be held Saturday, May 29, from 9 p.m. to 1 a.m., at Ridglea Country Club in Fort Worth.

A native of Texas, Schieffer has been White House Correspondent since October 1974, and is anchorman of the half-hour "CBS Evening News With Bob Schieffer" on Sundays. He served as CBS News' Pentagon Correspondent from July 1970 to October 1974, and he was anchorman of the Sunday fifteen-minute CBS News broadcast from July 1973 to October 1974.

In addition to contributing to numerous CBS News Special Reports, Schieffer has covered both the Democratic and Republican National Conventions. He was recently voted "best all-around television reporter in Washington, D.C.," in a poll conducted by and published in the Washingtonian magazine.

(more)

mental health 10-76
p. 2

      Before joining CBS News in 1969, Schieffer was a reporter for the Fort Worth *Star-Telegram* and, later, a news anchorman on WBAP-TV, Dallas-Fort Worth. As a reporter in Texas, he won a number of Sigma Delta Chi, Texas Associated Press Broadcasters and Associated Press Managing Editors awards. He was the first Texas newsman to report from Vietnam.

      Schieffer began his professional career in 1957, while a student at Texas Christian University, where he received a BA degree in journalism.

      Born in Austin, Schieffer is married to the former Patricia Penrose of Fort Worth. They have two daughters, Susan and Sharon, and live in Washington, D.C.

- 30 -

Remember that you will get only a few seconds, maybe a minute, of coverage. That gives you an opportunity to direct competing media to different facets of the event so they get better stories and you get better coverage. Be absolutely sure of all facts because there's no time for correction. The news media are not very forgiving of a PR source that causes them to broadcast an inaccuracy.

News Conferences

News conferences are called when a personality needs to interact with the news media. It might be a celebrity, for example, whose time in the area is limited, and you want to allow as many people as possible to ask questions. The opportunity to question is especially important if there is a controversy.

You may literally "call" a conference by using the telephone. But ordinarily an announcement is prepared, giving the reason for the conference, who the person is (background if a celebrity), the time, date and place, and who to contact if there are any questions—name, address and phone numbers. If the conference is being called to give information on a problem or to make an unexpected announcement, be sure you have prepared background materials to give to the media who attend. A package should contain a printed copy of the announcement, biographical background on the person (if appropriate), and background materials addressing the most significant questions. You should also have a "shooting schedule" for pictures. Be sure to have a still photographer, an audio recorder and someone shooting either film or videotape. You will need it for your own reference and might need to supply it to a medium that had mechanical problems.

(Remember, news conferences are not parties for the media. You might want to have coffee or soft drinks, but save the rest for a festive occasion that's not a working event.)

Crises

The crisis situation is a disorganized combination of the special event and the news conference. The media will need information that even you as an insider will have difficulty getting. The most important service you can perform is to get that information.

When time is critical and people are not where they usually can be found, a telephone operation becomes particularly important. You need to have someone skilled in getting facts, taking questions, and dispensing information accurately. You will have to be a reporter first and find out as much as you can about the event. Anticipate questions from the media. Have your own photographers and interviewers out gathering the story. If you don't, you won't have enough documentation later and will not know what the reporters are getting or how accurate it is.

The first thing to do is to get a statement on the severity of the disaster or crisis from someone in authority. You need it typed and on audiotape as well. Then you need a fact sheet telling what is known. Review this informtion with the attorney to assess the legal ramifications of information you will be releasing. All information given on the telephone should be from these prepared and checked sheets. No more than two people should be designated as spokespeople; otherwise you lose control of the situation. Conflicting information is highly likely at a time when no one is certain of events, and that jeopardizes your credibility. Your role is not censorship, but coordination.

NEWS RELEASES

News releases are either advance stories of something about to occur or stories telling what did occur or what is going on. Although no news medium is excited about doing your promotion for you, most will use well-done advance stories if the event has enough general public interest. News releases on upcoming events should be extremely brief for the broadcast media, no more than two or three short paragraphs. However, you can send along your longer print media version, a fact sheet, and, when appropriate, a brochure or printed program. If the event is likely to have regional interest, send a courtesy copy to the broadcast wire services, just to alert them to an event their reporters might be interested in. Be sure to say it is a courtesy copy when you deliver the release (or in a cover letter if you mail it). (See Example 8-1.)

Advance stories to the broadcast news media should be hand delivered when possible. If this is not possible, you should precede the release with a telephone call. Most of the time advance stories are given short shrift. If you have any visuals from a previous event, offer to make them available.

Stories about events that have already happened face the problem of timeliness. Nevertheless, most events of any significance—even past events—will be covered by the broadcast media. If you are supplying audio and visual materials, be sure you are aware of media deadlines and mechanical requirements. Let the news directors know, with a telephone call, that the material is coming. It should be hand delivered. If a speech was given, attach a complete copy to the brief release. You can file a courtesy copy with the wire service if the occurrence has regional interest, but, again, the wire services usually provide their own coverage.

For television you can offer graphs and charts that might help explain the occurrence, and you can offer radio broadcasters a telephone interview to flesh out their story and give it a sense of actuality. If you offer the phone interview, be sure you have all the facts and figures in front of you within easy reach. Your interview will be edited. If you are prepared, editors won't have to cut out dead air—gaps of silence—while you hunt down a fact. (See Example 8-2 for sample releases in the different styles—for TV, radio and print.)

TALK SHOWS

Public relations practitioners frequently arrange for people to appear on radio or television talk shows. Occasionally, the PR person is the talk show guest. Shows of this nature are not as fluid as they appear. Generally, they are structured by the host in a brief period before the show is aired.

Certain materials need to be prepared for such an event. The show's host needs to have a background sheet on the institution the individual represents, the event or occasion for the attention, and biographical information on the person being interviewed. All of this information must be very brief and in a form the show's host can take on the air—typed triple space on sheets of paper heavy enough so they don't rattle. The guest should have all the information he or she is going to present at hand *mentally*. This usually means a briefing session the day before and again just before air time so facts and figures will be fresh. The guest needs to alert the host to information that should be presented for the benefit of the listening audience. If the talk show is on television, take some slides or materials that can be shown. Remember the wiggle!

MINI-DOCS

A special type of news feature heard on radio stations is the mini-documentary ("mini-doc," for short). Mini-docs consist of a series of short features, generally on a significant issue needing public awareness and attention.

The mini-documentary developed from a realization on the part of broadcasters that longer news features of 30 to 60 minutes were not holding audiences. Breaking a long story up into serial form began in the print media, where it was discovered that such a format achieves a higher readership and sustains interest in a topic.

Broadcast mini-docs are about $3\frac{1}{2}$ minutes each. The research for the entire series is done all at one time, and usually the whole series is written at once. Some writers prefer to write the whole script as though it were one unit and then break off segments, writing an appropriate introduction and conclusion to identify each segment. (See Example 8-3.) Generally, the writer is also asked to write promotional

8-2 TV AND RADIO AND PRINT RELEASES

TO: Fernville Daily Star

NEWS FROM: Fernville Preservation League

FOR RELEASE: June 1, 1977, or thereafter

PRESERVATION LEAGUE RECEIVES GRANT

TO AID IN CHARTER HOUSE RESTORATION

Restoration of the Charter House, an 1842 house on 13th Street in Fernville, will proceed with the help of a $1,500 grant from the National Trust for Historic Preservation.

The money was awarded to the Fernville Preservation League under the National Trust Consultant Service Grant Program. The National Trust is a private nonprofit organization based in Washington, D.C.

"With this money, matched by a gift from the Fernville Rotary, we will be able to hire a qualified architect to prepare plans for the restoration of this important structure," said James Brady, president of the Fernville Restoration League.

Charter House was purchased by the league in 1974 when the city announced plans to demolish the structure to make way for a parking lot. The league raised $26,500 to buy the house and convinced the city to place its parking lot at a nearby site. The main floor of the two-story brick house has since been rented to a real estate firm, Landmarks, Inc., while the second floor has served as offices for the preservation league.

"For some time the house has been in need of repair and restoration," Brady said. "We want to do the job correctly, so we will hire Paul Richards, a restoration architect from Akron, to advise us. Our board is currently

-- more --

The examples above and following are from a sample media kit prepared by the National Trust for Historic Preservation. Representative materials from the kit, with directions for use and some other sample materials, appear as Example 8-4.

PRESERVATION LEAGUE RECEIVES GRANT
PAGE 2

attempting to raise the $18,000 that we estimate the restoration will cost."

Following restoration, Brady continued, the preservation league will offer the house for sale with covenants in the deed assuring preservation of the house.

The Charter House was built by Horace Charter, a local hardware and clothing merchant, soon after he established his business in 1839. After his death in 1879, his wife and two sons occupied the house. Mrs. Charter died in 1884, and the house was sold to Oliver W. Golden. Members of the Golden family resided there until 1970. The house stood vacant for four years until the city began condemnation proceedings. The preservation league made necessary repairs when it purchased the house from the city, but complete restoration was not possible at that time, for lack of funds.

"We are particularly pleased to have obtained this grant from a national preservation organization," Brady said. He noted that the National Trust for Historic Preservation was chartered by Congress to help Americans preserve buildings, sites and objects of historical and cultural significance.

Its matching grant to the Fernville Restoration League was made under its Consultant Service Grant Program, which has awarded nearly 350 such grants totaling more than $350,000 to preservation groups throughout the country since 1969.

The grants are matched by local money and are used to obtain the services of such professionals as architects, lawyers, city planners and preservation specialists. The grants cannot be used to pay for the purchase or renovation of properties or for administrative purposes.

-- more --

PRESERVATION LEAGUE RECEIVES GRANT
PAGE 3

In addition to its grant program, the National Trust publishes information about preservation methods and successes, owns and manages historic properties and house museums, provides advice on preservation problems, coordinates the efforts of private preservation groups and represents them on a national level.

The organization is supported by more than 115,000 members throughout the nation and by grants from private foundations and the federal government. In addition to its headquarters, the National Trust has five regional offices to serve the 50 states, District of Columbia and U.S. territories.

The Fernville Preservation League was organized in 1972 as a nonprofit group to encourage the preservation of historic buildings in the Fernville area. It has 140 members, according to Brady. Its headquarters, the Charter House, is listed in the National Register of Historic Places, the nation's official inventory of significant historic districts, sites, buildings, structures and objects.

# # #

CONTACT FOR ADDITIONAL INFORMATION: OR:

    James Brady   Mrs. John Hughey
    816 West Peach   1912 East Grand
    Fernville, Ohio   East Fernville, Ohio
    (216) 342-5508 -- from 9 a.m. to 5 p.m.   (216) 296-8866 -- all times
    (216) 381-1922 -- other times

8-2, CONTINUED

NEWS FROM: Fernville Preservation League

FOR RELEASE: June 1, 1977, or thereafter

RADIO ANNOUNCEMENT: (:30)

FERNVILLE PRESERVATION LEAGUE GETS NATIONAL GRANT

1   Today national recognition came to the Fernville Preservation

2   League restoration of the Charter House. The Washington-

3   based NATIONAL TRUST FOR HISTORIC PRESERVATION has awarded a

4    $1,500 matching grant to the league. The grant will be used to

5   hire an architect, who will prepare restoration plans for the

6   house. The house is located on 13th Street.

7   Following its restoration, the Charter House will be sold to

8   a new owner, who will guarantee its future preservation.##

CONTACT FOR FURTHER INFORMATION:

James Brady
816 West Peach
Fernville, Ohio
(216) 342-5508 - from 9 a.m. to 5 p.m.
(216) 381-1922 - other times

OR:
Mrs. John Hughey
1912 East Grand
East Fernville, Ohio
(216) 296-8866 - all times

CHAPTER 8
BROADCAST WRITING:
NEWS AND FEATURES

NEWS FROM: Fernville Preservation League

FOR RELEASE: June 1, 1977, or thereafter

TELEVISION ANNOUNCEMENT: (:30)

<u>FERNVILLE PRESERVATION LEAGUE GETS NATIONAL GRANT</u>

<u>Video</u>	<u>Audio</u>
Slide No. -- (exterior, Charter House)	Today national recognition came to the Fernville Preservation League restoration of the Charter House. The Washington-based NATIONAL TRUST FOR HISTORIC PRESERVATION has awarded a $1,500 matching grant to the league. The grant will be
Slide No. -- (interior, Charter House; architect measuring room)	used to hire an architect, who will prepare restoration plans for the 1842 house. The house is located on 13th Street. Following its restoration, the Charter House will be sold to a new owner, who will guarantee its future preservation.###

CONTACT FOR ADDITIONAL INFORMATION:

    James Brady   OR:
    816 West Peach   Mrs. John Hughey
    Fernville, Ohio   1912 East Grand
    (216) 342-5508 - from 9 a.m. to 5 p.m.   East Fernville, Ohio
    (216) 381-1922 - other times   (216) 296-8866 - all times

8-3 MINI-DOC OUTLINE

> Program One: Alcoholism is one of the nations' major health problems. It is an illness affecting the entire family. Help needs to be extended not only to the alcoholic, but to the members of the family as well.
>
> Program Two: How do you know when someone is an alcoholic? Identifying an alcoholic can be as simple as answering twenty questions. (Responses to twenty questions about drinking and behavior.)
>
> Program Three: Roles in the pattern of alcoholic behaviors: the alcoholic, the enabler, the victim, the provoker or adjuster.
>
> Program Four: Alcoholism is a physical, emotional, and spiritual disease. Patterns are the same, regardless of age or sex.
>
> Program Five: Avenues and agencies of help for the alcoholic and the lives he or she affects.
>
> Such an outline would be fleshed out by pulling out the research data that appears in the proposal and placing appropriate parts in each program content. The beginning of each series needs a separate introduction to identify it as a part of a whole. The conclusion should promote (promo) the next portion of the series. The introduction and the conclusion for each segment should be about 15 seconds each, for a total of 30 seconds per segment.

In developing a mini-doc, the problem needs to be stated clearly and concisely, then broken down into components. All questions about the problem must be included. A mini-doc outline is shown above.

announcements that the station can use during the day to call attention to the series.

There are many ways a public relations person can get involved in writing mini-docs. One is to work for a nonprofit organization at the national level, although local affiliates can also produce mini-docs. These organizations represent serious issues and concerns (mental health, heart disease, cancer, and so on)—that is usually why they exist. Another way is to prepare a series on an issue that is of vital concern to your commercial area. For example, a bank holding company did a series on how women can get credit in their own names, and another on how unemployed college students can get credit. An insurance company did a series on estate planning. These sound self-serving, and, of course, to a certain extent they are. But stations can be approached about using a series that only discusses the issue. Sometimes the only identification of the mini-doc with its source is a single script credit line.

To be successful (that is, to be used by the broadcast media), these mini-docs must follow the same rule as the well-written news release. They must be written as though prepared by the station—so neutral that no slant toward the source is perceived. Because documentaries should not be slanted, sometimes the first selling job is the most difficult: convincing management that the time and effort is worth the slight direct tie to the source. Enlightened managements generally see the benefit.

Some national associations and government agencies produce mini-docs and make them available to stations across the country. If you attempt a local mini-doc, you must first research the issue and prepare a proposal. Get management endorsement of the written proposal, and contact the most logical station in your area about the project. Choose a radio station if the subject matter does not lend itself to visual representation. If the proposal is going to a television station, be sure the proposal also outlines the visuals—what could be demonstrated in the studio, what needs to be filmed. You should approach the station as a resource person and writer. If the station is interested, you could provide all the information, write the scripts and submit them for editing by the station. Let the station provide the technical assistance and the talent. Stations at the local level are usually stretched for resources, but are also looking for good public service projects. If they have what they consider quality control over the project, they are more likely to go along.

BROADCAST WRITING STYLE

The basic difference in writing for broadcast media rather than print is that the copy must appeal to the ear. It has to attract attention with sound, and must be clear enough to be understood the first time through. The listener does not have a chance to review what is said. There's no looking back over a sentence to see what it meant, or going back to the one preceding it to figure out a sequence of ideas. Each offering is a one-time-only presentation. To compensate for that, broadcast writers first tell the listener (and viewer) what they are going to tell them, alerting them to the content so the listener can prepare by calling up frames of reference. Then the listener is told the content of the information. In the summary the writer again tells the listener what the message was. It takes a skillful writer to prepare material like this so it doesn't sound redundant. At the same time the writer is following this sequence, he or she must keep the time element in mind. Clarity and brevity are both important.

Broadcast style is conversational because of the intimacy of the medium. The listener or viewer experiences the broadcast media individually and responds to them personally. The relaxed style means that the leads or first paragraphs of broadcast stories, including news, are "soft." That is, the listener is introduced to the story before hearing it.

Other generalities are observed in broadcast writing. Because the tone is conversational, for instance, sentences are sometimes incomplete. We talk that way. In broadcast journalism it's acceptable to write that way. Another difference from print style is sentence length. Sentences are kept short in deference to the announcer, who has a limited amount of breath, and to the listener, whose attention span doesn't need to be taxed. For the same reason, subjects and verbs are kept close together. Also, sentences don't begin with a prepositional phrase because, by the time the announcer gets to the basic part of the information, the listener has forgotten the beginning.

Two peculiarities of newspaper style, sometimes called "journalese," should be avoided in preparing broadcast copy. One is inverted sentence structure, where the statement precedes the attribution: "Victims of the Wichita Falls tornado are all back in permanent housing, said Scott Smith, director of emergency disaster relief." Since broadcast audiences may not be attending to the first part of the sentence, the information should be presented the way it would probably be spoken in conversation: "The director of emergency disaster relief said all victims of the Wichita Falls tornado are now back in permanent housing." The name of the director is not important to the story, so just the title is used. If the story is a long one in which Smith is quoted, then his name would be used, but he would be identified in a separate sentence: "Scott Smith is the director of emergency relief."

The second peculiarity of newspaper style that should be avoided in broadcast writing is identification of subjects by age, job title and such. In newspapers this information usually follows the name and is set off by commas. But efficient newspaper style becomes cumbersome reading on the air. Again, the name of the individual is often not important at all—title identification is enough. (See Example 8-4 for media kit examples with tips for working with broadcast media.)

Physical Preparation

All broadcast copy is triple spaced and written on one side of the paper, as is newspaper copy. Some news departments prefer having copy typed in all caps (capital letters), others prefer upper- and lowercase letters. Most public relations people supplying information to the broadcast news media use caps and lowercase. For radio, typewriter margins should be set for a 70-space line to give an average of 10 words per line. Most announcers read at a rate of about 15 lines per minute. When you are writing for television and using only half the page (the audio side), set the margins between 35 and 80. The audio copy for the TV script goes on the right side of the page, opposite the video instructions. With the margins set like this, you'll get about six words to the line or about 21 lines a minute at an average reading speed.

8-4 MEDIA KIT SAMPLE

Press Kit

A new "Do-It-Yourself Press Kit" is now available to persons in charge of public relations for local preservation organizations.

The kit includes a guide to types of news, assistance in obtaining media coverage of preservation group activities and sample press releases for radio, television and publications. It is especially designed for persons unfamiliar with the workings of the media.

National Trust member organizations may obtain single copies free of charge by sending a self-addressed envelope, at least 10 by 12 inches, with 35 cents postage attached to Media Services Division, National Trust.

The National Trust for Historic Preservation is a nonprofit organization that helps people in communities throughout the nation save historic landmarks. The organization's newsletter (a newspaper) carried an item about the availability of a "press kit" (see the above clipping). The kit has excellent instructions and good examples that can be imitated (see following pages, as well as Examples 8-2 and 8-3, which are taken from the kit).

8-4, CONTINUED

Information:
from the National Trust for Historic Preservation

Public Relations for Local Preservation Organizations:
Press Relations, Public Education and Special Events

To be truly successful, preservation must be a communitywide activity. Building public support for preservation is the function of a solid public relations and public education program. While the tools needed to accomplish this are not unique to the preservation field, there are specific ways that nonprofit preservation organizations can best use them.

A comprehensive public relations program has three main elements: press relations, public education and special events. The three are interrelated and should be coordinated by one person within the organization. This person is responsible for insuring that the goals of specific public relations campaigns are met, whether they support fund-raising activities, education and general public awareness, social events or the saving of a building or neighborhood.

Unfortunately, one of the most visible public relations events is the worst enemy of preservation: the eleventh-hour attempt to save an endangered property. People who otherwise might not become involved in preservation are quick to rally in a crisis situation. But this last minute "call to arms," while it may show widespread support for preservation, cannot alone sustain a long-term commitment and too often does not result even in the preservation of the threatened property. The best public relations program, like the best preservation program, is well-planned, includes both short and long-range goals, and may include crisis strategies as part of its overall effort.

It is advisable to put down on paper a public relations plan consisting of specific goals, deadlines and ways to achieve them. This written plan serves as a reminder and is especially useful when other activities of the group threaten to crowd out public relations functions. The plan should include space for a progress report or checklist to insure that nothing goes undone in a sometimes hectic office.

Information sheet Number 24. © 1980 by the National Trust for Historic Preservation in the United States.

National Trust for Historic Preservation, 1785 Massachusetts Avenue, N.W., Washington, D.C. 20036

2

Organizing Public Relations

Proper structuring of the public relations program is critical, whether the organization has a paid public relations staff or, as in most cases, volunteers fill this role. There should be a single coordinator of all public relations activities, someone who has good organizational abilities and time to devote to the many tasks involved. The coordinator should be included, at least in an advisory capacity, in all decision-making of the organization -- not just that concerned with public relations. The coordinator should be kept informed of both the successes and failures of the group and be well versed in its goals and programs in order to present them clearly to the public.

At the same time, the public relations coordinator should know the community in order to serve as the group's "sounding board" on matters of public opinion. If a proposed action of the group might be controversial or subject to misinterpretation, the coordinator will need to inform the governing board of what the possible consequences will be. Because nonprofit organizations depend on public support, the public relations coordinator must be respected and able to provide concise, sound advice to the governing board.

Reporting to the public relations coordinator should be persons in charge of three specific areas: press relations, special events and public education. In the case of a small organization, the three might serve together with other volunteers on a public relations committee.

Volunteers working under the direction of the person in charge of each area can be assigned to carry out the details of producing promotional posters, flyers, banners and so on; sponsoring open houses, demonstrations, competitions and receptions; and handling arrangements for public speaking engagements, seminars, slide and videotape shows, films, displays and exhibits. How each of these three areas of public relations operates is detailed in the following sections. While the three are equally important, the press relations function will be dealt with in greater detail, as it is generally less familiar to nonprofit groups.

Press Considerations

The number one priority of the press relations component is getting the group's story in the news media. Television and radio stations, newspapers and magazines have differing requirements for news, but they have much in common as well.

Columnist and television commentator James J. Kilpatrick says of the media: "Not always, but very often, the essence of news is not accuracy, clarity, completeness, fairness or any of those good things. Very often the essence of news is now. In broadcasting or in newspapering, we are captives of the clock, prisoners of the next newscast or the next edition... . The time to answer the question, to make the impression, to leave the image is now." He urges organizations to make informed spokesmen available to the press when the press needs them.

Always, when talking to reporters, be truthful. If a story is embarrassing and a group attempts to cover up or lie, the results can be disastrous. If the story is important, sooner or later a reporter will dig out the truth, which means two stories instead of one and a loss of credibility that can outlast all the good done by a group.

What Is News? And Who Decides?

Published or broadcast information is "news," and newspaper editors and station news directors are those who decide what is published or broadcast. In general, the smaller the broadcast or newspaper operation, the more attention is given to community happenings. Large operations are more selective because they deal with a greater quantity of news.

For the purposes of preservation organizations seeking media recognition, news can be broadly categorized as follows:

Announcements of General Interest. These may be notices of newly elected officers, appointments, receipt of grants, forthcoming events and so on. Submitted announcements are not always published, because they may not be considered to have wide enough appeal. Thus, one community newspaper may publish advance announcements of all club and organization meetings, while another publishes only announcements of large groups or important speakers. Radio and television stations often set aside time each day, apart from regular newscasts, for "public service" announcements of local happenings. News releases sent to the station or newspaper are usually sufficient ways of presenting such information.

Hard News. Hard news is the journalist's term for a wide variety of events, from floods and fires to significant speeches, conferences and controversies. For preservation groups, such an event may be the decision to buy and restore an endangered property, the unveiling of a preservation master plan, a city hearing on a historic district ordinance or a significant court battle. Alerting a reporter in advance of an event may help to get coverage, and a follow-up phone call is helpful.

Features. There are several types of feature, including the personality or organizational profile and the background feature that goes beyond the immediate headlines of a situation to explore how the situation came about, what is being done about it and what is expected to happen next. Features present good opportunities for preservation organizations to tell their stories, promote their goals and increase their following. With newspapers and magazines increasingly concerned with personalities behind the news, an interview with the preservation group's president, or other representative, would make a strong candidate for a feature story.

The difference between a hard news story and a feature is somewhat blurred. Usually a hard news story is timely, referring to current events. Features, generally, can be printed at any time. Feature coverage is preferable, and preservation groups can attempt to gain such coverage by suggesting topics (how downtown is coming alive again, a survey of local old buildings now used for new purposes, etc.) supplemented with facts and names of persons involved who might be interviewed. The decision as to how a story will be handled rests entirely with the media.

4

Media Contacts

Making media contacts should be the first goal of the written public relations plan. Find out the name of the reporter who is most likely to cover preservation activities. Most media operations do not have anyone assigned to a preservation "beat." But usually some reporter will cover preservation news as it occurs. This may be the city hall reporter, a person assigned to community affairs or a general reporter with a special interest in history, preservation or neighborhood organizations. For broadcast media, call the station news manager to find out who would cover preservation news; for newspapers, telephone the city desk.

Next, arrange to meet and discuss your organization at a time when a reporter is not under deadline pressure. A fact sheet that lists the name, address and general purposes of your group can be given to the reporter for handy reference. Explain your organization's goals, its membership, relationship to other agencies and groups and to local government. Ask the reporter to explain the station's or newspaper's policies, procedures and deadline schedule. In turn, the reporter may have questions to ask and advice to give.

Allies at the local radio or television station and newspaper can do much more than assure a group's recognition. They often can provide advice on reaching the public, put you in touch with others in the community who have similar interests and perhaps be influential in the decision on what editorial stand the station or newspaper will take when a controversy arises.

When dealing with the media, always make sure you are fully armed with the facts. If you do not know the answer to a question, promise an answer as quickly as possible and make it your first priority to follow up--gather the information and tell the reporter.

The News Release

The news release (Appendixes A, B and C) is the backbone of communications with the media. Thus, an essential skill of the press information officer is writing ability. Most reporters prefer to have information provided to them in writing, even if they have also been telephoned or personally visited concerning the story.

The following 12 pointers are useful in all press relations work.

1. Make It Local. Local news media are not receptive to information that comes from sources outside the community. Place the organization's name or one of its members prominently in the story--in the first or second paragraph--and follow up with more local information in later paragraphs. For guidance, study the newspaper or broadcast station news. Learn what news makes the grade.

2. Have One Spokesperson. Nothing is more confusing to a reporter than too many people claiming to be spokespersons for a group. Appoint someone for that role and make sure that person always deals with the media as the official "press representative" or "information officer" of the organization.

8-4, CONTINUED

5

Avoid "publicity chairman" and similar titles. Radio and television stations and newspapers are in the business of informing, not publicizing.

    3. <u>Check and Observe Deadlines</u>. Obtain specific deadline schedules. If the story has a time element to it, make sure all information is provided well in advance of deadlines. In the case of "breaking news"--that which happens without notice--contact the media immediately. If you know when a newsworthy event will occur (such as election of officers), notify a reporter in advance. Stale news is no news to a reporter.

    4. <u>Ask Questions</u>. Most reporters would rather answer a question in advance than spend time trying to clarify a point after a news release is in their hands. Do not be afraid to call the newspaper or broadcast station to ask how to proceed or to ask what information is needed.

    5. <u>Provide Information Regularly</u>. You are the source of news and information for your organization. Just as you depend on adequate news coverage, reporters will come to depend on <u>you</u> for accurate, timely information. If your group is involved in a controversy, let the reporter know all sides of the story and then present your side. Keep the information flowing, even if all of it is not used. Do not expect your release to be used exactly as submitted. It will probably be rewritten. Radio and television time and newspaper space vary from day to day; what you consider a "big" story may not get in the news one day, whereas what appears to you to be a less important story may be played up another day.

    6. <u>Be Objective</u>. If you believe your news has been treated unfairly, tell the reporter. If you still have a complaint, write a letter to the editor or station manager setting forth your views. Stick to the facts and avoid harsh statements. If the reporter does a good job, express your appreciation in writing. A letter to the editor expressing appreciation for a job well done will gain further publicity for your organization.

    7. <u>Provide Complete Information</u>. Reporters and the areas assigned to them change, and you may be covered by a reporter who is a preservation novice. Start with the basic facts: who, what, where, when and why. Place this information first in any news release. Then add other items in order of priority. Background details go toward the end. Do not editorialize. Double-check dates, and indicate time of day with <u>a.m.</u> or <u>p.m.</u>

Double-check every spelling, especially of names. Use complete names, in most cases including middle initials. If the person prefers a nickname, put it in parentheses, e.g., John P. ("Red") Jones. Check titles and spell them out. Do not use abbreviations; they can be confusing. (Does "Assoc." mean "associates" or "association"?)

Be careful about corporate and educational titles. Note that college teachers often are not professors and that the title vice president can be vague. Use Dr., <u>Mr</u>., <u>Miss</u> or <u>Mrs</u>. Use <u>Ms</u>. only if the person prefers the designation and you know that the local news media accept it as a proper title. For foreign or unusual names or unusual spellings of common names (such as "Thom" instead of "Tom"), indicate that you have checked the spelling by writing "(Correct)" after the name. Following a name, indicate the home address. For persons from out of town, indicate home town and state.

> 6
>
> 8. <u>Use a Quote, If Possible</u>. Be sure the statement is newsworthy. If you receive a grant, let the president of your organization tell how the grant will be used. Expressing gratitude for a grant is not news. Instead, tell why the grant is important to the group and to people in the community.
>
> 9. <u>Type Double-spaced</u>. Never write press information in longhand. Type on one side of a clean white sheet on 8½ by 11-inch paper. Leave at least one-inch margins, with more space at the top for editor's markings.
>
> 10. <u>Provide Identifying Information</u>. Most reporters--and their audience-- are familiar with only a fraction of the thousands of organizations in existence. It is likely they do not know about the National Trust, for example, so the full name should be used, National Trust for Historic Preservation, followed by at least two sentences of explanatory material.
>
> 11. <u>Prepare a Fact Sheet</u>. With complicated subjects, a fact sheet with the important statistical and background information is helpful to reporters. One format is a question-and-answer sheet that amplifies statements made in a news release. The fact sheet should also provide basic information on the preservation group involved.
>
> 12. <u>Provide a Local Contact</u>. It is impossible to anticipate every question a reporter might have, so put in a prominent place (but not within the news story itself) the name and telephone number of one or two people who may be contacted for additional information. Include addresses and both daytime and evening telephone numbers.

The other markings are much like newspaper copy signals. In the upper right corner of the first page of each story is a slug line—the words identifying the story, the date, the name of the organization submitting the information, your name and phone numbers where you can be reached day or night. On the following pages, all you need is the page number, slug line and your last name. The story's end is marked by the traditional "30," and "more" goes at the bottom of pages in the story. Be sure to leave plenty of margin space—at least 2 inches at the top and bottom and 1 inch on either side for editing. The editing is done by the station, not you. *Never* give a broadcaster copy with editing marks. Type it over. And *never* mark broadcast copy with newspaper editing symbols.

To facilitate reading by announcers, do not split words between lines and don't split sentences between pages. If a word or name is difficult to pronounce, indicate the proper pronunciation in parentheses beside the word or name *each* time it appears. The announcer should not have to go back and look for your previous instructions. Do not use diacritical markings you find in dictionaries to indicate the proper pronunciation. Use popular phonetics like the newsmagazines employ (SHEE-fur for Schieffer, for example).

The AP Broadcast stylebook offers the following suggestions for phonetic symbols:

> The system used on The Associated Press broadcast wire is based on familiar principles of English usage with respect to the sound of vowels and consonants. For example:
>
> Guantanamo (Gwahn-tah'-nah-moh).
>
> Juan Martinez (Wahn Mahr-tee'-ness).
>
> Feisal—Fy'-sal.
>
> Note that the apostrophe is used to indicate where the accent falls.
>
> It has been found from long experience that the following will cover virtually all contingencies:
>
> AH is like the a in arm.
>
> A—is like the a in apple.
>
> EH—is like the ai in air.
>
> AY—is like the a in ace.
>
> E—is like the e in bed.
>
> EE—is like the ee in feel.
>
> I—is like the i in tin.
>
> Y—is like the i in time.
>
> OH—is like the o in go.
>
> OO—is like the oo in pool.
>
> UH—is like the u in puff.
>
> KH—is guttural.
>
> ZH—is like the g in rouge.
>
> J—is like the g in George.
>
> The symbol "ow" is subject to misunderstanding, since it can be pronounced as in "how" or as in "tow." Therefore it is necessary to handle some pronouncers like this: BLOUGH (rhymes with how).
>
> It will be recognized, of course, that approximations are necessary in indicating the pronunciation of some foreign names. It is almost impossible, for instance, to indicate the nasals common to the French tongue. It is equally difficult to indicate the exact pronunciation of the umlauted "o" or "u."

Remember, the audience can't see punctuation marks. These just help the announcer interpret the copy. Don't use them unless they are essential for the announcer. Don't use colons, semicolons, percentage signs, dollar signs, fractions, ampersands and other exotica. Just use commas, periods, question marks, dots and dashes, and quotation marks. Use quotation marks only when the use of the exact words is essential. It is better to rephrase a quote into indirect statements. If you feel a quote is necessary, precede it with something like "In his words" or "What she asked for was" or "The statement read."

Use hyphens only when you want the letters to be spelled out individually as Y-W-C-A, rather than being read, NASA. Don't use abbreviations unless you want them read on the air as abbreviations. Exceptions are titles such as Dr. and parts of names like St. Louis. If you don't know whether to write a word out or abbreviate it, write it out.

Numbers are difficult to follow if they're just heard and not seen, so avoid using them as much as possible. When you must, round numbers off and write them out—for example, "one thousand." Then there can be no risk of your having left off a digit. Broadcast stations have wire service stylebooks (and sometimes their own) telling how to deal with numbers. When you are supplying the material, it is best to spell them out. Broadcasters will change it if they want to. And to prevent errors, don't use A.M. or P.M. with times of the day. You should say, for example, "this morning" or "tomorrow night." However, since your copy is going to the news media for handling, you need to put the date in parentheses beside the designation (Monday, May 1). When the copy is processed, that information will be removed or designated not to be read on the air. But it will prevent errors. Another expression to be avoided regarding numbers is *per*, as in "miles per hour." Instead, use "miles an hour."

When using names and titles, don't begin sentences with the name, especially if it is unfamiliar. Use the title first. If it is a long, cumbersome title, break it up or shorten it. You generally do not use a person's middle initial in speech, so avoid using it in broadcast copy unless that middle initial is important for clarification and identification or is commonly associated with the name. On second reference use the surname only, except when you are referring to the president of the United States or a member of the clergy. Clergy retain their title on second reference—Rabbi Brown, for instance.

Watch obscurities. Be very careful about using pronouns. Listeners have trouble following the references. If you are dealing with specialized jargon, translate it. Use words and terms the audience can understand and relate to. Also, if you are writing about little-known groups, tell who they are and what they do. Don't assume the audience will know or understand. And do use contractions, like *don't*. We talk that way. Also, use the active voice. It gives life and movement to your writing.

Structure Considerations

The leads of broadcast stories are different from print leads, which often cram all of the *who, what, when, where, why* and *how* into the first paragraph. This is confusing for the listener and difficult for the announcer to read. First, alert listeners to what you are going to discuss, getting their attention with something they can relate to, something important to them. A summary statement is a good way to get into the story. Then you can give the essentials. Make your sentences simple; don't use long clauses at the beginning, end, or between the subject and verb. As you develop the story, look for ways to connect paragraphs with transitions that make the story emerge and flow logically. Keep the listener and the announcer in mind, and think about how each will be able to handle the words you write. (The difference in writing material to be spoken instead of read silently is illustrated by Examples 8–5 to 8–7.)

8-5 WIRE STORIES: BROADCAST AND NEWSPAPER VERSIONS

```
            U R G E N T


        SAKHAROV (TOPS)


     (MOSCOW) -- FAMILY MEMBERS SAY SOVIET AUTHORITIES SEIZED

DISSIDENT ANDREI SAKHAROV (AHN'-DRAY SAK'-HAH-ROHV) TODAY AND

PUT HIM ABOARD AN AIRPLANE. AND THEY SAY SAKHAROV APPARENTLY IS

HEADED FOR INTERNAL EXILE IN THE VOLGA RIVER CITY OF GORKY. THAT'S
 ABOUT 260 MILES EAST OF MOSCOW.
     SAKHAROV'S MOTHER-IN-LAW, RUTH BONNER, TOLD WESTERN REPORTERS
 SAKHAROV WAS PICKED UP IN MID-AFTERNOON OUTSIDE HIS MOSCOW APARTMENT,
 LATER REUNITED BRIEFLY WITH OTHER RELATIVES IN MOSCOW, AND FINALLY
 FLOWN OUT OF MOSCOW AT NIGHTFALL WITH HIS WIFE, YELENA BONNER.
     THERE'S NO OFFICIAL CONFIRMATION OF THE MOVE, BUT THE STATE-RUN
  MEDIA SAYS SAKHAROV HAD BEEN STRIPPED OF ALL HIS SOVIET HONORS FOR
  WHAT WAS CALLED ''SUBVERSIVE ACTIVITIES.''
      PLAINCLOTHES POLICE OUTSIDE SAKHAROV'S APARTMENT TOLD REPORTERS
  LOOKING FOR SAKHAROV EARLIER IN THE DAY TO GO TO MOSCOW'S
  INTERNATIONAL AIRPORT. AND THAT STARTED SPECULATION THAT HE'D BEEN
  SENT TO ANOTHER COUNTRY.
      BUT SAKHAROV'S MOTHER-IN-LAW QUOTED HIM AS SAYING HE WAS BEING
   TAKEN TO GORKY, AN INDUSTRIAL AND TRANSPORT CENTER. THAT CITY -- LIKE
  SEVERAL OTHER MAJOR SOVIET CITIES -- IS CLOSED TO FOREIGNERS.
  INTERNAL EXILE THERE WOULD CUT MANY OF SAKHAROV'S CONTACTS WITH
  FOREIGNERS.
      SAKHAROV HAS BEEN A MAIN SOURCE OF INFORMATION TO FOREIGNERS ON
  THE SOVIET DISSIDENT MOVEMENT.

AP-DN-0122 1415CST
```

Note the differences in these versions of the same story. The two moved on the wire at the same time. The newspaper wire story (by Steven Hurst) begins with a 23-word sentence, the broadcast story with 16. The broadcast story has what can be called a "soft start" since it begins with "Family members say," words that can be lost, not heard, and the loss would not be as significant as missing the first words of the newspaper story. If someone attempted to use that version on the air, listeners could not afford to miss "The Soviet government." Also, notice the phonetic spelling of Sakharov, which is in the broadcast story for the convenience of the announcer who may or may not be familiar with

a15

PM-Sakharov, 4th Ld,240
URGENT

    By STEVEN HURST
    Associated Press Writer
  MOSCOW AP — The Soviet government today stripped Nobel Peace Prize winner and dissident leader Andrei Sakharov of his state honors, accusing him of "subversive work." His family said he was seized and put aboard a plane, apparently headed for internal exile in the Volga River city of Gorky, 250 miles from Moscow.

  Sakharov's mother-in-law, Ruth Grigorievna Bonner, told Western reporters that he was picked up in mid-afternoon outside his Moscow apartment, reunited briefly with relatives in Moscow, and finally flown out at nightfall with his wife, Yelena Bonner. There was no official confirmation.

  In Washington, State Department spokesman Hodding Carter could not confirm absolutely that Sakharov has been arrested but said his well being is of "grave concern" to the United States.

  He noted that President Carter has expressed his personal admiration and respect for Sakharov.

  Asked whether the administration believes the Soviet action against Sakharov is linked to the Soviet invasion of Afghanistan, the spokesman said he did not know.

  He said, however, that there have been reports of increasing repression against dissidents dating back to last fall — well before the Afghanistan action. Carter noted that Amnesty International recently reported that 40 persons have been arrested in the last three months for non-violent exercise of human rights.

  The Tass, 2nd graf 3rd Ld
----- -----
01-22-80 02.22pcs

---

the name of the Nobel Prize winner. In the newspaper story's lead, quotation marks appear around "subversive work." The sense of quotation marks is difficult to convey verbally so generally quotes are avoided in broadcast copy. Although this broadcast story uses the quotes too, the audience is warned by the words "what was called" that quoted material follows. In the broadcast story, the mother-in-law's middle name is not used. Compare other sentences and see how the broadcast story is condensed, not just shortened.

8-6　FIRST LEAD ON THE BREAKING STORY IN EXAMPLE 8-5

```
HERE IS THE LATEST NEWS FROM THE ASSOCIATED PRESS:

   UNCONFIRMED REPORTS FROM MOSCOW SAY DISSIDENT LEADER ANDREI
SAKHAROV (AHN'-DRAY SAK'-HAH-ROHV) HAS BEEN ARRESTED AND POSSIBLY
EXPELLED FROM THE SOVIET UNION. ALL THAT'S KNOWN FOR SURE IS THAT THE
KREMLIN TODAY STRIPPED SAKHAROV -- A NOBEL PEACE PRIZE WINNER -- OF A
SERIES OF SOVIET AWARDS. HE WAS ACCUSED OF ''SUBVERSIVE WORK AGAINST
THE SOVIET STATE.''

   SAKHAROV CLIMBED TO THE TOP OF SOVIET SCIENCE THROUGH HIS WORK ON
RUSSIA'S FIRST HYDROGEN BOMB. BUT WHEN HE LATER FOUGHT AGAINST
TESTING THE WEAPON, HE LOST MUCH, BUT NOT ALL, OF HIS PRESTIGE. HE
BECAME A KEY CONTACT FOR WESTERN NEWS CORRESPONDENTS SEEKING
INFORMATION ABOUT SOVIET DISSIDENTS.

   SOME WESTERN OBSERVERS BELIEVE THE MOVE AGAINST SAKHAROV IS A
SIGNAL FROM MOSCOW THAT HUMAN RIGHTS IN THE SOVIET UNION WILL SUFFER
IF PRESIDENT CARTER PERSISTS IN TRYING TO FORCE THE SOVIETS OUT OF
AFGHANISTAN. COINCIDENTALLY, SAKHAROV HAD CALLED FOR A BOYCOTT OF THE
MOSCOW OLYMPICS LONG BEFORE THE AFGHANISTAN INVASION -- CITING
''FUNDAMENTAL HUMAN REASONS.''

   THE STATE DEPARTMENT COULD NOT CONFIRM ABSOLUTELY THAT SAKHAROV
HAS BEEN ARRESTED. BUT OFFICIALS SAID HIS WELL-BEING WAS OF ''GRAVE
CONCERN'' TO THE UNITED STATES.

AP-DN-0122 1358CST
```

Broadcast wire stories undergo a great deal more reworking than newspaper wire stories because the broadcast wire serves stations that use news directly from the wire on an hourly basis. One story, hour after hour, can get dull if the audience remains the same—and some offices have piped-in radio. Research can flesh out a breaking story both to give it depth and to keep the sparse facts from getting monotonous. See how this is handled in Example 8-6. (The status of this story is indicated in the last paragraph. The fuller, later story is in Example 8-5.)

8-7   ABBREVIATED PRINT MEDIA VERSION

**CHAPTER 8
BROADCAST WRITING:
NEWS AND FEATURES**

THE WALL STREET JOURNAL,
Wednesday, Jan. 23, 1980

What's News—

* * *

World-Wide

MOSCOW ARRESTED dissident Andrei Sakharov and stripped him of all honors.

The Soviet news agency charged that the Nobel Prize-winning physicist had ignored warnings to stop his "subversive activities." Sakharov had urged "reactionary circles of the imperialist states" to interfere in the Soviet Union's affairs, the report said.

Family sources said Sakharov, 58, and his wife were flown to internal exile in Gorky, 250 miles east of Moscow. The move was certain to keep him away from foreign journalists.

Sakharov had long urged an international boycott of the summer Olympic games in Moscow. After the Soviet invasion of Afghanistan, the idea was adopted by President Carter.

* * *

A condensed version of the same story, produced the same day as the broadcast story, appeared in the *Wall Street Journal* the following day. The story, condensed for column accommodation, has a different stress from the broadcast story.

CONCLUSION

Most people in the United States get their information about what's going on in the world from watching television. Another significant part of the population, especially those between 13 and 19, get theirs from radio. The two media are critical to communication. In times of crisis or a breaking news story, they assume even greater importance. PR people must know how to provide information to the broadcast media that is appropriate for the media and interesting to their audiences.

SELECTED BIBLIOGRAPHY

Rolf Gompertz, *Promotion and Publicity Handbook for Broadcasters* (Blue Ridge Summit, Pa.: TAB Books, 1979).

Mark W. Hall, *Broadcast Journalism* (New York: Hastings House, 1978).

Robert L. Hilliard, *Writing for Television and Radio,* 3d rev. ed. (New York: Hastings House, 1976).

Richard Weiner, *Professional's Guide to Publicity,* 2d ed. (New York: Richard Weiner, Inc., 1978).

9

ADVERTISING COPY

Advertising, by definition, is paid-for time or space in a communications medium. Two exceptions discussed in this chapter are public service announcements and house ads. No money is exchanged, but the two qualify in every other way as advertising.

Public service announcements (PSAs) are prepared like commercials, but they are the messages of nonprofit organizations and are aired at the discretion of the broadcast station (radio or television) when time is available. Sometimes stations help local nonprofit organizations develop and produce their PSAs. The stations provide facilities at times when they are not needed for regular business, but both the facilities and technical help are usually provided without charge. (After the PSAs have been aired, the station may send the nonprofit organization an invoice for the amount of air time given, with the number of hours and commercial rate typed on it, plus the notation: "Paid in full.")

A station will also use some air time to promote its own schedule or special events. There is no dollar exchange here either, but the station's own promotion department generally has a "budget" or an allowance to use. The print equivalent of such self-advertising within the medium is the house ad. The ad can be either for the publication in which it appears or for another medium held by the same owner.

ADVERTISING AS A PERSUASIVE FORCE

Public reaction to advertising is generally one of suspicion and a certain amount of skepticism, but just being aware of the persuasive effort does not make those exposed less vulnerable.[1] Vulnerability does not necessarily mean critics of advertising are correct in saying we are all being brainwashed by the mass media. On the contrary, advertising has its limitations. Advertising can help create awareness of a new product and thereby stimulate a demand. It also can help the larger advertisers dominate a market, and television advertising can increase purchases of low-cost items that are frequently replaced. There is some evidence that advertising is successful at image building.[2] In general, however, advertising copywriters should be aware that the public is sensitive to the persuasive effort, but can still be affected by an appropriate appeal.

Devising the appropriate appeal is part of advertising strategy. Strategists have to consider the product or service to be advertised in terms of who might be in the market. Demographics and psychographics are considered in such decisions. Often advertisers will artificially carve out a place in the market for their product or service by a technique called "positioning." For example, for products that are much the same—detergents for example—competitors appeal emotionally to a particular segment of the market, since there is no rational reason for selecting one product over another. A campaign might focus on those who must wash particularly dirty clothes, ones soiled by manual labor. A garage mechanic might be featured in such a commercial appeal. A whole series of ads could be built on those whose clothes are especially soiled by their work—or play, such as athletes.

Understanding what people in different parts of society think and do is critical to developing credible advertising. Good advertising copywriters never lose touch with everyday experiences and how people behave in them. They understand there is a little (maybe a lot of) snob in all of us because we see ourselves in relationship to something behaviorists call "reference groups." These are social groups, often organizations. We all want the comfort of belonging, of being accepted, so friends and family are important and we seek their approval. We can also be influenced by opinion leaders. These leaders differ among segments of society, and we react to them differently, based on our own personality characteristics. For example, authoritarian types are more vulnerable to appeals of status and authority.

If you are getting the idea that people don't respond rationally to advertising copy, you are on the right track. That's why good advertising is a complex blend of information (facts) and appeal (emotion). The best copywriters have minds that make unusual associations, see unique applications, and react to innovation with excitement and enthusiasm. Marvin M. Gropp, research director of the Magazine Publishers Association, concluded that "when it comes to advertising persuasion, what the consumer brings to the experience of reading/viewing can be as important as what the media brings to the consumer."[3]

Copy Approaches

Not all members of the public are going to react to something new with excitement and enthusiasm. If you have a new product or service, you are facing an uphill battle. Among the general public you will find a small group of innovators who want to be first, always. Behind them are those who will adopt something early, but not first. The majority of the public follows these front-runners, and a last group always brings up the rear. Being aware of the kinds of people in these different groups makes it possible to design effective messages for them. Psychographics are clearly significant here, much more so than demographics.

If your purpose is sustaining a product on the market and perhaps capturing a larger share of the audience, the approach must be very different from the new product appeal. If your product or service has been around quite a while or has little competition, or none (like utility companies), then a whole other creative approach is necessary.

Basic Considerations

As fundamental as determining the overall approach is deciding precisely what you want a particular piece of advertising copy to accomplish. You should have a single objective. The most successful ads are those with one reason for being. If you try to accomplish too much with a single ad, you are likely to be less effective. You have to ask yourself what you want the reader or viewer to *do* as a result of being exposed to your appeal. If you concentrate on the action you expect the audience to take, it will simplify your copywriting task.

You should also have a clear picture of the audience you want to appeal to. If you can visualize your audience, you will be able to design an appropriate message, something your audience can understand and relate to. You will know what the appeal should be and the appropriate language to use. You should respond to the needs and desires of a specific audience.

Keeping in mind the peculiarities of the medium is also a key to successful advertising copywriting. Visualize the medium as you write. Remember the advantages and use them; consider the disadvantages and work around them. Keep in mind how people react to the medium itself. For example, with television you can use fewer words because the audience has something to look at. But also remember that audiences regard TV as primarily an entertainment source, and you will have to adapt. In radio you can play on the imagination with exciting sounds and words that paint the pictures for you. With all broadcast media, though, there is a certain amount of audience inattention because listeners are distracted by other things going on around them. You must be compelling to both gain attention and hold it for the duration of the message.

The opposite is true of the print media. If attention is captured by an ad, there is a greater likelihood that attention will be maintained long enough for the reader to receive the message. That's the way we react to print. But we behave differently for newspapers and magazines. Newspapers are best for one-time messages. Magazine ads may be read and reread because the medium is retained. Advertising messages on outdoor media or transit vehicles must gain attention and tell the message quickly because exposure is often fleeting. In contrast, most direct response (coupon) and direct-mail advertising can afford long, detailed messages. Sales promotion pieces vary in form from advertising specialties (like campaign buttons) to brochures, and they rely heavily on symbols to be successful. Finding the right combination of medium and message is the key to success.

Research

A copywriter should collect research information on audiences from all the media in which the advertising will be placed. Most media have quite an investment in research since their job is selling time or space. Although these materials are self-serving, they can be useful. Add to them industry research from the Television Information Office, the Newspaper Foundation and the Magazine Publishers Association. Although the research generally reflects a favorable position for the particular medium involved, the research can be cross-referenced and applied. Scholarly journals in the behavioral sciences and in communication that print results of scientifically structured examinations have useful information that is "purer" in a sense because it is not written for popular audiences but for research use. Applying scholarly research is sometimes a problem, however, because the research may be fairly limited in scope.

A good copywriter will set up systems for evaluating the prepared copy. Most agencies will arrange for pretesting and posttesting ad copy. The pretesting helps choose among various messages and message-art combinations. The posttesting helps determine which appeals worked best with which audiences and why. But a copywriter has to do some personal testing, too. One is to go through a simple checklist to be sure all of the basic elements are there. Then, to do a "fog" count, to be sure the message is readable. Exposing the message to others often helps, too, especially if they are nonprofessionals and more likely to respond like people in the marketplace. Advertising messages often have to go through many adjustments, to the discouragement of their creators. A good copywriter puts aside proprietary feelings for the copy and works with it until it works for the advertiser.

BROADCAST ADVERTISING

Brevity, style and technique are the three important considerations in preparing broadcast copy designed to sell. Time slots vary with stations, but basically you will be writing for time segments of 10 seconds (about 25 words), 20 seconds (45 words), 30 seconds (65 words), or 60 seconds (125 words). The word limits vary with the medium and the technique, but you can see that words must be carefully chosen. Broadcast commercial writers have the same rigors placed on them as headline writers and poets: A story has to be told, and interest and imagination stirred, in a very few well-chosen words.

Because the attention of broadcast audiences is often diverted, copy must be very simple. Stick to a single point and use short sentences with easily recognized words to tell your story. Write clear, uncluttered sentences, avoiding cliches and slang that make copy seem stale. Be sure you have smooth, logical transitions to take the listener through the message easily. To keep audience attention, personalize the message with the frequent use of "you." Remember, people respond personally to the medium as if they were engaged in one-on-one communication, even though they can't talk back (or at least can't be heard when they do). Reward them for listening with some valuable information or entertainment, or both.

Keep the message credible by visualizing a direct conversation. Don't make any exaggerated claims you wouldn't state to a friend, face to face. Your persuasive appeal should have a distinctive element that makes it unique and recognizable when heard or seen again. Your copy must catch an audience's attention in the first few seconds and move through a persuasive appeal that climaxes with a reward, a promise of some benefit. Be sure to register the name of the product or service with the audience, and let the audience know what you want them to do. A sense of urgency may help motivate.

Techniques reflect the technical capabilities of the medium, but both television and radio share some approaches. You'll recognize them from your own familiarity with advertising. One approach is the slice of life, a sort of mini-drama that enacts a scene in which the product or service stars. Another is the jingle, a musical approach that gives the commercial identification and memorability as well as being entertaining. The music may introduce and close the copy (a donut format), may be sustained throughout the message, or the music (a song, for example) may be the message. A humor technique may be anything from a cartoon (on television) to a joke (usually radio only) to a mini sit-com (situation comedy). The difficulty is in finding universal themes. We all like to laugh, but not at the same things. A fourth technique is the customer interview, in which the announcer talks with real customers about the product or service. The straightforward approach is an announcer format, in which one announcer delivers the whole message or two announcers do so for a faster paced presentation. Occasionally an announcer may interact with an actor for a special effect. Sound effects may, of course, be employed with any or all of these techniques, and the techniques themselves may be combined.

Television has some additional visual techniques. One is the demonstration, sometimes used in a direct product comparison. TV can also use animation (which does not have to be tied to humor), and can combine animation with live action (rotoscope) so that a live actor may participate in a scene with something like the product's trademark character. Such possibilities must be kept in mind when drafting the copy approach.

Your choice of copy approach should be based first on the availability of resources, that is, money and facilities. The next decision is based on what techniques are currently being employed—by all products, your competition, your product. You don't want to copy other techniques, but you can borrow ideas from them. Also, you want to set your product apart from your competition, so you don't want a style too close to what is being used. Further, your own product may already be identified with a particular technique in the medium, or it may be involved in a campaign in other media. You will want to adapt to or follow such techniques. These considerations will limit your choice to some extent.

Next, what techniques have worked well for your product in the past? Given what you are advertising and the market you want to reach, what new behavioral research suggests a particularly effective approach? What does a look at the product itself suggest to you? Does it lend itself to a particular type of approach such as a demonstration, a side-by-side comparison or something like that? Once you have decided on the approach you are ready to write the script.

Commercials

When you are writing a commercial, imagine how it will sound (and look, if TV) in its final form. You have to produce it in your head as you compose. It helps to write out your message in one simple statement, and then write another statement of the commercial's objective. These two will keep you on track when you unleash your creativity.

TV Scripts Divide your paper down the middle into two columns. Caption the right side audio or script and the left, video or description. (See Example 9–1 for various ways to set up television scripts.) Begin in an informal way to write the words and sounds you want to use on the right side of the page. At the same time fill in the left side with the pictures the audience will see as they hear the words. Be sure to let the pictures carry some of the weight of telling the story. That's one of the assets of the medium. (Note Example 9–1.) Don't tell the audience what they are watching. Now go back and polish and edit your copy. Be precise in word choice.

Concentrate on conveying one basic idea with the pictures and the words. Be sure you reward the audience with some benefit—stated and supported.

Read your copy aloud to be sure it is easy to read and contains no hazards—such as tongue twisters like "five firefighters finished frying fish for 500 Boy Scouts"—for the announcers or actors. If you can, have a friend read the copy aloud without scanning it first. Try to get someone who is not a professional announcer accustomed to making cold copy sound good. The traps will emerge in the reading. As you listen, imagine the video. See if the audio will work with the pictures you have in mind.

Once you have the audio polished, turn your attention to the video. Don't forget that the scenes must have some movement. Avoid anything static. Be sure you have built in plenty of action. At the same time, don't clutter the video with too many scenes. If too much is going on, an audience paying only partial attention won't catch the message. Watch the transition from scene to scene to be sure the copy flows smoothly and develops logically. Remember, the product or service is the star of the show. Give it prominence. When you write the video description, describe the scene or action as completely as possible, because someone else is going to have to translate your words into pictures (see Example 9-2).

It may help if you draft your own storyboard. A storyboard—the intermediate step between script and production—is a series of rough illustrations showing segments of the action in sequence with the copy that will be heard with each segment. Although making a storyboard that will be used is the job of an art director, some copywriters find that filling in the video with stick figures and writing their copy under each segment helps them develop a commercial with unity. (See the presentation storyboard in Example 9-3.)

Radio Scripts Writing for radio seems deceptively easy. It isn't. In radio you can take advantage of the listener's imagination. And you must. You must search for words and phrases that evoke a scene, an atmosphere. You have to imagine what you want the listener to imagine. But calling up pictures in people's heads is not easy. For example, you may encounter regional inconsistencies in the use of words and in receptiveness to any dialects you may want to use for effect.

Be sure the imagery is created in a logical, easy-to-follow sequence or you'll lose the listeners. You'll have to build in excitement and drama to hold attention, and include a device for being sure the message—what the product is, what it does, what it is made of (if appropriate), where to get it and how much it costs—is conveyed. (See Example 9-4 for special effects.) Although most radio commercials are prerecorded, some are read live. If you are writing one that will be distributed in script form, be sure the words are simple to pronounce and flow smoothly so announcers will not foul things up by mispronouncing them. Placing the wrong inflection can also distort the message by giving elements of the copy the wrong emphasis.

Public Service Announcements

Public service announcements for nonprofit organizations can be elaborately produced videotapes, film with sound-on, or some type of pictures with an audio cassette. Many of these come from the national offices of nonprofit organizations, but they usually leave room for the local or regional agency's tagline to be added. More often, however, PSAs are produced locally for local agencies. Since the agency is begging for the time (and occasionally for the production time also), most PSA script writers try to keep things simple. See the examples of one nonprofit group's offering in Example 9-5.

**PART THREE
WRITING FOR
GENERAL AUDIENCES**

9-1 SET-UP OF COMMERCIAL SCRIPTS

Continental National Bank - :30 TV
"Image"

JRT
Jerre R. Todd & Associates, Inc.
Public Relations and Advertising

IF WE CAN FIND ANOTHER WAY. . .
    Male officer, early morning jogging scene, preparing for the day
    (Bill Chandler)

TO MAKE ANOTHER FRIEND TODAY. . .
    Jogging scene dissolves neatly from officer jogging to striding
    toward woman/child in lobby, he shakes hand and ushers toward
    his desk. (Bill Chandler, Melina and Byrdie)

YOU KNOW WE'RE GONNA FIND IT. . .
    Filing cabinet scene where girl has pencil in mouth looking
    through files. She looks up, takes pencil out of mouth and smiles.
    (Susan)

YOU KNOW WE'RE GONNA FIND IT. . .
    Girl at typewriter, types on beat, smiles. (Pat)

MORE HOURS. . .
    Mini Bank door, close-up of white type. Door or camera moves.

MORE PLACES. . .
    Motor Bank tube comes up from bottom of frame. Sign above it reads:
    "Continental National Bank - Motor Bank."

MORE SMILES ON OUR FACES. . .
    Main bank lobby with five tellers waiting on customers, three
    prominent tellers turn and smile on cue. (Cindy, Ellen, _____,
    _____, _____)

WE WON'T STOP. . .
    Late night work session in Trust library, one bank officer offers
    another cup of coffee. (Tom Turner, Frank McDowell)

UNTIL WE CAN. . .
    Line of Data Processing operators, all 15 look toward camera and
    smile on cue. (15 operators, plus supervisor)

SAY. . .
    Female officer whirls around in chair, phone at ear, smiles. (Nancy)

CONTINENTAL NATIONAL BANK. . .
    Bank officer (from earlier jogging scene) with child. (Bill Chandler,
    Byrdie)

MADE ANOTHER FRIEND TODAY.
    24-hour teller, guy in pajamas. Squeeze-Freeze, LOGO pops, Member
    FDIC, Member Southwest Bancshares, Inc. All out at music end.
    (Jerry Johnson)

###

1800 Continental National Bank Building, Fort Worth, Texas 76102, Phone: AC 817 335-2107 Metro 429-0348

Television commercials require a great deal of planning and work. Logistics often pose problems for commercials. The simple script of the bank commercial becomes more complex when you

**CHAPTER 9
ADVERTISING COPY**

```
                    JERRE R. TODD & ASSOCIATES, INC.
CONTINENTAL NATIONAL BANK -- :30 TV "Commercial"

     IF WE CAN FIND ANOTHER WAY. . .

          Speaker standing at front of room, setting is conference
          room, Club Tower.  Dissolve sequence into closeup of hand
          and figures on chalkboard or chart.  (Bob Shiels, Dan Gramatges,
          Dean Cochran, Jeff Harp, Ray Dickerson)

     TO MAKE ANOTHER FRIEND TODAY. . .

          Man at board dissolves out, hand dissolves out and into
          officers who have been listening in room.  Three officers
          at table will be prominent.

     YOU KNOW WE'RE GONNA FIND IT. . .

          Walkup of briefcase closing, in time with music percussion.
          Men get up to leave.

     YOU KNOW WE'RE GONNA FIND IT. . .

          Doors of conference room burst open in time with percussion.
          Floor-level shot of men walking briskly from room.
          Light blooms from windows behind.

     MORE HOURS, MORE PLACES. . .

          Newsteller "More Hours, More Places."

     MORE SMILES ON OUR FACES. . .

          Person buried in piles of books, finds his answer
          and offers triumphant smile. (Bryans Fitzhugh)

     WE WON'T STOP. . .

          (Dan Gramatges) at client location.

     UNTIL WE CAN. . .

          (Jeff Harp) at client location.

     SAY. . .

          (Dean Cochran) at client location, offers some
          figures and explanation to client.

     CONTINENTAL NATIONAL BANK. . .

          Client hears, acknowledges, looks extremely pleased.

     MADE ANOTHER FRIEND. . .

          (Dean) extends to shake with client.  Frame freezes
          on (Dean's) outstretched arm and his pleased look.

     TODAY. . .

          LOGO dissolves up into scene.  Both dissolve out at
          music's end.
     ###
```

look at the production schedule it demanded. The Dallas Morning News spot also required an involved production, although the simplicity of the script doesn't suggest it.

9-1, CONTINUED

```
PRODUCTION SCHEDULE
CONTINENTAL NATIONAL BANK


Thursday, December 6:
```

7:00 a.m.	Crew call at Rivercrest Country Club Golf Course. Talent (Bill Chandler) due at Country Club.
7:30 a.m.	Shoot jogger sequence.
8:00 a.m.	Crew to leave jogger location -- travel to Western Company, West Freeway and set up equipment.
8:45 a.m.	Talent (Dan Gramatges) due at Western Company along with Western Company official.
9:00 a.m.	Shoot sequence with Dan Gramatges and Western Company official.
9:30 a.m.	Crew to leave Western Company location -- travel to Speed Fabcrete, Mansfield Highway, Kennedale and set up equipment. Crew to arrange cranes and workers in background before arrival of talent.
10:45 a.m.	Talent (Jeff Harp and Fabcrete Exec.) due at Speed Fabcrete location.
11:00 a.m.	Shoot sequence with Jeff Harp and Fabcrete Exec.
	Lunch
12:30 p.m.	Crew to set up at Motor Bank (1st stall toward 6th). Need to arrange sign on unit and label on pneumatic tube.
1:00 p.m.	Shoot sequence at Motor Bank.
2:00 p.m.	Crew to leave Motor Bank location -- set up equipment at American Quasar Petroleum, 25th Floor, Fort Worth Natl. Bank Bldg.
2:15 p.m.	Talent (Dean Cochran and AQP official) due at AQP.
2:30 p.m.	Shoot sequences with Dean Cochran and AQP official.
5:00 p.m.	Crew to leave AQP location -- set up equipment at Newsteller, Houston Street.
5:30 p.m.	Shoot Newsteller sequence.

- more -

CNB Production Schedule -- Page Two

Friday, December 7:

7:30 a.m.	Crew call at Mini Bank (6th and Main) -- set up equipment at South entrance. Will need to hang black material behind glass.
8:00 a.m.	Shoot sequence at Mini Bank.
9:00 a.m.	Crew to set up equipment at empty office, 1st floor, CNB Bldg. (Commercial Dept.).
9:15 a.m.	Talent (Bryans Fitzhugh) due at Commercial Dept.
9:30 a.m.	Shoot sequence with Bryans Fitzhugh (stack of books).
9:30 a.m.	Crew to leave Commercial Dept. -- set up equipment in CNB main lobby (SE corner of teller area).
10:45 a.m.	Talent (5 tellers) due at teller area.
11:00 a.m.	Shoot teller sequence.
	Lunch
12:30 p.m.	Crew to set up equipment in Trust Dept. Filing room, 5th floor.
12:45 p.m.	Talent (Cindy Casstevens) due at filing room.
1:00 p.m.	Shoot sequence in Trust Dept. filing room.
1:45 p.m.	Crew to set up at Proof Dept., 3rd floor, VISA Center.
2:30 p.m.	Shoot sequence with computer operators.
4:30 p.m.	Crew to set up equipment in Trust Dept. conference room (night scene).
5:00 p.m.	Talent (Frank McDowell and Tom Turner) due in 5th floor conference room.
5:30 p.m.	Shoot sequence in conference room (late night work session).

- more -

9-1, CONTINUED

```
CNB Production Schedule -- Page Three

Saturday, December 8:

8:00 a.m.        Crew call at Club Tower Bank lobby.

8:15 a.m.        Talent (Pat _____) due at Club Tower Bank.

8:30 a.m.        Shoot Typist sequence.

9:45 a.m.        Talent (Bill Chandler, Melina Mahan, Byrdie
                 Williams) due at Club Tower Bank.

10:00 a.m.       Shoot Chandler/Woman/Child sequence.

11:45 a.m.       Talent (Nancy Magee) due at Club Tower Bank.

12:00 p.m.       Shoot whirling chair sequence.

                 Lunch

1:30 p.m.        Crew to set up in Club Tower conference room.

1:45 p.m.        Talent (Bob Shiels, Ray Dickerson, Dan Gramatges,
                 Jeff Harp, Dean Cochran) due in conference room.

2:00 p.m.        Shoot conference room sequence.

4:30 p.m.        Crew to set up in Club Tower Bank foyer.

5:00 p.m.        Shoot door-opening sequence.

5:45 p.m.        Talent (Jerry Johnson) due at Club Tower Bank.

6:00 p.m.        Shoot 24-hour Teller sequence.

                 WRAP.
```

KCBN

KCBN, INC.
ADVERTISING AND PUBLIC RELATIONS
3434 FAIRMOUNT
DALLAS, TEXAS 75219
(214) 521-6400

CLIENT	TITLE	JOB NO.
THE DALLAS MORNING NEWS	PACESETTER :30	
SLATE NO. bh/ct	MANUSCRIPT DATE 10/31/79	REVISION NO. 1/18/80

VIDEO	AUDIO
SCENE OF YOUNG PEOPLE JOGGING.	(SFX UNDER: NATURAL SOUNDS OF JOGGERS RUNNING, BREATHING.)
	ANNCR. (V.O.): You're a pacesetter. Active. Aware. Always wanting more.
CUT TO EDITOR'S MEETING.	(SFX: MUSIC BED UNDER.)
	EDITOR (SYNC): Fine. The Dallas Morning News will really wake them up with that!
CUT TO EMERGENCY HOSPITAL SCENE.	DOCTOR AND AMBULANCE DRIVER (SYNC UNDER)
	ANNCR: You need a newspaper that understands you. Keeps you up-to-date. The Dallas Morning News.
CUT TO REPORTER IN NEWSROOM.	SAM: (SYNC UNDER) He really said that? Great! (UP) Thanks for the tip.
CUT TO BUSINESSMAN'S LUNCH.	BUSINESSMAN (SYNC): That was Will. Now we've got the project and we can run it this afternoon.
CUT TO EDITOR & PHOTOGRAPHER IN DARK ROOM.	EDITOR (SYNC): OK, David. Now that's worth page one.
CUT TO DISCO SCENE.	(SFX: DISCO MUSIC.)
	ANNCR: An exciting paper for exciting people.

(continued)

9-1, CONTINUED

	(SFX: PRESS ROOM SOUND.)
CUT TO PRESSES RUNNING.	ANNCR: The Dallas Morning News.
	To give you that extra edge.
CUT TO DMN SIGNATURE.	(SFX: SOUND ID)
	ANNCR: Every morning.

TV Scripts Some local agencies can supply film footage of an event or services that can be edited for a PSA. The script is written and then an announcer, sometimes a recognized personality, records on audio cassette. If a noted personality does this, the copy must be appropriate to the individual. It has to be written in words the person would use. The personality may be filmed, but it is more likely that a slide of the personality will be used, or that he or she will be identified only in the voice-over. ("Voice-over" means that the voice is heard over any action but the person speaking is not involved in the action being shown.)

It's more likely, however, that the video will be a set of 35mm slides supplied to the station with a script that one of the station's announcers will read. For convenience, most stations record the script on audio cassette and use it with the slides. However, the script writer must recognize the lack of control over the audio and prepare a script that is infallible.

Radio Scripts Radio scripts of PSAs are most likely to be read live. Scripts are sent to the stations to be read by announcers. If the script is not good, the announcers will often improvise from the materials sent, sometimes with less than desirable results. To keep scripts from being "adapted," writers must be concerned with the number of words. If the script is being produced in a ready-to-air form, such as a tape recording, the writer can make changes if the person reading the copy reads faster or slower than average. When a script is sent out, however, it is in the hands of people with a wide variety of reading rates. The best policy is, when in doubt, *under* write. Use fewer words. Remember this is a PSA. If it is too long, it is likely to be thrown out.

In preparing PSAs for a local radio market, the writer can tailor the script to the style of the individual station—even to the style of certain deejays. Because radio stations do stress their individuality, attention to such details can yield high returns, but it also means a lot of work.

A shortcut that is sometimes attempted is pulling the audio off a television presentation to use on radio. This is seldom effective, however, because of the difference in writing styles demanded by the two media.

Most agencies and all media do research to measure the effectiveness of commercials, but copywriters have to turn to scholarly research to find out much about PSAs. An example of the type of research that can be useful is an article from *Journalism Quarterly*, "How Source Affects Response to Public Service Advertising."[4] The authors found that no source attribution at all on a PSA produced the greatest behavioral response. Further, the authors' research suggested that PSA message strategy should be tailored to specific goals, directed toward either a high message evaluation or a behavioral response. The two don't seem to work together. The authors concluded that PSAs have a more positive overall effect on individuals with a higher socioeconomic status. They also found that more careful placement of a PSA by the media might increase its effectiveness. Those who put out PSAs would like to see that happen, but it is not likely, given the low status of the PSA.

9-2 THE BEGINNINGS OF A STORYBOARD

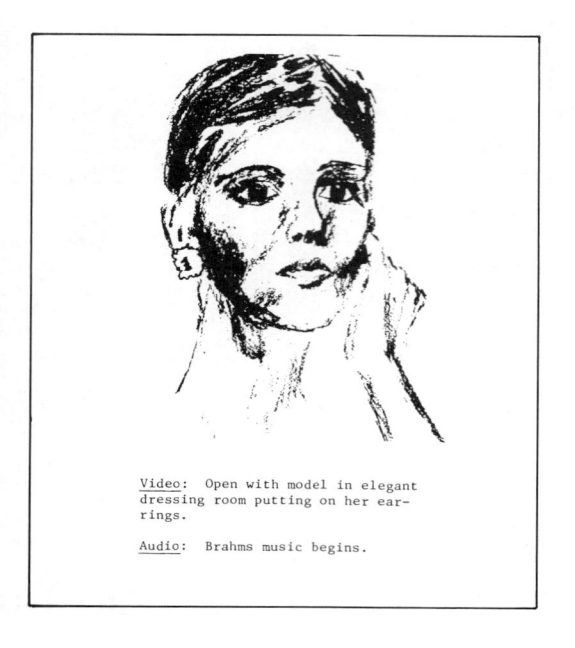

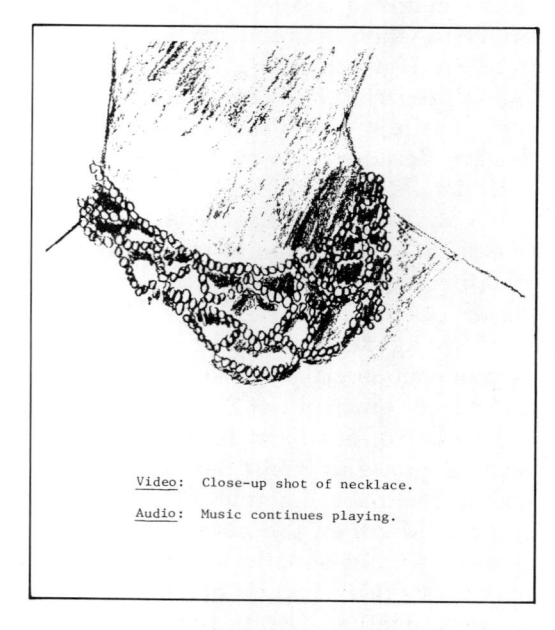

Video: Open with model in elegant dressing room putting on her earrings.

Audio: Brahms music begins.

Video: Model puts hand in Barnes Jewelry box with shining jewelry in it, takes out the necklace.

Audio: Music continues playing.

Video: Model puts on the necklace, with a look of admiration on her face.

Audio: Music continues playing.

Video: Close-up shot of necklace.

Audio: Music continues playing.

The beginnings of a storyboard often are very rough, like these art sketches and copy with suggested audio.

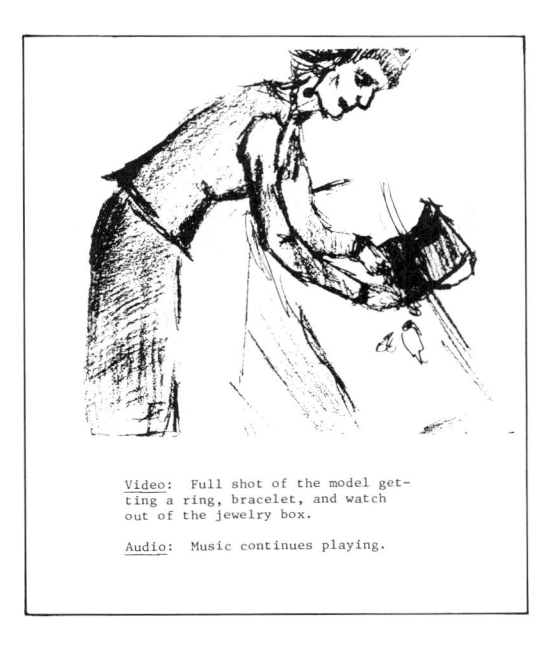

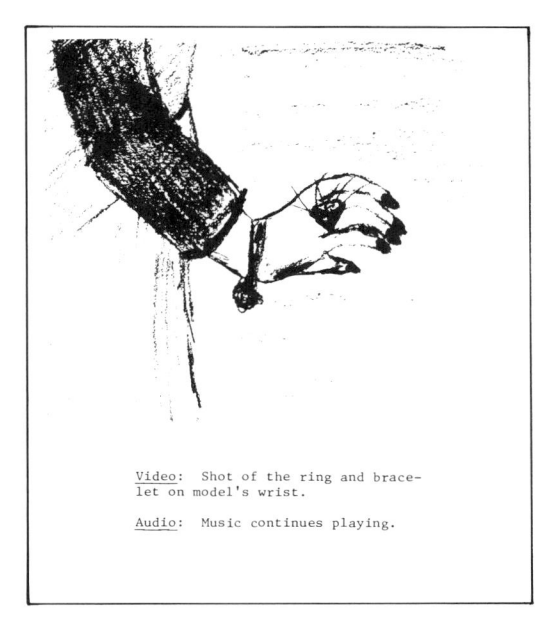

Video: Full shot of the model getting a ring, bracelet, and watch out of the jewelry box.

Audio: Music continues playing.

Video: Shot of the ring and bracelet on model's wrist.

Audio: Music continues playing.

Video: Model puts watch on and notices the time. Close-up shot of Rolex.

Audio: Music fades out. "Barnes Jewelry at 2611 Wolflin Village..."

Video: Model rushes out the door to her car.

Audio: "...for that added touch of distinction."

Sometimes a client is shown a storyboard to get a reaction to the concept, but clients who don't visualize well sometimes have difficulty reacting to an idea in such a rough form.

PART THREE
WRITING FOR
GENERAL AUDIENCES

9-3 TELEVISION COMMERCIAL

BBDO
Batten, Barton, Durstine & Osborn, Inc.

Client:	GENERAL ELECTRIC		Time:	60 SECONDS
Product:	CORPORATE	Title: "PROGRESS REPORT/EXPO-TECH"	Comml. No:	GEDO 8326

ANNCR. 1: Dear General Electric: Thank you for letting your traveling engineering exhibit visit Lincoln Junior High.

A Progress Report from General Electric. Subject: minority education.

VO 2: Our science teacher told us how GE is sending the van from school to school,

so kids can learn what engineering is all about.

VO 3: I made electricity by turning a crank...

VO 4: And I played tic-tac-toe with a computer...only it beat me!

VO 5: We learned about black people who were engineers and inventors, too.

VO 6: And we learned that if we want to be engineers,

we have to get good marks in science and math.

VO 4: So that's what I'm going to do...

so someday I can make a machine that will beat that dumb computer.

Yours truly, Jamie Mitchell.

ANNCR. 1: In 1977, less than five percent of all engineering graduates were Black, Hispanic or American Indian.

General Electric hopes this exhibit...called Expo-Tech ...will help improve that percentage.

100 YEARS OF PROGRESS FOR PEOPLE
GENERAL ELECTRIC

100 years of progress for people ...from General Electric.

After a television commercial's script is written, an effort is made to show what the commercial will look like to its audiences. That effort is called a storyboard. In its beginning stages, a storyboard has only artist sketches for the visual with copy lines below. This example is a presentation storyboard, showing pictures (photos) from the finished commercial.

9-4 WRITING RADIO SCRIPTS WITH SPECIAL EFFECTS

WA — WEEKLEY AND ASSOCIATES ADVERTISING GROUP, INC.
415 GREENLEAF STREET
FORT WORTH, TEXAS 76107
(817) 332-4546
METRO: 429-9107

COPY FOR:
☐ TV   ☐ Direct Mail
☐ Newspaper   ☐ Literature
☐ Outdoor   ☐ Display
☐ Magazine   ☐ Audio-Visual
☒ Radio

Date: January 19, 1979
Client: Champlin
Subject: 60 Sec. Radio
Ad or Script #: CMA-79R/2
M.C. #: CMA-426
Date Approved:
Date(s) to run:

((Typical quiz show bad music, reaching a quick cresendo))

((Applause and crowd noises up and under appropriately through entire spot))

((Anncr))   Now its time for the final round in our big giveaway contest, Win A Bundle!

((Host))   Okay, Mr. Kravitz, what title is held by Muhamed Ali?

((Kravitz, a nut)) Champlin of the world!

((Host))   Champlin? ((Buzzer)) Judges, what do you say?

((Judge))   Champlin...Champion...about the same. We accept. ((Drum Roll))

((Host))   Uh, oh...you wantta go for the whole bundle, Mr. Kravitz?

((Kravitz)) It's a gas!

((Host))   You think this contest is a gas?

((Kravitz)) No, Champlin's a gas...an oil too...and lots of service!

((Host))   ((Buzzer)) Judges?

((Judge))   We agree...Champlin's a gas.

((Host))   Okay, here's the question. What did Moses Part?

((Kravitz)) The Big Red C!

((Host))   Red sea would be sufficient.

((Kravitz)) No...it's gotta be a Big red C...so you can see it when you're comin' down the road and need gas.

((Host))   Moses didn't need gas! ((Buzzer)) Judges!

((Judge))   Our files show that a George C. Moses has a Champlin credit card. He must need gas.

((Host))   But that answer has nothing to do with the Red Sea.

((Krvitz))   Has ever'thin to do with the red C...when you need gas, you pull into the big red Champlin C.

((Host))   Ah-hah...you're changing your answer to the Champlin Sea?

In writing copy for radio commercials involving more than one voice and in writing scripts when dramatic effects such as noises or music are involved, the word count is reduced considerably, as these scripts illustrate.

9-4, CONTINUED

```
January 19, 1979
Champlin
60 Sec. Radio
CMA-79R/2
CMA-426

Page 2

((Kravitz))   Right...big red Champlin C.

((Host))      There's no such thing as a Champlin Sea.  ((Buzzer))
              Judges!

((Judge))     He's right.  There's more than 1200 big red Champlin C's
              all over mid-America.

              ((Applause up))

((Host - he's cracked))   I think I'll take gas...

((Anncr))     It's more than a gas.  The big red Champlin C
              is the sign of service to motorists all across
              mid-America.  That's a real gas, and more.
```

KERSS, CHAPMAN, BUA & NORSWORTHY, INC.

KCBN

CLIENT: Dallas Power & Light
TITLE: Unhandy Person Radio :30
JOB NO. _____ SLATE NO. _____
MANUSCRIPT DATE _____ REVISION NO. _____

ADVERTISING AND PUBLIC RELATIONS, 3434 FAIRMOUNT, DALLAS, TEXAS 75219, (214) 521-6400

1st Man: You're a home handyman?

2nd Man: Well actually, I'm the unhandiest man I know.

1st Man: But all the tools!

2nd Man: I'm teaching myself how to make my home more energy-efficient.

1st Man: You don't have to do that.

2nd Man: I don't have to do that?

1st Man: Dallas Power & Light presents the Unhandy Person's Guide to E-OK.

2nd Man: OK.

1st Man: Six booklets with tips and instructions on caulking...

2nd Man: Caulking!

1st Man: Insulation, storm windows, weatherstripping, maintenance and ductwork.

2nd Man: Where do I get the ducks? That's the first question...

1st Man: You don't understand.

2nd Man: I might after I read the booklets.

1st Man: Call Dallas Power & Light, 747-4011 and ask for the Unhandy Person's Guide to E-OK.

2nd Man: Well, let me write that number down. Say, is this a pencil?

1st Man: Hammer.

2nd Man: Oh hammer. Thank you.

KERSS, CHAPMAN, BUA & NORSWORTHY, INC.

KCBN

CLIENT: DALLAS POWER & LIGHT

COPY FOR: :30 Radio -- Summer Campaign -- Bandit

JOB: 23875

ACCOUNT EXECUTIVE: Solomon   DATE: 2-26-79

ss/bk

ADVERTISING AND PUBLIC RELATIONS, 3434 FAIRMOUNT, DALLAS, TEXAS 75219, (214) 521-6400

(SFX: CRICKETS, EERIE MUSIC, DRONE OF WINDOW UNIT AIR CONDITIONER)

ANNCR: (MYSTERIOUS WHISPER) Listen ... there may be a bandit at your window.

(SFX: TENSE MUSIC STAB, THEN UNDER)

ANNCR: Your air conditioner window unit could be an energy bandit, robbing you of energy dollars. If your unit's Energy Efficiency Rating is less than seven-point-five, your electric bill will be bigger than it needs to be. Call DP&L at 747-4011 for details on how to check your unit's Energy Efficiency Rating. You don't want to pay for energy you don't need. We don't want you to, either. At DP&L, we're still trying to help.

(SFX: A/C DRONE UP, THEN ALL SFX OUT)

9-5 PSA SPOT ANNOUNCEMENTS

```
Texas Boys Choir
Radio/TV public service announcement

                                        10 SECOND SPOT ANNOUNCEMENT

ANNOUNCER:

     A BOY CHOIR THAT COMBINES CONTINENTAL MUSICIANSHIP

     WITH AMERICAN SHOWMANSHIP---THAT'S THE TEXAS BOYS

     CHOIR OF FORT WORTH!  HEAR THEM THIS WEEK IN_____

     _____(NAME OF CONCERT HALL AND TOWN).

                           -0-
```

```
Texas Boys Choir
Radio/TV public service announcement

                                        10 SECOND SPOT ANNOUNCEMENT

ANNOUNCER:

     CHOIRBOYS IN STETSONS...THE TWENTY-SIX YOUNG TEXANS

     SINGING HERE_____(DATE) BELONG TO

     THE FAMOUS TEXAS BOYS CHOIR OF FORT WORTH.  THE TBC

     CONCERT IS SPONSORED BY_____.

                           -0-
```

Media kits for PSAs use the "swiss cheese" approach (also employed with new releases) when some information about the event must be supplied at the source. Included are two 10-second spots, two 15-second spots, one 20-second and one that could be a 20 or made into a 30-second spot if the final paragraph is used. There are two 30-second spots,

9-5, CONTINUED

```
Texas Boys Choir
Radio/TV public service announcement

                                        15 SECOND SPOT ANNOUNCEMENT


(APPLAUSE SOUND)

ANNOUNCER:
        THE APPLAUSE OF AUDIENCES ALL ACROSS THE NATION HAS
        SOUNDED FOR THE TEXAS BOYS CHOIR SCHEDULED TO SING
        IN_____(NAME OF TOWN)
        THIS WEEK.  SPONSOR OF THE SINGING YOUNG TEXANS' CONCERT
        IS_____.*


*(Give ticket information if public may attend.)
```

```
Texas Boys Choir
Radio/TV public service announcement

                                        15 SECOND SPOT ANNOUNCEMENT



ANNOUNCER:
        THEY'VE BEEN INVITED TO EUROPE.  THEY'VE TOURED THE U.S.
        COAST TO COAST.  THEY'RE COMING TO _____
        (NAME OF TOWN).  THE TOURING, SINGING YOUNG TEXANS CALLED
        THE TEXAS BOYS CHOIR OF FORT WORTH WILL APPEAR IN_____
        _____(LOCATION OF CONCERT)_____
        _____(DATE).

                             -0-
```

one 60 and one that could be 50 or 60 seconds, again if additional information is included or excluded. These spots were in media kits sent to sponsors of the artists on the Texas Boys Choir's national tours.

**CHAPTER 9
ADVERTISING COPY**

Texas Boys Choir
Radio/TV public service announcement

                                                         20 SECOND SPOT ANNOUNCEMENT

ANNOUNCER:

    THE TWENTY-SIX VOICES OF THE INTERNATIONALLY RENOWN TEXAS BOYS CHOIR WILL BE HEARD IN _____ _____(TOWN) ON _____(DATE). THE SINGING YOUNG TEXANS OFFER A VARIED PROGRAM DESIGNED TO APPEAL TO EVERYONE...WITH COSTUMES AND CHOREOGRAPHY TO ADD SHOWMANSHIP TO THEIR FAMED MUSICIANSHIP. HEAR THE TEXAS BOYS CHOIR, SPONSORED BY _____ _____.

                                     -0-

Texas Boys Choir
Radio/TV public service announcement

                                            20/30 SECOND SPOT ANNOUNCEMENT

ANNOUNCER:

    THE EYES OF TEXAS AND THE NATION ARE ON THE TOURING SINGING YOUNG TEXANS CALLED THE TEXAS BOY CHOIR OF FORT WORTH. THEY WILL PRESENT A CONCERT OF UNIVERSAL APPEAL_____(TIME AND DATE) IN _____(LOCATION). HEAR THIS GROUP...CALLED BY CRITICS "THE MOST VERSATILE... ENTERTAINING...AND UNIQUE BOY CHOIR IN THE WORLD."

    (Give ticket information if public may attend, and add 10 seconds to time of spot.)

    TICKETS PRICED FROM_____TO_____ ARE AVAILABLE AT_____(LOCATION).

9-5, CONTINUED

```
Texas Boys Choir
Radio/TV public service announcement

                                            30 SECOND ANNOUNCEMENT


ANNOUNCER:
            ONE OF THE MOST UNIQUE MUSICAL EXPERIENCES IN THE

            CONCERT WORLD IS SCHEDULED FOR LOCAL AUDIENCES

            _____(DATE). THE OCCASION

            IS A PERFORMANCE IN_____(LOCATION)

            OF THE TEXAS BOYS CHOIR OF FORT WORTH. THE SINGING

            YOUNG TEXANS HAVE TRAVELED ALL OVER TWO CONTINENTS

            SINGING FOR POPES, PRESIDENTS, AND JUST HOMEFOLKS WITH

            EQUAL MUSICIANSHIP AND CHARM. BE SURE TO MEET THEM...

            THE TEXAS BOYS CHOIR. THEIR CONCERT IS SPONSORED BY

            _____.

                              -0-
```

```
Texas Boys Choir
Radio/TV public service announcement

                                            30 SECOND SPOT ANNOUNCEMENT


ANNOUNCER:
            AMBASSADORS IN STETSONS...THAT'S WHAT MEMBERS OF THE

            GOVERNMENT HAVE CALLED THE SINGING YOUNG TEXANS WHO

            WILL BE IN TOWN THIS WEEK FOR A CONCERT IN_____

            _____(LOCATION). THE TEXAS BOYS CHOIR IS NOW

            MAKING A NATIONAL TOUR. THEY HAVE FULFILLED MORE THAN

            ONE THOUSAND-FOUR HUNDRED ENGAGEMENTS IN THIS COUNTRY AND

            ABROAD. INVITATIONS TO RETURN TO EUROPE ARE BEING CONSIDERED

            BY CHOIR DIRECTORS AND MANAGERS. THE CHOIRBOYS' PERFORMANCE

            HERE IS BEING SPONSORED BY_____.
```

Texas Boys Choir

Radio/TV public service announcement

                                      60 SECOND ANNOUNCEMENT

ANNOUNCER:

THE TEXAS BOYS CHOIR OF FORT WORTH BRINGS ITS CONCERT TOUR PROGRAM OF MADRIGALS AND COMIC OPERA...CONTEMPORARY RELIGIOUS MUSIC AND STAGE SHOW ENTERTAINMENT TO_____ ___(TOWN) ON_____(DATE).

THE TWENTY-SIX SINGING TEXANS HAVE WON CRITICAL ACCLAIM ON TWO CONTINENTS. EACH YEAR THE CHOIRBOYS TRAVEL THE U.S. COAST TO COAST. THE APPEARANCE OF THE TEXAS BOYS CHOIR IN_____ _____(TOWN) IS BEING SPONSORED BY_____ _____.

CHOIRBOYS TOURING WITH THE TBC ARE MEMBERS OF AN ELITE GROUP --- HAND-PICKED FOR PUBLIC PERFORMANCE FROM MORE THAN ONE HUNDRED AND FIFTY MEMBERS OF THE TEXAS BOYS CHOIR ORGANIZATION. THE CONCERT CHOIR IS COMPRISED OF YOUNGSTERS EIGHT TO FIFTEEN YEARS OLD. ALL HAVE SPENT AT LEAST A YEAR AND A HALF IN STUDY AT THE TEXAS BOYS CHOIR'S CONSERVATORY-STYLED SCHOOL IN FORT WORTH.

A LOVE OF SINGING IS AS MUCH A REQUIREMENT FOR CHOIR MEMBERSHIP AS A GOOD VOICE. THE CHOIRBOYS SINGING HERE WILL REFLECT BOTH ENTHUSIASM AND TRAINING IN THEIR_____(DATE) CONCERT IN_____(LOCATION).

                                      -0-

9-5, CONTINUED

Texas Boys Choir
Radio/TV public service announcement

50/60 SECOND SPOT ANNOUNCEMENT

ANNOUNCER:

FROM THE LONE STAR STATE TO THE CONCERT HALLS OF _____ _____(TOWN AND STATE) COMES ONE OF THE WORLD'S LEADING BOY CHOIRS. IN ONE THOUSAND FOUR HUNDRED CONCERTS AND TWO CONTINENTS, THE SINGING YOUNG TEXANS HAVE INDEED GIVEN THEIR STATE SOMETHING TO BRAG ABOUT. THE TEXAS BOYS CHOIR APPEARING HERE_____(DATE) HAS WON THE TRIBUTE OF AUDIENCES ALL ACROSS THE NATION DURING COAST TO COAST TOURS. FIVE FOREIGN COUNTRIES HAVE INVITED THE CHOIR TO SING IN THEIR PRINCIPAL CITIES NEXT SPRING. CRITICS ABROAD AND IN CITIES ALL ACROSS THE NATION HAVE PRAISED THE TEXAS BOYS CHOIR FOR PRECISE MUSICIANSHIP AND PROFESSIONAL PERFORMANCES...AUDIENCES HAVE APPLAUDED THE YOUNGSTERS FOR THEIR SHOWMANSHIP...THEIR WARMTH...THEIR VITALITY...THEIR OBVIOUS LOVE FOR SINGING. WHETHER ITS ENTERTAINMENT OR EXCELLENT MUSIC CONCERT GOERS ARE SEEKING, A TEXAS BOYS CHOIR PERFORMANCE FULFILLS BOTH QUESTS. THEIR APPEARANCE IN_____ _____(TOWN) IS BEING SPONSORED BY_____ _____.

(If open to the public add ticket information and allow 10 seconds to make this a 60 second spot.)

TICKETS PRICED FROM_____TO_____ARE AVAILABLE THROUGH
_____.

-0-

ADVERTISING IN THE PRINT MEDIA

In print media, the medium is the message. Determining what to say depends on where you are going to say it. The only element these various media have in common is that the message is printed; otherwise they are quite different. It is important to use your imagination to see the final product as you work on it.

Newspapers

Newspaper advertising falls into two categories: display and classified. There is something called "classified display," but it is really display advertising in the classified section. For display advertising, the words and art must present a unified concept, like the video and audio in the television commercials. Display advertising in newspapers is of two types: local (the bulk of it) and national (a small amount—10 to 15 percent—placed by national firms). Newspapers are read hurriedly and have a brief life. Although they have a reputation for hitting mass, rather than target, audiences, ads can be designed for special audiences among newspaper readers—such as those who read the sports pages—with some degree of success.

Display With display advertising, you want to convey a concept of the product or service and create an *immediate* demand for it. Newspaper display ads generally consist of a headline, copy blocks, art, information about the advertiser and a logo. The size of the space purchased determines the proportion and size of the components. Only when a great deal of space is bought, like a full page or half page, can the copywriter have an idea of the possible competition the ad will face. The more space you buy, of course, the less competition you have, at least from other ads being placed on the same page. The newspaper is a highly competitive medium; editorial content and other ads all on the same page vie for the reader's attention. Compelling headlines and creative art are the lures used to entice readers to the copy, which then has to be good enough to hold them and sell them. (See Example 9-6.)

Because most newspaper ads are for local audiences, a good copywriter takes advantage of research information about the area and about the readers of that particular medium. Compare some of the locally prepared ads with ones from national advertisers and note the difference in tone. Those from the national sources are more likely to be neutral in tone because they are usually prepared for publication in the *Los Angeles Times* and the *Atlanta Constitution,* although some national firms have ads that are tailored for different regions. Magazines, even national ones, also offer regional tailoring in their advertising, both classified and display.

9-6 CREATIVITY LURES CUSTOMERS

At last, a big fat juicy guarantee on big, fat, juicy produce.

If you aren't pleased with the produce you buy at Tom Thumb-Page, we'll give you double your money back. Because we stand behind everything we sell and that's a promise. Don't miss our special insert in this newspaper for outstanding produce values at Tom Thumb-Page.

TOM THUMB-PAGE
FOOD AND DRUG CENTERS

Creativity can make a produce promotion exciting, as these ads illustrate. The ads appeared in newspapers and magazines. The art appeared above the produce on display in the grocery stores, and a whole promotion was built around the emphasis on produce in this grocery store chain.

We really put our hearts into bringing you the best produce money can buy.

If you aren't pleased with the produce you buy at Tom Thumb-Page, we'll give you double your money back. Because we stand behind everything we sell and that's a promise. Don't miss our special insert in this newspaper for outstanding produce values at Tom Thumb-Page.

TOM THUMB-PAGE
FOOD AND DRUG CENTERS

182

9–6, CONTINUED

> # We believe great looks and good taste are the only ways to get a head.
>
> If you aren't pleased with the produce you buy at Tom Thumb-Page, we'll give you double your money back. Because we stand behind everything we sell and that's a promise. Don't miss our special insert in this newspaper for outstanding produce values at Tom Thumb-Page.
>
> **TOM THUMB-PAGE**
> FOOD AND DRUG CENTERS

One look at our quality selection of produce is enough to bring tears to your eyes.

If you aren't pleased with the produce you buy at Tom Thumb-Page, we'll give you double your money back. Because we stand behind everything we sell and that's a promise. Don't miss our special insert in this newspaper for outstanding produce values at Tom Thumb-Page.

TOM THUMB-PAGE
FOOD AND DRUG CENTERS

Classified In the classified sections there are some excellent demonstrations of the creative use of a few words. These sections are not just for those having garage sales. The classified section is used extensively by real estate firms and by transportation and recreation vehicle firms. A professional copywriter for an agency is very likely to prepare hundreds of such ads for clients. The technique of doing so is simple. Decide how many words you can get in the allotted space. Write down the words you have to include, such as the firm's name, address and phone number. The number of words you have left is the number you can be creative with! Read the classified columns before you begin writing. This will increase your appreciation for the ingenuity of others, and alert you to accepted abbreviations. It will also tell you what your competitors are doing.

Magazines

Magazine audiences are highly specialized, and production time for publication is long (5 to 7 weeks). Messages that go into magazines, therefore, are best when they address the specialized audience directly, or are written for rereading and reference, as opposed to announcements about new products. It is possible to buy placement for magazine ads so they appear only in certain editions—selected geographically or, in some cases, demographically.

A magazine ad allows the copywriter to address a target market that will probably spend some time reading the copy in a fairly leisurely way. The magazine also allows for more elaborate artwork and a more attractive setting for copy.

Again, the copywriter needs to know the size and placement of the ad before starting to work. Magazine ads can be columnar, if the page layout is in columns, but space is more usually apportioned by the full page, the half page—either vertical or horizontal—and the quarter page. Other variations are double-page spreads or half a double-page spread. Sometimes the two outside portions of the pages are used. Ads can also be placed in a checkerboard effect—upper left and lower right fourths, or vice versa. Another variation is the gatefold, an extra piece on the outside of a page. Some magazines sell a "junior page," which is a three-fourths inside position with editorial copy only in one outside column, and fewer sell an island, a center surrounded by editorial copy.

Having an image of the space, the copywriter should then look at several issues of the publication to see the character and tone of the other advertising. Looking at both the advertising and editorial content, plus reading material about the audience from the publication's advertising promotion department, will help the copywriter frame a message.

A major decision to be made is which will dominate—the words or the art. Once that decision is made, the other must be carefully designed to complement, not compete. The copywriter can sometimes get a better feel for the project by drawing to scale a rough sketch of the ad. This also helps in preparing copy that will fit precisely, as it must (although magazine copy has greater leeway than ads in our next topic).

Outdoor and Transit

Outdoor ads and transit ads are both posters. Writing poster copy is a challenge because the copy has a great deal of competition and often gets just a fleeting glance. The standard size billboard is 12-×-25 feet, and the most popular ad size is the 30-sheet poster. The term *sheet* is inherited from the days when it took sheets of paper as large as the presses could handle, 24 of them, to cover a billboard. Now the "24 sheets" are generally used for noncommercial messages, and the most extravagant billboard ad is the bleed, where art and copy go all of the way to the frame.

Messages for billboards are usually symbolic and simple, although a bank in one metropolitan city took advantage of its location at a traffic light reputed to be the longest in the world to write a 75-word message. It did get a high readership, but such a billboard on the highway would be a hazard, if it were read at all! Most billboard copy is 10 to 20 words, at the most, including the name of the advertiser. Imagery of both words and art is essential. Most billboard efforts are to attract attention and create memorability by a unique use of the language. (See Example 9-7.)

The same demand is made on the copywriter devising a message for the outside of transit vehicles. The type must be large and legible and create instant recognition for the advertiser. Messages inside buses and subway trains can have more words because the audiences are captive. But even here not many words can be used because the audiences must read the posters from a distance. These posters come in at least six different sizes, and, again, the copywriter needs some concept of the space in order to work effectively. It might be a good idea to design a full-sized mock-up.

Messages in these media are capsules, but they often offer many exposures, so they need to be done so they will become familiar but not tiresome.

Direct Response and Direct Mail

The true test of the persuasiveness of copy is the direct-response and direct-mail ad. Each ad is designed to stand alone and pull in sales. More research is available in this area than in any other; it is probably the most scientific area of advertising. Success is measured in the number of responses—coupons or order blanks returned. And once a successful ad has been designed and proven, it is not likely to be changed

9-7 BILLBOARD ADVERTISING

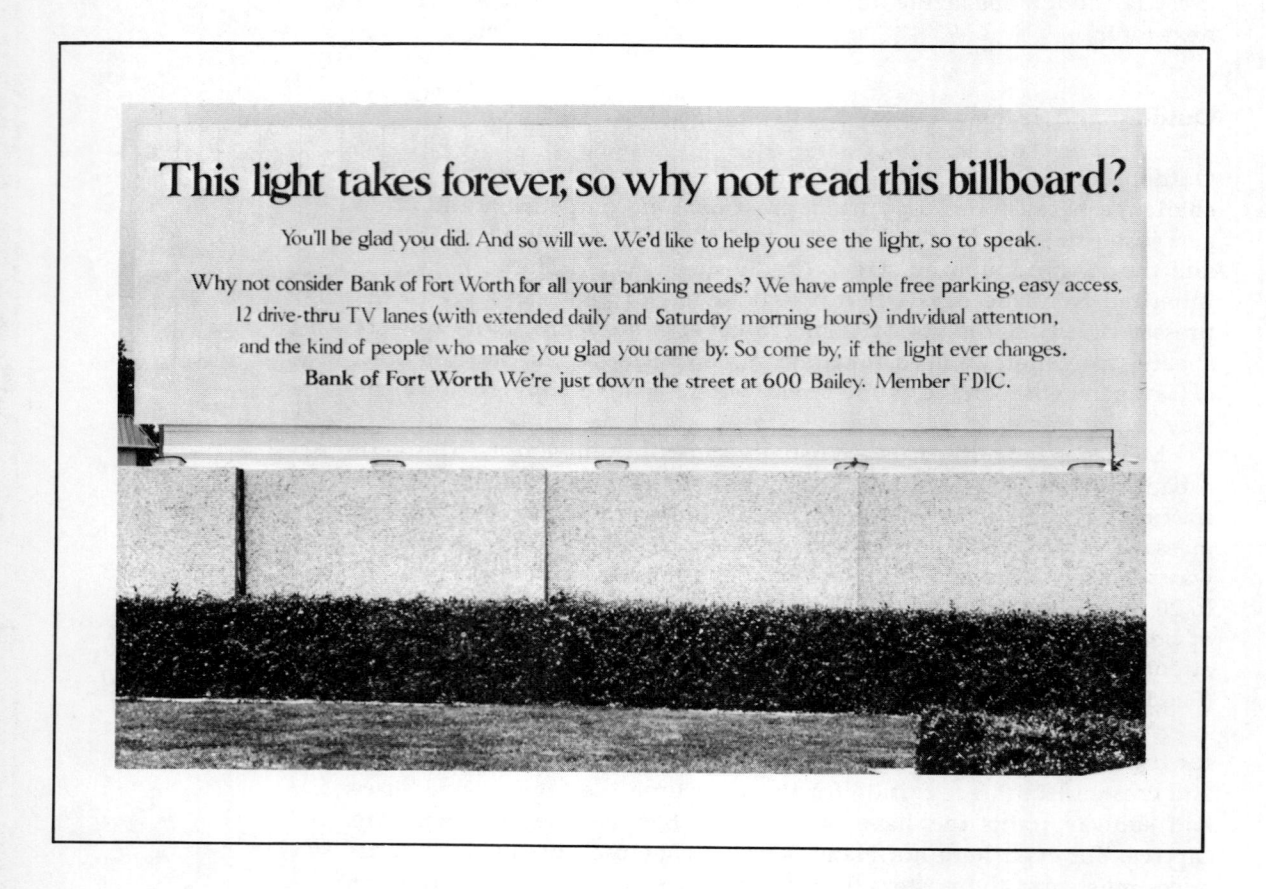

This light takes forever, so why not read this billboard?

You'll be glad you did. And so will we. We'd like to help you see the light, so to speak.

Why not consider Bank of Fort Worth for all your banking needs? We have ample free parking, easy access, 12 drive-thru TV lanes (with extended daily and Saturday morning hours) individual attention, and the kind of people who make you glad you came by. So come by, if the light ever changes.

Bank of Fort Worth We're just down the street at 600 Bailey. Member FDIC.

Most billboard copy is extraordinarily brief, but the traffic light at this intersection gives motorists plenty of time to read this—even if they are slow readers.

very much. Copywriters of direct-response ads have a big job in terms of the volume of words they must turn out and the dependence of the advertiser on the power of those words to sell the product. Design of the coupon or response is important, too. It has to be easy for the buyer to fill out, and complete enough for the advertiser to be able to fulfill the contract.

Not all direct-mail and direct-response ads are "single shots." Some are developed to attract customers before additional information is given to them. Items like insurance or expensive sets of books use this approach. The copywriter may prepare sequential materials, answering anticipated questions that research has shown may be asked.

Direct-response advertising can appear in newspapers, on television and radio, in magazines or books (including catalogs) and in other mailing pieces. Computerized analysis of responses gives copywriters of these pieces helpful information about target audiences.

Sales Promotion

Coupons, booklets, brochures and mailers are sales promotion pieces, as are point-of-purchase advertising, samples, contests and advertising specialties, as well as cooperative advertising.

Point-of-purchase advertising is designed to be displayed with the product to inspire a customer to buy on impulse. Most point-of-purchase advertising is strong on emotional impact, particularly symbolism, and ties in with other existing promotional materials to give recognition. Samples are sent with descriptive literature that informs the potential customer about the product. Copy for such literature often tries to inspire a sense of obligation to buy since the sample was free.

Contests are designed to offer customers something extra and to keep awareness of the product high through participation and anticipation. Advertising specialities can be anything with the corporate logo or product name, but generally they are useful pieces, like ice scrapers for windshields, or something with high visibility, like a match folder. Cooperative advertising is a combination of retail appeal for direct sale and manufacturer support. When you see a boat dealer advertising a line of boats and the manufacturer's logo appears in the ad, it is a cooperative piece with the manufacturer picking up part of the tab. There are specifications for the manufacturer's cooperation, and the copywriter has to be sure to follow these or the benefit will be lost.

Institutional

Advertising for the institution itself is sometimes called "image advertising," but a better name would be "identity advertising." (See the examples in 9-8 a-c.) An ad for a corporate entity, such as General Foods, may name all of the individual consumer companies under its umbrella, or a Tenneco ad (Example 9-8a) may name all of its units. This Tenneco ad appeared in *Time* magazine (April 28, 1980), but this type of advertising abounds in publications investors are likely to read, such as *Barron's, The Wall Street Journal, Fortune, Nation's Business*. The reason is obvious: the ad is meant to show the corporate strength of the company by calling attention to its well-known units.

Identity advertising also appears on television. Watch for commercials that tell you to look for labels in clothes that show the garment was made by union labor, or a nonprofit institution. Other identity ads from profit-making institutions—such as Boise Cascade—talk not of the parent company's commercial components, but of its corporate concerns, such as ecology. Some image or identity ads have won Clio Awards, the ad industry's equivalent to the film industry's Oscar. One public service ad—made by Marsteller, Inc. for the Advertising Council—depicted an American Indian going through modern society deploring the litter desecrating his homeland. Example 9-8d is a print ad from the Council urging support for the arts.

When you sell ideas, you lack a tangible benefit, and it's difficult to count the number of people who "bought" the idea. Included here are other types of institutional ads with a slightly different purpose. Example 9-8b, a natural gas company's ad found in an opera program, is simply designed to give opera goers a good feeling about the company.

Another example of institutional advertising is the second-line consumer advertising of companies such as De Beers. Consumer magazines carry their dramatic four-color ads for diamonds, although the diamonds are bought from jewelry stores, not from De Beers. However, most of the world's diamonds come from De Beers, so it is no wonder the company wants to encourage people to buy diamonds.

Nonprofit institutions advertise too, some with the idea of making you feel good so you'll support the institution, others hoping to have a more direct impact. For example, institutions of higher learning advertise to attract students and to get their parents' attention. More ads from colleges and universities are likely to appear in the next ten years, as the pool of available 18-year-old students decreases nationally. Trade associations, which are also nonprofit institutions, often advertise for their commercial members. (See Example 9-8c from the Chemical Manufacturers Association.) Some corporate and trade association advertising advocates an idea, but advocacy advertising is somewhat different from identity advertising.

Institutional advertising that tries to win public opinion to a particular point of view is more than just image advertising; it is "advocacy advertising." Examples of advocacy advertising are these ads from two oil companies trying to get public opinion on the side of the industry. Of the two, Exxon's ad (Example 9-8h) is more clearly advertising than is Mobil's, which uses the column layout (Example 9-8f). Mobil also employs an editorial page technique in its letter to the president (9–8e), although this ad is not likely to be mistaken for newspaper staff-originated material!

Advocacy advertising is a product of the late seventies, a bold gesture not all companies are willing to make. It has been reasonably successful, as the *New York Times* story indicates (Example 9–8g). However, it can cause problems too. In Fort Worth, the CEO of the Western Company, an oil equipment company among other things, broadcast a series of commercials attacking big government and other institutions. The commercials began with CEO Eddie Chiles saying "I am mad." He then described the particular cause of his anger. People who agreed with him could write the Western Company for bumper stickers that read: "I'm mad too, Eddie." The commercials drew national attention, as well as that of local attorney Don Gladden, who filed against the stations citing the fairness doctrine. Some advocacy advertising by Mobil has been rejected by network executives who cited the fairness doctrine and said they feared having to give equal time to "the other side." The issue of the rights of the corporate voice in advertising is one that will continue to be debated through the eighties.

House Ads

When a newspaper or magazine takes space to push one of its own projects, the ad is called a "house ad." It is "on the house" and no money changes hands. The promotion director for the medium has a budget of space to use each year and apportions it to various projects or campaigns. These ads are usually written by the promotion department's copywriters. They are prepared like any other ad. Their character is determined by their purpose and the medium involved. They may be a direct-response ad, as one newspaper used in selling American flag kits. Or they may urge attendance at some event, like an auto show, that the newspaper is sponsoring.

CONCLUSION

Most college students belong to a generation likely to recall more commercials than fairy tales. Yet, with all that exposure, few students analyze what they see and hear in ads with a critical view of what "works" and what doesn't. To perfect your own skills with this form of communication, look carefully at the persuasive art behind the message when viewing and listening.

9-8 IDENTITY AND ADVOCACY ADVERTISING

Another Tenneco Venture:
The Williston Basin.

This rugged region in the Dakotas and Montana is frontier territory again—for energy.

The Williston Basin is a geologic area in the upper Midwest, about two-thirds the size of Texas—and a promising source of oil and natural gas.

Tenneco has a $70 million investment in the Williston Basin and currently holds leases on more than a million acres there. The Company discovered six new oil fields in the Basin in 1979 alone; along with earlier finds, they have a total potential of more than 8,000 barrels a day. And Tenneco plans to accelerate exploration activity in the area, drilling more wildcat and development wells during the next few years.

The Basin doesn't give up its riches easily. Most finds are more than two miles deep and drilling is made more difficult by the remote location and the bitter winter weather, with temperatures sinking to 50 below.

But the effort is worthwhile, because every barrel of oil recovered can help reduce the billion dollars a week our nation is now spending on imported oil.

As part of our effort to build up domestic energy resources, Tenneco is also active in all other major energy-producing areas of the United States, both onshore and offshore. We helped develop the Yowlumne Field in California, one of the most productive oil strikes in the state in the last decade. Offshore, we are a leading producer of natural gas in the Gulf of Mexico and have discovered oil and natural gas in the Baltimore Canyon off New Jersey. We also drilled the first test wells off Georgia and Florida. Future exploration of the Atlantic Frontier will include drilling on newly acquired leases in the George's Bank area off New England.

Longer range, we're partners in a major oil-shale recovery project in Colorado and in a Louisiana project to recover natural gas from saline water in geopressurized zones.

We are making progress in our efforts to bring in additional natural gas from Canada and are already pipelining gas from Mexico. In addition, we are participating in a program to build the nation's first commercial-scale plant that will convert coal to synthetic natural gas, and are working to import liquefied natural gas.

These are giant ventures that require the expenditure of billions of dollars. In 1980 alone we have budgeted over $1 billion for energy projects.

Although energy makes up two-thirds of Tenneco's business, we continue to supply other basic needs, like food, automotive components, chemicals, ships, packaging, farm and construction equipment, and insurance.

That's Tenneco today: growing in energy ...and more.

For more information on Tenneco, write Box T-2, Tenneco Inc., Houston TX 77001.

TENNECO OIL TENNESSEE GAS TRANSMISSION J I CASE TENNECO AUTOMOTIVE
TENNECO CHEMICALS NEWPORT NEWS SHIPBUILDING PACKAGING CORP. OF AMERICA TENNECO WEST

Tenneco

9-8b

Opera is a gas!

AMERICAN QUASAR PETROLEUM CO.
2500 Fort Worth National Bank Building
Fort Worth, Texas 76102

American Quasar shares are traded over-the-counter under the symbol AQAS.

9–8c

Protecting Chemical Workers

How we're improving one of the best health and safety records in U.S. industry

According to National Safety Council figures, chemical workers are 2.3 times safer than the average employee in American industry. In fact, they are far safer on the job than off. But we're still not satisfied. Here are some of the steps we're taking to make the working environment healthier and safer:

1. Improving detection techniques

New and more sophisticated devices for monitoring the environment are worn by many workers. Many plants have "area monitoring devices" spotted in strategic locations. Some of these devices change color or sound an alarm to alert workers to even minute traces of contaminants. Others, like the gas chromatograph-mass spectrometer, measure contaminant quantities as low as one part per trillion—equivalent to one second in 32,000 years. Data from these and other measuring devices are analyzed by computer and compared with employee health records to help make sure that exposure is kept at safe levels. (See illustration.)

2. Upgrading educational programs

Chemical companies are intensifying their safety education programs, especially with videotapes and other visual aid techniques. One company has an 82-page listing of videotape cassettes. It also has an index of safety standards that runs to about 60 pages. And each standard can run as long as 50 pages. The effect of this training goes beyond the plant. Chemical workers learn to "think safety." So they have fewer accidents than the average industrial employee —not only at work, but also on their own time.

3. Expanding laboratory studies

Throughout the chemical industry, thousands of people are working on new and faster ways to determine the long-term effects of chemicals. It is not an easy job. Doing a study on just one chemical can take over three years and cost more than $1,000,000. To advance this work, 30 chemical com-

Worker Safety Protection System

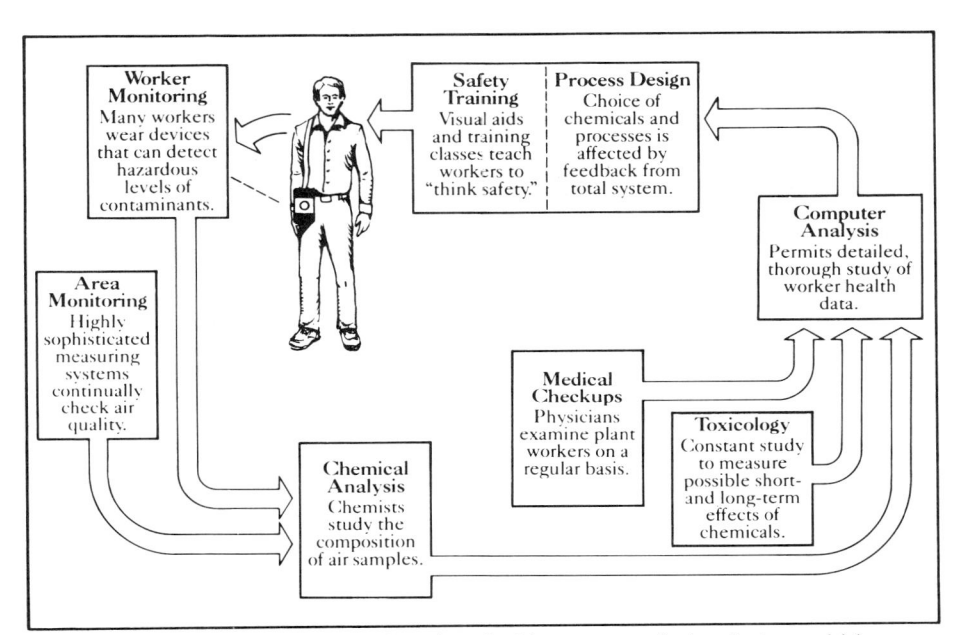

- **Worker Monitoring**: Many workers wear devices that can detect hazardous levels of contaminants.
- **Safety Training**: Visual aids and training classes teach workers to "think safety."
- **Process Design**: Choice of chemicals and processes is affected by feedback from total system.
- **Computer Analysis**: Permits detailed, thorough study of worker health data.
- **Area Monitoring**: Highly sophisticated measuring systems continually check air quality.
- **Chemical Analysis**: Chemists study the composition of air samples.
- **Medical Checkups**: Physicians examine plant workers on a regular basis.
- **Toxicology**: Constant study to measure possible short- and long-term effects of chemicals.

Worker Safety Protection System: Data from health exams, monitoring devices and laboratory studies are continually analyzed to identify situations that may require immediate action and to provide information for possible improvements in process design and safety training.

---

panies have joined to create the Chemical Industry Institute of Toxicology located near Raleigh, North Carolina. The Institute shares its findings with the entire industry, the U.S. Government and the public.

4. "Engineering out" risks

When tests cast suspicion on the safety of a substance, we often find substitutes. Example: At many plants, toxic materials have been replaced by safer chemicals. In other cases, we may redesign the entire manufacturing process to make it safer.

5. Closer monitoring of employee health

The number of industrial hygienists has tripled in the past 10 years. And they are only part of the picture. Chemical companies now use *interdisciplinary* teams to monitor employee health. A typical team consists of industrial hygienists, physicians, toxicologists and engineers. These teams then multiply their effectiveness by using the latest computer technology to process and study the data they collect. The results help chemical companies anticipate and control threats to worker health and safety better than ever before.

For more information, write: Chemical Manufacturers Association, Dept. BT-41, 1825 Connecticut Avenue, NW, Washington, D.C. 20009.

America's Chemical Industry

The member companies of the Chemical Manufacturers Association

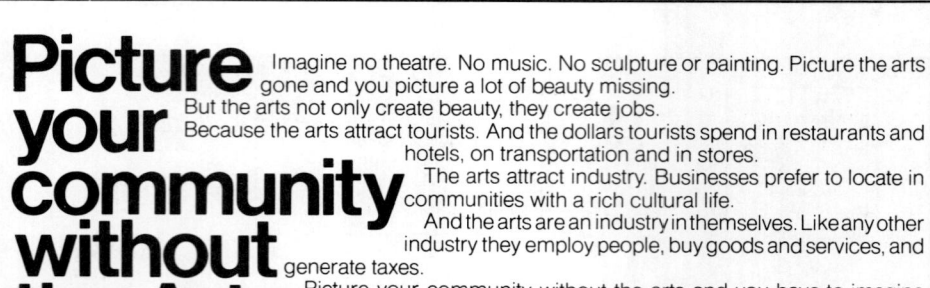

Picture your community without the Arts.

Imagine no theatre. No music. No sculpture or painting. Picture the arts gone and you picture a lot of beauty missing.

But the arts not only create beauty, they create jobs.

Because the arts attract tourists. And the dollars tourists spend in restaurants and hotels, on transportation and in stores.

The arts attract industry. Businesses prefer to locate in communities with a rich cultural life.

And the arts are an industry in themselves. Like any other industry they employ people, buy goods and services, and generate taxes.

Picture your community without the arts and you have to imagine industry and jobs gone, too. And after that, the people.

So it'd not only be pretty dull, it'd be pretty lonely.

Support The Arts. That's where the people are.

National Endowment for the Arts

A Public Service of The Advertising Council

Sorry, Mr. President, you've been misled

On Friday, March 28, you singled out Mobil Oil Corporation in a speech at the National Conference of State Legislatures, charging that our company had violated the Administration's price guidelines by $45 million. The White House said that Mobil was unwilling to refund this amount to consumers through a temporary reduction of 3 cents a gallon in the price of gasoline.

Our position, Mr. President, is very straightforward. We did not violate existing guidelines of the Council on Wage and Price Stability. And we were not asked by any government agency to reduce the price of gasoline by any particular amount per gallon. Further, we are most concerned that this charge—and your repetition of it last week—may represent a continuation of political maneuvering at the expense of our company, and our company alone, because of our policy of speaking out on energy issues, sometimes at variance with Administration policy.

Last year, you called for decontrol of domestic crude oil production subject to a so-called "windfall profits" tax. Shortly after Mobil disagreed publicly with the proposal—suggesting that controls might be continued on existing oil, providing newly discovered oil would be free from additional tax in order to encourage more exploration—it was reported that you called us the "most irresponsible company in America." We felt this allegation was unfair but decided not to answer because of the respect we have for the Office of the President of the United States. We felt at the time, however, that you had been poorly advised; and so, apparently, did the Congress, since its final version of the windfall measure favors new oil over old oil, accepting in substantial part the point we had made.

In this current situation, Mr. President, we are afraid that once again you have not been given the full facts; and, unlike the differing opinions we both have on the windfall profits tax, this time you have made the specific accusation that we overcharged our customers.

We present the facts here because we care about our reputation, not only as businessmen but also as honorable citizens trying to help solve America's energy problems:

1. At the time the COWPS guidelines were introduced in October, 1978, we were already (and still are) operating under Department of Energy mandatory price controls, in effect since 1971.

2. We found many of the new COWPS requirements in conflict with DOE requirements but struggled to live with both sets of controls.

3. Under the COWPS voluntary program, oil companies were permitted to recover increased costs in their prices for finished products, using either profit margin or gross margin standards. Each company was free to elect the standard suited to its circumstances; many opted for the profit margin standard while Mobil and a number of others elected gross margin. More than once, COWPS stated in writing that compliance under the gross margin test would be measured on an annual basis over the COWPS fiscal year ending each September 30.

4. When you and DOE urged the oil industry last June to build a large inventory of both gasoline and home heating oil simultaneously, Mobil bought supplies wherever we could, at higher-than-normal costs. We sold many of these products during the ensuing three months (COWPS' fiscal fourth quarter) at prices which helped us recover some of these extraordinary costs—exactly as the guidelines prescribed at that time.

5. Then, retroactively, in December 1979, COWPS changed these guidelines only for the companies using gross margin, requiring compliance on a quarterly basis for the fiscal year ended September 30, 1979. On the annual basis we had been working under, our prices were not only in compliance but well below COWPS guidelines. Under the retroactive rule change, COWPS announced on February 25 that Mobil was out of compliance and several other companies probably so. But COWPS named just Mobil.

6. Telegrams seeking clarification were sent by Mobil's president to COWPS and DOE but went unanswered. On February 27, Mobil's chairman wrote to you, Mr. President. On March 24, he received an answer from Alfred E. Kahn, your advisor on inflation, stating that he had asked R. Robert Russell, director of COWPS, "to give me an analysis of whether our standards, which set quarterly targets, unrealistically fail to take into account the normal flow into and out of inventories, and in so doing impose unreasonable burdens on petroleum refiners."

7. Midmorning on March 28, with White House encouragement, a Mobil director met with Mr. Russell, believing they would resolve the issue or at least get Mr. Russell's response to Mr. Kahn's request. Neither happened. It was really a non-meeting and we wonder why it was called.

8. Early that same afternoon, you leveled your attacks on our company, and the White House stated that Mobil had refused to reduce gasoline prices 3 cents a gallon for one quarter of 1980 to "repay" the alleged overcharges. The first time we were aware of such a figure was when we read it on the news wire that afternoon.

In summary, Mr. President, the rules of the game were changed retroactively. We were not out of compliance under the rules in effect when we were selling the products in question. Anybody can be thrown into violation when rules are made retroactively. We oppose retroactive rule changes which put companies into violation, particularly when they are applied selectively against companies that speak out

Mobil

© 1980 Mobil Corporation

9-8f

Observations

"National Nothing Day." It's coming up January 16, the one day set aside—we're told by its originator, retired California newsman Harold Coffin—for Americans to *"just sit without celebrating, observing or honoring anything."* Not a bad idea, considering that special periods proclaimed to get us to *"do something"* are getting pretty wearing. Or were you one of those rare people actually moved by President Carter's designation of last October as *"International Energy Conservation Month"*? (On October 29, for example, Washington's calendar asked you to *"make a grocery shopping trip without buying any items packaged in non-reusable plastic."*)

Non-practicing preachers. So what's Washington actually doing about saving energy? A fair question, because the 10 biggest energy-using agencies of the federal government consume enough energy to heat 11 million homes and fuel all the automobiles in California and New York. *"Regretfully, the federal government lags behind much of the nation in conservation,"* a House subcommittee reported; a failure of the feds *"to practice what they preach."* Other investigators criticized Uncle Sam's *"infrequent, inadequate and poorly organized"* efforts to save energy in federal buildings.

Sound and fury. By contrast, oil companies and other private industries are improving energy efficiency (some 16 percent since 1973). But you can be sure some politicians will continue to blame lack of energy progress on industry instead of on incoherent, contradictory government policies. As Brown University economics professor George H. Borts puts it: *"You could create a shortage of steak by having a law that said steak was worth 50 cents a pound. People wouldn't raise cattle...."* His recommendation is *"to leave the oil market alone, get rid of government price controls, get rid of the allocation system of the Department of Energy, (and) let the oil industry do its work...."*

"There must be some way we could blame it on the oil companies."

Nothing succeeds like... A Ford Foundation study concludes that the world energy problem is basically *"rising costs that will have to be accommodated by rising prices."* Not happy news, but the real facts. And more likely to solve the problem than *"letting government do it."* Both Energy Secretary Charles W. Duncan, Jr. and Deputy Energy Secretary John C. Sawhill have said the free market often works better than energy controls. Which is to say, sometimes the best government action is: Nothing.

It's a fact: Mobil's worldwide oil and gas earnings amounted to just 3.4 cents on every gallon of petroleum sold in the latest 12 months.

Mobil

THE NEW YORK TIMES, TUESDAY, MARCH 25, 1980

Advertising
Philip H. Dougherty

Bethlehem's Advocacy Campaign

IN recent years the Bethlehem Steel Corporation has been very serious about converting the public to its way of thinking on a number of controversial subjects. And its advocacy advertising, research shows, has been working.

Since it got on the corporate soapbox, the country's second-largest steelmaker has generally devoted an entire campaign to a single issue. For 1980 it is environmental controls.

"We believe at the present time that we and the steel industry are doing enough in the area of air and water pollution control and we believe that if we have to do what the Government is demanding, both Federal and state, we will have a difficult time investing in capital equipment," said Gene Cronin, Bethlehem's production and media director.

The campaign that breaks next month will not use all of the same media as last year's ads, which dealt with capital formation. In 1977, the company's ads concerned Bethlehem's attitudes on foreign trade. The change in media comes after the company has gone through a considerable amount of trouble to find out how the readers of certain magazines feel about particular subjects.

•

And it is not interested in reaching anyone who feels particularly strongly on either side of any of the issues, but rather the group it refers to as the "swayables," those who can be influenced. Since funds are limited, Bethlehem is also interested in reaching them as efficiently as possible.

That is why in 1975, with its corporate agency, Van Brunt & Company, and Manville Research, the steelmaker set out to discover attitudes of subscribers to 13 popular national magazines.

The idea behind it all is that while two magazines might attract similar audiences as far as their economic status is concerned, they could be far different as far as attitudes to issues. In an introduction to its latest research project, Bethlehem cites as an example the differences in views between the readers of The Daily Worker and those of the magazine of the John Birch Society.

"This difference," Bethlehem said, "is undoubtedly true in more subtle degrees in magazines such as Smithsonian, Atlantic and Saturday Review, as opposed to Business Week, Fortune and The Wall Street Journal. All of these magazines reach people of much the same demographic definition. But, because of their background, education, interests, or other reasons, their attitudes and opinions differ," it said.

•

The publications researched in 1975 were Atlantic, Business Week, Forbes, Fortune, Harper's, Newsweek, Saturday Review, Smithsonian, Sports Illustrated, Time, U.S. News & World Report and The New Yorker.

The New Yorker was dropped this time around, Mr. Cronin said, not because of the quality of the audience but because it was not cost efficient. The magazines added last year were Dun's Review, Industry Week, Iron Age, Money, National Geographic, Psychology Today and Reader's Digest.

With the exception of inflation, which was added to the list of topics, the others remained the same: environmental quality control, governmental overregulation, international trade and imports, energy-policy problems and capital formation.

The computer, which had been fed the results of the research, has recommended the following list of publications as the most cost efficient way of reaching the swayables on environmental quality control: Money, Reader's Digest, Psychology Today, National Geographic, Smithsonian, The Wall Street Journal and the three weekly news magazines.

•

Since the intent is, as Mr. Cronin put it, to "reach the people who might influence the masses," it is surprising to find Reader's Digest on the list because it is a mass publication itself. But it is apparently efficient, according to the research. And Mr. Cronin added, "I wish we had included TV Guide."

He said that, since the advertising started in 1976, awareness of Bethlehem Steel's advertising went from 23 percent of persons interviewed to 48 percent. And in all cases the campaigns had changed public opinion, "in some cases fantastically," he said.

No. 5 in a series.

Who profits from Exxon's profits? Millions of Americans. Perhaps you.

Exxon's profits are split two ways. So far this year, 42% of our profits have been paid out in the form of dividends on Exxon common stock. The remainder was retained by Exxon, primarily to help pay for new energy projects. You may benefit from both uses of our profits:

Dividends

Millions of Americans have either a direct or indirect share in Exxon profits in the form of dividends. Beyond the 625,000 individuals who have a direct ownership in Exxon, there are 60,000 institutions such as pension funds, trust funds, colleges, foundations and insurance companies in which millions of people have a stake.

In 1979, Exxon's total dividends will give our shareholders a return of about 7% on the current price of Exxon stock.

Reinvested Profits

Over the past ten years, more than half of Exxon's profits have been reinvested in the business, primarily to develop new supplies of oil and natural gas, coal, uranium, solar power and synthetic fuels. But the amount we must spend on these projects far exceeds our profits. We make up the difference mainly by borrowing money and from money set-aside to replace worn-out facilities.

So far in 1979, Exxon's investments in the energy business have been nearly 1½ times as large as our profits — investments that will help to supply energy to millions of consumers.

EXXON

NOTES

[1] Daryl L. Bem, *Beliefs, Attitudes and Human Affairs* (Belmont, Calif.: Brooks-Cole, 1970), pp. 70, 73.

[2] Robert C. Grass, "Measuring the Effects of Corporate Advertising," *Public Relations Review* 3 (Winter 1977): 39–50.

[3] Marvin M. Gropp, "Persuasion—From Perception to Purchase," *Magazine,* Newsletter of Research, no. 30, Magazine Publishers Association (December 1979): 5.

[4] Jerry R. Lynn, Robert O. Wyatt, Janet Gaines, Robert Pearce and Bruce Vanden Bergh, "How Source Affects Response to Public Service Advertising," *Journalism Quarterly* 55 (Winter 1978): 716–717.

SELECTED BIBLIOGRAPHY

Daryl L. Bem, *Beliefs, Attitudes and Human Affairs* (Belmont, Calif.: Brooks-Cole, 1970).

Elizabeth J. Heighton and Don R. Cunningham, *Advertising in the Broadcast Media* (Belmont, Calif.: Wadsworth, 1976).

Otto Kleppner, *Advertising Procedure,* 7th ed. (Englewood Cliffs, N.J.: Prentice-Hall, 1979).

C. Robert Patty, Albert Haring and Harvey L. Vredenburg, *Selling Direct to the Consumer* (Ft. Collins, Col.: Robinson Press, 1973).

Jack Z. Sissors and E. Reynold Petray, *Advertising Media Planning* (Chicago: Crain Books, 1976).

James Playstad Wood, *Magazines in the United States,* 3d ed. (New York: Ronald Press, 1971).

10

SPEECHES AND SCRIPTS

Giving a speech is a hazardous undertaking. It's never possible to convey ideas intact. A speaker can only send messages, verbally and nonverbally, to an audience. It's the audience that gives those messages meaning.

For this reason, writing speeches and scripts demands more attention and care from the public relations writer than almost any other writing task. You can't simply write down your thoughts on a subject and expect them to be delivered successfully by any speaker. Audiences react to speakers emotionally, based on their authority, trustworthiness, tolerance and friendliness. The image of the speaker that is perceived by the audience depends on these elements, so the speechwriter must consider these factors when writing a speech. In essence, this means that the speech must be personalized. The words must go with the person—the speaker must sound natural and not as though he or she were reading cue cards. A person who is comfortable with the words being spoken will be a more credible speaker.

Sometimes PR writers give speeches themselves, and in these cases it should be easy to write a natural sounding speech. But there's more to consider than just the speaker. Whether writing for another person or for yourself, the speechwriter must have an idea of what the audience will be like. What experiences do audience members bring with them? What do they expect from the speaker? What stereotypes do they hold—that is, what are the "pictures in their heads"? If you don't know these things, you won't be able to write an effective speech.

For example, stereotypes in the minds of the audience may lead them to perceive characteristics of the speaker that aren't there. Only if you know how people will perceive the speaker can you design the message either to reinforce the stereotype or contradict it.

You need to know the language patterns of the audience as well as of the speaker, because certain words used in particular ways can send thoughts down familiar paths. Remember that connotations of words are as important as denotations. And keep in mind that meanings change with time, and that the same words mean different things in different contexts or in different parts of the country. This simply means that you can't afford to write like you talk, or like the speaker talks, without considering how the audience talks.

Words, important as they are, aren't the only thing to be concerned with. Nonverbal cues can help emphasize points or obscure them. Audiences are sensitive to body movements, gestures, facial expressions, physical appearance, and displays of personality and emotion. Effective speakers use these nonverbal expressions to hold attention and help get the message across.

SPEECHES

Many speech writers get stalled at the beginning because they fail to ask some important questions: Why was the speaker invited to address this particular group? What does that group want to hear from the speaker? What do the group members expect to hear? What do you want to accomplish by having a speech given to that particular group? How can you choose a topic that will meet your needs and the group's expectations? You have to answer these questions before you start writing.

The next two questions have to be considered together: How long a speech should it be? And what is the physical setting? A luncheon group won't tolerate as long an address as a dinner group, for example. (The people attending luncheons usually have other obligations; the people who come to dinner are making an evening of it.) Are there other speakers? Who are they and what are their topics? These last questions are especially important if the speech is part of a seminar.

Planning

After you've answered the above questions, make a list of proposed topics and begin your research. One of the best places to begin is the *Readers' Guide to Periodical Literature* (especially if the audience is a general one). You can look up the articles listed and find out what the audience might have been exposed to recently. If the audience is a specialized group, go to the publications that group members receive and find out what is being written. You'll discover their current concerns and get an idea of what the group is like.

Most speeches written for public relations purposes are informative speeches. So you will need to do research on the topic chosen, after you have determined what the audience has already been exposed to. Although you may feel you know the material well enough to write a speech in your sleep, do some library research. All of your knowledge of the topic is likely to be from an insider's point of view. You probably have seen some materials that come from competitors and critics, but look at what has appeared in the mass media. The *New York Times Index* is a good source. Most public libraries in metropolitan areas and in cities with a university have electronic research capabilities. Select your topic and have the literature searched for sources. Remember that in writing an informative speech, you are charged with offering new and valuable information to the audience, helping them understand it and helping them retain it.

Paring

If you have done your research well, you have many more ideas than you can or should introduce in a single speech. Begin paring. Cut away until you have *three* items you want to communicate.

Select the three most important ideas you want people in the audience to carry away with them. Then make sure they do by presenting the ideas as something fresh and meaningful. (It helps if the ideas can be startling, but don't fake it.) Give the listeners some way to associate these ideas with others they hold. You'll have to repeat the ideas often to be sure they are retained, but don't be redundant. You don't want the audience thinking, "You just said that a few minutes ago." You also have to introduce the ideas in a logical sequence, using relationships that aid retention. It helps if you can add some visuals when appropriate. (Injecting humor also helps people retain information, as well as breaking the pace of the presentation.)

Persuading

As you convey these ideas, keep in mind what you want to accomplish with this message. Do you want to move the audience to take some action, to do something? If so, you'd better let them know what you want them to do, how they can do it and what their rewards will be if they do. Perhaps you want to change their belief about something. Remember, a belief is acceptance of a truth, an acceptance based on experience, evidence and opinions. If you are going to try to persuade them to change a belief, you'll have to offer both logical proof and some emotional appeals.

Or you may only want to reinforce a belief. Many public relations speeches are of this nature. Give the audience reasons for retaining their belief and inform them of reference groups who also hold the belief. This will reassure your listeners that they are right in believing what they do.

Mechanics of Organization

There are three parts to a speech: introduction, body and conclusion. Contrary to what you've probably done all your life, don't write the introduction first. You wouldn't write an introduction for a speaker until you knew who the speaker was; you shouldn't write an introduction for a speech until you know what's in it.

Start out simply with a title. The title should keep the main point of the speech in the forefront of your thinking. After you have a title write your purpose: entertain, explain, convince, or motivate. Then write the three ideas you want the audience to carry away. Next, state precisely what you want the audience to do as a result of hearing the speech. You should then be able to write a conclusion.

Go back now to the three main ideas you want to convey and devise a theme to tie them together. You ought to be able to tie this theme in with the purpose of the speech. At this point, you should be ready to prepare an outline.

Begin the outline by listing the three main points on separate sheets of paper. Under each point, list the pertinent things you have gathered by your research along with what you already knew. Keep this list on the left side of the page. On the right side write a key word for an anecdote or illustration to go with each point. Now arrange all of the ideas under each point in a logical sequence, and you are ready to write.

Style

To be effective in stimulating images in the minds of the audience, you need to employ vivid words and expressive language. Be clear. Choose your words with precision. Be specific. Keep a thesaurus on hand to find the missing word. For emphasis and retention, use repetition, but use it effectively. Use transitions not just to connect thoughts, but to remind, to underscore a point by reiterating it. Check that all of your words are appropriate to the purpose of the speech, the audience and the speaker. Involve the audience by using personal pronouns and asking questions the audience must answer for themselves. Find some way to establish rapport—cite common experiences or use familiar situations and imagery, for example. Use quotations if they are not long and if they can be integrated into the ideas to give authority. Be direct. If you are ambiguous, an audience may leave wondering what you meant and come up with the wrong answer.

When you deliver the speech, support your points with a variety of timely, meaningful material. It can be audio/visual aids, statistics (not too many), detailed illustrations and hypothetical or real situations. Comparison and contrast are effective too.

After you've completed the body, go back and write an introduction. The introduction is an integral part of the speech. It should lead smoothly, logically, and directly into the body. It shouldn't look as though it had been pasted on as an afterthought. The introduction must create attention and build rapport. It should give the audience some sign of the direction the rest of the speech will take.

Various devices can be used to create an effective introduction. You can start with an anecdote or illustration to capture the audience's interest. You can use a quotation or a bright one-liner, like a startling assertion or question. You might use a suspense gimmick. A gimmick used at the beginning can be referred to throughout the speech and finally tied into the conclusion. Some speakers begin with a compliment to help establish rapport, but there is some risk in this. You could come off as patronizing. You never want to apologize for yourself or the speech. You shouldn't have to!

After the speech, be prepared for response from the audience, either formal or informal. Think of questions the audience might ask and have your answers ready—written if necessary. It's good to jot down some examples you can develop extemporaneously—provided, of course, that you are the one giving the speech! For another speaker, develop some examples and write them down for review. Take a real example if possible from his or her own background or use that background to create a story or metaphor the speaker might have thought of himself or herself to illustrate the point. Summarize the three points so you can reiterate them.

If you are giving the speech, find out all you can about the physical location so you can think of appropriate gestures. If someone else is giving the speech, you need to inform them of the physical arrangements so delivery can be rehearsed and their normal expressions developed to reinforce the message. The physical situation is extremely important. For example, very subtle gestures are lost in a large auditorium. On the other hand, the slightest movement is magnified by television cameras. Be sure you are comfortable with any visual aids or demonstrations. If you are not giving the speech, go over these carefully with the person who is. Mechanical failures can undermine both a speaker's authority and poise. Eye contact is important. Audiences don't like to be talked at. Find some people to look at and direct your message to them. Be sure they are scattered about the room so that attention doesn't seem to be focused in one spot. On the other hand, if you're facing a television camera, the audience is the red light.

SCRIPTS

Speeches, as discussed here, are presentations that a single person delivers before a live audience or an electronic one. Scripts are formats for integrating visuals such as slides or film or videotape into a presentation.

Differences and Similarities

A major difference between preparing a script and a speech is the audience consideration. A script is not tailored as specifically for a single audience, or a single event, as a speech is. Approach script planning by first determining what you want to accomplish. Then think about the various publics who might be exposed to the presentation. After you have identified these publics, make a list of what each needs to know about the subject. Now you are ready to decide how to tell the story.

Planning

List the principal ideas you want to convey with the presentation. Arrange these logically so development is easy to follow. Use a narrative approach if you can. Make a master chart of the ideas, listing under each, as you do with a speech, the points you want to make. Beside each, describe in detail how you would present the point visually. Be sure each point has these elements: something to set the scene for the idea, something to carry the action of the line of thought forward, and something to relate to a common experience with which audiences can identify.

Implementing

At this point PR paths diverge dramatically. Some PR people, because of budget pressures, shoot their own slides. Others have to scurry about to find a photographer who might be talked into donating time or talent. Or a large company with close associations might be talked into supplying the technical assistance. Large-budget operations just draw up a proposal for what is needed—slides or film, sometimes videotape—and send it to studios for bids.

The script writer has to work closely with the person preparing the visuals because the visuals tell the story. The words are just there to help. There are two ways to go about this double-track operation. One is for the writer to prepare the script and for the script to be given to the photographers to "illustrate." This often occurs because the talent comes from outside the organization and it is logical for the writer to prepare the message that needs to be told and get the appropriate visuals to go with it.

If the studio is experienced in working with writers, the photographers may function best with a series of conferences. The first would add details not in the proposal. The writer could share with the photographers the outline of points and a description of how these could be told with visuals. The photographers then develop a shooting schedule, interpreting the intent of the script in terms of shots they would make to tell the story. A conference after their shooting is complete will help ensure the compatibility of the operation.

After the first pictures are ready, another conference should be held to ensure the story is developing in a parallel way in the minds of both the writer and the photographer(s). And when the shooting is complete, the writer and photographer(s) need to see what is missing. Also at this point the strongest art should be selected. The most compelling pictures need to be arranged in the best way to tell the story. At this stage the script may have to be revised. The importance of flexibility can't be overstated—although it is sometimes difficult to be objective about finding the best way to tell the story when one's creativity is being judged.

After the art is chosen and the sequences planned, the script is ready for polishing, if it has been written. If it has not been written, you are ready to start.

Matching Words and Sights

Visuals have the power to set a mood, inject drama, explain in powerful ways. The words of the script should help the visuals to do this. Most scripts are overwritten. There are so many words that the listener does not have time to absorb the visuals through the verbiage. Allow time for the pictures to have an impact.

With slides, the question arises whether the script should carry the same information as what is being seen, perhaps on charts or graphs. It's best to handle charts as they are handled in the print media. First the textual material prepares you for the illustration by discussing it. There usually is a caption explaining the graph or chart below the illustration. In the textual matter, readers then expect to see the relationship between the illustration and the point being made explained. This same system works well in handling charts or graphs in a slide show. (See Example 10-1 for an excerpt from a slide show script.)

Writers with television writing skills adjust easily to the slide presentation. Their experience with the medium makes writing the film or videotape script a natural style. Their only difficulty sometimes is the time period. Television writers are accustomed to working with fragments of time. In a visual presentation, the time is usually about 30 minutes, but may be twice that. Giving a presentation unity and pace over that extended period makes the job quite different from that of writing an ordinary television script. (See Example 10-2 for an excerpt from a film script.)

Pace can be varied by both the script and the visuals. But it is essential in keeping audience interest to employ some of the techniques of the dramatist—suspense, dramatic foreshadowing and comic relief are a few. The script is a dialogue with the visuals—both are essential to telling the story.

CONCLUSION

Direct interaction with an audience, either in a speech or a slide presentation, brings out the best in most of us who really want to please others. Preparing material especially for audiences is the key to pleasing them. But the person preparing the material must remember that although the audience is the ultimate receiver of the information, the person presenting it is most important.

Most PR people are in the business of preparing materials for others to use. Preparing material for presentation by others is a hazardous task, but a highly creative one. PR people must be skilled in preparing material for themselves or others to give. Also, they must be able to visualize the combination of pictures and words that will accommodate messages presented with slides.

SELECTED BIBLIOGRAPHY

David K. Berlo, *The Process of Communication: An Introduction to Theory and Practice* (New York: Holt, Rinehart and Winston, 1960).

Jack G. McAuley, *People to People: Essentials of Personal and Public Communication* (Belmont, Calif.: Wadsworth, 1979).

James C. McCroskey, *An Introduction to Rhetorical Communication*, 2d ed. (Englewood Cliffs, N.J.: Prentice-Hall, 1972).

Everett Shostrom, *Man, the Manipulator* (New York: Bantam, 1968).

Rudolph F. Verderber, *The Challenge of Effective Speaking*, 4th ed. (Belmont, Calif.: Wadsworth, 1979).

10-1 EXCERPT FROM SLIDE SHOW SCRIPT

SLIDE/SOUND PRESENTATION: Safety theme for new employees

Client: McKone & Co. Advertising/Ralph Wilson Plastics Co., Temple, Texas

TIME: 12'30"

VIDEO	AUDIO
1. Opaque slide	(MODIFIED ROCK/CONTEMPORARY JAZZ...SYMBOLIC "LAS VEGAS" THEME MUSIC)
2. Begin kaleidascope effect of night shots of Las Vegas strip.	MUSIC DOWN. NARRATOR:
2a- next shot of Vegas	There is NO gambling on "safety and you"
2b- next shot of Vegas	at the Ralph Wilson Plastics Company.
2c- next shot of Vegas	
3. Overhead shot of people at craps table	There's no playing the odds... Nor is there the concept of
4. ECU of dice: a "six" and a "one." Against deep green felt background	"good luck" or
5. ECU of dice: a "snakeyes" against same background	"bad luck" when it comes to your safety and employment....
6. Super" Safety is No Accident" against machinery background at Wilson Plastics.	Because we firmly believe that "Safety is No Accident." It's no fluke...
7. Blurred shot of spinning roulette wheel	No game of chance...
	BRIEF TRANSITIONAL PAUSE. SLOWER MUSICAL TEMPO

This example, from a slide show prepared to discuss on-the-job safety, illustrates the importance of coordinating the script with the pictures.

8. Exterior LD shot of Wilson Plastics. Company sign in foreground.

9. Exec. in working area with hardhat; business suit

10. Young employee at work

11. Cartoon: Sloppy worker carrying dripping oil can. Employee behind doing "prat-fall."

12. Meeting of Safety Committee

13. Art work: Bold picture of clock. ECU. Little hand at 12 hour mark. Big hand at 12 minute mark. Shadow in between.

For the company you have just joined is dedicated to your personal safety as being the prime responsibility of each of us...
from the highest executive...
to the newest employee...
For if a single person is "unsafe"--either in attitude or behavior--then none of us really safe...
No other activity of your company is more dependent upon both individual and collective effort than is the success of our safety program...

STOP MUSIC ABRUPTLY. COMPLETE SILENCE IN BACKGROUND. PICK UP SOMBER TICKING OF CLOCK. NARRATOR IN SERIOUS MEASURED CADENCE.

This brief orientation explaining to you the vital role that safety plays here at Wilson Plastics could prove to be the most important 12 minutes you will ever spend during your career at this company.

10-2 EXCERPT FROM FILM SCRIPT

MICHAEL O'SHEA CREATIVE SERVICES
COPY • VOICE • PRODUCTION

August 25, 1980

JET EAST, INC.

DESTINATION DALLAS

                                                      (sfx pilot #1)

1) cockpit shot with blue skyline visual through windshield

                                      Love approach lear 711 whiskey delta is with you at five.

                                              (sfx tower)

2) Chaser plane / helicopter animation sequence of lear exterior panning right to left. Iris to 40% blue to blend sequence.

                                      Roger turn right to 11 zero and descend to 3,000 and report the field in sight.

                                            (sfx pilot #1)

3) animation sequence continues with lear banking slightly. from inside cockpit. Dallas in view from cockpit.

                                      Roger descending to 3 - have the field in sight.

                                                  VO

4) Quick cut, 8 VTR frame Jet East fuel truck getting ready for arrival.

                                      Dallas, the New West.. And the best in the west for corporate aircraft service, repairs, and maintenance is Jet East.

                                            (sfx pilot #1)

5) Quick cut to shot of runway through lear windshield [sfx engine idle]

                                      Love tower lear 711 whiskey delta with you four miles out, requesting 3-1 left

2.

	VO
6) 8 VTR frame Jet East line crew running, and second stage fuel trucks getting ready.	Jet East: You can see from the sky that this is a special operation. And its expansive modern facility is only the beginning.
7) cockpit view of runway sequence final approach....	
8) sequence continued 6 sec. before touch down	(sfx tower) 711 whiskey delta, cleared to land 3-1 left.
9) Touch down [sfx tires, brakes]	
	VO
10) 8 VTR line crew ready and waiting on Jet East ramp.	Jet East has rapidly become one of the nation's top FBO's and much, much more--because it has been built from day one on service...
11) overhead shot of lear taxing to Jet East 9 shot sequence or multi-media animation. [sfx taxing lear]	(sfx pilot #1) Ground, lear 711 whiskey delta off the left going to Jet East....
	VO
12) Jet east line girl viewed from cockpit giving parking instructions. [sfx engine shutdown]	Service: At Jet East it's having everything you need before you need it.

10-2, CONTINUED

3.

VO

13) fade to black...

14) fade in shot of red carpet & line crew greeting passengers from inside fuselage, door open eye level perspective.

And it's also refreshingly human hospitality and a readiness to take care of your cares right on the spot.

15) customers deboarding, shot of line girl in background with limo door open and line girl ushering gesture...Jet East logo in background.

And that of course means affording your passengers a gracious reception and courtesies far beyond the expected.

16) shot of general manager greeting lear crew, hand extended.
17) multi-media animation of hand extending further to grasp pilot's hand....
18) hand 1 sec before grasping pilot's hand......

But the basic committment of Jet East is to serve corporate pilots and the aircraft they fly.

19) quick cut to tug tow bar clamp engaging nose gear of lear jet
 [sfx clamp]

20) cut to entry of Jet East lounge door opening, general manager inviting in from eye of pilot perspective

And this Jet East does by providing its corporate customers with precisely the kind of careful quality workmanship Jet East demands for its own fleet.

21) dissolve to hanger door opening by line crew, from lear fuselage perspective.
[sfx hanger door in track]
view of hanger with several maintenance function being performed

For starters, this means that Jet East is as dedicated to professionalism on the ground as it is to safety in the air.

22) zoom in on shot # 21 with functions of hot section, nose compartment repair, autopilot repair, milling maintenance personnel.

That's why you'll find state-of-the-art equipment and up-to-the-minute professionals throughout Jet East's 85,000 square foot facility.

4.

VO

23) quick cut to same shot as 21 and 22 from angle of hanger observation window with 711 whiskey delta being towed in.	Because of these capabilities, Jet East is equipped and certified to handle virtually every kind of aircraft maintenance, service, inspection, or repair.....
24) begin zoom in to maintenance function being performed on nose compartment of lear	From general inspection, to airframe repairs, to hot sections performed by fully certified FAA personnel.
25) pan over slightly, z-in to engine hot section being performed.	Jet East is furthermore an authorized GE service center with a complete inventory of GE parts.
26) zoom out slowly and pan right to cockpit with maintenance crew member inside	
27) dissolve to interior of aircraft cockpit, z-in on avionics, (autopilot)	One of the most distinctive strengths of Jet East is its advanced avionics lab-
28) dissolve, and z-out shot of same autopilot being tested in avionics department.	a facility which Jet East designed, engineered, and built. Here all phases of avionics trouble-shooting and repair take place---with special attention
29) cut to Avionics panels, wide view of services provided, mechanics, shot left from extreme right of avionics panel containing radio test equipment.	given to autopilot repair; and with additional expertise for retrofitting and avionics installation.

10-2, CONTINUED

5.

VO

30) zoom in on radio test panel of shot # 29 (slow zoom)

Jet East is thus totally at home in the jet age: And it therefore knows that this is an industry which thrives on speed....

radio frequency set on 131.05

(sfx pilot #2)

Jet East Airinc, this lear 36 mike whiskey, We'll be on your ramp in about 20 minutes, requesting 300 a side on a quick turn.

VO

31) quick cut to shot of fuel trucks ready to meet 36 MW.
32) quick cut to shot of chalking the lear.
33) fueling the craft
34) cleaning the aircraft windshield
35) cleaning the windshield cont..

That's why you'll find no quicker turn arounds around;
From refueling, to cleaning your plane from the outside in; always with spotless equipment and material.

36) Dissolve to shot of maintenance man cleaning the interior of the plane, from the isle shot angled so as to be able to z-in over his shoulder into the cockpit..
37) match-edit of cockpit zoom with pilots in seats(so that pilots appear instantly)

In jet aviation more than anywhere else time is money; and Jet East's rapid turn arounds help you save both

(sfx pilot #2)

Ground this is lear 36 mike whiskey IFR Nashville at Jet East with x-ray.

38) cut to 36 mike whiskey runway angle take off [sfx take off]

                                                                    6.
                                           VO

39) continue 36 MW take off   But whether your stay at Jet East
sequence [sfx fade out]
40) cut to pilot's lounge with   be brief or for a few days, you'll
pilots enjoying themselves.
                                   find attention to your needs everywhere

                                   you turn--from a pilot's private

                                   lounge, large screen tv, video

41) dissolve to pilot's dining area. cassette unit, fine food,

42) dissolve to courtesy car.
                                   courtesy cars, and added assistence

                                   if you like.

42) cut to pilot's sleeping facilities And that includes handsome complementary
slow zoom to color in bedspread.
                                   quarters--for overnight or for just a

                                   quick break.

43) rack focus dissolve to matching   So Jet East is unquestionably an FBO
color stripe in Jet East aircraft.
                                   of the first rank but it's also much,
44) Cut to series of split screen dissolve
shots....   much more.

45) random dissolve Jet East facilities It's a company with 24 hour charter service
46) random dissolve, or super of
crt and aircraft.   and computerized quotations.

                                   It stands ready at all times with

47) random dissolve of cargo conversion capabilities to convert planes from

48) overlapping split screen dissolves, of passengers to cargo or to emergency
emergency vehicle conversion and loading
to represent sequential events and speed. vehicles with unrivaled speed.
(left to right progression)
49) reverse progression of split screen It has established an enviable record
dissolves depicting aircraft management.
(administrative and aircraft)   of aircraft management for numerous

                                   private and corporate clients.

10-2, CONTINUED

7.

VO

50) aerial shot of jets on Jet East's ramp z- in as if landing on the ramp by helicopter.

And it maintains its own impressive fleet of more than a dozen aircraft. For jet and turbo prop charter or backup capacity whenever needed.

51) quick cut to 711 whiskey delta's passengers deboarding the helicopter [sfx helicopter]

Jet East also means helicopter support whenever required;

52) Cut to shot of customers' wives returning in limo with Neiman Marcus bags, "Ishot J.R. t-shirts" over arms.

courtesy limosine service for your passengers.--

53) cut to pilot's eye view of catering tray being brought out to aircraft.

and gourmet catering available for every flight.

54) dissolve to shot of crew, passengers, and line crew getting ready for departure. fade to black....
55) dissolve back into engine exhaust of lear at ignition (twilight with slightly out of focus)

Jet East: It's the best in the west for corporate aviation---

56) rack focus dissolve to sun at sunset from lear climb out perspective.

A facility where pilots, planes, and passengers are treated with unsurpassed courtesy and professional care twenty-four hours a day.

(pause)

57) dissolve to Jet East building with logo lit (twilight)

So jet--to Jet East and discover the difference a company actually built on service can really mean to you....

8.

                VO

          (sfx pilot #3)

58) match edit dissolve, with logo in right hand corner, so that Jet East building fades out, pan upward

Jet East Airinc this is falcon 12 Tango X-ray, we'll be arriving on your ramp.....

        (cross fade)

to bring skyline of Dallas at twilight into view, leaving Jet East logo supered in the right hand corner over skyline.
Aerial view panning skyline, logo remaining constant.

                VO

Jet East: Whenever your destination is Dallas.

59) slow fade to black

PART THREE EXERCISES

1. Rewrite the releases given in Examples 7–2 and 7–5 to make them suitable for a daily newspaper. Tell what facts are missing or would be helpful for a complete release.

2. A state legislator decides to release to the media a staff member's position paper arguing against a proposed bill to license lay midwives. (The paper is printed as Example 14–1 on pp. 268–273.) Prepare a news release to accompany the position paper. Assume the bill was introduced in the Texas House of Representatives and that committee hearings have not yet been scheduled. Make up a name for the legislator and choose any Texas city for the legislator's district.

3. Find articles in daily newspapers about businesses or nonprofit institutions. Try to determine which of these stories originated with a news release. Choose one and rewrite it, making sure you get the most important and most interesting points in the lead.

4. Prepare a broadcast news release from Example 7–3.

5. Outline a radio series (mini-doc) from Example 14–1.

6. Prepare a brief slide script from Example 14–1.

7. Develop a slide script to recruit students to your school.

8. Write a PSA promoting your own school to potential students.

9. Check through recent issues of major newsmagazines and find an article that treats a major public issue. Using this article as a starting place, do further research and then write a 15-minute speech to be delivered at a civic club luncheon. Before you begin writing the speech, list the three major points you want the speaker to make. Assume the speaker is president of a local company whose business is affected by the issue you've chosen.

PART

FOUR

WRITING FOR SPECIAL AUDIENCES

PR's special audiences are very particular readers who expect to be known, understood and communicated with through specifically directed media.

11

ANNUAL REPORTS

Annual report writing is the most maligned, parodied and laughed at writing anywhere. Its reputation is well deserved. Annual reports contain some of the worst written English prose in existence. And that's probably why few people bother to read them. As one writer observes, the annual report "is one of the most widely published, yet least read pieces of literature in the Western world."[1] One of America's best nonfiction writers, William Zinsser, calls annual report writing "the art of obfuscation raised high."[2]

Why are annual reports so bad? Probably because of a conflict between two very important considerations—truthfulness and "looking good." On the one hand, executives want people to like their company. Management wants investors to supply the money the company needs. Management wants the stockholders, who vote at stockholder meetings, to think that management is doing a good job. On the other hand, annual reports must, by law, tell the truth. And sometimes when the truth is told in a clear, understandable way, it doesn't look so good. By being technically accurate, yet verbose and complex, an annual report can meet the letter of the law by being truthful in such a way that no one can figure out what it all means.

A federal judge once commented, "What has developed is a literary art form calculated to communicate as little of the essential information as possible while exuding an air of total candor."[3]

There are, of course, other reasons why annual report writing is so bad. Some executives demand formality in writing to make their divisions sound important. Many company presidents, for example, wouldn't think of writing a letter that just anybody could understand. Furthermore, some presidents who know nothing about writing insist on writing their letters without help (or subsequent editing) because they feel that anybody in their position must know how to write.

CLARITY VERSUS ACCURACY

Writing expert Robert Gunning points out that problems unique to the annual report contribute to its lack of clarity. The foremost problem is the need for approval from many different departments before an annual report can go to press. Everybody wants to add extra words. "The legal department, the accounting department, and all the others tend to put in a few more terms or qualifications, just to show, if nothing else, that they are on the job," writes Gunning.[4]

What's worse, some trained writers begin to anticipate these changes before they occur and write gobbledygook to begin with. "Many writers," Gunning observes, "fool themselves into believing that they are writing for the public when they are actually writing to impress the boss."[5] No accountant would fake the net income figure just to make the boss feel better, Gunning points out. Yet writers do this sort of thing all the time in annual reports.

Whatever the reasons, annual report prose invariably ends up with long sentences, long words, and many words that aren't needed at all. A National Investor Relations Institute study of executive letters in annual reports found that a good copy editor giving the letters a once-through chopped out 18 percent of the words without losing meaning.[6]

Many executives scream, though, when you start shortening sentences and cutting out vague words. "You need those words to be accurate," they say. "It won't be correct if you say it any other way." Sometimes they're right. Annual report writers must respect the expertise of an executive and be sure they know what they're writing about. The point is not to say it right *or* say it simply but to say it right *and* say it simply.

In some cases saying it right and simply won't be easy, and you'll have to spend some time on one paragraph or even one sentence. But usually the fog in annual report writing is not caused by accuracy, but by the inclusion of details that don't bear on the main point of the message. If a detail alters the essence of your point, then that detail should certainly be included. But perhaps it could be added in another sentence, or in a footnote, instead of in a third conditional clause in an already unwieldy sentence. To quote U.S. Supreme Court Justice Benjamin Cardozo, "There is an accuracy that defeats itself by the overemphasis of details. . . . The sentence may be so overloaded with all its possible qualifications that it may tumble down of its own weight."[7]

We can't indict annual reports without giving a few specific examples. Take the following paragraphs from the annual report of a major oil company:

> These various government initiatives increasing participation, royalty and tax rates, or any other similar changes in arrangements increasing government take, result in increases in cost to the Company liftings. As a result of such government actions, the cost of the major representative crudes lifted by the Company had increased by the end of the year by about $6.85 a barrel, or about 196%, over the cost of those crudes at the end of the year 1973.
>
> Costs are necessarily a major factor in pricing crude oil and products, and, accordingly, increases in costs resulting from government participation, higher posted prices, and higher tax rates have to be recovered through increased petroleum prices if, and to the extent

that, competitive conditions and regulations permit. The materiality of the adverse effects on [the Company] of participation and unsettled Mid-East conditions cannot now be predicted.

This selection scores about 22 on the Gunning fog index (see Appendix A). In other words, it's at the reading level of a fourth-year Ph.D. student. And while it might be intelligible to a professor of petroleum economics, even he or she would probably rather read the *Wall Street Journal*. The second paragraph is especially bad, for it contains no technical details to warrant such obscurity. The writer could have said:

> When the cost of obtaining oil goes up, the company must charge higher prices for oil products. Such price increases cannot, of course, exceed the amount that competition and government regulations permit. [The Company] can't predict what effect Mid-East problems will have on business.

That's not flashy writing, but it is clear.

Let's look at another example—from the chief executive's letter in the same annual report:

> The industry responded by pointing out that there are no "windfall" profits, that much of the reported profits are nonrecurring "inventory profits" and thus unavailable for capital investment, that dividend payments have not been excessive, and that higher cash generation is needed and is being used for reinvestment in projects to provide more petroleum and satisfy the environmental laws and regulations. We have some basis to believe that our messages are finally beginning to be heard.

Heard? Maybe. But probably not understood. The fog level of this piece is nearly 23. Average sentence length is more than 36 words—an appropriate sentence length for a seventeenth-century novel, but not for twentieth-century nonfiction. Most prose read by the general public today has sentences averaging 16 to 17 words in length. The clearest sentence in this piece is the last one, and it's at least eight words too long. Why not: "We think people are beginning to listen"?

Here's a typical paragraph from a company with problems:

> The drain on [the Company's] cash resources resulting from disproportionate capital contributions to [subsidiary] and working capital support for its deficits, coupled with generally higher working capital requirements of other subsidiaries resulting from higher prices, have made it necessary to restrict budgeted capital expenditures in 1975.

This paragraph has the horrendous fog count of about 30. This is what it means: The company is cutting back on its spending plans because one of its subsidiaries has gone bankrupt (and is dragging down the whole operation with it, to add a qualifying detail).

Another company is having trouble selling some worthless land it owns in the West. But thanks to a deal made with another firm, the company may be able to dump its real estate soon. How did this relatively simple fact get reported?

> We were less successful than we had hoped last year in achieving our goal of disposing of the properties of our land division, located principally in the western part of the United States. While conditions in real estate were difficult, we did conclude an important joint venture with [another company], which we expect will facilitate the disposal of our real estate assets.

No wonder people laugh about the writing in annual reports. But this situation may not last. Government regulators are getting serious about making annual reports tell the truth, plainly. Corporations forced to face their public responsibilities are finding that times are changing, and they can't cover up company shortcomings in a cloud of words. As one observer puts it, "Companies are finding out that the report must *communicate* with shareholders instead of giving them only what management wants them to see."[8]

It's easier to point out what's wrong with annual reports than to give suggestions on how to do it right. The first step, though, is easy: Follow the principles of good writing. But even following the rules of good writing isn't always enough. For annual report writing to be successful, it must be done with a purpose. And defining the purpose requires some planning before the writing begins. After all, an annual report is "the most expensive, time-consuming, sensitive and important document that a corporate public relations . . . officer will be called upon to execute in the course of any given year."[9] It only makes sense that such an important task should be done with a plan, and done right.

PLANNING THE ANNUAL REPORT

Although our main concern here is writing, the annual report editor should never forget that the report is a publication much like a magazine. It takes careful planning to produce a unified product. Illustrations, pictures, design and writing must all mesh if communication is to be effective. Graphs and charts, photographs, type face and layout are all important.

But before the annual report editor decides on a format, chooses type, or begins to write, it is necessary to establish the report's purpose.

Purpose

The fundamental purpose of most annual reports is to provide investors with financial data and a description of the company's operations. But annual reports can do much more than that, and good ones do. Not only can the report tell the company story to investors, it can also be used to present the company's views to many other audiences—the media, community leaders, and employees, for example. No law says that annual reports must be sent only to stockholders.

Thus, the first step in annual report planning is answering the question: What should the annual report accomplish? Is the report's purpose to comfort investors, sell stock, or paint a glowing picture of the company in order to attract new customers or employees? Is the purpose merely to maintain good employee or investor relations? Will the report be used to convey the company's viewpoint on key issues to community leaders and the media?

Obviously the purpose is closely related to the audience. Whatever you want to say, you must know who will be reading the report so you can tailor your message to them. Stage two of annual report planning, then, is defining the audience.

Audience

In most cases, annual reports *are* written for stockholders, but stockholders are never the only audience and sometimes they aren't even the most important audience. Some companies, for example (such as those owned by holding companies) don't sell stock directly to the public. Annual reports for these firms might be directed to an entirely different audience—perhaps employees or legislators.

As with any piece of writing, then, it is important to define who the audience—or in this case audiences—is. You must also establish the relative importance of the various audiences. Among the possible audiences to consider are:

   Stockholders
   Potential stockholders
   Stockbrokers
   Financial analysts
   Employees
   Customers
   Potential customers
   Suppliers
   Legislators
   Regulators
   Reporters and business editors
   Editorial writers
   Community leaders
   Consumer advocates
   Educators

Various institutions may have other audiences to add to the list.

Before writing the report, list all the possible audiences. Then identify which audiences are most important. (A questionnaire to company executives, asking them to rate the importance of reaching each audience with the annual report, might accomplish this.) Direct the report's narrative to the most important audiences, but don't neglect the views of other possible audiences. Even if the report is sent only to stockholders, members of other groups may also read it. The writer must keep in mind, for example, that some stockholders are also employees. It would not help employee relations to stress how well your firm is holding costs down by paying low salaries.

WRITING THE REPORT

Once purpose is established and audience priorities set, the annual report writer can begin compiling information to be used in the report. The first question at this stage involves content: What features should the report contain?

Determining Content

Determining content is the biggest problem in writing annual reports. In probably no other writing job is determining content so difficult. An individual writer, composing a piece on a single topic, merely gathers information, decides what to say, and then says it. An annual report writer, however, must please many people while trying to present a true and complete picture of a multifaceted corporation or institution.

Fortunately, there are some guidelines to content, such as government rules specifying certain items that must be included (see Appendix B). Some of the essentials, either required by law or generally demanded by the investment community, are:

Financial summary
Letter from the chief executive
Narrative section describing operations
Balance sheet and income statement
Statement of sources and use of funds
Notes to financial statement
Auditor's statement
Ten-year statistical summary

Most of these are simply tables of numbers and aren't of immediate concern to the writer. Accountants supply the numbers; writers supply the words. Providing the words usually means writing the chief executive's letter and the narrative section of the report.

Executive's Letter In preparing the executive's letter, the writer must first meet with the chief executive and find out how he or she wants the letter written. Sometimes the executive will write a letter and turn it over to the writer for editing. Sometimes it works the other way around. In other cases the writer interviews the executive and then prepares a letter based on the executive's responses. Any of the procedures is acceptable as long as a good letter results.

What makes a good letter? There's no agreement on this—or even on what the letter should contain. Some simply summarize the year's financial results. Others ignore money and talk about the social problems facing the company and its industry. Many try to combine financial results and social commentary into a lengthy treatise designed to convince everybody that things are better than they seem. In different circumstances, different types of letters are appropriate.

The annual reports rated highest by financial analysts, however, usually contain letters adhering to a few basic principles. The best letters don't delve too deeply into money matters. Letters crowded with financial statistics aren't very readable. Except for brief mention of key results, the numbers are best left to the charts and tables. Brevity is another mark of a good letter. A brief letter that sums up the story is preferable to a lengthy dissertation that attempts to cover every aspect of the company's performance. Also, analysts generally expect a president's letter to discuss the past year and indicate expectations for the future of the business—including future problems as well as future successes.

In any event, the letter sets the stage for the rest of the report. It should in some way introduce the main body of the report, or narrative, where the company's operations are described in detail. (See Example 11-1.)

Narrative The body of the annual report is where the writer tells the company's story. This section includes a general description of the company or institution, its purpose, products, location and activities. The narrative reports the results of the past year and the plans for the future. All events, management decisions, sales, mergers and conditions having a significant effect on the company's operation should be disclosed and discussed.

At the same time, the narrative must also achieve the communications objectives set for it at the beginning of the planning process. If the report's purpose is to get people to buy stock, then the narrative must give the reasons why the company's stock is a good deal. It does this not in terms of dollars and cents, of course, but by describing the company's position, management philosophy, and record for success or foresight.

Most annual report narratives also cover things like plans for expansion, research and development programs, and the nature of the firm's customers or markets. But merely presenting basics like these isn't enough. Financial analysts want information on the problems facing the company and its industry, and a discussion of current economic conditions and their impact. As an Opinion Research Corporation survey of analysts discovered:[10]

> Analysts, in fact, are critical of companies that do not make some attempt to put their own strategy and plans into some industry perspective and historical context.... Analysts indicate a strong interest in how companies deal with general social and economic problems affecting their company or industry, as well as the impact of government regulation of their industry, another major theme in top-rated reports.

Thus, you should not attempt to write an annual report narrative that makes your firm appear to be a great company with no problems that is making more and more money every year. Discuss your company's problems frankly—then show that your company has a plan to solve them. Discuss the natural resources the company depends on, the possibility of shortages, and how the company will cope with them. Describe the advertising/marketing/public relations strategies that have been designed to communicate your firm's goals and objectives. Tell how the firm is responding to demands for corporate responsibility. These things belong in annual reports just as much as the bottom line figures of the income statement. (See Example 11-2.)

Inevitably, however, the annual report writer who sets out to include all these things faces the problem of lack of space. Something has to be left out. How do you decide what? First, check with the company's lawyers. They will point out certain things that *must* be included to satisfy government reporting requirements. Such items might include significant legal action the company is involved in or major financial transactions. Next, try to include things that most stockholders and analysts expect: financing, capital expenditures, consolidations, research, marketing, and energy supply, to name a few.

Choosing specific events to include in each category is more difficult. One approach is to go to the executives in charge of various company divisions and ask them what the most important events or actions of the past year are. This personal interview technique is used frequently; in fact annual reports have sometimes simply printed interviews with division heads verbatim—in a question-and-answer format—to cover those segments of the company's operations. If done well, such interviews can provide the necessary information. Note, however, that a survey of stockholders by Northern States Power Company found reaction to such interviews overwhelmingly negative.[11] Don't let this stop you from doing interviews, but keep in mind that the most valuable function of such interviews may be providing raw information.

Another approach to gathering information from executives is through a written questionnaire. A simple survey form can often help the writer get the information he or she needs to gauge the relative importance of different topics—and thereby decide what to put in and what to leave out.

11-1 CHIEF EXECUTIVE'S LETTER, EXXON CORPORATION 1974 ANNUAL REPORT

TO THE SHAREHOLDERS

For well over a year now, the world has been passing through a period of intense economic dislocation. In a search for historical guideposts, some observers see parallels with the excesses of the 1920s and the difficulties of the 1930s. We do not share their pessimism.

Better analogies might be drawn with the years immediately following World War II when the rebuilding of the world's economy was marked by inflation, unemployment, controls, distortions of supply and demand, and concern about the will of governments to work together for the common good. Eventually, the forces contributing to economic dislocation were brought under control and a long period of relative prosperity and stability emerged.

Today, unlike the period after World War II, energy considerations are so pervasive that there is a tendency to view all economic problems as being energy-related. While this view oversimplifies the situation, the relationship of rapidly rising energy costs to inflation and recession and the adequacy and security of the industrial world's energy supplies are rightly matters of compelling national and international concern. We are therefore taking this opportunity to state our views on the major changes taking place in the world which bear upon your investment in Exxon.

Most producing nations are moving to increase their control of oil and gas resources, although the methods used to attain this objective, the pace of implementation, and the actual ultimate degree of state ownership may differ from country to country. They are also using price mechanisms, taxes, royalties and production rates to further their national interests; the member nations of the Organization of Petroleum Exporting Countries (OPEC), for example, have increased their revenues from crude oil from 2.5 cents per gallon to 24 cents per gallon in four years. Despite such trends, we see no indication that any major producing country is about to eliminate private companies from the scene altogether. Quite the contrary. Companies like Exxon have the extensive and complex logistical systems needed to move petroleum into world markets and to distribute it to consumers. We have the technical and managerial skills backed by the research and development capabilities which these countries will need to develop their resources further. So we believe that there is a sound basis for continued relationships between producing countries and the industry, though the relationships will be different from those which existed when the companies were discovering and developing the oil and gas reserves from which those countries now derive their economic power. And in other parts of the world, the companies' exploration and production skills will be needed by countries where geological indications are favorable and petroleum development is just beginning.

Consuming countries are understandably concerned about ensuring themselves a steady supply of oil and gas. Some, as a matter of policy, are already favoring their own national oil companies as the instruments for bringing this about. Some may go a step further and attempt to conclude government-to-government supply arrangements with producing nations, but once again we see no indication that any major consuming country is about to eliminate private companies from the scene. For one thing, they recognize the risk that such bilateral arrangements may have ramifications which are more political than economic. Moreover, companies like Exxon have the terminals, refineries, pipelines and marketing facilities necessary to handle large volumes of petroleum economically and efficiently. We have the flexibility to cushion the normal imbalances which have always characterized the international oil business. Consuming countries also realize that there is a role for private companies within their borders which cannot be efficiently assumed by governments or agencies of government, a role which serves their national interests by the spur of competition it provides.

Conservation in the use of energy and an expansion of energy supplies are both essential if the world is to bring into balance some of the forces which are contributing to its present economic difficulties. Each of us can do something, in small and personal ways, to reduce our use of energy, whether in the form of electricity, heat or gasoline; on page 18 we describe the steps which Exxon has taken during

---

The executive's letter in an annual report can make a clear statement on important issues facing a company and its industry. In this annual report letter, Exxon made a straightforward presentation of its views on the international energy situation.

J. K. Jamieson, Chairman   *C. C. Garvin, Jr., President*

the past year to reduce consumption in its own operations. A major portion of the Review of Operations which follows is an accounting of the efforts we are making to discover and produce new supplies of oil and gas in many different parts of the world, to develop our coal and uranium reserves in the United States and find new reserves elsewhere, and, through research, to develop the technology necessary to make other sources of energy available.

Such efforts will take time and enormous amounts of money. Last year alone, we spent more than $3.6 billion on capital investments and exploration, 51 percent of it to find and develop new oil, gas and other energy supplies. Over the next four years we expect our outlays to total at least $17 billion.

These record expenditures reflect the basic change in the economics of finding and producing petroleum. As traditional producing areas have been more intensively explored, the search for major new petroleum deposits has necessarily been extended to deeper offshore waters, into the Arctic and to other regions where oil operations are inherently more expensive. There has also been a significant increase in the cost of leases which guarantee no more than the right to explore for petroleum on the leased acreage and to develop it. Increasingly, oil ventures are massive, complex projects which may take five years or more to produce any return on the sizable investments required. In the North Sea, for example, each daily barrel of producing capacity developed by the oil companies will require a capital investment of $5,000 to $7,000 for most of the fields, in contrast to capital expenditures of $500 to $700 per daily barrel in the vast, accessible producing areas of the Middle East.

Moreover, the escalating cost of labor, materials and services affects Exxon like everyone else. Adequate returns on our existing assets are essential if we are to generate funds for these more costly new investments. Only in the last two years—but not for a decade before then—have the oil industry and Exxon earned returns which could be characterized as adequate in this context. As shareholders, you have a vital stake in our ability to sustain earnings at acceptable levels in order to generate funds for reinvestment, to pay dividends to you, and to raise additional money in capital markets on favorable terms.

The role of governments in energy matters is an issue currently being debated in virtually every nation in the world. Even though it includes criticisms of companies like Exxon which are all too often based on misconceptions, active debate is understandable and desirable, for this is how national policies are developed in free societies. We need coherent energy policies here in the United States and in other countries. We need them soon. There is a danger, however, that political leaders will be tempted to advocate measures which in their simplicity have a great public appeal but which, if enacted, would only exacerbate the very problems they are designed to solve. Legislation—indeed, the threat of legislation—which casts doubt on the ability of companies to earn adequate rates of return on their present and future investments will be a deterrent to the vigorous development of energy supplies.

If we keep in mind the objective of expanding energy supplies, there will be plenty of room for constructive discussion on how best to achieve it. We still need greater understanding, a greater sense of common purpose, and the will to meet complex problems with unavoidably complex solutions. There will be honest differences of opinion in and between governments, the industry, and societies in general as to what to do. But we believe that the shock of recognition has passed and that all industrial nations have now begun a coordinated effort, both domestically and internationally, to conserve the use of energy and expand its supply. We intend to do all we can to help.

FOR THE BOARD OF DIRECTORS
March 3, 1975

J. K. JAMIESON, *Chairman*

C. C. GARVIN, JR., *President*

11-2 THE 1979 ANNUAL REPORT OF ARMSTRONG WORLD INDUSTRIES, INC.

1979 in Review

Armstrong is primarily a manufacturer and marketer of interior furnishings. Its products for The Indoor World include floor coverings (resilient flooring and carpets), ceiling systems, and furniture. Armstrong people also make and market a variety of specialty products for the building, automotive, textile, and other industries—an important part of Armstrong's business.

The next few pages present a review of how major Armstrong products performed during 1979, along with some statements about other developments of special significance for the Company's progress during last year and in the future.

Floor coverings

The year 1979 presented a variety of challenges within the floor coverings segment of the Company's worldwide business. Operating profit was affected by sizable new-product development costs, production cost variances and start-up costs in some areas, and inflationary costs that could not be fully recovered through price increases. Sales of Armstrong floor coverings maintained a high level, despite the failure of certain markets to retain their strength throughout the year.

In the resilient flooring portion of the floor covering business in North America, the trademark "Solarian" was extended in the spring of 1979 to apply to all of the Armstrong Mirabond no-wax flooring products. With this extension, Sundial Solarian and Premier Sundial Solarian sheet floorings were included in Armstrong's assortment of Solarian no-wax flooring materials. Consumers have responded favorably to the widened family of products bearing both the Armstrong and Solarian names.

The Interflex system of resilient sheet flooring installation, pioneered with the introduction of Tredway Vinyl Corlon in the mid-1970s, continued to gain in popularity, especially in residential construction. Many do-it-yourself customers also welcomed its easier and faster installation, since this type of resilient flooring needs no attachment to the subfloor except at seams and at the edges. The Interflex system, which also is applicable to Premier Sundial Solarian flooring, permits installation over particleboard underlayment and facilitates installation over other surfaces.

The most notable resilient floor product introduced in North America during 1979, Solarian Supreme flooring, combines the installation advantages of Interflex with the no-wax features of the Mirabond surface. It also offers inlaid construction and unprecedented styling opportunities. A high-fashion resilient sheet flooring introduced to retailers in the fall, it represents Armstrong's "top of the line." Although it is at the high end of the resilient flooring price scale, the quality features it offers have met with an excellent response from retailers and consumers. Solarian Supreme's designs make it especially appropriate for use in areas of the home in which resilient flooring has not traditionally been popular.

Consumers and retailers responding strongly to new "top of the line" no-wax Solarian Supreme flooring

The year also saw the expansion of Armstrong Mirabond no-wax tile selection with the introduction of Custom Solarian Tile in the spring and of Royal Solarian Tile during the summer. These resilient tile flooring products offer the consumer greatly improved styling at two price levels.

Early in 1979, a new commercial Vinyl Corlon sheet material was introduced, responding to the current design needs of architects and interior designers. It is Sandoval flooring, offering a terrazzo-like styling specifically for use in commercial and institutional interiors.

The do-it-yourself area continued strong for Armstrong products—led by Stylistik Vinyl Tile, a product introduced in 1977 that gained significant consumer acceptance as it replaced other more traditional types of flooring tile. This product's initial popularity required its being placed on allocation in its first year. To meet demand for Stylistik, the Company expanded production capability at its Kankakee, Illinois, factory. The new production line began producing at full capacity during the past summer, approximately doubling Stylistik production capacity and enabling Armstrong to offer improved delivery to its customers.

In the carpet portion of the business, a most significant event during 1979 was the inauguration of the

5

Armstrong's annual report narrative begins with a straightforward description of the company and its products and goes on to discuss results of the past year in the company's different areas of operations. Note the company's own description of the narrative section, provided in a "special edition" of

CHAPTER 11
ANNUAL REPORTS

Armstrong

1979 Annual Report
Special Edition

The Annual Report

- What it is
- Why it is published
- What you can find in it

An annual report is an accounting of financial stewardship, given each year by the managers of a company to those who have invested in the company's stock.

That was and is the essential purpose of such reports. But their scope has expanded. Companies, as well as the stockholding public, have grown in size and complexity. Public interest in business, as well as the public effects of business decisions, has broadened.

So the annual report today is usually much more than tables of figures. It describes the company—its performance, objectives, opportunities—to the world in which it operates. In addition to stockholders, that world includes employees, customers, suppliers, government officials and agencies, financial analysts, citizens of communities where the company does business, and others.

Financial Highlights (page 1)

As the term suggests, financial highlights give the reader a quick idea of how the company fared last year in comparison with the year before.

Some brief comments on the categories:

Net sales. This gives the dollar value of all the goods and services the company has sold to customers during the year, as described on page 23.

Net earnings. This is profit after taxes. It is what you want to know when you ask, "How much did the company make last year?" For this reason, the net earnings (or net loss) figure is one of the most important in any company's annual report.

Net earnings can be defined as what the company has left after deducting from its income all the costs and expenses, including income taxes, that went into producing the goods and services it sold. Another way to look at profits is to regard them as a return on investment earned by a customer-serving business. Seen in this light, it is clear that the profits earned by a successful business arise from the satisfying of customers' needs and wants. Out of a company's earnings come the dividends paid to its owners (shareholders) and the funds reinvested to maintain, strengthen, and expand its operations. Other groups also benefit from these profits. Generally, when earnings increase, a company is able to offer improved products and services to consumers, provide better jobs and greater job security for employees, and pay increased taxes for the support of government.

As % of sales. The ratio of net earnings to sales, expressed as a percentage, is one of several ways that investors can judge a company's performance, especially in relation to other companies in its industry.

As % of common stockholders' equity. The ratio of net earnings to the share of the equity belonging to holders of common stock is another measurement investors can use to judge a company's performance.

Total stockholders' equity. This can be described as how much the stockholders—the owners of the company—have put into the company from time to time. It includes not only their initial investment but also the funds that have

the report designed to help students and others understand more about an annual report's contents.

11-2, CONTINUED

Financial Highlights

	1979	1978
	(000)	(000)
Net sales	$1,341,067	$1,244,065
Net earnings (1)	66,044	61,132
As % of sales	4.9%	4.9%
Applicable to common stock as % of average common stockholders' equity	12.0%	11.7%
Total stockholders' equity	$ 567,657	$ 546,824
Common stockholders' equity	555,517	534,684
Capital additions	56,076	43,749
Per share of common stock:		
Net earnings	$ 2.58	$ 2.36
Dividends paid	1.075	1.00

(1) Includes after-tax unrealized exchange losses of $5.5 million in 1979 and $5.0 million in 1978.

Worldwide Net Sales by Industry Segments

	1975	1976	1977	1978	1979
Floor Coverings	59%	60%	59%	57%	54%
Ceilings	19%	18%	18%	19%	21%
Furniture	13%	13%	13%	15%	15%
Industry Products and Other	9%	9%	10%	9%	10%

Worldwide Operating Profit* by Industry Segments

*Earnings before general corporate expenses, interest expense, certain foreign exchange items, and taxes on income.

	1979	1978	1977	1976	1975
Floor Coverings	54%	65%	68%	68%	74%
Ceilings	23%	19%	16%	14%	13%
Furniture	6%	2%	1%	4%	3%
Industry Products and Other	17%	14%	15%	14%	10%

1

The opening page of the Armstrong Cork Report gives a table of contents, financial highlights, and graphs showing sales and income of the company's main divisions.

The simplest questionnaire merely asks executives to rate the importance of a few key areas. Such a form might look like this:

In Column A, rank the areas in which the company has achieved the greatest successes during the past year (1 = greatest success). In Column B, rank the areas in which the company has experienced the greatest problems in the past year (1 = greatest problem).

A		B
____	Marketing and sales	____
____	New product development	____
____	Employee relations	____
____	Community relations	____
____	Stockholder relations	____
____	Government relations	____
____	Energy supply	____
____	Public information	____
____	Customer service	____
____	Other: _____	____

To meet the needs of any given situation, categories can be added or deleted. In addition, space can be given for comments or observations about the problems or successes designated most important. A more extensive questionnaire can be given if the writer wants more detailed information. A series of short answer questions, for example, such as those in Table 11-3, might elicit more useful responses.

Responses to questionnaires like these will help the writer choose topics to include in the annual report. But the writer should never rely on such surveys exclusively. If your own research shows that something else is important, and should be in the annual report, don't leave it out simply because it didn't appear on the survey forms. Put it in—and be prepared to show why it's there.

Theme

Once you decide on content, you have to put the report together in a cohesive way. You want the company to appear to be a well-managed, well-organized, unified institution. The annual report should mirror these qualities, from cover to cover.

The best way to ensure cohesiveness is to find a theme, a central point that the various parts of the report can relate to. You may focus the report on a single outstanding problem facing your company's industry, or on a major event that affected your business. A new product can supply a theme, too, especially if it signifies a new direction for your company.

11-3   ANNUAL REPORT QUESTIONNAIRE FOR EXECUTIVES

1. Inside the company, what do you think was the most significant event of the past year?
2. Outside the company, what event of the past year do you think had the most significant impact on the company?
3. What event of the past year had the most significant impact on our company's industry?
4. What was the most important event or development in your division of the company during the past year?
5. What do you believe was the most significant accomplishment of your division of the company during the past year?
6. What do you believe was the most significant accomplishment of the company as a whole during the past year?
7. What do you believe to be the most important problem facing your division of the company?
8. What do you believe to be the most significant problem facing the company as a whole?
9. What do you believe to be the most important problem facing this company's industry?
10. What are the most significant things the company is doing to deal with these problems?

Style

After all else, you have to consider the preparation of the final draft and the polishing of the writing style. A major question about style is how formal the report should be. Many annual report writers, and most corporate executives, might object that the informal style advocated by readability experts like Flesch and Gunning is not appropriate for so serious a document as an annual report. And it's true that writing style must be appropriate for the document and the audience.

In practice, though, neither the document nor the audience determines style. Style is part of what you want to say. If your company wants to portray itself as a friendly, informal neighborhood firm eager to do business with just plain folks, then stilted and stuffy writing is as inappropriate in an annual report as it is in TV advertising. A firm wishing to be viewed as formal and sophisticated could reasonably be expected to employ formal writing, with few contractions and less humor, in its annual report.

In any event, formality is no excuse for fog. A formal report can still be readable. No company likes to be thought of as complex and confusing. And no company wants to give the impression that nobody in the business can think clearly enough to say something understandable. Many people have made the observation that fuzzy writing is a sign of fuzzy thinking. Annual report writers should keep that in mind. (And they should pass the word on to company lawyers.)

Frequently, the ultimate wording of an annual report is determined only after a clash between writer and lawyer. In matters of law, the lawyers should have the last word, of course. But too often the lawyer is given the last word, period—even regarding writing style. Gunning points out that this works to the detriment of clarity, since lawyers have a vested interest in complexity. "If a man draws a document that only he can interpret," Gunning writes, "he has built himself a degree of security. He must be retained to interpret it."[12]

Of course, lawyers wouldn't all lose their jobs if writing became understandable, and certainly there are lawyers who don't intentionally confuse things. But most lawyers aren't trained in the art of written communication and simply aren't very good at it. When it comes to style, the professional writer should have the last word.

One annual report critic summed it up rather well: "I don't know whether it would be better for PR men to redraft what the lawyers have written, or for the lawyers to review the work product of the communication expert, but I do know that we must do a better job of telling the company's story—good or bad—if the purpose of the securities laws are to be fulfilled."[13]

11-4 ANNUAL REPORT TIMETABLE

This is a sample production timetable for the annual report of a company whose regulatory agencies require a copy of the report by March 31.

September (previous year): Begin preliminary planning.

October: Send questionnaires to company executives. Compile research from company publications and other sources on events of the year.

November: Interview executives. Decide on theme and approach. Begin cover design. Collect photographs and assign additional needed photographs to the photographer. Begin production of charts and graphs and other artwork.

December: Begin writing preliminary draft of chief executive's letter and narrative. Complete photographs and artwork, except for financial charts.

January: Circulate draft of narrative for review by various company departments. Begin layout and design. Revise draft of chief executive's letter and narrative as required.

February: Circulate final draft of letter and narrative for approval by executives, lawyers, auditors and other company departments. Make final corrections. Complete layout and design. Have type set on narrative, letter and financial tables (if available). Deliver camera-ready copy to printer by end of the month.

March: Review proofs provided by printer. Make final corrections.

CONCLUSION

Annual reports are often foggy and confusing, partly because companies fear that a clear, understandable description of their operations might reveal their weaknesses.

Today, companies are under more and more pressure to produce annual reports that are readable. By making them readable, companies may find that annual reports can be a valuable part of an overall communications program—but they also have to be carefully planned (see Table 11-4) and well written.

NOTES

[1] Joseph Graves, "Critical Questions and Honest Answers: Spice for Effective Annual Reports," *Public Relations Journal* 33 (September 1977): 17.

[2] William Zinsser, *On Writing Well* (New York: Harper and Row, 1976), p. 139.

[3] Darrell Luery, "Keeping a Finger on the Public Pulse and the Corporate Thumb Off the Scale," *Public Relations Journal* 28 (February 1972): 15.

[4] Robert Gunning, *The Technique of Clear Writing* (New York: McGraw-Hill, 1968), p. 227.

[5] Ibid., p. 227.

[6] Robert Mayall, "Sensitizing Your Management to the Needs of the Annual Report," *Public Relations Journal* 33 (September 1977): 16.

[7] Rudolf Flesch, *The Art of Readable Writing*, 25th anniversary ed. (New York: Harper and Row, 1974), p. 135.

[8] Peg Dardenne, "Emerging Trends in Annual Reports," *Public Relations Journal* 33 (September 1977): 8.

[9] Mayall, "Sensitizing Your Management," p. 13.

[10] Opinion Research Corporation, "Guidelines for Communicating Effectively with the Investment World," October 1975, p. 6.

[11] Leo Northart, "Editor's Notebook," *Public Relations Journal* 33 (September 1977): 6.

[12] Gunning, *Technique of Clear Writing*, p. 244.

[13] Luery, "Keeping a Finger on the Public Pulse," p. 16.

SELECTED BIBLIOGRAPHY

Peg Dardenne, "Emerging Trends in Annual Reports," *Public Relations Journal* 33 (September 1977): 8 and 48.

Joseph J. Graves, "Critical Questions and Honest Answers: Spice for Effective Annual Reports," *Public Relations Journal* 33 (September 1977): 17–18.

Robert Gunning, *The Technique of Clear Writing*, rev. ed. (New York: McGraw-Hill, 1968).

Darrell Luery, "Keeping a Finger on the Public Pulse and the Corporate Thumb Off the Scale," *Public Relations Journal* 28 (February 1972): 14–16, 45–46.

Robert L. Mayall, "Sensitizing Your Management to the Needs of the Annual Report," *Public Relations Journal* 33 (September 1977): 12–16.

Leo J. Northart, "Editor's Notebook, *Public Relations Journal* 33 (September 1977): 6.

Opinion Research Corporation, "Guidelines for Communicating Effectively with the Investment World," October 1975.

12

MAGAZINES AND EMPLOYEE PUBLICATIONS

Magazines can be a powerful public relations tool. They allow greater depth of treatment than most other media, permit more vivid and attractive display, and enable writers to compose a message for a specific target audience.

Sometimes that audience is internal—when a magazine is published for the employees of an institution, for example. Sometimes it is external, as with magazines like EXXON USA that go to the media and to community leaders. By one estimate more than 10,000 public relations magazines are published in the United States.

The success of such publications is determined in part by format, illustrations and design, editing, and proper distribution. But the most important element of any magazine is the writing—its quality, its relevance, its appropriateness for the target audience. The slickest looking magazine will not be successful—that is, it won't communicate ideas—without well-written articles.

TOPICS

When you start to write a magazine article, you need to have a topic in mind. Occasionally, topics are predetermined for you by your superiors. But more often than not, the writer is responsible for article ideas.

Finding Topics

If you know your readers, and know what's important to them, certain topics will suggest themselves automatically. But such flashes of insight may not fill every issue. Fortunately, therefore, you can turn to many other sources for article ideas.

Public opinion surveys, for example, can tell you what's on the minds of various groups of people. This is a clue to the kinds of articles they'd be interested in reading. Newspapers and newsletters can also give you article ideas. Frequently a three-paragraph short buried in the back pages of the daily paper can be developed into an interesting full-length magazine article if properly pursued. You can get ideas also from the trade and technical journals that serve your industry. Even conversations with people inside the company, or in other organizations, can reveal new developments that will interest your readers.

Evaluating Topics

Finding ideas for articles isn't that difficult. The hard part is separating the good ideas from the bad. Once you get an idea for an article, you must evaluate it by considering two things: reader interest and reader consequence.

Reader Interest The first question to ask about a topic is: Will the audience be interested? You have to know who you're writing for—their interests, their likes and dislikes, their predispositions. Are you writing for unskilled employees with less than a high school education? Are you writing for business leaders who are intensely concerned about the state of the economy? Is your magazine aimed at consumer advocates, government regulators, university professors? Unless you know who your audience is, you won't be very successful in evaluating article ideas. If you print articles on topics that don't interest the readers, you're wasting ink.

Consequence In addition to being interesting to your audience, the article must also have "consequence" for the reader—that is, it must be about something that affects his or her life in some way.

Some topics, of course, that don't interest your readers might be critically important, whether the readers know it or not. In this case, write the article, but do it so the importance of the article is made clear.

Angle

Sometimes, making clear the importance of a topic is not easy. Readers may not recognize immediately, for example, that an article has consequence for them. You have to grab the readers' attention and draw them into the story by informing them, at the outset, that there is some point to the article. That is, you must tell the story with a specific approach, called the *angle* or *slant*. The angle must hook readers, get them interested, and lead naturally into the main topic of the article.

It is very difficult to write a good article without a good angle. Magazine articles can't simply be "about" something. An article that is merely "about" federal regulations doesn't sound too interesting. But an article with an angle such as "federal regulations are costing you money every day" immediately gets the readers involved with a subject that is of concern to them—their pocketbooks.

Or consider the writer preparing an article for a university magazine on research in the biology department. Several biology professors were collaborating on a research project on Asian clams. The topic "Asian clams" was considerably more specific than the topic "research in the biology department," but it still didn't provide an angle. After interviewing the biologists, though, the writer found that the clams reproduced at a rapid rate, and were becoming so populous that they threatened to block certain waterways such as irrigation ditches and industrial water pipes. Here was an angle: Small clams the size of a half dollar threatened to disrupt the water supply of giant industries. Notice that the writer didn't come up with this angle immediately. First came the general topic. The specific angle required research.

RESEARCH

Once you choose a general topic for an article, you have to research it. Research must come early—before you start writing and before you have a firm idea of what you want to say. If you already have a conclusion in mind, your research is bound to be selective, and you may ignore information that doesn't support your case. The result will be an article that is one-sided and probably inaccurate—and therefore not very effective.*

Research techniques for writing magazine articles are similar to the general techniques of PR research (see Chapter 3). But there are a few steps basic to article research that it always helps to follow.

Background Research

First, you should do general background research on the topic. You may already know a lot about your subject. If you don't, however, find out how your topic fits into the overall scheme of things. An article about inflation, for example, requires some general knowledge of economics.

Next, become more specific—narrow your research down to the topic of your article. You should check the *Readers' Guide to Periodical Literature* (or other appropriate bibliographies) to find out what has

---

*This isn't to say that your article shouldn't make a point, or that it shouldn't come down on one side of an issue or the other. Most articles in PR magazines should and do take one side. But you still must research the subject first to decide precisely what position you should take, and to find out whether the position you *want* to take can be supported by the evidence. If a preordained conclusion leads you to ignore certain information in the course of your research, the article will fail to address important points on the other side of the question. And, as the findings reported in Chapter 2 have shown, writing that deals only with one side of an issue is not likely, in most cases, to be very persuasive.

been written on the topic recently (as with speeches—see Chapter 10). Reviewing these articles will give you helpful background on the topic, and also tell you what your audience has been reading on the subject (assuming that you know which magazines they read—and you should). For example, if your audience includes university science professors you know they probably read *Science*. Ministers probably read *The Christian Century*. You need to know what your audience reads so you can avoid duplicating what is now old news. Offer them something new, something they haven't read before.

After reviewing what your audience has probably read, go on to what they probably haven't read—technical and trade journals, limited circulation newsletters, or government documents, for example. Compile from these sources the facts and figures you will need to build your article.

Pay special attention to figures. The right statistics here or there can help an article tremendously, and if you don't write them down when you come across them you'll have trouble finding them later. It's hard to know ahead of time which statistics you'll need, so keep all you find that are possibly relevant.

At this stage you are probably ready to form some possible approaches to the article. Try to find angles that haven't been explored in publications to date. Once you've arrived at some tentative angles, focus your research to gather specific material on those aspects of the topic. When you have enough material to decide on the best angle, you're ready for step two of the research process: interviewing.

Interviewing

Some of the best material for an article will come from interviews with experts on the topic. They not only provide additional information and insight, but they can also give you the direct quotations and anecdotes you need to bring a dull article to life.

In most PR settings, there are experts within your organization you can call on for information. Occasionally you might need to call an outside expert, like a university professor. Or, for example, if you're writing about federal regulations, you might want to call one of the regulators.

There are a few basic interviewing guidelines you should follow whether you're talking to someone inside or outside your organization. If possible, let the person know ahead of time what you want to talk about. Give him or her a chance to prepare, especially if you will be asking specific questions that might require a little research. Make sure you ask all the important questions you have on specific points, but be sure to give the person an opportunity to expand on the answers or to talk about things you hadn't thought to ask. It's not a bad idea to use a tape recorder, as long as you also take notes—machines sometimes don't work like they're supposed to.

WRITING

Once you've researched the subject and determined the angle, you're ready to write. And the best place to start is at the beginning, with the lead.

Lead

"The most important sentence in any article," says magazine writer William Zinsser, "is the first one."[1] If readers don't finish the first sentence, they won't go on to the second. And they'll never know what it was you wanted to say.

So the lead must do two things. It must grab the readers' attention, and it must tell the readers what the article is going to say.

A bland, dull lead that says nothing a reader doesn't already know isn't likely to induce anyone to read on. To attract attention leads should be concrete and visual. They should offer something that readers can relate to and understand. If the lead is about completely unfamiliar things, the reader is likely to think the article won't be of interest. You must link an unfamiliar topic, in the lead, to something that *is* familiar.

The lead must also state the central point of the piece. Let the reader know at the outset what the article is about and what the point is. You can't expect a reader to read through several sentences or paragraphs to find out what the topic is.

The lead can be the first sentence, the first few sentences or, in some cases, the first few paragraphs. It can be a simple, direct statement, it can be a quotation, it can even be an anecdote that illustrates the main point of the article. Any device can be used, as long as it gets the reader's attention and tells the reader what the point of the article is.

Here, for example, is a simple lead that makes an article about Easter eggs seem interesting:[2]

> In the southwestern corner of the Soviet Union, decorating Easter eggs is not child's play. In fact, children there are often forbidden to touch the Easter eggs, much less hide them and play with them.

This first paragraph creates interest, and the next paragraph immediately discloses the subject of the article:

> The reason for this "adults only" egg is because Ukrainian Easter eggs are unlike any other decorated eggs you have ever seen. These gaily colored, intricately designed eggs are, indeed, works of art that often remain on display for decades. Called *pysanky*, the Ukrainian eggs are carefully, and even secretly, designed and dyed each year as a part of a religious tradition that dates to 988 A.D., when the Ukraine accepted Christianity.*

---

*Proper editing would have changed "988 A.D." to "A.D. 988." B.C. follows dates; A.D. precedes them.

This lead succeeds because the writer didn't simply write "Easter eggs are something special in the Ukraine." Instead, he found an interesting angle—Easter eggs that children aren't allowed to hide or play with. And he didn't let the angle he selected get in the way of telling readers exactly what the article was about. In other words, the lead flowed naturally into the body of the story.

Once the flow of the lead to the body gets the reader going, the flow must continue to keep the reader going all the way through the article. To accomplish this, the article must be properly developed.

Development

The purpose of the body of the article is to support and develop the point made in the lead. The point must be amplified and extended so that its implications and importance are clear. The story must flow smoothly and logically, with each paragraph leading naturally to the next, and each paragraph adding something to the story.

As the article develops, you should answer the questions that will naturally come into the readers' minds. Make sure these answers are linked closely with what comes before and what follows, so the reader will be able to see how each bit of information fits into the picture. This requires close attention to transition between sentences and between paragraphs.

Besides amplifying the point made in the lead, the body of the article must also verify and illustrate it. It is one thing to make a bold statement in an interesting manner to grab the readers' attention. It is something else to convince the readers that your view has merit.

Verification and Illustration

You can't communicate effectively by assuming readers will accept your statements and absorb them as given. Generalizations must be supported with specific examples. Statements of fact that are not general knowledge should be attributed to an appropriate source. Contentions should be backed up with solid evidence.

Frequently you can support your position simply by stating the relevant facts. Just make sure you remember that "facts" are not opinions. They are undisputable, observable or recorded pieces of information that can be readily verified.

Some facts can be used without any specific attribution or further verification because they are so well known—"George Washington was the first President," for example. Feel free to use similar facts that can be found in any standard reference work, like "Columbus is the capital of Ohio" or "Alaska is the largest state in the Union."

Other facts—like statistics and survey results, for example—are also useful, but in most instances these should be attributed to their source. If you use the result of a public opinion poll, include important information like who took the poll and when it was taken. Furthermore, when using survey results or statistics take care that the figures you cite are really applicable to the situation at hand.

For less well-known facts you should also give a source, whether a document or an expert in the field. A quote from an authority can be used to verify statements of opinion as well. But be sure the person you quote has the expertise necessary for forming an intelligent opinion on the topic.

Sometimes straight facts won't make your case, especially if they are unfamiliar. So you must illustrate your point with specific examples. If you are writing about marine geology and want to make the point that vast mountain chains are found beneath the oceans, it might not be enough just to say so. Point out an example—the Mid-Atlantic Ridge, say, which winds down the Atlantic and even pierces the surface as the island of Iceland.

Another device that might help you illustrate your case is the analogy—an example of a parallel relationship between your subject and an unrelated, but easier to grasp idea. For example, if you are trying to explain how utility rates are set, you might draw an analogy with the charges for renting a car, something more readily understood by most people. Remember, though, that analogies don't prove anything—they merely illustrate a point.

A good lead, logical development and adequate verification are the skeleton of an article. Good articles must then be fleshed out; the story must be brought to life. Readers must be given pictures to help them visualize what you are telling them.

Good writers use devices that involve the readers in the article. Some of the methods for doing this include anecdotes, direct quotations, humanization, dramatization, and description.

Anecdotes

One of the best devices for involving the reader in a piece of writing is the anecdote. As Stanford professor Bill Rivers says, "No other element of an article is more important."[3] Anecdotes break monotony, illustrate points, and give the readers something to visualize. If they deal with familiar things, anecdotes can help people relate to the subject of the article. Anecdotes "show" readers something rather than merely tell about it.

Quotations

Another way to break monotony and make writing more natural is to use direct quotations. Quotations help make the writing more personal, more like conversation, and therefore more readable.

Be careful about using too many quotations, however. They can add to interest, but often a direct quote doesn't make the point in the clearest possible way. Often it is best to make a point in your own words and then use a quotation to amplify or illustrate.

Stylistically it is usually most effective when the quote begins the sentence and the source is identified in the middle (if it's a long quote) or at the end.

Humanization

Whenever you write, you are writing for people. And people are more interested in people than in things. So when you write, look for the human element. Always look for the aspects of a subject that touch people's lives. Use personal words and phrases where you can, and address the reader directly if it fits the situation.

One of the best places to find examples of humanizing is the pages of the *Wall Street Journal*. The *Journal*'s front page feature stories invariably begin, not with economic facts and figures, but with an example of a specific person in a specific city. The person's problems or business or economic situation introduces a subject of more general scope. The facts and figures follow to verify and illustrate the point of the article. But the story is introduced and told in human terms.

When a *Journal* writer did a piece on a trend toward the four-day workweek, for example, she had at her disposal such statistics as 1.2 million Americans (2 percent of the full-time labor force) already work four-day weeks. The lead, though, began like this:

> South Padre Island, a Texas resort area, was nearly deserted when Terry and Vicki Shea and their two sons arrived for a winter weekend late last year. They had driven 300 miles to the national seashore from their San Antonio home on Thursday night. They had the whole place to themselves the next day, but by noon Saturday hordes of sunseekers were swarming over the beach....
>
> Ralph and Cindee Hurlburt also have their Fridays off....
>
> What Mr. Shea and the Hurlburts have in common is that their Fridays are free regularly, and so are their Saturdays and Sundays. They are among an estimated 1.2 million Americans for whom the four-day workweek, with all its attendant problems and pleasures, has become a reality....

Dramatization

Frequently the humanization of writing is best accomplished by placing the topic in some dramatic context. A discussion of a new medicine, for example, could be limited to a dry description of the chemical composition of the medicine and its biochemical action inside the body. Or the story could be told in the context of a doctor treating patients. Often such dramatization can keep a reader involved with an article that would otherwise not get read.

Description

Good description can be hard to write, but it can also be one of the most important factors in getting a complete picture across to your readers. Readers will understand and retain more information if you can place a picture in their heads.

One way to illustrate or describe something unfamiliar is by comparing it with familiar things. It's not very helpful to say that a new machine is "big." But "as big as a house" says something that the reader can understand and relate to. Skillful use of simile and metaphor can make your message clearer, livelier, and more interesting to read.

All these devices for involving readers apply to magazine articles for just about any audience. But for certain specific audiences, there is more to consider. One audience of special concern to most organizations is the employees.

EMPLOYEE PUBLICATIONS

Most companies or institutions have an employee publication of some sort. Often the employee publication is a full-fledged magazine; sometimes it looks more like a newspaper or newsletter. But whatever the format, the writing in employee publications should follow most closely the style of magazine articles.

Why? Because even if an employee publication looks like a newspaper, it rarely functions as a medium for hard news. Unless it comes out daily (and few, if any, do), an employee publication cannot compete with other information sources available to employees. Informal communications networks among supervisors and secretaries can spread news faster than the UPI wire. And when important events occur or major decisions are made, they are generally announced at once rather than held for the next month's employee publication to be printed.

Furthermore, employee publications can be an extremely potent tool of internal public relations, and they should be used to accomplish more than telling of the shop foreman's new baby or the vice president's successful fishing trip. (This is known as the "dead fish and live babies" syndrome.) As experienced employee publication editor Don Fabun points out, employee publications today must appeal not only to the switchboard operator, but "to an atomic physicist, a systems engineer, a market analyst, and an operations analyst. These latter are not likely to be interested in, or motivated by, bowling scores and a detailed account of the company picnic."[4]

Employee publications can help generate support among employees for corporate goals and objectives. Articles can build employee morale, enhance job satisfaction, and thus boost productivity. Publications can create a broader understanding among employees of the problems a company faces.

How can these things be accomplished? Mainly by keeping such objectives in mind when you're writing articles for employees, and by following the principles of magazine writing outlined earlier in the chapter (see Table 12-1). Specifically, you must orient the writing to the reader. Explain the significance of events from the viewpoint of the employee, not from the viewpoint of the board of directors. In other words, don't relate verbatim a new company policy as handed down from on high. *Explain* the policy and tell what it means to the reader. But explain it in an interesting way—find a good angle, write a good lead, and make the article as human and dramatic as possible.

With this approach, an employee publication can be a valuable asset to any organization. Articles about a company's achievements in research can generate pride among the employees, giving them a good feeling about being a part of the company. Articles about the need to save energy or improve safety records can motivate employees to improve performance in those areas. Articles about the relationship between your company and the well-being of the community can give employees a sense of involvement in a socially useful occupation. Articles emphasizing the accomplishments of individuals can be an incentive to other workers.

If you write articles on such subjects skillfully, so that employees will read them, you can accomplish much more than you can with a publication written strictly for entertainment or for relating social fluff. This does *not* mean that an employee publication should be a propaganda piece for the views of management. Rather, such a publication can be mutually beneficial to the individual employees and the organization as a whole.

12-1 MAGAZINE ARTICLE WRITING CHECKLIST

1. Is the lead interesting and specific? Does it approach the story from a slant or angle designed to catch the reader's interest?
2. Is the idea in the lead developed and supported by the rest of the article?
3. Are statements verified or properly attributed? Are general statements supported with specific examples?
4. Are anecdotes used throughout the article, both as illustrations and as devices to increase reader interest?
5. Has sufficient use been made of direct quotations?
6. Is the writing dramatic? Has the story been told in human terms?
7. Is description adequate to give the reader an accurate picture of the subject?

CONCLUSION

Magazines offer a vast opportunity to the PR writer. They can reach many audiences, ranging from influential public officials to company employees. By selecting topics wisely, researching thoroughly, and writing clear, lively and well-supported articles, PR writers can use magazines to accomplish a great many PR goals and objectives.

NOTES

[1] William Zinsser, *On Writing Well* (New York: Harper and Row, 1980), p. 59.

[2] B. R. Hughes, "Ukrainian Easter Eggs," *Fort Worth*, April 1976, p. 35.

[3] William L. Rivers, *Free-Lancer and Staff Writer* (Belmont, Calif.: Wadsworth, 1972), p. 93.

[4] Don Fabun, "Company Publications," in *Lesly's Public Relations Handbook*, ed. Philip Lesly (Englewood Cliffs, N.J.: Prentice-Hall, 1971), p. 135.

SELECTED BIBLIOGRAPHY

Don Fabun, "Company Publications," in *Lesly's Public Relations Handbook*, ed. Philip Lesly (Englewood Cliffs, N.J.: Prentice-Hall, 1971), pp. 134-143.

William L. Rivers, *Free-Lancer and Staff Writer*, 3d ed. (Belmont, Calif.: Wadsworth, 1981).

13

NEWSLETTERS AND BROCHURES

Among the PR media most often used for communicating with specific audiences are newsletters and brochures. A newsletter is a printed sheet (or sheets), often resembling a small newspaper, used to disseminate news to a special interest group, usually on a regular basis. Brochures are generally one-time printed pieces on a specific subject.

Often the term *brochure* is restricted to printed pieces of six pages or more, but many people use *brochure* loosely to include pamphlets, booklets, flyers, circulars, leaflets and tracts. *Pamphlets* are generally smaller and have less color and fewer illustrations than a full-fledged brochure. Booklets range from pamphletlike publications of a few pages to those the size of small books. Flyers and circulars are usually single-sheet mailing pieces or items distributed for free (like the various printed messages you find stuck under your windshield wiper). Leaflets are similar, but are usually folded though not stitched or trimmed. Tracts are pamphlets or booklets containing religious or political propaganda.

NEWSLETTERS

One of the principal purposes for newsletters is organizational communication—keeping in touch with the members of an organization or the employees of an institution. Associations of individuals with a single interest in common are likely to use newsletters to keep in touch because meetings are relatively rare. For example, owners of various types of aircraft and different makes and models of cars are often members of an association. The association may meet only once a year, if at all, but the members maintain contact and benefit from the exchange of information in their newsletter.

The Cessna 120/140 newsletter, for example, goes to all owners of these two types of aircraft. Because most of the planes are old, information about restorations and improvements is important. The group has meetings, called "fly-ins," but even the one designated as the annual meeting is not likely to attract all the members. These are scattered around the country and the speed and fuel limitations of their airplanes prevent their going great distances in a brief time.

Even clubs whose members are more likely to have direct contact use newsletters to keep in touch. Many PR people are members of press clubs, places where members can go individually for meals and where many activities are held. The newsletter tells of events scheduled for the club and gives news of various members. Church events are conveyed to the congregations through newsletters. These are usually mailed, but they may be distributed at church, to notify members of other functions during the week. Community groups like civic organizations also use newsletters to keep in touch with members and to stimulate attendance at events. Encouraging member participation is the primary persuasive element in all of these newsletters, but it is most apparent, perhaps, in social group newsletters. Examples 13–1 through 13–4 show a variety of newsletters.

Persuading people to become involved, to participate, is less apparent in the newsletters used as internal communication for institutional groups. Usually institutional newsletters for employees are designed more to inform than to persuade. Corporate employee newsletters do not differ significantly from nonprofit employee internal communication pieces. Both are designed to give employees a common experience, a feeling of belonging, and to offer them information about each other and the institution so there will be a feeling of cohesiveness and unity.

Unlike institutional newsletters, which already have a clearly defined public, some newsletters are developed to create a public. Examples include newsletters prepared for publicity campaigns in the areas of entertainment or politics. The newsletter can be for a resort, for example. A resort in the Bahamas keeps all former residents on its mailing list and also offers the newsletter to tourists in the islands who, even if they don't visit as residents, might come in for some of the nightclub entertainment or special meals. Television and film stars often develop newsletters for their fan clubs. These newsletters bring additional publicity and make people feel they know the stars personally. Politicians use the same device to build a constituency, especially during an election year. Even elected officials try to keep in touch with their constituency through newsletters, especially when the seat of government is outside the district. One U.S. Senator has a policy of sending a letter a month to "the people back home" (in addition to supplying local radio stations with a tape a week to be used in "public service time").

A political constituency can be built for a cause or an issue just as it can for a politician. Many groups, such as those opposed to nuclear power plants, have built a constituency through the publication and distribution of newsletters. Consumer groups built by newsletters include Common Cause, which has achieved national recognition. With consumer issues the newsletter often unifies a public rather than creating one, as with an entertainer.

Newsletters for some special interest groups are money-makers for the group, although that was not their original intent. Some consumer

13-1   CUB SCOUT NEWSLETTER

NEWSLETTER

Cub Scout Pack 350

January 1980

PINEWOOD DERBY

This is it! Saturday is Pinewood Derby Day! Don't miss it. This is one of the most fun-filled days of our Cub activity year.

The place is the Precinct 1 Garage on Cleburne Road. (Go out Hulen Street south and turn left on Cleburne Road.)

Be there at 9 a.m. for weigh-in. Racing cars must not weigh more than 5 ounces. Generally you have to add weight to get the cars up to 5 ounces.

We want to start the racing at 9:30 and finish as quickly as possible because another group will be using the building when we finish.

After cars are weighed-in and numbered, boys are not allowed to make any changes or adjustments until racing is completed.

If you don't yet have a racing kit, get it tonight and start working on it.

SCOUT SUNDAY

Since this is the 50th year of Cub Scouting, Pack 350 would like to make a special effort to show its appreciation to Overton Park United Methodist Church, sponsors of the pack.

The Pack Executive Committee wants to urge each boy and all parents to attend the Scout Sunday service at Overton Park Church at 10:45 a.m., Feb. 10.

Boys should come in uniform, and we will sit as a group. This is really our only way to say "thanks" to the church for the use of its facilities.

BLUE & GOLD

Be sure and reserve Thursday, Feb. 28, on your calendar. That's the date of the annual Blue & Gold Banquet. It will be held at Colonial in the Park (Jetton's).

You can start through the food lines between 6:30 and 7 p.m. Everyone buys his own food.

Everyone is invited to this banquet--ma, pa, all the kids, aunts, uncles, grandparents and friends. The banquet takes the place of our pack meeting in February. Let us know if you plan to attend.

SME

Also at the Blue & Gold Banquet will be our annual Sustaining Membership Enrollment (SME). We will be asking parents to contribute to the fund which helps keep Scouting alive in this area

Give $5 or $6 or $10 or even more if you can afford it. This is a very important fund-raising event for Scouting--do what you can to help.

FAMILY CAMPOUT

Everybody likes to go camping, especially Cub Scouts. Our family campout this year will be held April 19-20 at Sid Richardson Scout Ranch on Lake Bridgeport.

We need to know as soon as possible who will be going on this really-fun overnight trip. (See coupon below.)

Most boys like to sleep in tents. However, there are a limited number of cabins that sleep six (or more if you sleep on the floor). Reservations for the cabins will be on a first-paid, first-served basis. The cabin rent is $4 per person. Other costs are $1.50 each for Saturday dinner and $2 each for Sunday breakfast.

FAMILY CAMPOUT RESERVATION FORM

Sid Richardson Scout Ranch, April 19-20

Family name............................Phone............................

Adults going camping...................Children going camping...................

Please turn in money with this reservation.

Cabin @ $4 per person.................
Dinner @ $1.50 per person.............
Breakfast @ $2 per person.............
Tent rental @ $2......................

TOTAL $............

Even small organizations with limited budgets put out newsletters to keep club members aware of group activities.

PART FOUR WRITING FOR SPECIAL AUDIENCES

13-2 PR AGENCY NEWSLETTER

WA communique

A newsletter by Witherspoon & Associates Advertising/Public Relations, 321 S. Henderson, Fort Worth, Texas 76101, Telephone (817) 335-1373   April 1978

May the best foot you put forward be your own.

A few days before Christmas the chief executive of a large firm we like to think of as a potential client volunteered that he had received our Christmas card and thought it clever. Nice of him to say, I thought. A positive acknowledgement. Then he really surprised me. "I guess you guys can't afford to send out just any kind of card," he said. "It *really* has to be good."

That told me he perceived, better than most managers, the importance of communication. Anything and everything that a company sends out in its name — from people to printed materials — should be consistent with the identity that company seeks to maintain among its publics. And, of course, that goes double for a firm like ours whose stock in trade is telling other companies how to put their best foot forward.

Launching this newsletter poses the same challenge as the Christmas card. We can't afford to send out just any kind of newsletter. It really had better be good, because effective communications is supposed to be our bag.

Communique is designed to give greater insight into the broad field of communications and where Witherspoon & Associates stands in that field. It will be published quarterly, which is something of a challenge in itself. (Like the cobbler and his children, we find all too little time for our own.) I am aware we must compete for your attention. But if we can practice what we preach, it will be compelling enough to spark your interest.

We can't afford to do anything less.

— *Roger Rienstra*

Public Relations: what you don't know *can* hurt.

Of all management functions, public relations may be at once the most potent, and the most misunderstood and misused. Most companies — with notable exceptions — have still to gain enough understanding of and confidence in public relations to use it with anything approaching its full potential.

You say you don't need it anyway? You have public relations whether you like it or not. You are what people think you are.

I've been asked many questions about public relations during two decades in the business. The answers — as I see them — might help you make better public relations decisions in your own business.

Q. *Isn't PR the business of image building?*

A. The first maxim of public relations is that a good image begins with good performance. Do not go to a public relations counselor and ask him to make out of you or your product something you aren't. Do ask him how he would propose to make your sound performance more widely known and appreciated, through the use of his professional communications skills.

Q. *Aren't advertising and publicity the same thing?*

A. In a broad sense, they are part of public relations, but by no means synonymous. Public relations is at the same time the communications effort through which a business seeks to build and maintain a good name, and the public's evaluation of that effort (or lack of effort) in terms of what people think about the company, its products, and its services.

Publicity is that element of public relations which seeks to provide to the media information which will stand on its own feet as legitimate news or feature material.

Advertising is, essentially, paid publicity: the purchase of time or space (radio, TV, newspapers, magazines, outdoor) to call public attention to one's company, product, service or need.

Q. *If I have a good name already, why do I need public relations?*

A. Are you the only company in town doing well in your line of business? If you're publicly held, are you the only company in your industry with good performance? Are you sure you're getting the attention of everyone you want to reach? How much better might you do with a planned program to build on the good name you already have?

This newsletter was designed for clients and potential clients of a major advertising/public relations agency. This issue included information about the firm as well as some excellent advice on public relations.

13-3 BANK NEWSLETTER

First of Fort Worth

The First National Bank of Fort Worth
One Burnett Plaza / 390-6161
Fort Worth, Texas 76102

First Impressions

Vol. 3, No. 1

A Newsletter to help you utilize money wisely

If Uncle Sam says "You paid too much income tax! You're entitled to a refund!"

What will you do with the money?

Some day soon, if the postman should bring you a small, tan-colored envelope with the familiar IRS trademark up in the corner, don't panic!

Chances are, it's not a request for an audit. Only 2% of U.S. taxpayers are invited to "come in and bring your papers."

You would be amazed to know how many people overpay their tax — actually three out of four, according to H&R Block, the firm of tax accountants.

A surprisingly large percentage of taxpayers get a refund check from the U.S. Treasury because their W-2 payments amounted to more than their tax.

So, if you experience a pleasant thrill when you open the letter from the IRS — and out pops a check for $25 or $150 or $800 — you have to decide — what to do with the money!

You can spend it

Spending is the easiest solution — but not necessarily the wisest. Spending, of course, helps the economy — but it may not be the best policy for your individual situation.

You could buy a camera. An electric typewriter. Make a down payment on a new car. Or, if it is only a modest check, you could take your spouse out for a night on the town. Tempting ideas — but maybe not the best.

You can invest it

If your tax refund is large enough, you may decide to invest it in real estate, the Stock Market or another investment that seems to promise a good return. But such an investment usually involves a risk. Even stockbrokers tell you that you should have an adequate amount in savings before you invest money.

You can save it

Adding money to your savings account makes a lot of sense. It gives you a feeling of security.

Consumer counselors recommend you should have as much as 3 to 6 months of your annual income in savings — a fund to meet the financial emergencies every family faces from time to time — even unemployment.

Put your tax refund in your Regular Savings — where it is readily accessible and earns 5% per annum interest compounded daily.

If you already have a savings account at First of Fort Worth, all you need to do is fill out a deposit slip, step up to the teller's window — and that's the end of your "what-to-do-with-my-refund" problem.

When you stop to think about it, the best place of all to put that income tax refund may be your Regular Savings Account.

If you're between 17 and 21, check on our First Account
—see page 4 for details

This newsletter is sent to bank customers along with their monthly statement. It focuses on money matters, giving customers helpful tips and advice (as well as pointing out ways the bank can be of service).

13-4 A CONGRESSMAN'S NEWSLETTER

House of Representatives
Washington, D.C. 20515
Official Business

POSTAL PATRON — LOCAL
6th DISTRICT
TEXAS

Phil Gramm
M.C.
Blk. Rt.

CONGRESSMAN PHIL GRAMM'S
WASHINGTON REPORT

Number 2   96th Congress, 1st Session   July, 1979

ACTION ON ENERGY

Congress took a hard look at the energy crisis last week and took one first bold step toward a solution. It won't solve things overnight, but it is an honest start.

U.S. PRODUCTION AND CONSUMPTION, ALL OILS, 1920-1977
(Billions of barrels per year)

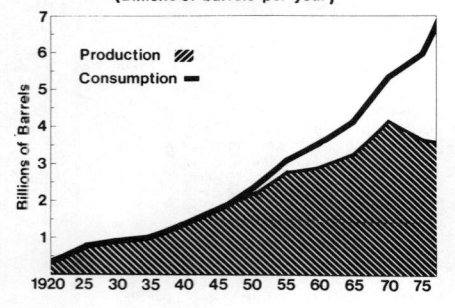

THE PROBLEM . . .

is plain. The hard truth is that we use more oil than we produce. Each day we consume nearly nine million barrels that have to be imported. That problem has been getting worse.

Gasoline lines are symptoms of the disease. The disease is the growing domestic shortage.

Until we take steps to increase our production and cut our dependence on foreign supplies, we will be dangerously—and increasingly—vulnerable to the whims and greed of the OPEC nations.

And the gas lines will grow longer—and more frequent.

U.S. Representative Phil Gramm used this issue of his newsletter to give voters information on a pressing national issue—energy. The newsletter not only informed citizens of Gramm's opinion on the issue, it also provided facts and figures and charts and graphs to support his case.

---

groups find, for example, that subscriptions to their newsletters help pay for their other expenses. This situation came about because the newsletters began to offer information others considered valuable enough to pay for.

THE COST...

of imports is enormous and growing.

The Arab embargo of 1973 should have shocked us into action. That year, we paid $8 billion for petroleum imports. By the most recent estimate, oil imports will cost us $60 billion this year. That's nearly an **eight-fold increase** in six years.

It fuels inflation, hurts the dollar, and drains thousands of jobs out of the U.S. economy. Unless we stop this trend, it could bring on a serious recession.

COST OF PETROLEUM IMPORTS
Billions of U.S. Dollars

Year	1973	1974	1975	1976	1977	1978	1979
Billions $	8	26	25	32	44	40	60
mbd	6.2						8.6

U.S. ESTIMATED IMPORTS OF CRUDE OIL AND REFINED PRODUCTS

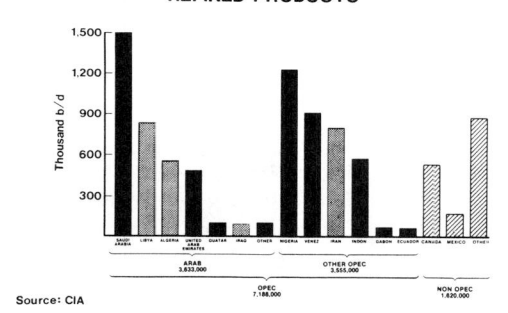

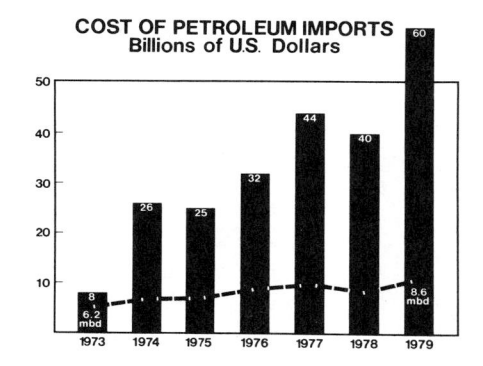

Source: CIA

ARAB 3,633,000 — OTHER OPEC 3,555,000 — OPEC 7,188,000 — NON OPEC 1,620,000

OUR SOURCES...

are increasingly undependable.

OPEC controls the price and the supply. We get 26 percent of our imports from nations openly hostile to us—Libya, Algeria, Iran and Iraq.

In recent weeks Nigeria, our second largest supplier, has threatened to cut exports if our Rhodesian policy is not to their liking.

And Saudi Arabia, the largest, hints darkly that it's time for the U.S. to negotiate with the P.L.O.

Other newsletters are started by individuals for the purpose of making money. These people decide they have information valuable enough that others will pay for it. They sell this information in the form of a newsletter. An example is an investment letter that offers advice to people daring enough to buy when the market is down. The developer of the newsletter is a person who has been working the down cycle of the market long enough that he thinks he can offer others sound advice for doing the same. The newsletter was deliberately designed as a money-making project. Other examples like this summarize occurrences in Washington, D.C., that affect the business climate. The most famous of these is the *Kiplinger Report*. Some professional newsletters are designed with the same intent: offering information good enough that people will pay for it. The PR professional has a few: *pr reporter, PR News, O'Dwyer's Newsletter* and others.

A newsletter that offers enough information to carry a price tag but is primarily for publicity is the sports newsletter. Almost all sports—even the minor ones—have newsletters. The scope of the newsletters can be national, regional, or limited to the constituency for one institution, such as a bank, university or health agency like American Heart Association, but the purpose is mainly publicity. A side benefit is making money and getting enthusiastic support for the players.

Whatever the intent of the newsletter, its effect is to develop an audience, usually dispersed, with a common experience—often one that begins to share common viewpoints.

BROCHURES

Many brochures are developed to sell a product, service or idea. Such brochures present what is to be sold to the best advantage. Real estate agents use brochures to show property and describe the advantages of owning it. Sometimes realtors use a brochure to sell the services of the company, rather than specific properties. Most professional PR people get at least one brochure a week describing some seminar that has been designed to help them improve their skills. PR professional groups also publish brochures offering members as speakers to other interested groups. Selling talent is selling a service in that others will benefit.

Brochures sell intangibles by describing the worth of the ideas. An example is brochures designed to garner support (usually financial) for foundations. One mental health foundation sends out brochures "selling" its publications and audiovisual materials at prices that barely cover mailing. The foundation offers the materials to justify its existence, its reason for being, by selling ideas for sound mental health.

Publicity can also be informational in a stricter sense. A brochure was developed, for example, to tell citizens in a community about a health service they can dial to have various illnesses described and recommendations made. The brochure for the service, Tel-Med, lists all the tapes available in the community and gives the phone number (as well as hours to call, since the service is handled by volunteers). Informational brochures are often produced too for other community services, such as hotlines (phone service) for suicide prevention, accident reports, crime deterrence and so on. A druggist may dispense, along with prescriptions, a brochure on how to prevent poisoning accidents and describing what to do if an accident occurs. Such informational brochures perform a service and generate goodwill for those who distribute them. (Example 13–5 is an informational brochure.)

In developing brochures, the primary consideration is concept. Art and words have to work together to convey an idea, to sell the message. In a brochure for a new apartment or office complex, for example, you must carefully choose what to show and what to tell. One consideration in choosing is determining what art is available. If the facility is under construction, you can use a photograph of the architect's model or a reproduction of the architect's sketches, together with copy that stresses what advantages this *new* facility has over other existing facilities. Characteristics that it has in common with other facilities need to be given for comparison. Emphasis, though, should be placed on what is new and different. If the facilities exist already and are known, the brochure must consider the desired image of the facility and compare this with its accepted image. If your presentation is too remote from the commonly held view, you will have a problem with believability and acceptance.

However, presenting a known product in a new way often succeeds. Approach the task with insight and imagination. Try to think of symbols in words and art that will evoke the image you want to convey. Remember that image in your choice of art, color and design.

The validity of your representation is always a consideration. PR writers are accountable for the accuracy of their presentation. You must be careful in collecting information about the subject of the brochure. Make certain, for example, that each office in the complex described in the brochure does indeed have thermostat control if the brochure shows it. If a firm rents space and installs computer components that need a special temperature—and there is no thermostat control—you can be challenged for misrepresenting the situation in the literature you produced.

Brochures about investment opportunities are particularly hazardous. You need to spell out carefully all the financial considerations, and review the copy with both an accountant and an attorney before going into production. The underlying reason for this is the same as for the office or apartment complex—people should be assured of getting their money's worth. A professional organization's foundation offered a brochure detailing for potential contributors the benefits of membership in the foundation. The group's attorney was adamant that the mechanism for providing these benefits be in place before the publication went to press. Colleges and universities have begun looking carefully at their catalogs and promotional literature after being warned by counsel of cases where institutions had been taken to court for promising more than they could deliver.

Strictly informational pieces are easier to prepare. Some schools and departments of journalism—or communication—produce and cir-

13-5 INFORMATIONAL BROCHURE

WHAT DOES HEART DISEASE MEAN TO YOU...?

One out of every two people will die of Heart and Circulatory Diseases if present rates are allowed to continue.

Over one million children and adults will die of Cardiovascular Diseases this year—that's a city about the size of Dallas.

Cardiovascular Disease costs our nation 19 1/2 billion dollars annually....through lost production, retraining, medical care, premature retirement and losses in management skills. In addition, approximately 52 million man-days of production are lost each year.

Yet, real progress is being made. There has been a 21% decline in cardiovascular deaths in the under 65 year old age bracket since 1965. A majority of the nation's hospitals have installed coronary care units which have reduced heart attack deaths from 15% to 30%.

What is the American Heart Association doing to insure continued progress against our nation's #1 health threat?

RESEARCH:
To probe the unknown to find the causes, cures, treatment and prevention of diseases of the heart and circulatory system.

PUBLIC EDUCATION:
To reduce premature death and disability from cardiovascular disease by educating the public to the risk factors of heart disease—such as proper weight, diet and exercise programs—the need for regular medical examinations, and the early warning signs of heart attack and stroke. Programs are conducted in clubs, organizations, schools, colleges, industries and neighborhoods.

Preparing brochures to advertise resorts, new buildings, apartment complexes and such is usually a problem of deciding what to show and condensing what you want to tell. When you prepare an informational brochure designed

culate a prospectus of graduates to employers. The students are shown and described with thumbnail resumes, but no promise of expectations is given! Other types of informational pieces are technical brochures that describe how something works—such as the instruction brochure that came with your clock-radio or stereo. The only catch to preparing information brochures is that you must be sure all necessary information is included *and* that it is specific and absolutely accurate. In dealing with processes, be sure you haven't left anything to the reader's imagination or the information user won't be able to put the parts together correctly and get the equipment to work.

PROFESSIONAL EDUCATION:

To provide for the continuing education of physicians, nurses and paramedical personnel. Up-to-date information on diagnosis, treatment and rehabilitation is provided through films, conferences and publications.

COMMUNITY SERVICE:

To meet the needs and concerns of many publics—patients, medical personnel, hospitals, and community health centers—through heart screening programs, blood pressure clinics, heart information centers, rehabilitation clubs, and instruction in cardiopulmonary resuscitation.

WHY IS MORE MONEY NEEDED:

Nationally, 499 scientifically approved research grants totalling $5,466,000 went unfunded last year because the money was simply not available.

And in Texas, an additional $1,540,000 is needed—

- *$490,000 to provide rehabilitation for thousands of stroke victims through therapy, counselling and loan equipment
- *$213,000 to train one person in every ten in cardiopulmonary resuscitation (closed chest massage and mouth to mouth breathing)
- *$77,000 to provide three blood pressure recording devices in each of the Texas service centers
- *$190,000 to reach 8,000 more coronary care nurses in training and retraining programs
- *$350,000 to fund approved research grants in Texas that went unfunded last year
- *$220,000 to reach approximately 90% of the Texas population with information on the risk factors of Cardiovascular Disease

What can you do to protect yourself against heart attack, stroke or related Cardiovascular Diseases?

- *Don't smoke cigarettes
- *Eat foods low in saturated fats and cholesterol
- *Maintain normal weight
- *Exercise regularly
- *Control high blood pressure
- *Have regular check ups

What are the warning signs of heart attack?

- *Prolonged, heavy pressure or squeezing pain in the center of the chest, behind the breastbone
- *Pain which may spread to the shoulder, arm, neck or jaw
- *Pain or discomfort is often accompanied by sweating. Nausea, vomiting or shortness of breath may also occur
- *Symptoms may subside and then return

What are the warning signs of stroke?

- *Sudden, temporary weakness or numbness of the face, arm or leg
- *Temporary difficulty or loss of speech, or trouble understanding speech
- *Transient dimness or loss of vision, particularly in one eye
- *An episode of double vision
- *Unexplained headaches, or a change in the pattern of your headaches
- *Temporary dizziness or unsteadiness
- *A recent change in personality or mental ability

American Heart Association
Texas Affiliate, Inc.
P.O. Box 15186
Austin, Texas 78761

FR120 rev. 9/74

to teach, you have other problems—making readers want to read and learn, and writing the material so it will be easy to comprehend. The American Heart Association's brochure is an example of such an effort.

Regardless of the type of brochure you are writing, you need to prepare the copy first. Write everything you want to tell. Next, see what you can show. Perhaps you can delete some copy. Then try to find a way to represent the rest of the information in easy-to-read ways such as with graphs, charts or boxes. Finally, look at the piece itself as a whole to determine how big you want it and how you are going to use the space—what should be words and what should be art. After you know what you want the finished brochure to look like, you can go back to your copy again to cut and polish before you get to the biggest job—copyfitting.

DESIGNING LAYOUTS AND WRITING COPY TO FIT

Designing newsletters and brochures to display information attractively is important in order to gain attention. Newsletters have a great deal of room for copy since they do not use many, if any, illustrations. The danger is crowding the piece with too much copy. Headlines, indentations and generous paragraphing as well as tables and charts will help tell the story in a word-heavy piece. Brochures are the medium to use when pictures can tell the story better than words or when the piece is mostly a reference work, as in speakers' bureau brochures or medical information pieces.

Audiences for newsletters are likely to be a fairly cohesive group. Either they are already members of the audience because they belong to the club or are employees of the firm, or because they are philosophically aligned or at least inclined toward the group. Brochures are more likely to go to those who are unreceptive.

However, brochures often have a longer life than newsletters. Newsletters, as their name suggests, have much in common with newspapers and are often read for their content and discarded. Brochures are more like magazines in that they are likely to be kept and referred to more than once—even passed along to others.

Use has something to do with the purpose for publication. When you are deciding how to communicate with an audience, you have to determine what you want to accomplish, then go about achieving that goal in the way most likely to be successful. If you have a diving shop in the Virgin Islands, for example, you can excite the imagination and probably stimulate business better with pictures than words. On the other hand, if you want to keep in touch with all of the Corvette owners in your state, you're better off with a newsletter, where you can talk about rallies and parts.

How you are going to send the piece has a great deal to do with the design. If you intend the newsletter or brochure to be a self-mailer, one side of it will have to carry your return address, postage and the label space. Furthermore, the whole piece will have to meet the specifications of the U.S. Postal Department, including how you seal it.

If the newsletter or brochure is going to be an enclosure, stop and think before you design it. How are you most likely to send it? with what? in what? when? to whom? All of these questions are likely to dictate a design that deserves its own envelope, with a design matching the piece.

What will happen to the piece also has bearing on the design—will it wind up on a bulletin board, for example? Some organization newsletters are mailed to the president to be posted. Such newsletters should be designed to stand out in a display. Some brochures are distributed through rack-card or countertop display units. The unit will have to be designed to call attention to the brochures; they, in turn, will have to be designed so that the part visible in the rack is attractive and inviting. Some brochures are designed for point-of-sale displays. Brochures about microwave ovens, for example, are put beside the oven in the hope that the additional sales pitch will move the merchandise. But the brochure may also be taken by someone wanting the oven and used to help to make a decision. Selling pieces like this have to be informational, too.

Some pieces are designed for personal distribution—for one person to give another. Many health information pieces are like this. A physician may give a mother-to-be information about prenatal care or a counselor may give a high school student information about how to choose a college. These pieces are designed to stand alone, but should also be supplemental and complementary to advice from the individual giving them.

When you are writing the copy, you have to prepare the message to say what you think needs to be said in an appropriate way. Then you have to decide how you are going to convey that message in the available space. Some PR practitioners are experienced enough to "write to fit" the space, but not many. Most prepare the message and then spend a great deal of time trimming it to fit, substituting illustrations for words, if appropriate, and generally tailoring the message to the medium. With a newsletter, there is somewhat more flexibility in that you can add pages, but that usually costs money. A better solution is to determine your information hole and fit the message to it.

In fitting copy to a design the first step is to find out the size and type face to be used in the printed piece. Then count the characters and spaces in your typed copy. To do this, you count the number of lines per paragraph and the number of paragraphs. Or you can use a ruler and just measure the width of the typed copy. If your typewriter has pica type, it has 10 characters to the inch. If it's elite, you have 12 characters to the inch. When you know how much copy you have, you must then find out the size of the area the copy will be going into. Measure the actual size of the copy block once the piece is printed. Remember margins and space for headlines, indentations and such.

Next, consult a type book to get the characters per pica of the type size you are using. There are 6 picas to the inch. Take the total number of lines the copy will make and see how much space the copy will be, set in that type style and size, when you divide the characters per pica figure into the total number of characters in your typed copy. Copy may be specially spaced for legibility. If so, the space is placed between the lines, and will affect the depth. Type styles come in regular, expanded or condensed. You can use an expanded to give more space between letters, or use the condensed for closer fitting copy. However, the important consideration is the readability of the piece. Cut words, rather than crowd. (See Appendix C for copyfitting examples.)

Make words count for you. Select words that tell the story best, words that stir the imagination and excite interest. Emphasize the most significant elements in the information you want to convey through both word choice and graphics. Active verbs will convey emphasis and so will italics, all capital letters, color and other design ingredients. A brochure to call attention to the dangers of common household items that are poisonous had only the word P-o-i-s-o-n in bright red letters across the front of a box easily recognizable as a detergent package. The word and the graphics combined to make a powerful statement about common items in the home we don't normally think of as poisonous, and that's what the brochure was all about. Internally, in the copy, words can be used just as significantly and graphically. A brochure on investments had columns of *Do*s and *Don't*s. Other brochures and newsletters use checklists effectively.

CONCLUSION

The effective, efficient use of language creates a climate for credibility and comprehension. Words in newsletters and brochures need to be chosen to tell a story in a limited space with maximum utility. Newsletters are often the principal communication medium for people networks. Brochures have long, often important, lives as reference pieces. Both deserve a writer's commitment.

14

BACKGROUNDERS AND POSITION PAPERS

For some companies, it happens several times a week. For others it might be every month or so. Some organizations face it once a year or less. But sometime, sooner or later, every company gets a call from a reporter.

The reporter is likely to ask something like this: "What's your position on the Smith and Jones Act and how will it affect your company?" Or "What's your stand on the latest rules change by the Environmental Protection Agency?" Or "I'm doing a story on declining innovation in industry. Can you give me some information on that?"

Your company's spokesperson needs to be able to respond to such questions. A firm's credibility won't be enhanced if it has nothing to say on important issues that affect it. A "no comment" or a "let me call you back" response is no way to get a reputation as a sharp, top-notch organization that knows what's going on.

For these reasons PR people have to keep company executives armed with the facts. Good PR departments monitor the media and the polls and government activities to stay aware of the latest public issues. PR people research these issues and prepare information on them ahead of time, so when a reporter calls, the company executive will be able to offer a well-informed and unequivocal answer.

This sort of work is somewhat different from the everyday tasks of writing news releases, ads, or brochure copy. It usually involves some in-depth research and preparing a report of some kind. Such reports are generally called *backgrounders* or *position papers*.

Sometimes these documents are prepared and then filed until needed. But frequently preparing position papers and backgrounders is the first step in a public relations campaign. For example, assume that an electric utility plans to offer a new way of charging for electricity, giving very low rates on weekends and at night but very high rates during the day—a system known as time-of-day pricing. The first step in a PR department's action plan would be to prepare a backgrounder describing time-of-day pricing concepts and their history, where they've been tried before, results of those experiments, the availability and cost of special electric meters, and so on. Such a backgrounder would probably also discuss the various types of time-of-day pricing systems and the advantages and disadvantages of each.

At some point, the company management would decide which of the systems to implement. PR writers would then prepare a position paper stating the specific system to be used and giving the reasons why it was chosen. From this point, the copywriters would use the material in the backgrounder and position paper to prepare brochures, ads, news releases, and perhaps an article for the employee magazine, describing the new pricing system.

Backgrounders, in general, tend to be heavy on information but light on opinion while position papers are mainly statements of an organization's position on an issue. In either case the topic can be broad or specific, but usually backgrounders deal with general subjects and position papers treat specific questions, like a proposed new law.

For example, a backgrounder might be prepared on "coal transportation," discussing the various methods for transporting coal from mines to the point of use. The backgrounder would discuss the technological, economic and environmental considerations involved with each transportation option. A position paper, however, might be concerned specifically with a proposed law regulating coal slurry pipelines. The position paper would take a pro or con position on the proposal and present arguments for its case.

Ordinarily a position paper does not provide a comprehensive background of the subject. When it does, it takes on many of the characteristics of a backgrounder. Sometimes the term *position paper* is applied to a lengthy document that spells out a viewpoint on a general topic. A political candidate, for example, is likely to have a position paper prepared on "the economy" or "foreign affairs." (Also see Example 14–1, the position paper on licensing of lay midwives.) In this chapter, however, we'll assume that a backgrounder's purpose is to provide information while a position paper's purpose is to defend a position.

BACKGROUNDERS

Backgrounders have many purposes. They can serve as information sheets for company executives or employees. They provide source material for copywriters preparing ads, news releases, brochures, speeches or articles for the employee magazine. They can be used as documents to hand out to reporters or members of the public who inquire about a certain subject. And company speakers can use backgrounders to brush up on a subject so they'll be ready to answer questions from the audience. In writing backgrounders, keep all these potential uses in mind.

Backgrounders must be accurate and comprehensive. The first rule in writing a backgrounder, then, is to research the subject thoroughly.

Research

Researching a backgrounder requires full use of all the resources discussed in Chapter 3. You can't afford to leave any source unread, especially if the backgrounder is to be used as an information source by executives or speakers who must answer questions from the media or the general public. It can be embarrassing if the questioner knows more than the executive.

Remember that research is a never-ending process. Once a backgrounder is completed, keep a file of all new newspaper articles, magazine stories, reports or other documents on the subject so that the backgrounder can be updated at regular intervals. Backgrounders that don't include the latest important developments are virtually worthless.

Writing

Most backgrounders begin simply with a statement of what the issue is and why it is important. This opening statement should be concise and to the point, but it should also give the reader an accurate impression of the significance of the subject. The writer should then give the history of the issue, describe the current situation, and discuss implications for the future.

Background As its name states, a backgrounder must give the background of the issue or subject under discussion. It should provide a fairly complete historical overview so a reader not familiar with the issue can see how the current situation evolved. You must answer the question: Why are things the way they are today? You can't do that without giving some details about how things used to be and why they changed.

The history of an issue includes significant historical events, enactment of legislation, changes in government or company policy. And it names books, articles or government reports that played an important role in the development of the issue. In essence, this section should describe the evolution of the current situation.

Current Situation When you reach the present, you should discuss the current status of the issue. This might include a description of current public policy on the issue (or your organization's policy), or a discussion of various policy alternatives now being considered. Do not defend or condemn any policy, however. The purpose of a backgrounder is to analyze and explain policy. Stick to the facts. Describe policy options, discuss their good and bad points, but don't make value judgments.

For example, if the issue is the high cost of home heating and its effects on poor people, one policy to consider might be the use of fuel

14-1 POSITION PAPER ON THE LICENSING OF LAY MIDWIVES

THE CASE AGAINST LICENSING LAY MIDWIVES

In 1975 midwives delivered 5,050 babies in Texas. This figure was only 2.3 percent of all the live births in the State that year, but it represented an increase of 90 percent over the number of midwife deliveries in 1970. Since 1975 the rate has continued to increase. Reasons for this increase are unclear, but two general trends are apparent. First, more and more babies are being delivered by midwives in counties along the Mexican border. And second, many young urban couples are choosing to have their babies delivered at home by midwives.

Many persons believe the first of these trends is caused by alien mothers crossing the border to have their babies. Babies born in Texas have the benefit of U.S. citizenship or, if taken back to Mexico, have dual citizenship until age 18. This practice may or may not be the reason for the large number of deliveries in the valley. At any rate, the statistics point to the fact that large numbers of Mexican-American babies are delivered by midwives.

The second trend can be attributed to a number of things--the women's movement, rising hospital and doctor fees, the growing disaffection from the medical profession in general, the return by many young couples to a pioneer, do-it-yourself lifestyle. For whatever reasons, the number of home births among young urban women is increasing, and the number of midwives along with it.

This growth in the number of midwives has raised questions about regulating the practice of midwifery by some type of licensing. The chief argument given for regulation has been the need to safeguard the public from unskilled or incompetent practitioners. There are flaws in this argument, however, and in fact the weight of the evidence indicates that licensing of lay midwives is not desirable. The arguments against regulation include: (1) restriction of practice, (2) problems of enforcement, (3) problems associated with midwifery being a cultural practice, (4) side effects such as rising fees and maldistribution of personnel, and (5) the new negative sentiment in the state towards professional licensing.

Each of these arguments is discussed below.

The Need to Safeguard the Public

Safeguarding the public has been a common rationale for professional licensing legislation. In the case of midwives, however, safety figures are too sketchy and conflicting to build a strong case for regulation.

Critics of lay midwifery, for example, talk of the dangers involved in unsupervised deliveries made by lay persons of unknown training and skills. Figures collected by Texas Department of Health for 1974 do not substantiate these fears. Out of 4,421 midwife deliveries, only 36 or 0.81 percent resulted in fetal deaths. This figure compares to 2,473 fetal deaths or 1.2 percent for nonmidwife deliveries. Not only do these figures fail to build a case for regulation of lay midwives, but they appear to suggest that midwife deliveries are safer than others. (Along these lines, one study

---

This paper begins by giving statistics to establish the significance of the issue—the growing use of midwives in parts of Texas and rising interest in the need for midwife regulation. The position taken—that midwife regulation should not be adopted—is stated, with five supporting reasons. The five points

published recently in *International Childbirth News* compared home births to an equal number of hospital births and found home births to have fewer cases of infant distress, maternal high blood pressure, postpartum hemorrhage and birth injuries.[1] Furthermore, some countries that use midwives extensively, like The Netherlands, have lower infant mortality rates than the U.S.)

Critics of lay midwifery point out that lay midwives do not have the skills to recognize or cope with birth complications. These critics fail to mention that prenatal screening can identify those births most likely to need specialized care and that 90 percent of all births occur without any major complications.[2] In addition, many urban midwives deliver babies only if they have easy access to a hospital.

The American College of Obstetricians and Gynecologists (ACOG) recently sent out a news release saying that "out-of-hospital births pose a two to five times greater risk to a baby's life than hospital births."[3] This assertion is based on data from only eleven state health departments, however. And of this eleven "only four . . . identified stillbirths occurring at home." This sparsity of data finally leads the ACOG to conclude that it cannot make an accurate comparison.

Two other points need to be made about figures like those put out by the ACOG. First, no attempt is made to correlate the number of fetal deaths with economic status of the mother or with data about the availability of prenatal care. Good prenatal care will greatly improve the life chances of mother and baby. And second, it cannot be assumed that all "out of hospital births" occur in private homes or that all are attended by lay midwives. The statistics simply are not broken down to a degree that allows meaningful comparisons to be made.

One final point to be made about the safety argument is found in Patrick O'Donoghue's book *Evidence about the Effect of Health Care Regulations: An Evaluation and Synopsis of Policy Relevant Research*. O'Donoghue points out that "licensure stops at least one step short of actually assuring on a continuing basis the quality of health care delivered by a practitioner."[4] This is because it does little to ensure safe practice over the professional lifetime of the health care practitioner. Most licensing laws operate to ensure certain entering qualifications, but few can assure the continued competence of the practitioner. There are no mechanisms to protect the public from the licensed practitioner who is no longer competent to practice.

Restriction of Practice

Any legislation aimed at regulating lay midwives may ultimately restrict their practice. Among certain population groups and in areas where obstetrical services are scarce, this may prove to be a great disservice.

The two groups of women making the greatest use of lay midwives are Mexican Americans and young feminists. Mexican Americans use midwives partly out of cultural tradition but also because other health personnel are unavailable to them. Last year the *Corpus Christi Caller* reported that "20 percent of all the children born in the Lower Rio Grande Valley were delivered by

are then discussed in more detail throughout the paper. Note that the paper does not simply give figures and arguments against midwife licensing. The writer also discusses evidence that seems to favor licensing and analyzes that evidence to show its shortcomings.

14-1, CONTINUED

parteras outside hospital facilities."[5] (*Parteras* is the Spanish word for midwife.) The *Caller* went on to point out that parteras are used because other types of professional health care are "too often financially and geographically inaccessible. Most *parteras* charge what the family can afford."

Until more health professionals agree to serve in underserved rural areas and barrios, poor Mexican Americans will continue to rely heavily on the services of lay midwives. Regulation of midwives may help to further cut off this group from needed health services.

For young feminists, the regulation issue involves rights and individual freedoms. Feminists say that women should have more control over the birthing process and that the medical profession is largely responsible for taking childbirth out of the warm, home environment and placing it in the cold confines of a hospital delivery room. Moreover, many young women believe it is important to the psychological strengthening of the family unit to have the entire family present at the birth of a new family member. Few hospitals allow this practice.

Of course, regulation would not have to mean an end to the practice of lay midwifery. (Though in other states this has often been the case.) But, depending on how legislation is drawn, it can severely limit how and when and under what conditions midwives practice. For example, Connecticut prohibits midwives from attending any women in labor who are not at least seven months pregnant. Many states have laws that prohibit midwives from attending any except cases of normal childbirth. Still other states prohibit midwives from practicing without sponsorship or medical backup from a physician. Not only do regulations like these restrict practice of midwives, but they make criminals of midwives who deliver babies due to the unavailability of other medical personnel.

The groups supporting regulation are a clue to the function regulation would serve. Frequently, the group to be regulated promotes regulation because it has the most to gain from controlling entrance into the profession. In this case, however, it is not lay midwives but the dominant health professionals--doctors, nurses, and nurse midwives--who are supporting regulation. Needless to say, the beliefs of most of these health professionals about home births and midwifery are antithetical to those of lay midwives.

Doctors and nurses also have a financial motive for promoting regulation. According to *Time* magazine, "Obstetrics is one of the largest and most lucrative specialties in U.S. medicine."[6] Midwives present a threat to the income of those who practice obstetrics. Obviously doctors hope to keep their stranglehold on this specialty by making it more difficult for midwives to practice.

Problem of Enforcement

There are at least two reasons why any mechanism to regulate the practice of lay midwives will not be easy to enforce. First, the Texas Department of Health will be the enforcing body, and it is not funded or structured adequately to permit enforcement. Some rural counties in South Texas, for example, have only a single health officer to oversee all public health functions for the county.

The second thing that will make enforcement difficult is the nature of the practice of midwifery. Midwives seldom advertise their practice or solicit business. Many midwives have practiced in the same community for years, and customers learn about them chiefly by word of mouth. Though Texas law requires all midwives to register with the local registrar, very few of them do so now. These facts taken together seem to suggest that any attempts to enforce regulation would run into difficulties.

One other point about enforcement should be made. Because of the nature of midwifery and the limited resources the state would probably commit to enforcement, any regulation is bound to be differentially enforced. The Department of Health will have to depend largely upon complaints to inform it of unsafe practices of a midwife. And those people who have chosen to use the services of an unlicensed midwife will not be likely to file a complaint. In fact, even those who use the licensed midwives will not be likely to complain if they are young, poor, or Spanish-speaking.

On top of this, licensed midwives would be reporting on unlicensed ones. This would clearly work against the elderly, Spanish-speaking parteras who have practiced for years, because they are the persons least likely to comply with new regulations.

In short, the enforcement problems accompanying regulation of the midwife practice are monumental. And the wisdom of passing regulating legislation that has a poor chance of operating effectively is questionable.

Midwifery as a Cultural Practice

Still another argument against licensing can be made on the grounds that midwives are an intricate part of the Mexican-American culture. For years, lower-class Mexicans and Mexican Americans have used neighborhood parteras to deliver their babies. Part of the reason for this is financial. The partera, however, is a well-established and widely accepted part of the community support system. She may be preferred even by those who can afford other medical personnel because she is known by the mother and the family, operates in a familiar setting, speaks Spanish, and because she is female. Childbirth can be a frightening experience, especially for young mothers. The partera has the ability to transmit warmth and comfort to young females that they cannot receive from Anglo male doctors in a hospital setting.

Regulating midwives, then, may amount to regulating a long-held cultural practice.

Side Effects of Regulating Health Personnel

O'Donoghue mentions a number of side effects that result from licensing health personnel. Most of these side effects are detrimental to the consumers of health services.

First of all, personnel licensing almost always serves to reduce the supply of health practitioners, and the resulting manpower shortage almost always brings about rising fees. Second, as a general rule, licensed practitioners prefer to practice in urban areas where they can make more money. This means that after they are licensed, health personnel often leave the

14-1, CONTINUED

rural areas where they are needed most. Still a third drawback to licensing health personnel is the reluctance of states to accept licenses issued by other states. This reluctance limits interstate mobility of health personnel and also exacerbates the maldistribution problem.

It is not clear how many of these side effects will result from the licensing of lay midwives. Undoubtedly, those midwives who have practiced for years in the same community will want to remain there. But with the growth of the practice, some of those events mentioned above would be likely to occur. So, once again, licensing may be an ultimate disservice to the public.

Negative Sentiment about Licensing

One final argument against regulations is the growing sentiment among many legislators to curtail professional licensing. Although more and more professions are petitioning the state legislature for licensing ordinances, recent activities of the Sunset Commission have cast a shadow of doubt over their chances for getting bills passed. The pattern in the past has been for the legislature to create an independent licensing board to oversee all functions related to testing, issuing, and revoking professional licenses. Recent investigations by members of the Sunset Commission, however, have revealed that many independent licensing boards do very little to regulate their professions. The commission is recommending combining some boards, abolishing others, and putting still others under the auspices of state agencies.

The midwife licensing bill (H.B. 1314) introduced last session placed the responsibility for granting licenses directly under the Department of Health. Placing the licensing responsibility within a state agency rather than with a board probably made the bill more palatable to House members. But at the same time, this approach gave control of the licensing process to a profession whose beliefs and practices are antithetical to those of lay midwives. Any future attempt to set up a licensing mechanism for midwives should avoid giving complete control of the licensing process to the medical profession. (One way this might be done is to set up a board of lay midwives under the Health Department and to give this board direct regulatory responsibility. After all, lay midwives operate with principles that are different from those of other health practitioners who render obstetrical care, and they are in the best position to judge the practices of other lay midwives.)

Recommendations

For the reasons given above and others, regulation of lay midwives is not advisable. Lay midwifery exists and will continue to be used by certain population groups despite efforts to regulate or do away with it. If physicians and others are truly concerned about public safety they should give their assistance to lay midwives in the form of training or medical backup. In addition, the Texas Department of Health should set as its priority not introducing measures to regulate midwives but providing good prenatal care clinics so that every woman in Texas has a greater chance to have a safe pregnancy and delivery. Measures taken to help update and improve the practice of midwifery and measures taken to upgrade prenatal care services will be a far greater service to the people of Texas than regulation will be.

NOTES

[1] "Home Births Might Be Better," Fort Worth Morning *Star-Telegram,* December 13, 1977, p. 19A.

[2] "Rebirth for Midwifery," *Time,* August 29, 1977, p. 66.

[3] American College of Obstetricians and Gynecologists, "Health Department Data Shows Danger of Home Births," January 4, 1978 (news release).

[4] Patrick O'Donoghue, *Evidence about the Effect of Health Care Regulation: An Evaluation and Synopsis of Policy Relevant Research* (Denver, Colo.: Spectrum Research, Inc., 1974), p. 91.

[5] Hilary Hilton, "Working toward a Better Beginning," *Corpus Christi Caller,* June 26, 1977, p. 8a.

[6] "Rebirth for Midwifery," p. 66.

stamps to help people pay their utility bills. This idea has its good points and bad points. Some writers might say:

> Using fuel stamps is a poor way to solve this problem, because stamps would require a massive wasteful bureaucracy and excessive government funding.

Others might argue:

> Using fuel stamps is an excellent solution to the problem, because stamps could be easily administered by existing service organizations.

Such statements might be OK in a position paper, but they would be out of place in an informational backgrounder. Instead of defending one side or another, merely write to inform:

> Fuel stamps are one proposed solution to this problem. A fuel stamp program would require government funding and a system for administering the funds. Such a program possibly could be managed by existing service organizations.

Implications What are the consequences of choosing one policy over another? A good backgrounder either answers that question or points out some of the things to consider.

A backgrounder on national energy policy, for example, might discuss synthetic fuel production from coal as a method of replacing diminishing oil reserves. The discussion should include the background (oil supply and demand situation), the state of synthetic fuel technology, the economics of synthetic fuel production, environmental effects, and the prospects for meeting the country's fuel needs. But in addition to all that, implications not obvious at first glance must be mentioned. For example, the use of coal to make liquid fuels might solve the problem of fuel for transportation. But such a program might also diminish the amount of coal available to make electricity. For another thing, the production and use of synthetic fuels releases more carbon dioxide than direct burning of coal. Too much carbon dioxide in the air could cause serious future climate changes.

Identifying the implications of a certain policy includes anticipating future developments. A backgrounder should point out whether an issue is likely to grow more important or fade away—if such predictions are possible. Perhaps a major government study is under way with a report due next year, or perhaps the issue is to be a topic of discussion at a forthcoming convention. If so, the issue is likely to be in the news in the future and thus become more visible.

Documentation

When you prepare a backgrounder, you must provide documentation for the information you use. You should list articles, books and other source material in a bibliography at the end of the paper, and also provide footnotes for specific facts or statistics. People using the backgrounder may want to pursue a specific point more fully. Or they might find a discrepancy between facts in the backgrounder and some other source, in which case they'll want to check out the original source.

POSITION PAPERS

Position papers are documents designed to give an organization's position on an issue. The issue may be general and national in scope—like national health insurance—or it might be a state or local matter. The position might be taken on a general subject or on one specific aspect of it—like one senator's proposal on a national health insurance program.

Like the backgrounder, a position paper requires extensive research. But it also requires consultation with the management of the company or organization to determine just what the position should be. In some cases, management determines a position, then asks the PR writer to prepare a position paper supporting that particular stand. In other cases, the PR writer will prepare a paper giving a proposed position, and management may accept it, reject it or modify it.

Frequently the PR person's role is simply to call management's attention to the existence of an issue on which the company should take a position. The first step in writing a position paper is just that: stating the issue.

Stating the Issue

No position paper will be of any value if the issue it addresses is not clearly stated. The writer must have a clear idea of what the real issue is, and the issue must be described fairly and honestly. *Don't* distort the issue to suit your purposes or to make it easier to form—or defend—an opinion. The purpose of a position paper is to address an issue squarely, not skirt it.

For example, assume an oil company addresses the issue of excess profits by pointing out that profits are important for attracting investment capital and for reinvestment in the business to create jobs. Such a response does not speak to the issue. The real issue is not whether profits are needed, but whether the company is making more than is fair or needed. To avoid such pitfalls, the position paper should state clearly, near the beginning of the paper, just what the issue is. One of the best ways to do this is to provide some relevant background.

Background

In order for the position paper to make any sense, you have to provide some background. Position papers are not history papers, though, so don't write the entire chronology of an issue. Be sure, though, that you provide enough background for readers to understand why the subject under discussion has become "an issue."

In many cases the nature of the issue is fairly obvious and the need for background minimal. Sometimes, however, a position cannot be defended adequately without going into the background in some detail. This was the case in a paper prepared by a state legislator's staff member on the licensing of lay midwives in Texas (see Example 14–1). The purpose of this paper was to defend a position against licensing, but to do so the writer had to go into the circumstances surrounding the practice of lay midwifery. Notice that although this paper is like a backgrounder in many ways, its main purpose is to defend a position.

Ordinarily, a position paper need not be so lengthy. Once a minimum amount of background is provided, the writer should immediately make the position clear and then defend it.

Position

The "position" in a position paper should be stated at once. Don't launch into an elaborate recitation of facts and figures that culminate in an eloquent conclusion, keeping your readers in suspense throughout. State the position clearly first so the reader will know where you stand. Then go on to support it with appropriate facts and figures. Organize your points logically so readers can follow your chain of reasoning. Use examples or illustrations that readers can understand and relate to. Use statistics and other factual data to support and reinforce your points.

Be careful, though, not to overwork statistics. While a long list of numbers and percentages might be needed in a backgrounder, they just fog up your message in a position paper. An endless list of figures will simply bore readers—or confuse them. So make your point in clear, plain language, and then select just the right statistic to support the point. Additional figures can be relegated to a table or appendix. (Also, use footnotes or an appendix to provide the source for statistics and other factual material. Numbers carry greater weight with some readers if they come from an authoritative source.)

Consider Both Sides Although a position paper should come down strongly on one side of an issue, don't ignore the other side. It is appropriate to marshal all the evidence you can to support your view. But don't stack cards.

"Cardstacking" is the propaganda device whereby all the supporting arguments are given but none of the opposition points are mentioned. This gives the impression that the evidence is more overwhelming than it really is. It might make a good first impression, but as soon as readers find out there's another side to the story they may begin to distrust your message.

It is far better to raise objections to your view and then refute them, if possible. If the other side has some good points, acknowledge them, but show why you think they are outweighed by other considerations.

Consider the Audience Sometimes position papers are written for distribution to various publics; often they are written just for management. But even when management is the initial audience, position papers must be prepared with the ultimate audience in mind. For example, some position papers will be used by management to explain company policy to stockholders. Others might be written to help management explain company policy to employees, or to the media and general public. In each case, the explanation of the position must be written considering the ultimate audience.

That doesn't mean you give conflicting stories to different groups. But you must explain your position in a way that makes sense to the audience—and often the things that make sense to employees or stockholders or the public are not the same things that make sense to management.

Remember, too, that different audiences are likely to have different questions about any given issue and the position you have taken. You should anticipate such questions and answer them in the paper.

Recommendations

One question will come up frequently when you take a position against some program or proposed law: What do you recommend? If a problem exists, and you take a position against someone's proposed solution, it is not enough just to show that the proposal is bad. Take national health insurance, for example. If Congress is considering a bill to address the problem that many Americans can't afford good health care, your organization may oppose the bill because it will cost taxpayers too much money. But if that's all you say, you really haven't faced the problem. Part of your position should be the recommendation of alternate solutions to the problem.

FORMAT

When you've finished the writing, you must consider the question of format. Often backgrounders and position papers designed for internal use are simply typed on regular paper with appropriate headings, and the pages are stapled or clipped together. Backgrounders and position papers for handing out to the public may be prepared in forms ranging from plain paper to elaborate printed booklets.

Some companies prepare backgrounders for the public on a special form (see Example 14–2). For internal use, the same company prepares backgrounders and position papers in loose-leaf form so they can be included in a comprehensive notebook. Extensive backgrounders on subjects of major importance (like a request for a large increase in electric rates) are printed and bound in spiral binders.

Often backgrounders include charts and graphs to help explain the subject or provide additional information. Preparing charts and graphs goes beyond writing, but the writer should always be aware of places where a clear chart can supplement words and get the message across more readily.

CONCLUSION

At the heart of successful public relations programs is good information, and such information is often prepared in the form of a backgrounder. At the same time, communicating an organization's viewpoint requires first a clear, well-defended statement of that viewpoint—that's what position papers should provide. Good PR writers know the value of well-prepared backgrounders and position papers to the entire PR operation, and they know that preparing such documents requires just as much skill and care as preparing news releases, ads, brochures, speeches, and any of the other various writing projects that PR people take on.

SELECTED BIBLIOGRAPHY

William L. Rivers, *Writing: Craft and Art* (Englewood Cliffs, N.J.: Prentice-Hall, 1975).

Heil Sheehan, Hedrick Smith, E. W. Kenworthy and Fox Butterfield, *The Pentagon Papers* (Chicago, Ill.: Quadrangle Books, 1971). Besides being of historical interest, this book is amply illustrated with backgrounders and position papers.

14-2 BACKGROUNDER FORMATS

Background Info
Texas Electric Service Company
HOW NUCLEAR POWER WORKS

There are many ways to make electricity. Hydro power, batteries, and solar cells, for example, can be used to make electricity in varying amounts. But the most common method for making large amounts of electricity in a power plant is to use a steam turbine and generator.

With this arrangement, steam at a very high temperature and pressure passes through the steam turbine. The energy from the steam drives the blades of the turbine, which is connected to an electric generator. The rotation of the turbine turns the generator which makes the electricity that is carried away from the plant by transmission wires.

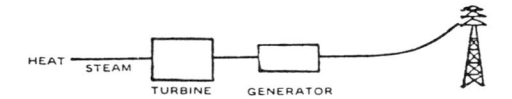

HEAT — STEAM — TURBINE — GENERATOR

For this method of making electricity to work, you need a source of steam. And that means you have to create sufficient heat to boil water and heat the steam to even higher temperatures.

In conventional power plants, the heat comes from burning a fuel. The fuel can be natural gas, oil, or coal, such as lignite. When the fuel is burned in a boiler, heat is created, water is converted into steam, and the steam passes through the steam turbine which drives the generator.

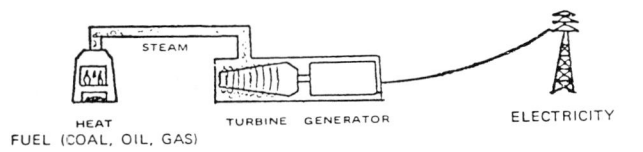

STEAM — TURBINE GENERATOR — ELECTRICITY
HEAT
FUEL (COAL, OIL, GAS)

A Texas electric ultility company uses one format for backgrounders to be distributed to the public and another format for employees. Backgrounders for employees are coded for use in a loose-leaf notebook that covers various issues.

14-2, CONTINUED

Nuclear Information

SECTION: GENERAL INFORMATION

SUBJECT: HOW NUCLEAR POWER WORKS

DATE: 8/25/77

ITEM: 4

PAGE: 1

Q: *How Nuclear Power Works*

A: Nuclear power plants work very much like fossil fuel plants. In a fossil fuel plant, fuel is burned to generate heat, and the heat is used to make steam. The steam passes through a turbine connected to a generator. The force of the steam causes the turbine to spin, which then turns the generator to make an electric current. A nuclear plant operates in the same way except for the heat source. Instead of burning a fuel, the heat comes from uranium fuel in the reactor core. The uranium gives off heat by the process of nuclear fission, which is simply the breaking in two, or splitting, of the nucleus of a uranium atom.

Fossil Fuel Plant

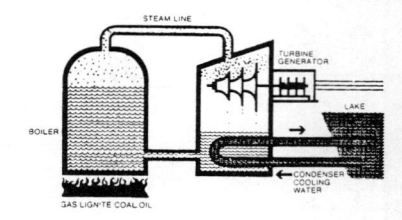

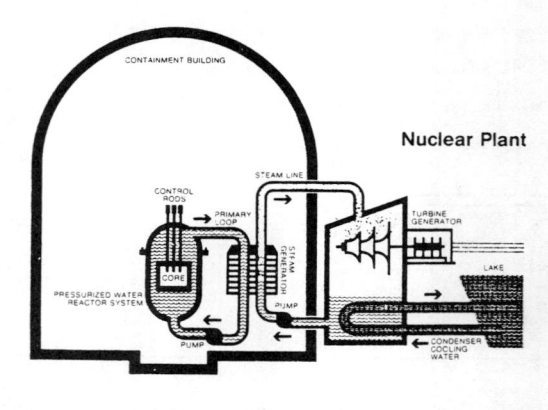

Nuclear Plant

15

MEMOS AND LETTERS/REPORTS AND PROPOSALS

Business correspondence is often drafted by the public relations specialist because usually such correspondence is persuasive communication of some sort, regardless of the format. Four formats are discussed in this chapter: memos and letters, which may be addressed either to individuals or groups, and the more formal reports and proposals.

SIMILARITIES

Memos and Letters

Memo comes from *memorandum* and means an informal note written as a reminder of something important, something recorded to help remember the details of something that has occurred (like an agreement or transaction), or something that is to occur. Memo has also come to mean an informal communication, generally used between offices, to give directions or to exchange information.

A more formal means of communication is a letter. It usually has a form of address, internal format and closing that follows an accepted style found in standard manuals.

Memos or letters may be directed from one individual to another. In this case the purpose of the communication and the relationship between the individuals determine the tone and style of the communication. A person of higher status generally feels freer to be informal with a person of lower status, so the tone of a memo from a PR executive to the office secretary may be more informal than a memo from the PR executive to the president of the company, unless the president is also a tennis partner. Then the personal relationship makes for a more relaxed language.

Memos and letters may be produced for larger audiences, but received by people as individuals. For example, a PR executive may want to remind the creative department that an important campaign is going to come during the summer when many intend to go on vacation. The memo is on a subject affecting all of them, so it will be written in a single form, but distributed to each member of the creative department. Each member of that audience has to be considered when writing the memo. The reactions of each must be anticipated because it is addressed to each.

The same thing is true of letters. Most of us have received Christmas letters—letters written by a friend to a large number of us who are expected to react as we would to correspondence written especially for us and sent only to us. Obviously such letters, either personal or business, are not like personal correspondence because they are, in effect, "published" correspondence. In business, sophisticated machines make it possible for these "mass" letters to be very personalized, with your name not only in the address but also within the letter. Nevertheless, individualized mass letters are more formal in tone and remote in approach than one-on-one letters or memos.

The terms *formal* and *informal* refer mostly to physical format because the language of an internal memo addressed to all employees from management may be much more formal in tone and language than the business letters between two corporation presidents who are close friends. As always, the intended audience and the purpose of the communication make the difference.

Reports and Proposals

The purpose is particularly significant when we look at the difference between reports and proposals. A report may be a review of a meeting, a series of meetings, an event, or progress on a project. It is an informative document. Proposals are selling pieces. A proposal may be a few pages or it may be hundreds of papers, but its purpose is always to win agreement from the person to whom the proposal is submitted. Both reports and proposals often include illustrations that help tell the story: either artists' sketches, photographs, charts or tables. Usually the audience for a report or proposal is more than one person.

DIFFERENCES

Memos and Letters

One memo in the office mail reminds account group members of a meeting, another calls attention to a new policy on billings, and still another is a whimsical piece on the function of committees. All are technically memos, but their different purposes set them apart. Their different purposes—to inform, to educate or to entertain—also suggest a difference in style.

Letters with different purposes also reflect stylistic differences. A letter explaining a change in management philosophy, policy or procedure might be done in a bright, lively style to attract attention so it will be read and remembered, but its principal purpose is not to entertain. The devices used to make it bright and lively must not detract from the point the letter is trying to make, or diminish the seriousness with which the letter should be taken.

Knowing the audience well often makes the difference between selecting exactly the right tone and losing effectiveness because of an inappropriate approach. A PR student hired as an intern by a Florida company was told to "do something about the terrible internal communications problem." Management said no one paid any attention to directives being issued weekly, if not daily, on very important matters about plant safety. It didn't take the student very long to locate the problem. All of the letters and memos were in English and 80 percent of the employees spoke only Spanish. Usually, the communicator has a better awareness of the audience than that, but sometimes the audience is not given as careful attention as necessary.

Reports and Proposals

The purpose for a report or proposal is usually specific, and the style is set by style manuals or corporate policy. Remember, however, in preparing a report or proposal, that all of those who will be reading it must be considered. If you are writing a proposal for promoting a special event, for instance, and you know that the potential sponsor is a sailing enthusiast, your chances of getting support are greater if you work the sport into your event. Or perhaps the person you are writing the proposal for is known to be a real penny pincher. If you can design a proposal so every activity in the event has multiple benefits, you are more likely to get the attention of that person, who looks to get the ultimate out of every investment. People with big egos enjoy events that are "first" or "only" or "biggest." The most salable part of the proposal may occur in a single sentence.

MEMOS

The tone and tempo of a memo depends on its purpose, style and audience. There are five general categories for classifying memos: bulletin, essay, informative, action and summary.

1. The bulletin has a sense of urgency and immediacy about it. Generally it is brief and may be somewhat terse in style. It is the telegram of the memo world.

2. An essay memo is more discursive; it is used for "let's talk it over" material. The essay may be on management philosophy or it may be nothing weightier than getting people to clean up the coffee room after using it. The style is often conversational and flowing.

3. The informative memo is usually a detailed descriptive piece, like the progress report an account group might prepare for a client. It documents action already taken and its results, and projects what is to occur and what effects might be anticipated.

4. The action memo describes either action that was taken or action planned. There may be a place on the memo for a response from recipients—a place where they can indicate approval or disapproval of actions or where they can indicate their assumption of responsibilities for an activity. Perhaps you have belonged to an organization and received a memo outlining what needed to be done for an event. Beside each event was a dash and you were to sign your name beside one of the areas of responsibility—you risked being "assigned" a duty if you did not respond voluntarily. This form of "persuasion" is implied coercion, but it works if the person doing the assigning has some power over you. (See 15–1 for an example of an action memo.)

5. A summary memo is a detailed descriptive in essay or outline format. Discussions and actions are collected under appropriate topical headings so that progress made during the meeting is easy to determine. The discussions usually provide the reasons for the actions taken or planned.

Memos, because they are informal pieces of communication, generally reflect the personality of the person writing them. They are seldom impersonal, stiff or remote. There are exceptions, however. In large companies and often in branches of government a memo is circulated that appears to have been written by a machine, and sometimes not a very literate one. Navy personnel stationed at a base in the Philippines once got a memo sent to all residents in the housing complex advising them "to secure all unaffixed waste disposal units by placing same in permanently uninhabited designated space in quarters" because there was "a predicted turbulence which could result in their dispersal." Although it took a while to decode the memo, what it meant was a tropical storm was brewing and all garbage cans should be placed in the utility rooms so the cans wouldn't blow away.

Memos should be personalized, not only by being intelligible, but also by involving the reader through the use of "you." The direct form of address generally gets our attention and involves us in the message. Not only is it a pleasant way to write, it is effective.

The way a message is disseminated often has some impact on the attention it gets. An office trying to conserve time and paper, yet inform everyone, often resorts to the routing slip. A routing slip contains the names of everyone who should see the material typed on it. The slip is attached to the material to be routed. As the people read the material, they check or initial the space opposite their name. Often, such materials are simply moved instead of being read. A frustrated executive once threatened to hold morning memo quizzes to see who—if anyone—had read materials signed.

Posting memos is often less effective than routing. Unless the posted material has some attention-getting graphics the message is likely to be missed. Important directives may be routed and posted—the posting would help ensure that they were seen. However, if a memo is prepared especially for posting, it should be designed like a poster and treated like a bulletin.

Printing many copies of a memo puts you in the publishing business, and you need to look at whether you have the appropriate medium for your message. If you do have to publish a memo for a large circulation, then you have to decide the best way to send it to get attention and to be timely and effective. You could, for example, have it carried to department heads and have them hand it out to employees in a meeting or at their desks. You might want to put a memo about changes in insurance coverage in with paychecks to be sure it will be read. Or you might want to mail a memo about the company picnic to the employee's home to be sure the family has an opportunity to plan for the event.

The setting in which the memo is received has a great deal to do with its impact. A fund-raising agency found this out in a negative way. The agency sent letters describing procedures to department heads in a large company, and attached donation cards to memos that the department heads were to distribute to the employees. The employees were to hand their pledge cards or donations back to the department heads. The department heads were under considerable pressure from management to get 100 percent "volunteered." Some of the employees complained about the implied coercion and management reacted by refusing to cooperate with the fund-raising agency the following year.

LETTERS

A letter can be one-to-one in intent, but may either be to an individual or to a mass of individuals, like the one you got last week from a car insurance company—you and thousands of other car owners. In either case, the recipient will react as if being addressed individually by the correspondence. (See unusual use of letters in Examples 15-2 and 15-3.)

15-1 AN ACTION MEMO: PR PLANNING MEMO

MEMORANDUM

To: S. Adams

Re: Independence and Necessary Public Relations Programs

OBJECTIVES

To begin with, we must formulate objectives more specific than "independence." Saying what we want is easy; saying what we have to do to get it is a little more difficult. As with the PR campaign against the Stamp Act, we must specify the objective in terms that tell us what we must do. With the Stamp Act, we wanted repeal. But our specific objective was to prevent the act's enforcement.

If we rephrase "independence" to describe what we really want, we might say "to establish home rule and prevent the interference of the British in the internal affairs of the colonies." In a sense, we had "home rule" before 1763. But our research on British attitudes shows that return to the pre-1763 days is impossible. Hence, complete separation is the only way to achieve home rule.

But what will this require? Above all, it will require unification of the colonies and belief in a common purpose: independence from Britain. No plan for separation will succeed unless all the colonies join together. Thus our primary objective is:

To effect a unification of the colonies.

Achieving this objective will require a massive, well-coordinated PR campaign throughout the colonies. The objective of such a campaign should be:

1. To generate common attitudes among the inhabitants of the various colonies.

2. To sustain and organize popular sentiment.

3. To change the attitude of the people toward Great Britain from one of allegiance to one of repudiation.

RESEARCH

A thorough examination of English common law, colonial charters, newspapers of the last decade and British and colonial history formed the major portion of the research effort for this project. In addition, during my recent tour of the colonies I interviewed a number of key political figures to gather their insights into the current situation. To this has been added the report from Benjamin Franklin on opinions in Britain and France. I list below the major research findings.

One of the most important kinds of memos PR people write is the memo outlining a major PR program. This mock memo is prepared as though a single PR consultant was in charge of planning the public relations for the American Revolution. Note that the first step is to give a clear statement

Legal Basis for Independence

There can be no doubt that taxation of an Englishman without his consent (through representation in the taxing body) is a violation of his rights. This is the clear message of the Glorious Revolution (1689), and it is reaffirmed in various ways by the colonial charters. Furthermore, during the reign of Queen Anne, the crown agreed to recall the provincial governor after the New York assembly complained that he had taxed the subjects without the consent of the assembly. This action seems to have established royal consent to the doctrine that taxation without representation is unconstitutional.

No responsible person, in the colonies or England, argues that direct representation of the colonies in Parliament is feasible (see the resolutions of the Stamp Act Congress). Thus if Parliament persists in taxing us, we have no administrative remedies, as our lawyer friends would say. It thus becomes a clear case of Parliament's violating our rights through unconstitutional action; they are the lawbreakers. We are thus legally--and morally--justified in breaking our ties to the empire.

Current State of Opinion in the Colonies

Despite the anti-British feelings displayed at the time of the Stamp Act, ties to Britain remain strong. We are, for the most part, Englishmen who just happen to live on the other side of the Atlantic. The physical distance is trifling compared to the closeness of language, history and culture.

In fact, it is not an exaggeration to say that the colonies feel closer to England than they do to each other. At first glance, barriers to achieving unification would seem almost insurmountable.

But research has turned up some encouraging signs. Since the beginning of this century the colonies have joined in several wars, most recently the seven years' battle against the French. Fighting on the same side brings peoples together, and joining in battle again would not be a completely novel affair. Furthermore, the colonists have in common their "rights as Englishmen," along with the heritage of fighting for these rights, which have been passed down from 17th-century England. Most of us share a common language, and we hold a common allegiance to the crown. Upon these common beliefs and traits we should be able to build a movement for unity.

True, these common features have not led the way to unity so far. In essence, this is because the tie to Britain has been strong; each colony needed Britain more than it needed any other colony. But this need was largely due to the threatening presence of the French on our western borders. With France gone, the tie to England can be weakened.

One further point should be made about weakening ties to Britain. A great many of our people came to America because they didn't like things in Britain. Thus we have a ready-made broad base of support for any anti-British movements we undertake.

of the campaign objectives; this is followed by a synopsis of the research findings. Target audiences are designated next, followed by a discussion of "vehicles" of communication (we'd call them "media" today). Finally, the strategy for implementing the program is discussed.

15-1, CONTINUED

Support will also come from certain specific groups. Printers and lawyers, with the memory of the oppressive Stamp Act fresh in their minds, will back efforts for home rule. An extremely important group that will favor self-rule is the clergy. The faith of Protestant Christianity is one of the most central characteristics of colonial culture. It sets us apart from the English, and is perhaps the best spot through which to drive a wedge between the colonies and the crown. After all, the church is a most powerful social institution. The colonies have at least 3,000 churches serving a dozen and a half denominations. And most church leaders fear above all else the establishment of an Anglican episcopate on the North American continent. By promoting such fears we can increase the clergy's hostility toward Britain.

Opinion in England

Opinion toward the colonies in England has changed dramatically since the French and Indian War. English officials view the colonists as spoiled children, and they are determined to crack down on the colonists and bring them "into line." Parliament may have repealed the Stamp Act, but further measures are sure to follow.

The person in England whose opinion is most important, of course, is the king. Most colonists see the king as wise and just; it's Parliament that is to blame for the tyrannical taxation. Our research indicates that this view is rather naive.

King George is certainly a courageous and resolute ruler. He does not lack intelligence. But, without being too unkind, we must report that the king suffers from moral obtuseness and is also stubborn and vain. Most colonists don't know that George favors suppression of the colonies by whatever means might be needed. He has absolutely no sympathy for our appeals in the name of "liberty."

The king's views are shared by many in Parliament. But also in Parliament are those who support the American cause and understand our arguments. Such procolonial voices can be quite important; their protests will no doubt inhibit the ministry from pressing an all-out war against the colonies, at least at first.

Feasibility of Achieving Independence

Research shows that independence is possible. It will not be granted by the king without a fight. But a war for independence can be won. The English army is not in top shape; George will probably have to hire mercenaries to invade the colonies, and mercenaries do not make the best fighters. We have an exceptional military weapon in the backwoods riflemen, who, as marksmen, far surpass anything the British can put in the field.

AUDIENCES

My research findings indicate that certain obvious key audiences should be the primary targets of our PR efforts. These include:
1. Printers
2. Clergy
3. Colonial leaders
4. Certain Members of Parliament
5. The French government

Printers are obviously among the most influential people in the colonies. By controlling the press, they control the flow of information to the public. They constitute our highest priority target audience.

Clergymen, as noted above, can also be of great value in swaying public opinion. They are generally experienced orators and have captive audiences every Sunday.

If we are to achieve unification of the colonies, it is imperative that political leaders in each province be subjected to our communication efforts. Those who already agree must be provided information to support their view; those who are undecided must be persuaded to join the cause.

Members of Parliament who are inclined to support the colonies should be kept informed of our problems. They may be helpful in moderating any possible punitive acts by Parliament. Eventually, of course, war will break out despite the help of our friends in Parliament. At that point we must hope to receive aid from France. Thus, the French government must also be persuaded of the merits of our case.

We must also be aware of certain groups making up the colonial public. Some communications must be designed for the intellectuals, those who make up the colonial assemblies and the like. The lower classes, the backwoods farmers, and the illiterate and poorly educated are other groups we must consider. Special interest groups like mechanics and merchants must also be persuaded, and we must obtain the support--or at least the neutrality--of blacks, Indians, and French Canadians.

VEHICLES

To be effective, our PR program must use the proper vehicles of communication to reach each of our target audiences. Such vehicles can be of three types: written, verbal, and visual.

Written Vehicles of Communication

Beyond any doubt, newspapers will be our most important and most effective method of communicating to large audiences. More than 20 newspapers are published now, and that number is growing; more than 40 should be in operation ten years from now. It is essential that we develop good working relations with the press, for without its cooperation we can never

15-1, CONTINUED

hope to unify opinion across the colonies. We must use this medium in all ways possible.

Primarily, we will use newspapers as an outlet for political essays designed to promote unity among the colonies and animosity toward Great Britain. Newspapers will also be valuable as a medium for reprinting letters and documents helpful to our cause. We may, for example, want to print the Magna Carta, the Bill of Rights, and perhaps parts of some colonial charters. Resolutions passed by colonial assemblies can be reprinted across all the colonies.

Newspapers do have serious limitations, however. Space restrictions force essays to be briefer than we would sometimes like. Developing our arguments in sufficient depth to convince the intellectual classes will require a different medium--the pamphlet. Pamphlets give writers the space they need to build a thorough and complete case for their propositions. Most colonial (and British) leaders are avid pamphlet readers, and propagating our ideas in this form will help develop unified thinking among the key citizens in each colony. Pamphlets will serve to present the overall, complete statement of the American position while newspaper essays can attack more specific points.

While pamphlets are an excellent device for reaching the upper classes, they usually are not read by the majority of the people. In addition to the newspapers, then, we must have a vehicle designed specifically to reach the lower classes. The broadside, or handbill, is perfect for this purpose. It's ideal for rallying crowds and inciting the emotions, since it can be distributed quickly or posted in gathering places. Broadsides rarely identify any source or author, so they can be as inflammatory as we like without fear of reprisal. Broadsides can reach many more people than newspapers can, and they are more effective in gaining attention to a specific issue. They are also easily distributed by clandestine methods, making censorship impossible.

Broadsides and newspapers both reach many townspeople. But seldom do they fall into the hands of our rural citizens. The country people have no regular means of communication with the city, yet it is important that they get our message also. The best possibility with them is the almanac. It is not a timely medium; people get new almanacs no more than once a year. But the only printed matter many rural citizens own is an almanac and a Bible. Indeed, nearly every household has an almanac. While newspaper circulation commonly numbers in the hundreds, Ames of Boston sells 60,000 copies of his almanac each year. Almanacs can't present news, but they can place our general arguments before the country people.

Verbal Vehicles

While written material will be the most important device for disseminating information, we must realize that only about half the men in the colonies can read (and only about a fourth of the women are literate). Furthermore, not everyone who *can* read actually *does* read. So we must devise means for reaching the nonreaders.

The most obvious way is through speeches. Public addresses can gather large crowds. Sermons can also get our message across; here we must enlist the aid of the sympathetic clergy. The best of the speeches and sermons can be reprinted in the newspapers or in pamphlet form.

We must remember that the great majority of the public is not interested in the philosophical and constitutional issues. In fact, most of them can't grasp such complexities. But we must communicate some flavor of the substance of these issues, and verbal communication can help accomplish this. One device especially well-suited to this goal is the slogan--the short, simple but expressive phrase that condenses volumes of elaborate reasoning into a quick, emotional, potent statement of feeling and fact. "No taxation without representation!" is an example. It coveys a substantial amount of the essence of an important issue, but nobody needs to be able to read to understand and remember it.

Taking the brevity of the slogan one step further, we can instruct our speakers to use certain key words again and again, some evoking the positive aspects of our position and others calling forth images of British unfairness. Words standing alone can be just as powerful as slogans. "Tyranny" or "Oppression" or "Slavery" can be the words that characterize the practices of the British; "Liberty" or "Freedom" or "Independence" can be the watchwords of the revolution.

One other verbal device we might try is the song. People who can't read a word can remember uncountable verses of song lyrics. If we can introduce songs that carry our message, and if the songs become popular, we can reach a far greater audience than we can with newspapers, pamphlets and speeches.

Visual Vehicles

Complementing the verbal approach toward those who don't read should be devices aimed at the eyes rather than the ears. Illustrations can be used on broadsides to depict the British in an unfavorable light. Almanac covers are convenient spots for cartoonlike drawings either to idolize the heroes of our side or lampoon the British. One of our most successful illustrative devices during the Stamp Act campaign was the snake cut in pieces. Used with the slogan "Join or Die," this can be a most persuasive cartoon.

Other visual symbols can be created and ingrained in the public consciousness. Liberty trees and liberty poles can be the rallying points for demonstrations, serving as focal points for public attention to the issues.

Other Vehicles

Several miscellaneous devices can add to the overall effect of our communications program. Town meetings, for example, can be forums for publicizing our views. We can coordinate town meetings throughout New England so the same message is received by many audiences at once.

Other less formal methods can be used for communicating ideas and information. Certain taverns can be designated information centers where those in support of our cause can gather to discuss the latest news.

15-1, CONTINUED

STRATEGY

Our research shows that popular sentiment favoring independence will come about only after war breaks out with Britain. The first phase of our PR strategy, then, must be geared to preparing the people for war by building up ill feelings toward Britain and by promoting a sense of intercolonial unity. A second phase of PR strategy will be used after war breaks out, with a third phase to be put into effect after independence is actually declared.

Strategy before War

Our most important objective is to effect a sense of unity among the colonies. This will, of course, be difficult. The diversity of the colonies is well known. However, we have noted two major common threads running through the colonies (aside from the fact that almost everyone speaks English). They are: (1) Every colonial charter guarantees its citizens the rights of Englishmen; and (2) colonists from north to south share a common allegiance to the crown.

We must use these common threads to create a new consciousness, a new spirit of American nationalism among the colonists. Distinctions between New Englanders, New Yorkers, Georgians and Virginians must be made to appear trivial.

Our heritage as Englishmen is a common bond that must be used to turn the colonies against England. We must champion our rights as Englishmen. The early years of our communication efforts must arouse opposition to all those acts of Parliament that ignore our rights. We must heavily emphasize that parliamentary acts denying our rights are unconstitutional, and that if we are to be true to our common heritage, we must oppose them.

This is, of course, an appeal to principle. Some people are motivated by high principle, others by self-interest. Interests differ, but principle is universal and unifying, so appeal to principle must be our primary thrust. We must also, however, provide arguments for those susceptible to self-interest appeals. If one group in particular is taxed or oppressed, we must stress to others that they may be the next to be stung by the ministry's punitive measures. By creating a common bond of subordination to an unjust Parliament, we can create another unifying element--the sharing of a common enemy--and further our objectives.

In pursuing this strategy, we can enhance feelings of unity while encouraging derisive attitudes toward Britain. In generating these ill feelings we must be careful not to break one of our common bonds--allegiance to the crown. King George must not become the object of our attacks during this phase of the campaign. Though we know better, we must appear to believe that the king is good and wise, merely out of touch with the situation in America, and kept in the dark by the ministry. All our wrath should be directed at Parliament. In this way we will avoid severing too soon one of the strongest ties among the colonies.

With these considerations in mind, we can outline the following elements of our PR strategy in the prewar years:

1. Prepare pamphlets aimed at political leaders that detail the legal and moral arguments opposing parliamentary acts of taxation or oppression.

2. Prepare a continuous flow of newspaper essays designed for the general public, stressing the *principle* that Parliament has no right to tax, and emphasizing possible future taxes that might damage each group's particular interests.

3. Stress in all messages our common heritage as Englishmen and our determination to stand on the rights of Englishmen, as loyal subjects of the king.

4. Direct all expressions of outrage at Parliament, the ministry, or colonial governors, but not the king.

Finally, as soon as general sentiment warrants, a conference similar to the Stamp Act Congress should be convened. As soon as armed conflict breaks out, such a congress should become permanent in order to coordinate colonial opposition to the British forces.

Wartime Strategy, before Independence

Until war begins, public statements favoring independence will be useless; in fact, they would damage our cause by appearing too radical. Once war begins, however, the idea of independence might be mentioned. But it will take at least a year of fighting before colonial leaders will be willing to vote for independence. Thus, our strategy for the early part of the war should follow this outline:

1. During the first six months, mention the possibility of independence in newspaper essays but do not promote an immediate vote at this time.

2. During this time allow a small amount of criticism of the king to appear.

3. Six to eight months after the war starts, prepare a pamphlet setting forth the case for independence in strong terms. Distribute the pamphlet widely and have large portions of it reprinted in the newspapers.

4. Use newspapers during the following months to support the ideas of the pamphlet and generate vocal public support for independence.

Our pamphlet calling for independence must address the question of loyalty to the king. This will be the time to sever all ties to the crown. Attacking George personally might prove difficult; instead, we should attack the very notion of kingship, saying, in effect, that no matter how nice a guy George is, all kings are bad because the very idea of "king" is bad.

15-1, CONTINUED

Postindependence Strategy

After the colonies vote for independence, it will still be necessary to win the war to keep it. In large measure, strategy during this period will be typical war strategy: engender hatred for the enemy, boost national morale, induce desertions of enemy soldiers. Of special importance during this period will be communications abroad. We must persuade other countries, especially France, that we are worthy of diplomatic recognition and military aid.

The above has been a bare outline of what we must do to achieve our objectives. I will proceed at once with the planning details. If all goes well, we should have independence in ten years.

15-2 THANK YOU LETTER

Season's Greetings

WE SINCERELY THANK YOU

One of our real joys this holiday season, as we recollect the activities of the North Texas Commission over the past four years, is to be reminded once again that our greatest asset is the strength and unity of the people who live in this region.

We are most grateful to the Commission's membership and our many other friends who have helped this program to produce results as our founders intended.

This holiday season we are thankful for the opportunity to say "Thank You" to our friends and supporters who have participated in this program since 1971 and to many new friendships we enjoy along the way.

We firmly believe that, with your support and participation, Dallas/Fort Worth: The Southwest Metroplex is in a more enviable position as a fine place where people live better, fuller, happier lives.

With your continued participation, we hope to add to the region's assets and quality of life. Working together, we will be able to position the Metroplex as "The Sensible Alternative" in the minds of executives of selected corporations that can contribute to our region's economic and cultural base without disrupting our favorable lifestyle.

We pause to count our many blessings and to be thankful for the opportunity to work with you during each year to build a better Southwest Metroplex.

May you and all whom you hold dear be graced with the blessings of good health and happiness, peace, freedom, and security at this holiday time and in the coming new year.

NORTH TEXAS COMMISSION
Board of Directors
and Staff

NORTH TEXAS COMMISSION • 600 Avenue H East, Suite 101 • Arlington, Texas 76011 • 817/265-7101

Sending a letter instead of a Christmas card is the policy of many institutions who want to use the holiday to thank a constituency for support. The North Texas Commission letter is a good example.

296

PART FOUR
WRITING FOR
SPECIAL AUDIENCES

15-3 PROCLAMATION

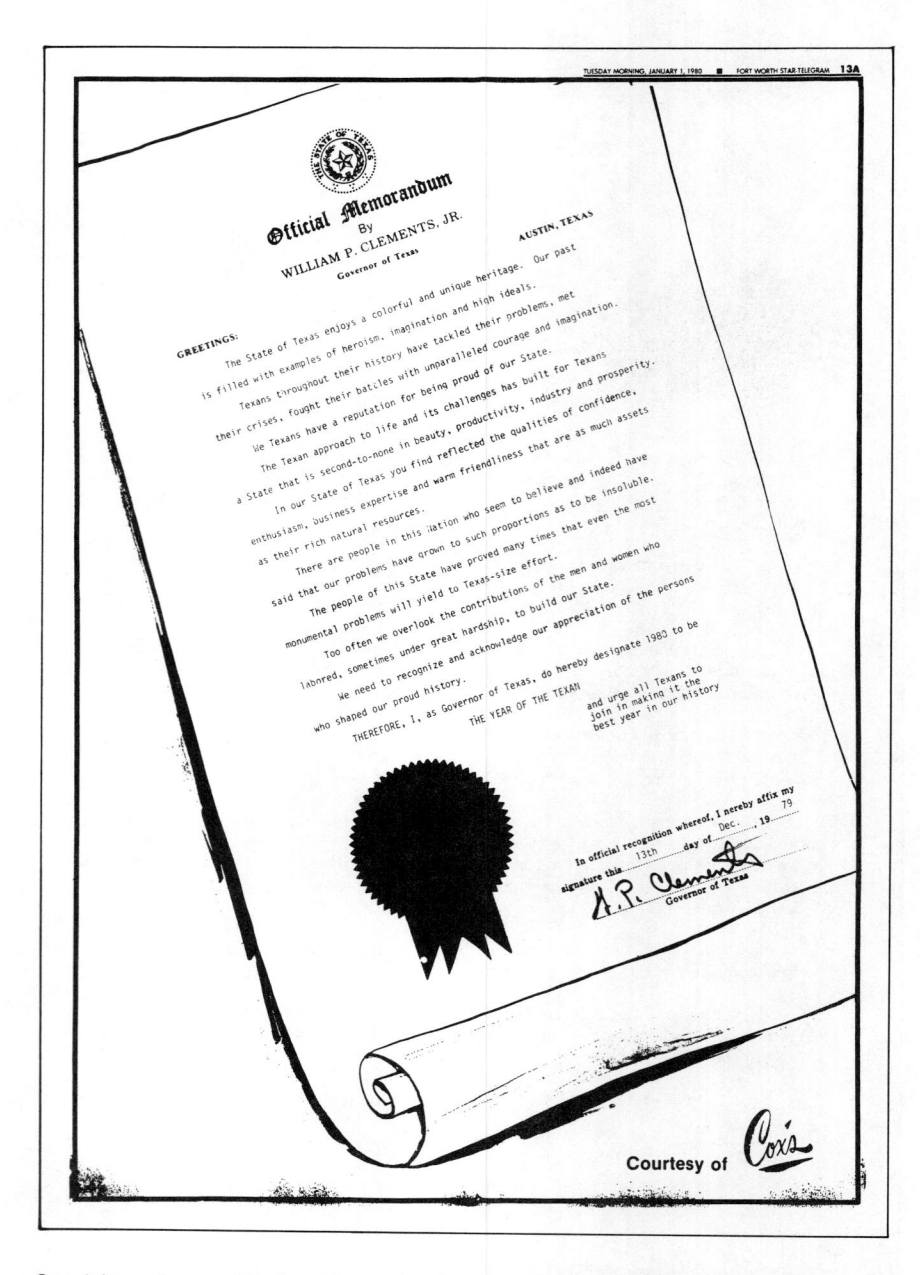

> **Official Memorandum**
> By
> **WILLIAM P. CLEMENTS, JR.**
> Governor of Texas
> AUSTIN, TEXAS
>
> GREETINGS:
>
> The State of Texas enjoys a colorful and unique heritage. Our past is filled with examples of heroism, imagination and high ideals. Texans throughout their history have tackled their problems, met their crises, fought their battles with unparalleled courage and imagination.
>
> We Texans have a reputation for being proud of our State. The Texan approach to life and its challenges has built for Texans a State that is second-to-none in beauty, productivity, industry and prosperity.
>
> In our State of Texas you find reflected the qualities of confidence, enthusiasm, business expertise and warm friendliness that are as much assets as their rich natural resources.
>
> There are people in this Nation who seem to believe and indeed have said that our problems have grown to such proportions as to be insoluble. The people of this State have proved many times that even the most monumental problems will yield to Texas-size effort.
>
> Too often we overlook the contributions of the men and women who labored, sometimes under great hardship, to build our State. We need to recognize and acknowledge our appreciation of the persons who shaped our proud history.
>
> THEREFORE, I, as Governor of Texas, do hereby designate 1980 to be THE YEAR OF THE TEXAN and urge all Texans to join in making it the best year in our history.
>
> In official recognition whereof, I hereby affix my signature this 13th day of Dec., 1979
>
> *W. P. Clements*
> Governor of Texas

Courtesy of *Cox's*

Special events are often based on a proclamation from some government official. In this case, the text of the proclamation was written by the advertising department of a department store chain, which then used it to focus an event. Of course, the officials involved

**CHAPTER 15
MEMOS AND LETTERS/
REPORTS AND PROPOSALS**

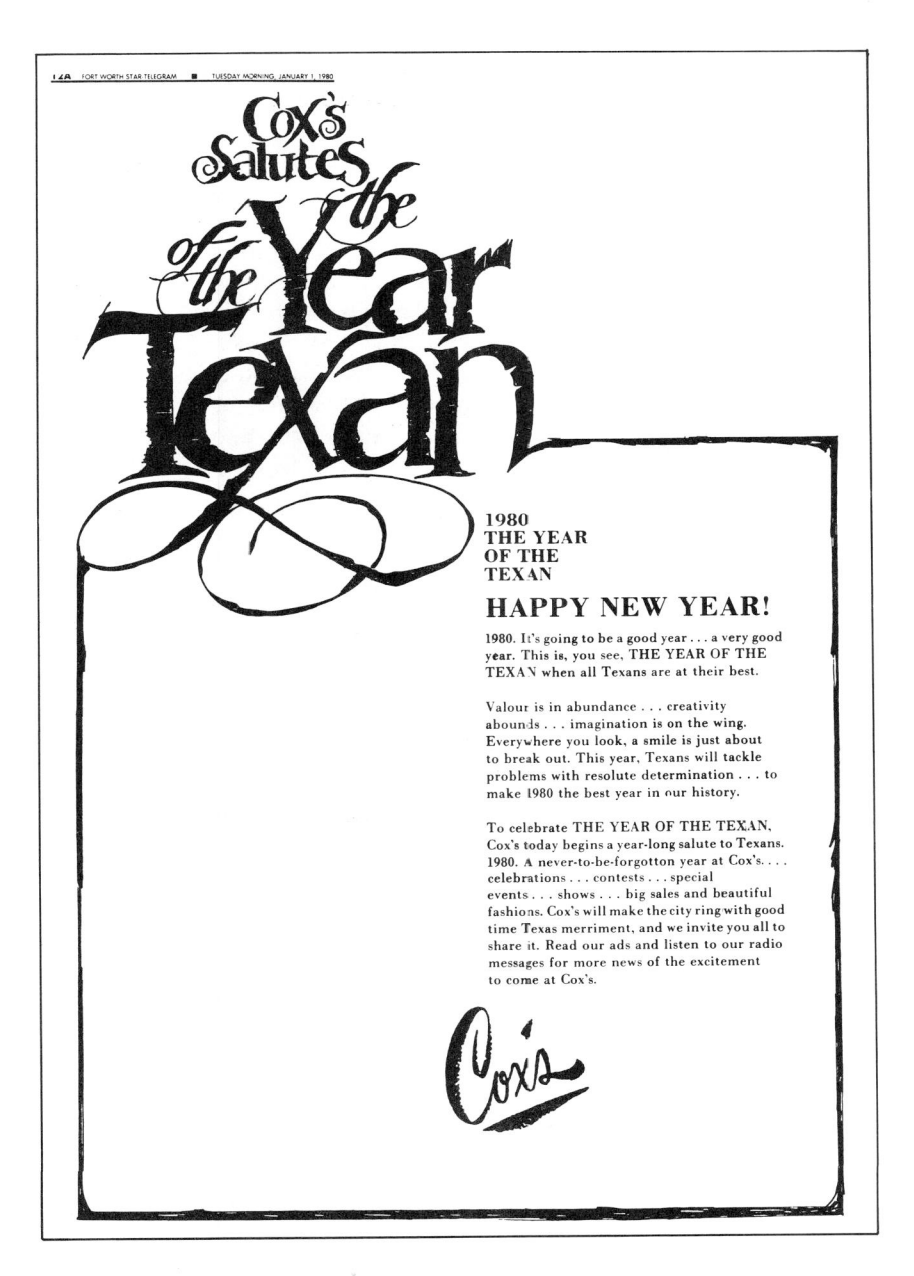

> **Cox's Salutes the Year of the Texan**
>
> *FORT WORTH STAR-TELEGRAM — TUESDAY MORNING, JANUARY 1, 1980*
>
> **1980
> THE YEAR
> OF THE
> TEXAN**
>
> **HAPPY NEW YEAR!**
>
> 1980. It's going to be a good year... a very good year. This is, you see, THE YEAR OF THE TEXAN when all Texans are at their best.
>
> Valour is in abundance... creativity abounds... imagination is on the wing. Everywhere you look, a smile is just about to break out. This year, Texans will tackle problems with resolute determination... to make 1980 the best year in our history.
>
> To celebrate THE YEAR OF THE TEXAN, Cox's today begins a year-long salute to Texans. 1980. A never-to-be-forgotton year at Cox's.... celebrations... contests... special events... shows... big sales and beautiful fashions. Cox's will make the city ring with good time Texas merriment, and we invite you all to share it. Read our ads and listen to our radio messages for more news of the excitement to come at Cox's.
>
> *Cox's*

had to be convinced the project was worthwhile. Usually, convincing officials is no problem with nonprofit events like those put on by the March of Dimes. Note that there is nothing commercial in this proclamation. It is used only to give the event a tag.

When a person is individually addressed, the form of address becomes important, especially if you want to attract attention and establish rapport with the individual. Many business writing texts suggest using "Dear Sir" when writing a letter to someone you don't know. That's fine, if a man receives it. It's not safe to assume that business correspondence is going to a man. Furthermore, you've said something about your own attitude toward women by making that assumption. If you are going to use an impersonal title instead of the person's name, use "Dear Customer," or something else that's appropriate but does not designate sex. Finding an appropriate word to call the persons you are addressing in a mass mailing or in a form letter response to an inquiry is a good idea. The format of the letter is easier to develop with a standard opening, and you avoid having to decide sex on the basis of name. Sometimes it is difficult to tell from a name what sex a person is. There are men named "Carol" and "Shirley" and "Evelyn" and women named "Billie" and "Leslie" and even "Douglas." If you do decide to use the name, find an appropriate title other than Mr., Mrs. and Ms. or Miss. In the academic world students often worry about whether to address a professor as "Dr." if they don't know the degree. A simple solution is always to use, "Dear Prof. Jones." There are many ways to avoid the social title of Mr., Mrs., Ms. or Miss.

What follows the form of address is the most important. Some readers who get past the address may read a letter or not depending on its length. An advertising executive we know won't mail a letter longer than one page. He says if it's longer than a page, then he needs to get on either the phone or a plane and explain the situation in person.

Some letters may be longer than one page and be effective if they look easy to read. One way to make them easy to read is to break them up with topical headlines and indented material set in boldface or italics. Readers can scan a letter like this more easily, select what seems most important and react to portions of the message.

The style of each portion is important too because each should be understandable by itself, apart from the bulk of the letter. Thus, each must be a smoothly polished part, fitting together with the whole, but capable of standing alone to offer a special insight into the situation or problem. A university's admissions office has a three-page letter it sends to high school students who are probably not too eager to read. However, the letter is divided into enticing bits: "What about Your Social Life?" and "How's the Food?"—all designed to attract attention and describe one facet of life at the school. For style to be effective, whether you're talking to high school seniors or senior executives, a clean and uncluttered prose is essential. Appendix A contains readability formulas—apply them to your letters.

For promotions, the public relations person will address letters to a particular audience, "Dear Subscribers," "Dear Channel 13 Listeners." It is difficult to be specific and creative, but a letter from the credit union that begins "Dear Millionaire-to-Be" is sure to have a readership. Such exaggeration might appear to be either oversell or gross assumption, but it will call attention to a savings plan that might otherwise have been discounted.

Most promotional letters are generally no longer than two pages unless a very expensive item or idea is involved. A letter soliciting memberships in the university's President's Club at $1,000 a year was four pages, but its length was necessary to explain why the president of a state university needed private funds and describe how these would be spent. A letter inviting subscription to a series of porcelain plates was also four pages, inside a handsome four-color cover of almost framable quality. The format of the piece said something about the quality implied by the offer.

The more you are asking for, in donations of time or money, the clearer your appeal needs to be. Readers are doing you a favor by reading your material. Reward them with clarity and simplicity, as well as easy-to-follow directions for a response.

Every letter should make clear how the reader should respond. That's common courtesy. Ease of response should be a part of the design of the communication. There should also be adequate reference in the communication to the message source. Provide, too, for unanticipated responses. For years a mail order company gave only a post office box; that made it impossible for customers to call to find out what had happened to an order. If the company had not been a well-established, reputable one, quite a few customers would probably have been one-time customers—they would be suspicious of a mail order operation you couldn't reach by telephone. For years after zip codes were introduced, another well-established but conservative company kept "using up" old letterheads that did not have the zip code, much to the frustration of all correspondents.

The best way to test both memos and letters is to read the finished piece from the point of view of someone who knows nothing about the subject matter. If you are good at role-playing, the problems your memo or letter is likely to cause will become apparent. If you're not a good actor, find a subject for the experiment. This is also a good way to test reports and proposals. Line up as many readers as you can to help you debug your reports and letters.

REPORTS AND PROPOSALS

The organization and requirements of reports and proposals are similar enough for both to be considered together.

Organization

Front Matter At the beginning of any formal presentation of a report or proposal is a collection of material, much like what appears at the beginning of a book, called "front matter." The front matter for a presentation includes a cover page, a letter directing attention to the document, a table of contents and a list of illustrations, charts and tables. All of these are familiar and probably self-explanatory, except the letter. Two types of letters may be involved.

One letter is a simple cover letter addressed to the person in charge of the group considering the document. The cover letter simply describes the document and who put it together: the people who did the research, planning, writing and illustrating. At the end is a brief summary of the findings or conclusions. The letter also lists the title and perhaps other credentials of the person responsible for the organization of the document, and indicates where this person, who signed the letter, may be contacted.

Another type of letter is called a "letter of transmittal." A transmittal letter is needed when a group has been authorized to do a study or report or asked to submit a proposal. The letter should state the problem and note the authorization given the group or person to address the problem and transmit the findings, which will be the report or proposal itself. The transmittal letter should also include a brief summary of results. And a list of acknowledgments in the letter shows resources used and gives recognition to helpful people and institutions, as well as establishes credibility for the report. The letter also allows you to include material that did not belong in the body of the report, but that will give the reader an additional perspective or an interesting sidelight. A discussion in your letter of how the material in the report was organized will prepare the reader for what follows. Additional discussion, of how the research was done, allows you to call attention to any limitations in the study. This also gives you a base for explaining your recommendations.

When you include information like this in a letter to be read before a document is examined, you have used the letter as a way of educating the reader of the document; you have told that reader how to interpret the material in the document.

Synopsis Next the reader encounters a synopsis. If you have written scholarly papers, or had to read them for classes, you know about abstracts. An abstract is a summary of the paper, with the information appearing in exactly the order in which it appears in the document. A synopsis is similar. Every element in the document doesn't get equal treatment in a synopsis, though. You have to give special emphasis to results and recommendations.

Body The paper itself follows. You have probably been doing term papers for what seems like all of your life, so you don't need to be reminded of their basic organization: introduction, body and conclusion. This internal introduction should advise the reader of what you intend to do, the scope of the effort, and how you intend to go about it. You need to explain to the reader why the paper is significant and identify areas of discussion in the order in which they appear. You may also use the introduction to include background material and discuss problems you had in doing research in order to prepare the reader for any limitations.

The body of the paper should be built around a simple statement of fact. You have heard it called a thesis sentence. That single idea gives unity to your discussion. You can organize the points that relate to it in a logical sequence. Develop each point and support it with facts and illustrations. Use headings and subheadings to help guide the reader.

A conclusion should summarize findings and make recommendations based on them. Make clear recommendations that are feasible, responsible and appropriate. Sometimes it takes courage to be clear and not cagey, but a report or proposal that is subject to many interpretations is not very useful.

References Following the document itself should be a bibliography that cites all of your references, including interviews. Any style manual has illustrations. Just adopt one style manual for the whole paper and don't borrow bits and pieces of several. Style manuals are designed with logic and consistency, and you corrupt their intent by appropriating various parts. Use the same style manual for your table of contents, and other sections of the document.

Appendix An appendix is a place to put all charts, tables and illustrations you could not weave into the text successfully. The only ones you should use in the text are simple charts that illustrate a point. Save the longer, more complex matters for appendices. Be sure all tabular matter is clearly labeled and carries a brief description, if necessary, for easy reference. Tabular materials are used to further explain textual materials, and a reader shouldn't find a complex puzzle instead of an illustration.

Readability and Applicability

A reader of your reports and proposals should register this reaction: This is meaningful to me. To succeed in getting this, you have to convey meaning in simple, familiar terms. Use examples and illustrations to make a point. Include anecdotes, but be sure to preserve the general tone of the presentation—formal and serious. In a report you will use more neutral expressions than you will in a proposal, which is a persuasive piece. In a proposal, you want to sell your reader on the idea or project. In either, your illustrations should contribute to the text, not compete for attention. You should prepare the reader for the appearance of illustrations or charts and tables and give enough information in the body of the report to make the illustration easy to understand. You may use type as an illustration or for emphasis in writing a report or proposal. You do not have to adhere to strict rules of English composition, and you can use headings and indentations for emphasis when appropriate and meaningful.

In many ways, writing a proposal is more like writing ad copy than editorial matter. Your showmanship with words counts. Your ability to relate the meaningfulness of the report, the significance of the findings, is measured by the acceptance the report gains.

Use lists to your advantage, especially in making your recommendations. You can provide a pattern for action for if the report is adopted that is almost a checklist of things to do. The easier you make its accomplishment appear, the more likely you are to win adoption for your proposal. For a report, you may find the best way to order the results, the findings, is through a list that may then be a reference for action that should be taken.

In writing reports and proposals, it is important not to fall into the jargon of any professional group. Say what you mean as simply and directly as possible in words used the way most people use them, not in jargon. If you must use technical terms, define and describe them. If words unique to the situation appear often in the text, either identify them each time they appear or add a brief and simple glossary of terms.

The easiest way to clarify is to use examples and references within the experience of your readers. Remember in writing your report: simplify and clarify, reiterate and reinforce the points you want to make.

CONCLUSION

Many public relations students receive little business experience before going into a public relations job. But even a nonprofit organization is a part of the business world. Thus, you are going to have to be a business communicator in a very literal sense if you are going to accomplish goals you set for your organization and goals the organization requires of you. Critical to all internal and external communication are memos and letters. A PR function concerned with both internal and external audiences is the preparation of reports and proposals. Skill in preparing such communications will take you a long way toward the successful management of your PR responsibilities.

PART FOUR EXERCISES

1. Imagine you are the PR writer for a medical organization that *favors* licensing of lay midwives. Prepare the opening paragraphs of a position paper you might compose on the subject to support your organization's position. In outline form indicate what you might put in the rest of the document.

2. You're a PR writer for a hotel in a major resort community. Next week extensive remodeling work will begin on the west wing of the ninth floor. West wing rooms will be closed, but guests in the east wing will have to put up with some noise and unsightly construction equipment. Prepare a letter to send to people who have reservations for this next week in the east wing on the ninth floor. Explain that the inconvenience will be kept to a minimum.

3. You edit a newsletter for the state legislator who opposes licensing of lay midwives. Prepare a brief article for the newsletter based on the position paper in Example 14-1. (The newsletter is sent to the legislator's constituents, in an urban area.)

4. You are the PR writer for a company that makes pocket calculators. Last year was a record year for sales, but market research indicates the calculator market is getting saturated and that future sales will drop. It is time to prepare the annual report. List questions you will ask the company's chief executive before preparing the CEO's letter for the annual report. What advice would you give the CEO?

5. You have written an article for the company magazine on new employee insurance benefits. The president says to pull the article and replace it with a long story on a new product the company is bringing out. What arguments would you use to persuade the president to use the story on insurance benefits?

6. Develop an inquiry form to help an editor gather news for an employee publication or an organization's newsletter.

P A R T

FIVE

WRITING FOR PR—A PROJECT

Familiarity builds confidence, so this exercise attempts to incorporate the aspects of PR writing that are treated separately in earlier chapters.

PART FIVE
WRITING FOR PR—A PROJECT

You are the head PR writer for a giant electric utility conglomerate, Serendipity Electric Power Company. The utility is based in Barton, capital and largest city of Serendip, a large southwestern state. Your company provides electricity to Barton and other cities and towns over most of the northern half of Serendip.

The use of electricity has grown much faster in Serendip than in the rest of the country in recent years because many businesses, industries and people have been moving into the state. Last summer the demand for electricity reached a high point of 5.2 million kilowatts, compared to the utility's total power-producing capacity of 6 million kilowatts. Projections show that within 10 years the demand for power will reach 7 million kilowatts.

Engineers have calculated that the company needs a capacity of 15 to 20 percent more than the expected peak load to prevent blackouts. Therefore, in 10 years the company will need a capacity of about 8 million kilowatts.

Fortunately, your company has been planning ahead. Serendipity Electric already produces 90 percent of its electricity by burning coal (the other 10 percent comes from oil) and a new 1-million-kilowatt coal plant is under construction—to be completed in five years.

But the company will need still another million-kilowatt plant to meet the need for 8 million kilowatts 10 years from now. All the coal fields in Serendip have already been developed, and the company can get no guarantee that rail transportation will be available to haul coal in from out-of-state. Serendipity Electric's management committee has decided, therefore, to build a nuclear power plant.

The plant will be built in Leavitt, a small farming community of about 2,000 people located 75 miles west of Barton. People in Leavitt are aware that the electric company has acquired land to build a power plant, but they don't know it is to be a nuclear plant.

Company executives have been considering the nuclear plant decision for a year, so the PR research staff has had time to prepare in-depth backgrounders on nuclear power and the issues surrounding it (these backgrounders are provided on pp. 309–331). Researchers have also provided a list of articles and books for additional information on page 330 (Table V–1). Some tables, charts and statistical material have also been provided. Using this material—and whatever other information you can find on your own—you are to produce various PR materials for use in the company's communication program explaining the need for nuclear power.

PROJECT TASK 1

The vice president in charge of public relations tells you that the nuclear plant decision will be announced publicly in one month. The VP asks you for advice in handling the PR on this project. Prepare a detailed memo for the VP outlining what needs to be considered in planning such PR. Make sure you discuss messages, audiences and media. (You will not be expected to deal with the Nuclear Regulatory Commission or other government agencies. Your responsibility is to consider audiences in Barton and Leavitt.)

After reviewing your memo, the VP decides that the announcement of the nuclear plant should be made in a speech by the company president (call him Bryan Hall) at a Barton Chamber of Commerce luncheon. On the same day, a slide show is to be presented to the people of Leavitt at 7:30 P.M.

PROJECT TASK 2

Prepare a speech for the company president to deliver at the Barton Chamber of Commerce luncheon. The speech should explain why nuclear power is needed and address some of the questions about nuclear safety. The audience will be made up mostly of city business leaders, but also will include members of the news media and several state government officials.

PROJECT TASK 3

Prepare a slide show to be shown to a general audience in Leavitt. The slide show should explain what a nuclear power plant is and why it is being built. Keep in mind that this audience has not been exposed to much information about nuclear power. Carefully consider whether to address the question of nuclear safety, including possible accidents and the emission of small amounts of radiation from the plant. Write a brief memo to the VP explaining your decision to address (or not to address) those issues. Cite research findings from Chapter 2 of this book to support your position.

PROJECT TASK 4

Prepare a news release for Barton's daily newspapers, based on the president's speech to the chamber of commerce. Prepare a broadcast version of the release for the city's TV and radio stations. Also, prepare a news release for Leavitt's weekly newspaper, giving the details of the decision to build a nuclear plant.

PROJECT TASK 5

Suggest possible illustrations and write copy for a newspaper ad discussing the nuclear plant. Prepare one version for Barton's dailies and one for Leavitt's weekly. Then adapt the copy for a 60-second TV spot, a 30-second TV spot, and a 60-second radio spot. Design and write the ads to answer the question: Why is Serendipity Electric building a nuclear plant?

PROJECT TASK 6

Design and write copy for a small insert to be mailed to customers with their electric bills. Tell why Serendipity Electric is building a nuclear plant.

PROJECT TASK 7

Write an in-depth feature article on nuclear power for the company's employee magazine. Remember that many of the company's employees are technically trained engineers, but many others are accountants, secretaries and mechanics. Also remember that employees' friends and relatives will be asking them questions about nuclear power; the article should help give them answers.

As soon as the announcement of the nuclear plant is made, a number of groups express interest: some pro, some con, some just curious. A consumer group issues a statement denouncing nuclear power and marches in protest in front of Serendipity headquarters. A newspaper reporter wants to interview the company president about the dangers of nuclear waste. The editor of the chamber of commerce magazine asks for an article about nuclear power for the next month's issue. People in Leavitt want more information about the plant—how big will it be, how many people will it employ, for example. The state's politicians have begun to choose sides on the issue, yet only a few have made public comments against the plant so far.

It is your job to prepare material to help deal with these situations. The VP lets you know that you'll have to put in a lot of overtime this week.

PROJECT TASK 8

Write a statement and issue a news release in response to the protests of the antinuclear group. The group has charged that "nuclear power is dangerous, expensive, and unnecessary." Their statement adds that "solar power can easily meet our electricity needs at a much lower cost and with no danger to the environment."

PROJECT TASK 9

Prepare a three-page backgrounder on the question of nuclear waste disposal for use by the company president in talking to a reporter. The backgrounder should be informational.

PROJECT TASK 10

Your company regularly sends a four-page newsletter to legislators, regulators and community leaders in the cities and towns served by Serendipity Electric. Prepare one major article on nuclear power for a special edition of the newsletter and one or two smaller articles discussing specific points.

PROJECT TASK 11

Prepare copy for a small folder or pamphlet that describes the nuclear plant, giving details of its construction schedule, cost, size, and so on.

Shortly after the plant is announced, a bill is introduced in Congress that would prohibit forever the reprocessing of spent nuclear fuel because of the danger of proliferation of nuclear weapons. The company VP asks you to recommend a position for the company to take on the reprocessing-proliferation question.

PROJECT TASK 12

Using the information provided as well as information from the references listed in Table V-1, decide what position—either for or against reprocessing—your company should take on the reprocessing-proliferation issue. Write a position paper defending that position.

PROJECT TASK 13

Assume the VP rejects your decision. Prepare *another* position, taking the opposite side of the issue.

PROJECT BACKGROUND INFORMATION 1

NUCLEAR POWER AND U.S. ENERGY SUPPLY*

In 1978 nuclear power plants generated 300 billion kilowatt-hours of electricity in the United States, about 12.5 percent of the nation's electricity production.[1]

---

*Copyright 1980 Browder & Associates Public Relations. Reprinted by permission.

Some areas of the country depend on nuclear power more than others. For example, 35 percent of the electricity used in New England is produced by nuclear plants.[2] In the Chicago area, Commonwealth Edison generated 45 percent of its electricity with nuclear plants in 1978.[3]

Reliance on nuclear power is expected to increase in the future. Today, nuclear plants with operating licenses have a total capability of producing about 50 million kilowatts. (Plant capacity, given in kilowatts, indicates the maximum power available at any one time. Total energy production, measured in kilowatt-hours, depends on both the amount of power demanded and the length of time it is used.) Nuclear plants under construction have a total capacity of twice that much. Completion of nuclear plants now under construction or planned would bring the total U.S. nuclear capacity to about 190 million kilowatts by the early 1990s. Estimates for the year 2000 place nuclear capacity between 300 million and 400 million kilowatts. Even at the lower end of that range, nuclear plants could produce 2 trillion kilowatt-hours of electricity annually by the end of the century.

The need for this electricity from nuclear power stems from two causes: decreases in the supply of other fuels, and increases in the demand for energy.

Decreasing Supply

Whether short-term shortages of gasoline are real or not, the simple fact is that production of oil in the United States has declined every year since 1970. And while production is diminishing, the rate of new discoveries is falling off even faster, so that the nation's proved reserves of oil have also been steadily declining. In fact, proved reserves of oil *and* natural gas have fallen every year since 1970.

Americans' use of oil has not dropped along with production, however, and increasing imports of foreign oil have been required to meet the nation's needs. This imported oil increases the country's vulnerability to an embargo and exacerbates the U.S. balance of payments deficit.

In 1978, for example, domestic oil production accounted for less than 11 million barrels a day, while consumption reached 19 million barrels daily. More than 8 billion barrels a day were imported, at a cost exceeding $40 billion.

Increasing Demand

At the same time oil supplies are diminishing, the demand for energy in the United States is going up. In 1978 domestic energy use (from all fuel sources) totaled 78 quadrillion Btu (78 quads)[4], and most studies project consumption of 90 to 100 quads by 1985 and 100 to 120 quads by 2000.[5]

The demand for electricity is going up even faster than the increase in total energy consumption. Since 1974 the growth in electricity use has averaged more than 4 percent per year.[6]

Of course, some of the increased demand can be provided by burning more coal. Coal already accounts for 44 percent of U.S. electricity production.[7] And new technologies may provide some help in the future, though they probably will not provide more than a few percent of the nation's electricity in the year 2000.

A report to Congress by the General Accounting Office puts the situation in perspective. Even if coal production increases steadily, reaching 2 billion tons annually by 2000, all nuclear plants now under construction must be completed to meet the expected growth in electricity demand.

This assumes that the entire national coal production will be used to generate electricity. But the GAO report points out that much coal will be needed to make synthetic fuels to support the U.S. transportation system. If no new nuclear plants are built, the nation could face either shortages of electricity or shortages of fuel for transportation.[8]

Conservation

Some suggest that any shortfall in energy supply caused by loss of nuclear power can be compensated for by intense conservation. Most studies of future energy needs already take conservation into account,[9] but some people believe conservation can shave more from energy demand levels than usually estimated. They point to Sweden, a country that uses roughly half as much energy per capita as the United States, but has a GNP per capita that is comparable to this country's.

To be sure, increased efficiency can save much wasted energy in the United States, but there are reasons other than waste for the differences in energy consumption between Sweden and the United States. A study of energy use in the two countries[10] showed that transportation, which accounts for 26 percent of U.S. energy use, is the main difference. In European countries population density is high, and in Sweden most of the population is concentrated in a small part of the country. Thus, transportation of people and goods requires relatively little energy. The United States is spread out over a continent, population density is low, and transportation requirements are high. Added to that, European vehicles get better gas mileage than U.S. vehicles, and public transportation is less available here.

The study identified other factors behind the differences in energy use. The United States requires more energy for space heating and cooling, due mainly to the large number of single family homes here compared to Sweden, and the lack of insulation and proper design of buildings here.

Furthermore, a large amount of U.S. energy is poured into farming, producing food not only for the U.S. population but for large numbers of people abroad. Countries that don't have to export food don't have this energy burden. By one study, 15 percent of U.S. energy use involves food in some way.

Alternate Sources of Energy

If nuclear power is abandoned, other sources of energy must be found to take its place. In the short run, there is little choice other than burning more oil, an unsatisfactory solution because it would require importing more foreign oil or reducing the amount of oil available for gasoline.

In the long run, other resources can be developed. Attention has focused on coal and solar power, along with fusion, an advanced form of nuclear energy that avoids many of the problems of today's nuclear plants. Fusion, however, is much farther from feasibility than other sources and is not considered an option for the rest of this century.[11]

The most realistic of the long-term prospects are coal and solar power. The United States does possess large amounts of coal and sunshine. But the use of these resources is constrained by factors other than supply.

With coal, the technology for using it to produce electricity is in place. Supplies are adequate; minable coal deposits in the United States total at least 250 billion tons, more than 300 years' worth at the current rate of use.[12] But a large step-up in coal production means training many miners, building new mining equipment, and vastly expanding the coal transportation system. Various studies estimate coal production by 1985 at 900–1,100 tons annually; by year 2000, perhaps, 1,700 tons per year.[13] Even that amount would provide only 30 to 35 percent of total U.S. energy needs, however.

With solar power, technology exists to provide space and water heating for some homes and businesses. The cost of solar heating is comparable to electric resistance heating in some areas.[14]

But the technology for producing electricity with solar power on a large scale has not yet been demonstrated. The first full-scale solar demonstration plant is scheduled for completion in the mid-1980s.

Certainly it would be desirable to develop solar-electric plants as rapidly as possible. But the fact is it takes many years to introduce any new technology, and solar power is no exception. Writing in *Science* magazine, C. Pierre L.-Zaleski points out that it takes 10 to 20 years from the start of research before a technical demonstration is possible. It takes 10 to 30 more years before the new technology becomes economically feasible. And then it takes several years to build an individual power plant.[15]

Nuclear power, for example, was born in 1938 when Hahn and Strassmann discovered nuclear fission. Nearly 20 years passed before the first commercial nuclear power plant began operation, and eight more years went by before nuclear power became economically competitive. Forty years after the discovery of fission, nuclear power provided 12 percent of the nation's electricity.

Research in solar power began in earnest only after the 1973 Arab oil embargo, though some research had been under way before then. With an accelerated effort the first commercial solar-electric plants—each with a maximum capacity of perhaps 100,000 kilowatts—could be completed by about 1990.

By one estimate, 110 of these plants could be built in the years from 1990 to 2000.[16] The Electric Power Research Institute believes that 250 plants could be built by the year 2000,[17] and one study suggests the equivalent of 400 such plants could be on line by 2000.[18] These 400 plants could provide about 2 percent of the nation's electricity.

All in all, the various forms of solar power (including wind power, biomass, and hydroelectric power) can supply a considerable amount of energy by the year 2000—up to 10 quads, by some estimates. The Council on Environmental Quality suggests that rapid expansion of solar power could boost that amount to 19 quads.[19] In 1979 the Carter administration called for efforts to see that we get 20 percent of our energy from the sun by the year 2000. But that still leaves 80 percent that must be supplied from other sources.

Economic Considerations

Nuclear power plants are extremely expensive to build, compared to what they used to cost. The cost of uranium to fuel the plants is much higher than it used to be, too.

Yet coal plants are also expensive to build. And the cost of coal for fuel has also gone up, as has the cost of oil and natural gas. Compared to a few years ago, electricity from *any* type of power plant is now very expensive.

Coal plants usually cost less to build than nuclear plants. But the cost of nuclear fuel is less than the cost of coal in most parts of the country. The costs of both fuel and building the plant must be considered when the costs of two electricity sources are compared.

Taking all factors into account, the average cost for a kilowatt-hour of electricity from a nuclear plant in 1978 was 1.5 cents, compared to 2 cents for coal and 4 cents for oil.[20] These are national figures.

Similar comparisons are found in an electric utility company that uses both coal and nuclear plants—Commonwealth Edison of Chicago. In 1978 that utility's nuclear plants produced electricity at an average cost of 1.3 cents per kilowatt-hour, compared to 2.5 cents per kilowatt-hour for coal plants.[21]

As for future costs, Commonwealth Edison's planners estimate that the cost of nuclear power for plants coming on line in the late 1980s will be 3.5 cents per kilowatt-hour, compared to 4.2 cents for coal.[22]

Similar results were obtained by a Ford Foundation-Mitre Corporation study on nuclear power. The report's power cost projections for 1985 are shown in Table P1-8 (p. 317).

Of course, a slight difference one way or the other does not imply that the more expensive source should be eliminated. As Lewis Perl of the National Economic Research Associates points out, "If you abandon one form of energy, the others become more expensive."[23] Removing one source puts strain on the supply of the other; diminished supply means increased price. Even if nuclear power cost more than coal, banning nuclear would simply make coal cost more.

Furthermore, uranium is a domestic resource. Doing without nuclear power in the United States in 1978 would have required 500 million barrels of oil for replacement electricity—about $7 billion worth at foreign oil prices.[24]

In the long run, solar power may become an economic source of electricity. But it will be many years before mass production can bring costs down to competitive levels. For solar cells, an American Physical Society report says that sufficient cost reduction may take decades.[25] A solar-electric power plant using mirrors will also be expensive; a demonstration plant now under construction will cost more than $100 million and will produce, at peak power, 10,000 kilowatts (1 percent as much as a large coal or nuclear plant). Using a simple formula for estimating the cost of power production,[26] electricity from such a plant will cost 88 cents per kilowatt-hour. That cost should fall quickly as more plants are built in the 1990s, but it may still be many years before solar economics are competitive.

Until solar power becomes economically competitive, less use of nuclear power means more use of coal and oil, at a higher cost to consumers of electricity. The price tag will be in the billions of dollars.

According to a National Economic Research Associates study, electricity users will pay an extra $119 billion over the rest of this century if no new nuclear plants are licensed to operate. If existing nuclear plants are phased out by 1990, the additional costs over the rest of the century will be $181 billion.[27] As the NERA report points out, "cost information alone cannot tell us what the future of nuclear power should be." Nevertheless cost is one thing to consider, and without nuclear power, the cost of energy will be higher. It may not be prohibitively higher—the NERA price increase estimates represent something like a 5 to 10 percent increase in electric bills—but the higher costs could still be a significant burden on people who already have trouble coping with inflation.

NOTES

[1] U.S. Department of Energy figures as reported in *Newsweek*, April 16, 1979, p. 41.

[2] Ibid.

[3] "U.S. Electrical Generating Costs and Power Plant Performance in 1978," *Atomic Industrial Forum*, May 14, 1979.

[4]"Energy Use Increased Modestly in 1978," *Chemical & Engineering News* 57 (March 1979): 18. A report on statistics released by the U.S. Department of Energy.

[5]*The National Energy Plan,* Executive Office of the President, April 29, 1977, p. 95. The National Energy Plan projected energy use exceeding 100 quads by 1985 and estimated that with strict conservation that amount could be cut to 95 quads. The plan's energy growth rate goal of 2 percent per year would produce by the year 2000 energy use of about 120 quads.

[6]"Nuclear Power: Facts and Figures," *Atomic Industrial Forum,* May 1979.

[7]*Newsweek,* April 16, 1979, p. 41.

[8]"GAO Points Up Need for Nuclear Plants," *Chemical & Engineering News* 57 (June 1979): 17.

[9]One of the most optimistic studies of the U.S. energy future, by the Council on Environmental Quality, suggested a possible year 2000 energy use of 85 quads in the "low demand" scenario. This study assumed very successful conservation efforts. See "CEQ Optimistic on U.S. Energy Future," *Chemical & Engineering News* 57 (February 1979): 8.

[10]J. Darmstadter, J. Dunkerley and J. Alterman, *How Industrial Societies Use Energy: A Comparative Analysis* (Baltimore, Md.: Johns Hopkins University Press, 1977), cited in Philip Abelson, "Intercountry Energy Comparison," *Science* 199 (February 1978): 605.

[11]The potential and problems of fusion are discussed in depth in David A. Dingee, "Fusion Power," *Chemical & Engineering News* 57 (April 1979): 32–47.

[12]E. T. Hayes, "Energy Resources Available to the United States, 1985 to 2000," *Science* 203 (January 1979): 236.

[13]Ibid. Some studies suggest that 2,000 million tons could be mined in the year 2000.

[14]Roger H. Bezdek, Alan S. Hirshberg and William H. Babcock, "Economic Feasibility of Solar Water and Space Heating," *Science* 203 (March 1979): 1214–1220.

[15]C. Pierre L.-Zaleski, "Energy Choices for the Next 15 Years: A View from Europe," *Science* 203 (March 1979): 849–851.

[16]Dwain F. Spencer, "Solar Energy, A View from an Electric Utility Standpoint," *American Nuclear Society,* 1976, p. 20.

[17]Chauncey Starr, "Role of Solar Energy in Electric Power Generation," paper presented at the annual meeting of the American Association for the Advancement of Science, Denver, Colorado, February 20–25, 1977, p. 3.

[18]Alvin F. Hildebrandt and Lorin L. Vant-Hull, "Power with Heliostats," *Science* 197 (1977): 1145.

[19]See note 9.

[20]Eliot Marshall, "Assessing the Damage at TMI," *Science* 204 (May 1979): 596.

[21]See note 3.

[22]A. D. Rossin and T. A. Beck, "Economics of Nuclear Power," *Science* 201 (August 1978): 582–589.

[23]Quoted in *Weekly Energy Report,* June 14, 1976, p. 7.

[24]At $14 per barrel. OPEC oil prices are now considerably higher.

[25]Arthur L. Robinson, "American Physical Society Gives a Long-Term Yes to Electricity from the Sun," *Science* 203 (February 1979): 629.

[26]Marc W. Goldsmith et al., *New Energy Sources: Dreams and Promises* (Framingham, Mass.: Energy Research Group, 1976), p. 30. The formula is: electricity cost (cents/kwh) = $0.002 \times K/C + 0.3 + F$, where K is capital cost in dollars per kilowatt and C is the capacity factor (for solar thermal plants, 0.23, as given on p. 16 of *New Energy Sources*). F, fuel cost, does not enter into solar plant calculations. For a nuclear plant, F would be $0.25 + 1$ percent of the price of uranium ore in dollars per pound. Capacity factors for nuclear plants range from about 0.50 to 0.80.

[27]"The Economic and Energy Impact of Further Constraints on Nuclear Power in the U.S.," National Economic Research Associates, April 16, 1979.

TABLE P1-1 U.S. OIL AND GAS PRODUCTION

Year	Oil*	Gas*
1970	4.07	21.9
1971	4.01	22.5
1972	4.04	22.5
1973	3.93	22.5
1974	3.76	21.4
1975	3.59	19.7
1976	3.53	19.5
1977	3.56	19.4

*Oil production is given in billions of barrels; natural gas production is given in trillions of cubic feet. Petroleum liquids are included in oil production.

TABLE P1-2 U.S. OIL AND GAS PROVED RESERVES

Year	Oil*	Gas*
1970	46.7	290.4
1971	45.4	278.8
1972	43.09	266.1
1973	41.75	250.0
1974	40.55	237.1
1975	38.97	228.2
1976	37.3	216.0
1977	35.49	208.9

*Oil reserves are given in billions of barrels; natural gas reserves are given in trillions of cubic feet. Petroleum liquids are included in oil reserves.

TABLE P1-3 U.S. ELECTRICITY SOURCES, 1978

Coal	44.3%
Oil	16.5%
Natural gas	13.8%
Nuclear	12.5%
Hydroelectric	12.7%

TABLE P1-4 ENERGY USE AND FOOD IN THE U.S., 1970

Activity	Energy Consumed
Farming	2.1 quads
Processing and packaging	2.1 quads
Transportation	2.6 quads
Refrigeration and cooking	3.2 quads
Total	10.0 quads
Total U.S. Energy Consumption	67.1 quads
Food-related energy use as percentage of total energy use	14.9%

Sources

Tables P1-1 and P1-2: E. T. Hayes, "Energy Resources Available to the United States, 1985 to 2000," *Science* 203 (January 19, 1979): 234.
    Table P1-3: U.S. Department of Energy data reported in *Newsweek*, April 16, 1979, p. 41.
    Table P1-4: Based on data in J. S. Steinhart and C. E. Steinhart, "Energy Use in the U.S. Food System," in *Energy: Use, Conservation and Supply* (American Association for the Advancement of Science, 1974), p. 48.

TABLE P1-5 U.S. ENERGY RESOURCES—QUADS*

Resource	Proved Recoverable	Estimated Total
Crude oil (includes) natural gas liquids)	170–200	670–2100
Natural gas	210–220	700–1200
Shale and tar sands	400	3600–6000
Coal	4800–6000	20,000–80,000
Uranium (LWRs)	276	452
Total	5856–7096	25,422–89,752

*One quad is equal to one quadrillion British thermal units. Total energy use in the United States in 1978 was about 78 quads.

TABLE P1-6 U.S. ENERGY SUPPLY, YEAR 2000

Source	Quads
High Demand	
Oil and gas	46
Solar*	19
Nuclear	18
Coal	37
Total	120
Low Demand	
Oil and gas	40
Solar*	19
Nuclear	8
Coal	18
Total	85

*Includes hydro

Sources

Table P1-5: "U.S. Has Ample Resources for Synthetic Fuels," *Chemical & Engineering News* 57 (August 27, 1979): 24, and National Academy of Sciences, *Energy in Transition 1985–2010* (San Francisco: W. H. Freeman, 1980).
    Table P1-6: "CEQ Optimistic on U.S. Energy Future," *Chemical & Engineering News* 57 (February 26, 1979): 8.

TABLE P1-7 1978 ELECTRICAL GENERATING COSTS

Fuel	Cents/kilowatt-hour
Nuclear	1.54
Coal (base load)	2.15
Coal (overall)	2.32
Oil (base load)	3.46
Oil (overall)	3.95

TABLE P1-8 PROJECTED 1985 GENERATING COSTS

Fuel	Cents/kilowatt-hour
Midwest location	
Nuclear	2.39
Coal with scrubbers	2.85
Coal without scrubbers	2.72
Estimated range, all locations	
Nuclear	1.8–2.8
Coal with scrubbers	2.5–3.4
Coal without scrubbers	1.6–3.1

TABLE P1-9 GENERATION COST FOR SOLAR ELECTRICITY

Construction cost of plant	Generation cost
$10,000/kw	88.3¢/kwh
$ 2,000/kw	17.7¢/kwh
$ 1,000/kw	9.0¢/kwh

TABLE P1-10 NUCLEAR POWER CONSTRAINTS AND TOTAL ADDITIONAL COST FOR ELECTRICITY, 1979–2000

Case	Total cost
No nuclear plants permitted beyond those already under construction	$ 29.7 billion
No new nuclear plants beyond those already operating	$118.7 billion
Phase out of existing plants by 1990	$180.8 billion
Phase out of existing plants by 1985	$195.1 billion

Sources

Table P1-7: "U.S. Electrical Generating Costs and Power Plant Performance in 1978," *Atomic Industrial Forum,* May 1979. Figures are based on a survey of 43 utilities owning a nuclear plant or purchasing substantial amounts of nuclear power. Generating costs include only the cost of producing electricity at the power plant and do not include the cost of transmission and distribution to customers.
    Table P1-8: Nuclear Energy Policy Study Group, *Nuclear Power Issues and Choices* (Cambridge, Mass.: Ballinger, 1977), p. 127. (This report, commonly referred to as the Ford-Mitre study, was sponsored by the Ford Foundation and administered by the Mitre Corporation.)
    Table P1-9: Based on data and formulas in Marc W. Goldsmith et al. *New Energy Sources: Dreams and Promises* (Framingham, Mass.: Energy Research Group, 1976), pp. 16, 30.
    Table P1-10: "The Economic and Energy Impact of Further Constraints on Nuclear Power in the U.S.," National Economic Research Associates, April 16, 1979.

PROJECT BACKGROUND INFORMATION 2

NUCLEAR POWER AND PUBLIC RISK*

Perhaps the only major point of agreement between nuclear advocates and critics is that nuclear plants cannot explode like atomic bombs. The laws of physics prohibit such an explosion. Nuclear bombs must contain more than 90 percent uranium-235 (the explosive form of uranium); the fuel in nuclear power plants contains only 3 percent uranium-235.

Yet, as the Three Mile Island accident demonstrated, the fact that nuclear power plants are not bombs does not mean that there are no risks. While the fuel initially placed in a nuclear reactor is virtually harmless, the process of nuclear fission—which provides energy—also produces a variety of intensely radioactive substances. If released to the public in large amounts, these substances can be very dangerous.

---

*Copyright 1980 Browder & Associates Public Relations. Reprinted by permission.

Radiation

Under normal operating conditions, nuclear power plants release only small amounts of radiation to the environment. Most of this release consists of the inert gases krypton and xenon, which are released into the air, and radioactive hydrogen, which is released into the water.[1]

Because krypton and xenon are inert, they don't combine with other substances and thus don't become entangled in the food chain. And most of the radioactivity of these gases decays away to negligible levels in a matter of hours or days.[2]

The amount of radioactivity in the water discharged from nuclear plants is less than half the amount of radioactivity found in ordinary drinking water, and far below the amount in other common beverages (see Table P2-1).

It is tempting, then, to conclude that the radiation released from nuclear plants is so low that it must be safe. But in fact all we can say is that routine radiation from nuclear power is much less than the radiation received from many common activities—like watching TV, getting a tooth X-ray, or living at high altitudes.

People living in Denver, for example, are exposed to twice the radiation from cosmic rays as people living at sea level.[3] People everywhere are exposed to radiation from radioactive minerals in the ground and the wood and bricks of our houses and buildings. Food, water and air contain trace amounts of radioactive substances as well. Thus, we receive much more radiation from natural sources than from anything connected with nuclear energy (see Tables P2-1 and P2-2).

While natural "background" radiation is relatively unavoidable, people voluntarily subject themselves to many additional sources of radiation. In addition to TV viewing and medical X-rays, such activities as jet airplane travel or taking a vacation in the mountains increases an individual's radiation dose.[4] A one-week vacation in the Sierra Nevada or watching TV for three hours a day during a year gives twice as much radiation as living a mile from a nuclear plant for a year.

Such statistics may be reassuring, yet they do not prove that the small amount of radiation released by nuclear power is safe. It is true that the amount of radiation released by the nuclear power industry is only a small fraction of background radiation levels. Yet even background radiation can cause cancer.

So even the very small amounts of radiation released to the environment by nuclear plants (and other steps in the nuclear fuel cycle) could conceivably increase the incidence of cancer. One estimate suggests that over the rest of this century an additional 90 cancer deaths might be caused by the nuclear power industry.[5] Another study, assuming 400 reactors in use (only 72 are licensed today) estimates 20 deaths per year by the year 2000[6]; another study suggests 16 deaths per year for every 100 reactors.[7]

Some scientists believe that these figures overstate the risk. On the other hand, several recent studies (disputed by some experts) tend to show that low levels of radiation are more dangerous than most scientists believe.[8] Most of these studies are concerned with bomb fallout or with workers at nuclear facilities, and not with exposure to members of the public living near nuclear power plants.

One recent study, which includes workers in all nuclear facilities as well as the public, concludes that 100 plants operating at full power might lead to 50 cancer deaths per year—or one death for every two plants.[9] This figure is higher than estimates from other studies and might suggest the need for stricter exposure standards for plant workers.

In any event, the number of cancer deaths in the United States each year is approaching 400,000 (a total of 387,430 in 1977). The BEIR committee estimated that background radiation causes between 2,000 and 9,000 cancers each year, with a most likely value of between 3,000 and 4,000—or about 1 percent of all cancers.[10] Adding the effects of manmade radiation (primarily from medical exposures), the cancer death toll from radiation comes to between 3,000 and 15,000 each year, most likely in the range of 5,000 to 7,000.

So it is clear that radiation is far from the most serious inducer of cancer. More than 95 percent—and perhaps as many as 99 percent—of all cancer deaths are caused by things other than radiation.

Furthermore, most of this radiation comes from the ground and air and the walls of our buildings. The use of nuclear power to generate electricity contributes a fraction of a percent to our total radiation dose. By one recent estimate, all the radiation released by nuclear power last year—from every facility in the fuel cycle, to workers as well as the public—might eventually cause 17 fatal cancers.[11] That's 0.004 percent of the current annual number of cancer deaths.

Risk from Accidents

For many modern technologies, statistics for evaluating risks are readily available. We know that about 50,000 people die each year in motor vehicle accidents and hundreds more die in airplane crashes. We can calculate death rates per 100 million passenger miles: about 1.36 for cars, 0.04 for airlines.

With nuclear power, however, there are no statistics—outside of the fact that accidents at commercial nuclear power plants have caused no public fatalities.

For this reason the risk from nuclear power is often judged in terms of the "worst case accident"—the most terrible catastrophe imaginable. Other technologies are not judged in this way. But nuclear power is no ordinary technology, and a full assessment of the risks requires an examination of the potential for a severe accident.

The "worst accident" in a nuclear plant would start with the loss of cooling water from the reactor core, which contains the nuclear fuel. There are several back-up systems to provide more water, but if all failed the fuel would melt.

If the fuel melted, large amounts of radiation might be released to the environment. But not necessarily. The fuel would most likely melt down through the floor of the containment building and the radioactivity would be trapped in the ground beneath the plant.[12]

Under the most severe accident conditions, though, some radiation could escape into the air. The containment building, for example, might crack, allowing some of the gaseous radioactive substances to get out. "If the weather conditions include a strong inversion that keeps the cloud of released radioactivity close to the ground," writes nuclear physicist Bernard Cohen, "and if the wind is blowing toward a densely populated area, thousands of fatalities would result."[13]

How many fatalities? About 3,300 in the weeks immediately following the accident, according to the Reactor Safety Study directed by MIT nuclear engineering professor Norman Rasmussen. The 2,300-page Rasmussen study, released in 1975, estimated the odds of such an accident at any given plant at once in a billion years. However, a Nuclear Regulatory Commission review panel concluded in 1978 that the odds calculations were highly uncertain, so nobody can say for sure just how likely such a major accident is.

The report did establish that, as with other technologies, the probability for a large accident is less than a probability for a small accident. Small fires happen more often than large fires, car accidents with minor injuries happen more often than fatal wrecks. The same is true for nuclear plants.

Even if Rasmussen's odds are a thousand times off, the chance of such a major accident at a nuclear plant is still only once in a million years. But nuclear critics, even if they concede that the chance for such an accident is small, say the consequences are so great that even a small chance cannot be accepted.

If this "worst case accident" method of judging risk were applied to all technologies, others could be found with consequences equally great. An airliner crashing into a crowded football stadium would probably kill thousands; a large dam failure could kill hundreds of thousands.[14]

Critics point out, though, that radiation left over from a large nuclear accident would produce long-term effects, perhaps an "epidemic" of cancer during the period 15 to 45 years after the accident. Under certain assumptions it is true that the radiation released by a major accident would increase the cancer rate in the area. By Rasmussen's calculations, up to 1,500 extra cancer cases per year might occur in the affected population, compared to the 17,000 cancer deaths expected annually without the accident.[15]

Since the incidence of cancer fluctuates from year to year, such an increase would not be noticed in the cancer statistics. This is not to say that statistics are more important than people; it is only to point out that these risks from a hypothetical accident should be compared to the risks of cancer that people are exposed to now. A major nuclear accident in Mississippi would still leave the cancer rate there less than it is now in New England.[16]

Three Mile Island

Beyond any doubt, the nuclear accident at Three Mile Island was the worst commercial nuclear plant accident in U.S. history. Some people called it a "disaster."

The effects of the nation's worst nuclear accident were not visibly disastrous, however. Nobody was killed. Nevertheless, some radiation was released to the atmosphere.

The health effects of that radiation can be estimated based on measurements of the amount released around the plant. All in all, the radiation dose received by the 2 million persons living within 50 miles of Three Mile Island was roughly 5,000 person-rems, an average of 0.002 rems per person.[17] This is about one-tenth the dose received from a tooth X-ray. This is only an average; some people would have received lower doses and some higher. A person standing at the plant gate for three weeks after the accident might have received 0.09 rems.[18]

According to the latest BEIR report of the National Academy of Sciences, each 1 million person-rems of radiation might cause an eventual 70 to 353 cancer deaths.[19] At that rate, the 5,000 person-rems released by Three Mile Island would be expected to cause 0.4 to 1.8 eventual cancer deaths.

Before the accident, the number of cancer deaths expected among the 2 million persons in the area was 325,000. Thus, the accident increased the risk of cancer in the area by 0.0005 percent.

Risks of Alternatives

All energy sources pose some risk. Consider natural gas. It's a clean fuel, as fossil fuels go, and offers very little hazard from air pollution. Yet natural gas explosions are not uncommon and many deaths result. A catastrophic natural gas explosion in 1937 took 413 lives.

Another source of electricity, hydroelectric power, generates very little pollution. Yet the potential for a catastrophic accident is great. Dam failures are common; in 1976 alone six dam failures around the world claimed 700 lives. In the United States more than 30 dams failed in the period from 1918 to 1958; the five largest of those failures took 1,680 lives.[20] The potential for disaster is much greater; by one estimate, failure of the Folsom Dam in California (above Sacramento) would take 260,000 lives.[21]

Oil refinery fires and explosions have caused large-scale death and destruction. An oil town fire in Venezuela in 1939 took 500 lives. Coal mine explosions and cave-ins have killed thousands of mine workers.

Of course, the dangers of coal mine disasters are limited to the miners and don't threaten the general public. But the public is threatened from the normal operation of coal plants. A typical coal plant emits just as much radioactivity into the air as a nuclear plant does because of trace amounts of uranium and thorium in the coal.[22] But unlike nuclear plants, coal plants pour sulfur dioxide and other pollutants into the air. By one estimate air pollution from 100 coal plants leads to 2,500 deaths per year.[23] Other studies give lower estimates; some give higher.[24]

Pollution control technology can cut emissions to a fraction of what they would otherwise be, but even the best controls don't screen out everything. And though controls may reduce deaths from air pollutants, there is one gas emitted from fossil fuel plants that pollution controls don't touch—carbon dioxide (CO_2).

In itself, CO_2 is harmless. But the vast quantities emitted by burning fossil fuels seems to be changing the amount of carbon dioxide in the atmosphere. Over the past 25 years the amount of CO_2 in the air has risen by 10 percent. If it keeps going up, scientists say, the excess CO_2 will trap heat in the atmosphere and possibly cause large parts of the polar icecaps to melt. Sea level would rise by 15 to 25 feet. One study estimated that 11 million people—including 40 percent of the population of Florida—would be displaced as water covered low-lying land along the sea coast. Much of southern Louisiana, including New Orleans, would be submerged.[25]

In addition, the increased global temperature might cause severe climatic changes in various parts of the world, possibly affecting food production.

The CO_2 issue is complex and is currently the subject of several studies. Other sources of carbon dioxide are involved. But the possibility remains that large increases in coal burning could have serious, irreversible effects.

Solar power, on the other hand, seems to be perfectly safe. While solar plants aren't completely free from environmental effect (land use, the need for cooling water), they are certainly much safer than conventional energy technologies.

A recent Canadian study points out, however, that you must measure more than the risk of the power plant alone. You must consider the entire operation, from the mining of materials to build the plant, to construction and operation, to the disposal of any waste products. For systems like solar and wind power, which only work part of the time, the risks of a back-up power source must also be considered.

When all these things are considered, solar and wind power also pose some risk to the public. The Canadian study rated natural gas as extremely safe, nuclear as somewhat more dangerous, and various forms of solar energy as still more dangerous, though not quite so dangerous as coal or oil.[26]

These calculations have been criticized, and according to one critic the differences between solar and nuclear disappear when corrections are made and different assumptions are used.[27] That may be. The point is that all energy sources pose some risk, though sometimes that risk isn't immediately visible.

Thus, substituting one energy source for another does not eliminate risk. Eliminating all sources of risk is simply not possible.

Furthermore, the risks from nuclear power and other energy sources must be viewed in light of the many other risks that people routinely accept. More than 100,000 Americans die each year from accidental causes, and in 1978 50,145 people died in motor vehicle accidents—more than six vehicle-related deaths each *hour.*

It is true that some risks are voluntary, in theory. People can choose not to ride in automobiles or airplanes, for example. In practice, however, it is very difficult for most people to avoid these dangers, and in any event cars kill pedestrians and airplane crashes kill people on the ground. There is no way to avoid all risk.

Some of the risks we take are indicated by the fatality figures in Tables P2-5, P2-6, and P2-7. There is every reason to improve safety standards to reduce the number of people who meet with accidental death. No level of fatalities is low enough.

At the same time, we must recognize that reducing one risk sometimes entails the substitute of a greater risk. Ultimately, people must decide what risks are worth taking in order to obtain certain benefits—or avoid worse risks.

NOTES

[1] Anthony V. Nero Jr., *A Guidebook to Nuclear Reactors* (Berkeley: University of California Press, 1979), p. 36.

[2] Ibid., p. 41.

[3] American Nuclear Society, *Nuclear Power and the Environment* (Hinsdale, Ill., 1976), p. 26. Annual radiation dose to individuals from cosmic rays ranges from 38 millirems per year in Florida to 75 millirems per year in Wyoming. See Advisory Committee on Biological Effects of Ionizing Radiation (BEIR), *The Effects on Populations of Exposure to Low Levels of Ionizing Radiation* (Washington, D.C.: National Academy of Sciences, 1972), p. 12.

[4] Ibid., p. 26.

[5] Ralph Lapp, *The Nuclear Controversy* (Greenwich, Conn.: Fact Systems, 1974), pp. 26-28. Lapp's estimate is based on data from the BEIR report for 1,000 reactors in operation by the year 2000; the estimate given above is based on a more realistic figure of 300 reactors, as calculated in note 3, p. 35.

[6] Bernard L. Cohen, "Impacts of the Nuclear Energy Industry on Human Health and Safety," *American Scientist* 64 (September–October 1976): 552.

[7] David J. Rose, Patrick W. Walsh and Larry L. Leskovjan, "Nuclear Power—Compared to What?" *American Scientist* 64 (May–June 1976): 293.

[8] Jean L. Marx, "Low-Level Radiation: Just How Bad Is It?" *Science* 204 (April 1979): 160–164.

[9] Eliot Marshall, "Nuclear Risks: Still Uncertain," *Science* 204 (May 1979): 714.

[10] In the 1972 BEIR report mentioned in note 3, p. 168.

[11] As calculated from data in note 9.

[12] Reactor Safety Study (WASH-1400), U.S. Nuclear Regulatory Commission, 1975.

[13] Bernard L. Cohen, "Some Issues in the Nuclear Power Controversy," *Public Utilities Fortnightly*, August 12, 1976.

[14] Alvin M. Weinberg, "The Maturity and Future of Nuclear Energy," *American Scientist* 64 (January–February 1976): 19.

[15] Norman Rasmussen, speech given at the University of Akron, July 27, 1976, printed in *Proceedings of the National Energy Forum*, University of Akron, Akron, Ohio, Vol. 1.

[16] Cancer rates by state are given in *The Statistical Abstract of the United States 1977*, p. 72.

[17] Based on various measurements, estimates of the total population dose ranged from 1,000 to 5,300 person-rems. See "Three Mile Island Dose Estimates," *Science News* 115 (June 1979): 360.

[18] Eliot Marshall, "NAS Study on Radiation Takes the Middle Road," *Science* 204 (May 1979): 711–714.

[19] Ibid.

[20] R. K. Mark and D. E. Stuart-Alexander, "Disasters as a Necessary Part of Benefit-Cost Analyses," *Science* 197 (September 1977): 1160.

[21] See note 14, p. 9.

[22] J. P. McBride et al., "Radiological Impact of Airborne Effluents of Coal and Nuclear Plants," *Science* 202 (December 1978): 1045–1050.

[23] See note 6, p. 558. Cohen's estimate of 10,000 deaths per year from 400 plants is based on data from the National Academy of Sciences report mentioned in note 24.

[24] Nuclear Energy Policy Study Group, *Nuclear Power Issues and Choices* (Cambridge, Mass.: Ballinger, 1977), pp. 188–196. These pages discuss various estimates of mortality from coal-fired plants, including data from National Academy of Sciences, "Air Quality and Stationary Source Emission Controls," March 1975. (The Nuclear Energy Policy Study Group report was sponsored by the Ford Foundation and administered by the Mitre Corporation and is commonly referred to as the Ford-Mitre study.)

[25] "Costing the CO_2," *Technology Review* 81 (March–April 1979): 72.

[26] Herbert Inhaber, "Risk with Energy from Conventional and Nonconventional Sources," *Science* 203 (February 1979): 564–568.

[27] John P. Holdren, Kirk R. Smith and Gregory Morris, "Energy: Calculating the Risks (II)," *Science* 204 (May 1979): 564–568.

TABLE P2-1 LIQUID RADIOACTIVITY LEVELS

Liquid	Picocuries/liter
Nuclear power waste discharge	1–10
Tap water	20
River water	10–100
Beer (4%)	130
Ocean water	350
Whisky	1,200
Milk	1,400
Salad oil	4,900

TABLE P2-2 RADIATION EXPOSURE TO U.S. POPULATION, 1978

Source	Person-rems/year
Natural background	20,000,000
Healing arts	17,000,000
Nuclear weapons fallout	1,000,000–1,600,000
Nuclear Energy	56,000
Consumer products	6,000

Sources
Table P2-1: American Nuclear Society, *Nuclear Power and the Environment* (Hinsdale, Ill.: 1976), p. 30.
Table P2-2: Data from the Interagency Task Force on Ionizing Radiation as reported in "The Sources of Ionizing Radiation," *Science* 204 (April 13, 1979): 162.

TABLE P2-3 ANNUAL HEALTH EFFECTS OF NUCLEAR-GENERATED ELECTRICITY (Per 1,000 Megawatt Plant)

Activity	Accidental deaths (nonradiation)	Deaths from radiation
Uranium mining & milling	.173	.001
Fuel processing & reprocessing	.048	.040
Design and manufacture of reactors	.040	—
Reactor operation and maintenance	.037	.117
Waste disposal	—	.0003
Transport of nuclear fuel	.036	.010
Total	.334	.168

TABLE P2-4   HEALTH EFFECTS OF COAL PLANTS
(Per 1,000 Megawatt Plant)

Sulfur content	Premature deaths per year
3%, no scrubbers	2–100
Urban	50
Remote	18
3%, with scrubbers	0.2–10
0.8%, no scrubbers	0.4–25
0.8%, with scrubbers	0.04–2.5

Sources

Table P2-3: David J. Rose, Patrick W. Walsh and Larry L. Leskovjan, "Nuclear Power—Compared to What?" *American Scientist* 64 (May–June 1976): 293.
Table P2-4: Based on data in *Nuclear Power Issues and Choices* (Cambridge, Mass.: Ballinger, 1977), pp. 188–196.

TABLE P2-5   LEADING CAUSES OF DEATH, 1977

Cause	Total deaths
Heart and artery disease	777,550
Cancer	387,430
Stroke	182,840
Accidents	105,020
Motor Vehicle	50,380
Other	54,640

TABLE P2-6   ACCIDENTAL DEATHS, 1976

Cause	Total deaths
All accidents	100,761
Motor vehicle	47,038
Accidental falls	14,136
Fire	6,338
Accidental poisoning	5,730
Drowning	5,645
Firearms	2,059
Air travel accidents	1,445
Water travel accidents	1,371
Electric current	1,041
Railway accidents	552

TABLE P2-7   DEATHS FROM CATASTROPHIC ACCIDENTS,* 1971–1976

Cause	Total deaths
Fire and explosion	1,633
Air travel	1,473
Tornadoes, floods, hurricanes	1,456
Motor vehicle	1,178
Mines and quarries	137

*Accidents in which five or more fatalities occurred.

Sources

Table P2-5: Reader's Digest Almanac, 1979, p. 452.
Tables P2-6 and P2-7: Statistical Abstract of the United States, 1978.

PROJECT BACKGROUND INFORMATION 3

NUCLEAR WASTE, PLUTONIUM AND PROLIFERATION*

Waste Disposal

One of the major public issues connected with nuclear power involves the fact that nuclear power plants produce large quantities of radioactive waste.

For the most part this issue is concerned with high-level radioactive wastes produced within the nuclear fuel pellets in the core of a nuclear reactor. There are two main types of this waste: (1) fission products—intensely radioactive elements like iodine, strontium and cesium, and (2) actinides—elements whose atoms are about as heavy

*Copyright 1980 Browder & Associates Public Relations. Reprinted by permission.

or heavier than uranium. Actinides are not as radioactive as fission products but have very long lives, some remaining radioactive for a million years or more. Compared to the actinides, fission products decay very quickly, so that after a few hundred years the hazard is very small.[1] In either case, these wastes must be disposed of in some safe place.

Before disposal, most of the actinides (which include plutonium) could be separated from the spent fuel and reused as fuel in nuclear power plants. The remaining fission products could be solidified, embedded in glass or ceramic pellets, and buried in some deep, stable geological formation.

Whether such reprocessing of fuel will be allowed is a question the government has not yet decided. But even if reprocessing does take place, some traces of the actinides will remain in the waste. Thus, the wastes will remain radioactive for hundreds of thousands of years or more.

Critics fear that water will reach the wastes and carry them to the surface, contaminating the environment. And no geologist can guarantee that any burial site will remain dry for a million years. But if water did reach the wastes it would first have to dissolve them out of the water-resistant glass or ceramic. The dissolving process would be very slow, as would the movement upward to the surface, giving the fission products plenty of time to decay.[2]

The principal question, then, is: What is the hazard of the remaining actinides? Several scientists have studied this question, using a variety of approaches. A Dutch scientist, for example, found the remaining radioactivity of the actinides to be less than the uranium ore taken from the ground to make the nuclear fuel in the first place.[3]

Using another approach, Bernard Cohen of the University of Pittsburgh calculated how fast a radioactive element occurring naturally (radium) gets out of the ground and into people.[4] He assumed that an atom of radioactive waste, buried 600 meters deep, could get to the surface no faster than the radium atoms above it. He then calculated how much of the waste would reach people and concluded that, over the next million years, the waste produced annually by 400 nuclear power plants would kill 0.4 people.

One group of researchers say it isn't proper to compare waste to natural deposits of radioactive minerals because the waste will be concentrated in a small area compared to the original ore bodies.[5] This group made a series of elaborate calculations of the dangers from a few of the longest-lived radioactive elements. After assuming various characteristics for a disposal site, the authors calculated the speed with which water could dissolve wastes and carry them to the surface, and determined whether the radioactivity in that water would exceed the maximum permissible concentration for drinking water. The calculations showed, in most cases, that the radioactivity would be a small fraction of the maximum permitted amount. When the calculations were repeated, with the assumption that the glass material containing the wastes broke apart, the eventual release of radioactivity was still small for most of the formations considered (see Tables P3-1 and P3-2).

This study indicated that even if a burial site "fails" and admits water, the results need not be catastrophic. But the study also shows that a disposal site must be selected carefully. Government research is now focusing on salt beds; salt domes, shale and granite formations are also being considered.

The government has not been prompt in its search for a disposal site, though studies are under way at a number of possible sites in several states. A report by a 14-agency federal review group concluded that current knowledge is sufficient to identify potential burial sites, but specific studies are needed at proposed sites before a final decision on a waste disposal location can be made.[6]

Eventually, a waste disposal site may be developed far from any populated area. Recent research indicates that red clay in the central areas of the ocean floor has many desirable characteristics for waste disposal.[7] Energy consultant R. Philip Hammond suggests that wastes could be stored in the tunnels carved out of Nevada mountains for underground nuclear weapons testing.[8]

Nuclear waste disposal is a serious concern. More research is needed before the technology for disposing of these wastes can be put completely in place. This is not, however, equivalent to saying "there is no solution." As the Ford Foundation-sponsored study of nuclear power issues concluded, "Nuclear wastes and plutonium can be disposed of permanently in a safe manner. If properly buried deep underground in geologically stable formations, there is little chance that these materials will reenter the environment in dangerous quantities."[9]

Plutonium and Proliferation

One of the most publicized of the risks of nuclear power is the hazard of plutonium.

Plutonium is a radioactive element unavoidably produced in the reactors of today's nuclear power plants. It is considered dangerous for two reasons: (1) It is highly toxic, and (2) it can be used to make nuclear explosives.

The toxicity of plutonium arises only from its radioactivity and not from its chemical properties.[10] And it is dangerous only if taken internally. Since the radioactivity from plutonium is rather weak, it cannot penetrate the skin. You could hold a small lump of plutonium oxide in your hand with no ill effects.

Animal experiments indicate that plutonium is very dangerous if ground up and ingested or inhaled. Small amounts can cause cancer (though probably not for 20 years or so). Larger doses can cause death within hours or days, as with other poisons.

Plutonium is not, as sometimes stated, the most toxic substance known to man. Some industrial chemicals are comparably toxic and botulism toxin is considerably more potent.[11] Comparisons of the lethal dose for plutonium and some other substances are given in Table P3-3.

It is also untrue that spreading a few pounds of plutonium through the air would kill billions of people. Nuclear weapons testing in the 1950s and early 1960s spread more than 5 tons of plutonium through the atmosphere. The amount of this plutonium that reaches the lungs of a given individual is 80,000 times less than the maximum permissible dose.[12]

During World War II, 25 workers in a government laboratory received doses of plutonium ranging up to 10 times the maximum permitted amount. No cancer deaths have been recorded in this group.[13]

As for bombs, it is true that the plutonium produced in nuclear power plants can be made into a nuclear explosive. Such a bomb would not approach the power of a sophisticated military weapon, since the plutonium from a power plant differs in composition from the plutonium used in military bombs. Dr. Theodore Taylor, a former atomic bomb designer, points out that a bomb made from reactor plutonium could level a city block, but not a whole city. Nevertheless, the bomb could cause considerable loss of life if detonated in a large office building.[14]

The fear that terrorists might steal plutonium and build a nuclear weapon is one of the main reasons that the Carter administration has not yet decided whether to allow the reprocessing of spent fuel to separate plutonium. The plutonium recovered during reprocessing could be used as fuel in nuclear plants, conserving uranium and reducing the overall cost of nuclear fuel.[15] However, separating plutonium also means it would be in a form more easily made into a bomb.

The Ford Foundation-Mitre Corporation study of nuclear power issues concluded that reprocessing should be deferred indefinitely, emphasizing the danger from terrorists and questioning the economic benefits.[16] The report also concluded, though, that the danger of plutonium proliferation arises from the reprocessing of fuel exclusively and not from the normal operation of nuclear power plants.

Plutonium produced in nuclear power plant fuel is not accessible to terrorists, because it is mixed with the highly radioactive fission products in the fuel rods. The fuel rods, which come in bundles weighing at least one ton each, must be handled by remote control and are encased in a steel shipping cask weighing from 20 to 100 tons before removal from the power plant.

Anyone attempting to steal the spent fuel rods before they are placed in the protective shipping cask would be killed by the radiation. Anyone managing to steal a 20-ton shipping cask would not be able to extract plutonium from the spent fuel without the use of a large chemical reprocessing facility. Only if plutonium is first recycled could terrorists build a bomb in a small laboratory.

The Ford-Mitre study, while recommending deferral of reprocessing, concluded the danger of terrorists' theft of plutonium involves reprocessing and not the operation of nuclear power plants alone. "If plutonium is not recycled," the report stated, "the opportunities for plutonium theft in civilian industry are essentially eliminated."[17]

NOTES

[1] For the major fission products strontium and cesium, only a millionth of the original radioactivity remains after 600 years. See Ralph Lapp, *Radioactive Waste: Society's Problem Child* (Greenwich, Conn.: Reddy Communications, 1977), p. 71.

[2] G. de Marsily et al., "Nuclear Waste Disposal: Can the Geologist Guarantee Isolation?" *Science* 197 (August 5, 1977): 519–527.

[3] Jan Hamstra, "Radiotoxic Hazard Measure for Buried Solid Radioactive Waste," *Nuclear Safety* 16 (March–April 1975).

[4] Bernard L. Cohen, "The Impacts of the Nuclear Industry on Human Health and Safety," *American Scientist* 64 (September–October 1976): 556.

[5] See note 2, pp. 519–527.

[6] Luther J. Carter, "Interagency Group Cautious on Nuclear Waste Disposal," *Science* 203 (March 1979): 1320–1321.

[7] Richard A. Kerr, "Geologic Disposal of Nuclear Wastes: Salt's Lead Is Challenged," *Science* 204 (May 1979): 146–150. See also "Subgroup Report on Alternative Technology Strategies for the Isolation of Nuclear Waste" (draft), Interagency Review Group on Nuclear Waste Management, October 1978.

[8] R. Philip Hammond, "Nuclear Wastes and Public Acceptance, *American Scientist* 67 (March–April 1979): 146–150. See also an objection to this proposal raised in note 1, pp. 81–82.

[9] Nuclear Energy Policy Study Group, *Nuclear Power Issues and Choices* (Cambridge, Mass.: Ballinger, 1977), pp. 19–20. (This report, sponsored by the Ford Foundation and administered by the Mitre Corporation, is commonly referred to as the Ford-Mitre study.)

[10] Leonard A. Sagan, "The Plutonium Controversy," *Journal of the American Medical Association* 234 (December 1975): 1267.

[11] American Nuclear Society, *Nuclear Power and the Environment* (Hinsdale, Ill., 1976), p. 53.

[12] Refer to note 1, p. 31.

[13] Refer to note 10.

[14] Theodore Taylor, speech at the University of Akron, July 27, 1976, printed in *Proceedings of the National Energy Forum*, University of Akron, Akron, Ohio, Vol. 1.

[15] The economic benefits of plutonium recycle are discussed and calculated in W. J. Dollard, "Plutonium Recycle—A Perspective," paper presented at the Atomic Industrial Forum Fuel Cycle Conference in Phoenix, Arizona, March 21–24, 1976, and printed in *Summary Report: Fuel Cycle Conference '76*, Atomic Industrial Forum, June 1976.

[16] Refer to note 9, p. 333.

[17] Ibid., p. 302.

TABLE P3-1   POSSIBLE WATER CONTAMINATION FROM LONG-LIVED NUCLEAR WASTES (Glass Intact)

Isotope	% of maximum permissible concentration
Iodine-129	1.4%
Neptunium-237	0.02%
Plutonium-239	0.00%
Plutonium-239*	0.05%

*Assumes that plutonium is not adsorbed by surrounding materials. Calculations are based on the assumption that groundwater reaches solidified waste and slowly dissolves the glass in which wastes are impregnated.

TABLE P3-2   POSSIBLE WATER CONTAMINATION FROM LONG-LIVED NUCLEAR WASTES (Glass Breaks)

Isotope	% of maximum permissible concentration
Iodine-129	58%
Neptunium-237	67%
Plutonium-239	0.0000003%
Plutonium-239*	130%

*Assumes that plutonium is not adsorbed by surrounding materials. Calculations presume that groundwater reaches solidified waste and that glass structure in which wastes are impregnated disintegrates after 10,000 years.

TABLE P3-3   TOXICITY OF INGESTED POISONS

Poison	Lethal dose
Anthrax spores	0.0001 mg
Botulism	0.001 mg
Lead arsenate	100 mg
Potassium cyanide	700 mg
Reactor plutonium	1150 mg

Note: Time to death is over 15 years for plutonium, hours to days (or less) for other poisons. Doses are given in milligrams.

Sources

Tables P3-1 and P3-2: G. de Marsily et al., "Nuclear Waste Disposal: Can the Geologist Guarantee Isolation?" *Science* 197 (August 4, 1977): 519–527. Data given is for one of the five geological formation types considered by the study. Maximum permissible concentrations are set at levels far below the point where serious health effects would be expected.
   Table P3-3: American Nuclear Society, *Nuclear Power and the Environment* (Hinsdale, Ill.: 1976), p. 53.

TABLE V-1

Here is a brief list of books and articles that discuss some of the issues of nuclear power in more depth than the backgrounders included in this section.

American Nuclear Society, *Nuclear Power and the Environment* (Hinsdale, Ill.: American Nuclear Society, 1976).
   A thorough booklet that examines all the major nuclear issues, using a question-and-answer format. Outdated in some areas, the book still has many valuable discussions and numerous charts and tables.

H. A. Bethe, "The Necessity of Fission Power," *Scientific American* 234 (January 1976): 21–31.
   A readable analysis of the nuclear power controversy by a Nobel Prize-winning physicist.

Bernard L. Cohen, "Impacts of the Nuclear Energy Industry on Human Health and Safety," *American Scientist* 64 (September–October 1976): 550–559.
   Cohen, a pro-nuclear physicist, computes the expected effects of an all-nuclear electricity production system and uses mathematical comparisons to the risks from other sources to argue for the relative safety of nuclear energy.

Anthony V. Nero Jr., *A Guidebook to Nuclear Reactors* (Berkeley: University of California Press, 1979).
   Nero, a physicist, provides a factual and objective account of the mechanics of nuclear reactors, their safety, their environmental effects, and the various proposed fuel cycles.

Nuclear Energy Policy Study Group, *Nuclear Power Issues and Choices* (Cambridge, Mass.: Ballinger, 1977).
   This study provides a thorough examination of all important nuclear energy issues; it is done by an independent group and sponsored by the Ford Foundation. This study takes a position against allowing reprocessing of nuclear fuel.

TABLE V-2 NUCLEAR POWER PLANT FACT SHEET

Cost: $1.15 billion
Construction scheduled to begin: Two years from today.
Scheduled date of operation: Nine years from today.
Generating capacity: 1.15 million kilowatts.
Number of generating units: One
Type of reactor: Pressurized water reactor, manufactured by Northinghouse Corp.
Construction force: Average 1,000 workers; maximum of 3,000 workers during peak years of construction activity.
Cooling water: A man-made reservoir will provide cooling water. Surface area of the lake will be 3,000 acres; water volume will be 150,000 acre-feet.

Reactor Characteristics

Core thermal power: 3,411 megawatts thermal.
Plant electrical output: 1,150 megawatts electrical (1.15 million kilowatts).
Plant efficiency: 34 percent.
Reactor vessel size: 43 feet, 10 inches tall; 157 inches in diameter.
Reactor vessel weight: 450 tons.
Weight of fuel: 222,739 pounds.
Number of fuel assemblies: 193.
Number of fuel rods per assembly: 264.
Total number of fuel rods: 50,952.
Coolant temperature, inlet: 557.3 F (at full power).
Coolant temperature, outlet: 619.6 F.
Average temperature increase of coolant in core: 62.3 F.
Coolant: water.
Refueling: One-third of fuel replaced each year.
Refueling time: 17 days (minimum).

Containment Building

Walls: 4½ feet thick, steel-reinforced concrete.
Height: 265 feet.
Inside diameter: 135 feet.
Foundations: 12 feet thick.

APPENDICES

APPENDIX A

READABILITY FORMULAS

Research in readability goes back at least to the 1920s. Early work identified various factors—like sentence length, word length, prepositional phrases—that affected the readability of prose.

In *What Makes a Book Readable,* published in 1935, William Gray and Bernice Leary discussed 64 different aspects of prose that seemed to affect reading difficulty. It would have been nearly impossible to devise a usable formula covering that many variables, so when readability formulas were developed, most emphasized two of the most important factors: sentence length and word length.

Dozens of formulas have been designed to measure readability. In 1959 George Klare identified 31 formulas and 10 variations, and he didn't cover all the different types of formulas. More formulas have been designed since then. Only a handful of these formulas are in general use, however. The three best-known formulas are those devised by Rudolf Flesch, by Robert Gunning, and by Edgar Dale and Jeanne Chall.

FLESCH

The first formula to gain much notice was the one proposed by Flesch in the late 1940s. His formula is based on the average sentence length and the average number of syllables per word.

To use the Flesch formula, select 100-word samples at random from your text. Divide the number of words by the number of sentences to obtain an average sentence length (asl) expressed in words per sentence. Next count the number of syllables in the sample and divide by the number of words to obtain an average word length (awl) expressed in syllables per word. Then insert these values into the Flesch "Reading Ease" formula:

$$\text{Reading Ease} = 206.835 - (.846 \times \text{awl}) - (1.015 \times \text{asl})$$

The resulting score should fall between 0 and 100; the higher the score, the easier the material is to read. A score in the 70–80 range is "fairly easy"; a sixth-grader could understand it. Scores below 50 are considered difficult reading. Scores below 30 are generally found only in scientific and technical journals.

When using the Flesch formula, count contractions and hyphenated words as one word. When counting sentences, count clauses separated by colons or semicolons as separate sentences.

Recognizing that there is more to easy reading than short words and sentences, Flesch devised a "Human Interest" formula that measures the degree of reader interest. It is not used as often as the reading ease formula. It is based on the number of personal words (pw) per 100 words and personal sentences (ps) per 100 sentences. Personal words include personal pronouns and any other words that are either masculine or feminine. Personal sentences are direct quotations, exclamations, questions—sentences that address the reader directly. The formula:

$$\text{Human Interest} = \text{pw}/100 \text{ words} \times 3.635 + \text{ps}/100 \text{ sentences} \times 0.314$$

A score below 10 is dull; 20 to 40 is interesting; above 40 is very interesting.

GUNNING

Gunning's formula is much simpler to apply than Flesch's. The "fog index," as Gunning calls it, measures reading difficulty rather than reading ease.

Gunning also counts words and divides by the number of sentences to find an average sentence length. But rather than counting syllables, Gunning's method is to count the number of "long words"—those of three syllables or more. He excludes from this count all proper nouns, verbs where the third syllable is an *-ed* or *-es*, and compound words made from two short words, like "manpower."

To apply the formula, take the average sentence length and add to it the number of long words per 100 words. Multiply the total by 0.4.

The resulting score is roughly equal to the grade level of difficulty. A score of 12, for example, indicates that an average high school senior should be able to read the material. In practice, no general audience magazine would rate above 12 on the Gunning index. *Time* magazine probably rates about 10, *Reader's Digest* would score about 9, and comic books would score around 6.

DALE-CHALL

The Dale-Chall formula is more difficult to apply because it requires the use of a list of 3,000 words. Words on the list are known by 80 percent of fourth graders. [The list is included as an appendix to Gunning's book, *The Technique of Clear Writing*, rev. ed. (New York: McGraw-Hill, 1968).]

To use the Dale-Chall formula, select 100-word samples and determine the average sentence length (as with the Gunning and Flesch tests). Then count the number of words not on the Dale list. The formula:

> average sentence length $\times$ 0.0496
> $+$ words not on Dale list $\times$ 0.1579
> $+$ 3.6365

Dale-Chall scores will typically be lower than Gunning scores for a given piece of writing. A Gunning index of 16, for example, indicates readability on the college graduate level; the same piece would score about 10 on the Dale-Chall test.

Keep in mind that readability scores do not reflect a "recommended" level of reading difficulty. They only indicate the readability level that an average reader (average seventh-grader, average high school senior, or whatever) is likely to understand. To make the reading *easy*, the writing level should be a couple of steps below the educational level of the intended audience. Rarely do popular magazines—even those read by college graduates—score higher than a high school senior readability level.

OTHER READABILITY TESTS

A completely different type of readability test is Wilson Taylor's "Cloze" procedure. This test, first used in the early 1950s, was developed from concepts of Gestalt psychology. It tests readability by seeing how easily a reader can "fill in the blanks" when words are left out of a passage.

For example, readers might be given a passage with every fifth word deleted. From the context, the reader should be able to fill in some of the missing words. The more words the reader can fill in, the more readable the selection is.

This unique readability test has one major drawback: It can't be applied simply by making calculations. The prose must be tested on real readers, and those readers must be representative of the intended audience.

All readability formulas are approximations, because no single formula can cover all the variables that affect readability. With the increased use of computers, though, more complicated formulas may soon come into use. Computers can be programmed to calculate readability automatically when a sample of a story is typed in at a computer keyboard.

An early formula appropriate for computerized use is the Danielson-Bryan formula. It is based on the total number of characters (letters) per word and per sentence. The formula:

1.0364 × characters per word
+ 0.0194 × characters per sentence
− 0.6059

An even more elaborate formula has been devised by Danielson to measure the probable time period of prose. It has long been known that English sentences have, on average, become shorter over the centuries. Taking a random sample of novels published between 1740 and 1977, Danielson found several other variables that change with time, such as paragraph length (shorter now than in the past), presence of long words (less frequent now than in the past), and presence of "internal apostrophes" for possessives and contractions (more frequent now than in the past).

Using data from his sample of novels, Danielson produced a formula that would "predict" the publication date for a fiction selection. These predictions work with a fair degree of accuracy on fiction, but the formula in no way predicts publication year for nonfiction, since only novels were included in the original sample. However, any prose can be given a "stylistic year" rating by applying the formula. And while the formula is not a readability measure by design, "style year" scores show a very high correlation to readability scores obtained by standard formulas.

A computer program has been written to apply this formula, and tests show that a selection with a style year of 1900 or later rates "very readable" on standard readability tests. Style year scores of before 1850 are not very readable.

The formula, which must be applied to an integral number of paragraphs, is:

Style year =
1949
+ 36.41 × internal apostrophes per sentence
− 2.57 × words per sentence
− 2.92 × sentences per paragraph
− 16.71 × long words per sentence

Long words are defined as words with 10 or more letters.

TABLE A-1 COMPARISON OF READABILITY SCORES WITH STYLE YEAR

Gunning score (fog index)	Grade level	Style year
4	fourth	1948
5	fifth	1939
6	sixth	1929
7–8	seventh–eighth	1916
9–10	ninth–tenth	1897
11–12	eleventh–twelfth	1879
13–15	college	1856
16 and up	college graduate	1838

APPENDIX B

CORPORATE REPORTING REQUIREMENTS

Corporate Reporting Requirements

Prepared by Robert W. Taft and Cullen Couch, Hill and Knowlton, Inc.

Reporting Required For	Securities and Exchange Commission	New York Stock Exchange	American Stock Exchange	Generally Recommended Publicity Practice All Companies
Accounting: Change in auditors	8-K; include information on disputes over past two years and whether opinions in last two years were adverse or qualified. Departing accountant files letter as exhibit commenting on company explanation. Disclose impact of any changes made by new firm. In proxy statement give name of current accountant and of accountant of the previous year, if changed, along with details of disagreements. Note whether accountant will be available at annual meeting.	Prompt notice to Exchange, 8-K when filed. The NYSE recommends that the independent audit firm be represented at annual meeting to answer questions.	Same as NYSE.	Press release desirable at time of filing 8-K if differences are major. Consider discussion of change in annual or quarterly reports to shareholders. Consider clear statement in annual report or elsewhere on when and how company rotates auditing firms and on steps to insure continued independence of auditors including their reporting relationship to Board's audit committee.

Reprinted with permission of Hill and Knowlton, Inc., New York, New York 10017.

Reporting Required For	Securities and Exchange Commission	New York Stock Exchange	American Stock Exchange	Generally Recommended Publicity Practice All Companies
Accounting: Change in method	10-Q. Independent public accountant must file letter indicating whether he approves of "improved method of measuring business operations."	Prompt notification to Exchange required.	Notify Exchange before change is made and disclose the impact in succeeding interim and annual reports.	Statement of accounting policies is required in annual report. To be consistent with 10-K and new SEC requirements, give some publicity to accounting changes; be prepared to illustrate how alternative accounting methods would affect earnings. Also effect of alternatives, where company's accounting method differs from that prevailing in its industry, and differences in tax and financial reporting. Special problems arise in charging LIFO/FIFO methods of accounting for inventory.
Amendment of charter or bylaws	10-Q if matter subject to stockholders' approval, or if change materially modifies rights of holders of any class of registered securities.	Four copies of any material sent to stockholders in respect to proposed changes. Appropriately certified copy of changes when effective.	Ten copies of any material sent to stockholders. 10-Q must be filed with Exchange when effective with certified copy of (a) charter amendments; (b) directors' resolution as to charter or bylaws.	Recommend immediate publicity if change significantly alters rights or interests of shareholders. "Defensive" provision to make takeovers more difficult likely to face new legal challenges.
Annual (or special) meeting of stockholders	10-Q following meeting when security holders' vote required except as to procedural matters, selection of auditors or uncontested election of management nominees as listed in proxy statement.	Four copies of all proxy material sent to shareholders. Prompt notice of calling of meeting; publicity on material actions at meeting. Ten days' advance notice of record date or closing transfer books to Exchange.	Ten copies of all material sent to shareholders. Other requirements same as NYSE.	Press release at time of meeting. Competition for news space minimizes public coverage except on actively contested issues. Recommend wide distribution of post-meeting report to shareholders.

Reporting Required For	Securities and Exchange Commission	New York Stock Exchange	American Stock Exchange	Generally Recommended Publicity Practice All Companies
Annual report: Form 10-K	Required by Section 13 or 15 (d) of Securities Exchange Act of 1934 on Form 10-K. Three complete copies and five copies without exhibits to be filed with SEC and one copy with exchanges where listed no later than 90 days after close of fiscal year. (Some schedules may be filed 120 days thereafter.) Companies which file pursuant to Section 15 (d) must submit four copies of printed annual report with 10-K.	One signed copy must be filed with Exchange.	Three copies must be filed with Exchange. (See Company Guide, p. 253.)	Publicity usually not necessary unless 10-K contains previously unreported material information.
Annual report to shareholders: Contents	Certified financial statements for last two years. Explanation of any differences between financial statements in annual report and statements filed with the SEC. Summary of operations for last five years and accompanying management analysis. Identification of directors' principal occupations. Stock market and dividend information for past two years. Notice of Form 10-K availability. Brief description of business and line-of-business breakout similar to 10-K. Summary of quarterly results in "audited footnote." Material differences reflected in financial statements, from established accounting principles. Supplementary inflation accounting.	Requirements are more than satisfied by compliance with SEC requirements.	Requirements are more than satisfied by compliance with SEC requirements.	Check printed annual report and appropriate news releases to insure they conform to information reported on Form 10-K. News releases will be needed if annual report contains previously undisclosed material information.

Reporting Required For	Securities and Exchange Commission	New York Stock Exchange	American Stock Exchange	Generally Recommended Publicity Practice All Companies
Annual report to shareholders: Distribution	Annual report to shareholders must precede or accompany delivery of proxy material. Seven copies to SEC with preliminary proxy material or when given holders, whichever is later.	Published and submitted to shareholders at least 15 days before annual meeting but no later than three months after close of fiscal year. PROMPTEST POSSIBLE ISSUANCE URGED. Three copies to Exchange. Recommend release of audited figures as soon as available.	Published and submitted to shareholders at least 10 days before meeting but no later than four months after close of fiscal year. PROMPTEST POSSIBLE ISSUANCE URGED. Ten copies to Exchange, Securities Division. Recommend release of audited figures as soon as available.	Financial information should be released as soon as available; second release at time printed report is issued if report contains other material information. NYSE and Amex urge broad distribution of report to include statistical services so company information is available for "ready public reference."
Bankruptcy or receivership	8-K immediately after appointment of receiver. Identify proceeding, court, date of event, name of receiver and date of appointment. Proposed amendment to 8-K would require information as to confirmation of plan of reorganization, arrangement or liquidation. Form 10-Q requires description of any bankruptcy, receivership or similar proceeding.	Immediate notice to Exchange.	Same as NYSE.	Recommend press release at time of 8-K filing. Purpose is to tell creditors how to secure claims, not to notify stockholders of a material development.
Contracts: Defense and major long-term	Progress on material contracts should be disclosed in such filings as 10-K, 10-Q and registrations. Should include earnings losses, anticipated losses and material cost overruns.	Immediate publicity as soon as news spreads beyond top management and confidential advisors.	Acquisition or loss of material contract requires prompt publicity.	SEC urges that annual reports include disclosure on contract progress as complete as Commission filings. News release should be issued when any material developments affecting contracts become known. (See also "Extraordinary charge or credit.")

Reporting Required For	Securities and Exchange Commission	New York Stock Exchange	American Stock Exchange	Generally Recommended Publicity Practice All Companies
Conversion rate: Changes in	10-Q if material change.	Prompt publicity on any change in convertible security, or termination of conversion privilege when conversions have been occurring or appear imminent. Timely notice by mail to holders of record. Immediate notice to Exchange.	Prompt notice to stockholders and to Exchange.	Publicity should be timed to the event causing the change or termination of the conversion privilege, immediate notice to statistical services.
Default upon senior securities	10-Q if actual material default in principal, interest, sinking fund installment, arrearage in dividends for preferred, registered or ranking securities not cured within 30 days of any stated grace period and if indebtedness exceeds 5 percent of total assets.	Immediate publicity and notice to the Exchange.	Immediate publicity and notice to the Exchange.	Immediate disclosure probably required at time default condition is known.

Reporting Required For	Securities and Exchange Commission	New York Stock Exchange	American Stock Exchange	Generally Recommended Publicity Practice All Companies
Directors or officers: Change in, change in control	8-K if change in control of corporation. Report who acquired from whom; terms; terms of any loan involved; and the amount and source of consideration used to gain control. Statement on Schedule 13D may be required by new controlling persons. Where there is a stockholder vote involving the election of directors, 10-Q requires disclosure of names of newly elected directors and names of all directors still in office after the meeting unless proxies were solicited, there was no opposition to management's nominees, and all such nominees were elected. New directors and officers must personally file Form 3 upon election. New proxy rules (11-31-79) requires certain disclosures about votes cast for or withheld from individual directors. New rule requires disclosure of vote on all directors if one or more directors receive 5% plus negative vote.	Prompt written notice to Exchange of any change. Immediate release, if material. Recommends Audit Committee for Board. Recommends directors be identified in annual report.	PROMPT written notice to Exchange. Immediate release, if material. Recommends that company with no outside directors nominate at least two independent directors.	Recommend immediate announcement of any change in directors, officers. However, no technical requirement for publicity except where control of company changes or key person is added or lost. Expect problems in reporting on vote cast for each director this year.
Dividends	All issuers of publicly traded securities are required to give notice of dividend declarations pursuant to Rule 10B-17. Over-the-counter companies must provide advance notice of record date for subsequent dissemination to investors, extending comparable stock exchange requirements to OTC market. Failure to comply places issuer in violation of Section 10 (b) of the Securities Exchange Act of 1934.	Prompt notice to Exchange and immediate publicity. "Telephone Alert" to Exchange when the action is unusual and during market hours. "Immediate" means even while directors' meeting is still in progress. Ten days' advance notice of record date.	Same as NYSE. Notification to Exchange by telephone or telegram with confirmation by letter.	Prepare publicity in advance and release immediately by a designated officer on word of declaration. Publicity especially important when dividend rate changes. NYSE manual implies announcement of management intention prior to formal board action may be required in case of a "leak" or rumor.

Reporting Required For	Securities and Exchange Commission	New York Stock Exchange	American Stock Exchange	Generally Recommended Publicity Practice All Companies
Earnings	Form 10-Q required for each of first three fiscal quarters. Include unaudited income statement for current quarter, same quarter of prior year, year-to-date data for two years; balance sheet for end of latest and year ago quarter's source and application of funds for year-to-date for two years; management analysis of changes between current and prior quarter, quarter a year ago, and comparison of two years-to-date. Summary of quarterly results for two years in "unaudited" annual report footnote. Form 10-K required to report full year's earnings.	Quarterly. Publicity required. Shareholder mailing recommended. No set time limit but four to five weeks after close of period considered usual. NYSE urges breakout of fourth quarter results for AP and UPI P/E ratio computation. NYSE recommends that insiders trade only after quarter report is published.	Quarterly. Should be published within 45 days after end of fiscal quarter for all four quarters.	Immediate publicity; do not hold data until printed quarterly report is published and mailed. Release no later than 10-Q filing; annual results as soon as available. Information in news as available. Information in news release must be consistent with 10-Q. Breakout of current quarter results together with year-to-date totals desirable in 2nd, 3rd and 4th quarter releases.
Earnings: Forecast or estimate	SEC policy is to permit "reasonably based and adequately presented projections." Underlying assumptions should be disclosed. Recent SEC guidelines permit inclusion of forecast in such filings as registration statements and prospectuses. New "safe harbor rule" effective August '79 limits liability for incorrect forecast. SEC is "encouraging experimentation."	Immediate public disclosure when news goes beyond insiders and their confidential advisors.	Public disclosure not required initially, but if earnings forecast released, and later appears to be wrong, issuer must correct promptly and publicly.	Forecasts should be either avoided altogether or widely circulated with all assumptions stated. Forecasts by others may require correction by company if wrong but widely believed. Once having made forecast, issuer has obligation to "update" it promptly if assumptions prove wrong. Press releases and other communications should include all information necessary to an understanding of the forecast. Legal counsel should be consulted.
Employee stock purchase and saving plans	Form 11-K may be required under 15 (d) of '34 Act. Form S-8 may also be required.	No specific rules.	No specific rules.	Generally no publicity required or recommended. There is increasing trend to mention program in annual report.

Reporting Required For	Securities and Exchange Commission	New York Stock Exchange	American Stock Exchange	Generally Recommended Publicity Practice All Companies
Energy problems	Disclose possible impact of fuel shortages and fuel cost increases if material.	No specific rules.	No specific rules.	Watch out for material disclosures on energy matters in speeches, interviews, other unexpected sources. Distribute in same channels as traditional material information.
Environmental matters	Where material, appropriate disclosure in Forms 10, 10-K and 10-Q under sections pertaining to description of company's business and legal proceedings. Any environmental proceeding of any size by governmental authorities is deemed material and must be reported on 10-Q. Environmental suits by others where damages claimed exceed 10 percent of current assets must be reported in 10-Q.	No specific provision.	No specific provision.	Immediate public disclosure where material, or required to be reported. Subject matter may include impact that compliance with various laws would have on company expenses, earnings and competitive position. Recent U.S. Steel decision probably expands need for careful disclosure of environmental plans.
Extraordinary charge or credit; charge to retained earnings	SEC expects discussion of nature of and reason for charge in "Management Discussion and Analysis."	Disclosure recommended for material provisions for future losses, discontinued operations, foreign operations, future costs. Include detail on amounts reserved, subsequently used and remaining available at year-end. Prior notice to Exchange required for any proposed substantial charge to retained earnings by company or by directly controlled subsidiary.	Same as NYSE for charge.	Generally material. Requires immediate disclosure. Press release should precede SEC filings. There is increasing "enterprise" reporting of impact of extraordinary items on earnings per share.

Reporting Required For	Securities and Exchange Commission	New York Stock Exchange	American Stock Exchange	Generally Recommended Publicity Practice All Companies
Float: Increase or decrease in	10-Q if an outstanding "class" of securities is changed more than 5 percent by issuance or purchase of securities, or payment of indebtedness. Include this information in 10-K. New rules specify timing and method for company to tender for own shares.	Prompt notice when occasioned by actual or proposed deposit under voting trust agreements, etc., and brought to "official attention" of officers or directors. The NYSE requires prompt announcement of a program to purchase the company's own shares. See "Treasury stock—increase or decrease."	Prompt announcement upon establishing program to acquire the company's own shares.	Company statement on its intention to purchase stock in open market. Ads and releases where company tenders for own shares must conform with SEC filings. Publicity if change in control is involved or there is a sharp decrease in floating supply which could affect the market in the company's securities.
Foreign currency translation	New SEC requirements. FASB 8 requires report of foreign currency translation gains or losses as they occur (quarterly).	No requirements.	No requirements.	Recommend clear discussion of effect of translation gains or losses in quarterly and annual earnings release where applicable. Few companies yet report this information in a way which SEC and security analysts consider adequate.
Form, nature, rights or privileges of listed securities changed	10-Q if constituent instruments defining rights of shareholders have been materially modified or if rights are otherwise limited—including restrictions on working capital or dividend payments.	At least 20 days prior notice of change in form, nature or right of securities or certificates.	Same as NYSE.	Timely disclosure of all relevant information as soon as those other than insiders are involved in planning discussions.

Reporting Required For	Securities and Exchange Commission	New York Stock Exchange	American Stock Exchange	Generally Recommended Publicity Practice All Companies
Inflation: Impact of	SEC requires adherence to FASB Statement No. 33. Companies must include in shareholder annual reports current cost and constant dollar disclosures for fiscal periods ending after December 25, 1979. Current cost disclosures not required until 1980 annual reports. Disclosures include separate one-year income information and five-year comparison of selected financial data holding gains or losses, net of inflation, statement of current cost of inventory and property, plant and equipment, inflation gain or loss on net monetary items, and foreign exchange gain or loss. Notes explaining information also required.	No requirement.	No requirement.	Publicity generally not necessary. However expect considerable shareholder and press interest in this section of annual report during next two years.
Legal proceedings: See also "Environmental matters"	10-Q at start and termination of material proceedings (generally damage claims in excess of 10 percent of current assets); also any bankruptcy or receivership proceeding involving any part of company; also any suit against company by an officer, director or major stockholder. Consider filing 8-K if suit is of major importance. 8-K required if bankruptcy or receivership proceeding initiated.	No notice to NYSE required unless proceedings bears on ownership, dividends, interest or principal of listed securities, or start of receivership, bankruptcy, reorganization proceedings.	Public disclosure if material. Prompt notice to Exchange.	Public disclosure recommended if outcome of legal proceeding could have material effect on company and news of proceeding has not already become public. Wall Street seeks expanded discussion of pending anti-trust and other major suits in annual report.
Listing: Initially or on another Exchange	Involved and extensive legal work is required.	See listing requirements. Dual listing now permitted.	See listing requirements. Dual listing now permitted.	Bulk of routine publicity handled by exchanges. Discuss other special opportunities with legal and public relations counsel.

Reporting Required For	Securities and Exchange Commission	New York Stock Exchange	American Stock Exchange	Generally Recommended Publicity Practice All Companies
Merger, acquisition or disposition of assets	8-K if company or majority-owned subsidiary acquires or disposes of a significant (10 percent of total assets) amount of assets or business other than in course of business. Proxy soliciting material or registration statement may also be required. Check application of Rule 145 (b) to any such transaction involving exchange of stock.	8-K if filed (where assets acquired). Immediate public disclosure. Prompt notice to Exchange where assets disposed of.	8-K if filed, for acquisition or disposition of assets. Immediate public disclosure.	NYSE policy requires immediate announcement as soon as confidential disclosures relating to such important matters are made to "outsiders" (i.e., other than "top management" and "their individual confidential advisors"). Immediate publicity, especially when assets to be sold consist of an entire product line division, operating unit or a substantial part of the business.
Options granted to purchase securities	Include options granted and exercised in 10-K. If previously reported on 10-Q, may be incorporated by reference. New rules on executive compensation require survey of option information in proxy statement.	Before issuing options, unissued securities must be authorized for trading on Exchange. Stockholders' authorization also is required. No notice of granting of options required. Summarize information on options in annual report.	Same as NYSE.	Generally no publicity for options to insiders.
Policy statement on handling inside information	Not specifically required by any regulatory authority. However, recent cases involving insider information have turned on whether company had developed and implemented a written statement of policy on disclosure of material, non-public corporate information. SEC frequently requires submission of such statements as part of consent decree.	Same as SEC.	Same as SEC.	Same as SEC.

Reporting Required For	Securities and Exchange Commission	New York Stock Exchange	American Stock Exchange	Generally Recommended Publicity Practice All Companies
Prospectus	Prospectus must be filed as part of registration statement. Copies distributed to underwriters and dealers in securities offerings, and in turn to investors. Photos of management, products, maps, other visuals now permitted. Under recent SEC guidelines, forecasts may be included in prospectuses and registration statements.	Seven copies of final prospectus to Exchange. May be used as part of listing application covering the new securities.	Copy of complete registration filing to Exchange. Recent prospectus may be used as part of listing application covering the new securities.	News release, if issued at time of registration, must state from whom prospectus may be obtained. See SEC Rule 134 for permitted content of release at or after initial filing, and SEC Rule 135 for permitted content of release before filing.
Proxy material	Five preliminary copies of proxy form and statement filed with SEC at least 10 days prior to shareholder mailing. Eight finals when sent to holders, plus three to each exchange where listed. Five preliminary copies of additional soliciting material subsequent to proxy to be filed with SEC two days prior to mailing; eight finals, when mailed. See also "Stockholder proposals." SEC has broadened disclosure requirements to include additional information on directors, and has changed form of proxy to provide shareholders greater voice in corporate governance. (11-31-79). Issuer must also disclose in proxy final date for receipt of shareholder proposals.	Immediate newspaper publicity on controversial issues, especially when there is a contest. Four copies of definitive proxy material to Exchange. Ask for advance review in major matters, e.g., to determine Exchange policy; also whether brokers may vote "street name" shares without instructions from customers.	Same as NYSE. Ten copies of all proxy material are required when sent to shareholders.	Normally publicity not needed on routine matters. Press release at time proxy is mailed becoming more common. Press release may constitute "soliciting" material, so caution is advised. Special rules apply in contests; use caution. Corporate responsibility issues: no requirement to identify shareholder proposals by press release prior to meeting. Expanded information on executive compensation is widely used for round-up stories in spring. Review carefully prior to inquiries.

Reporting Required For	Securities and Exchange Commission	New York Stock Exchange	American Stock Exchange	Generally Recommended Publicity Practice All Companies
Questionable or illegal payments	"Voluntary" program requires filing under miscellaneous item of Form 8-K. Guidelines for content published by SEC in May '76. Current proposals would make any management involvement the subject of mandatory disclosure to shareholders. Current proposals also would require management comments on adequacy of internal accounting controls.	No requirement.	No requirement.	Recommend press release conforming to 8-K at time 8-K is filed. However, no technical requirement for publicity. Recommend adoption of company policy statement on ethical business practices.
Redemption, repurchase, cancellation, retirement of listed securities	File 10-Q if amount of securities decrease is greater than 5 percent of amount outstanding. File 8-K and full general disclosure if the transaction is material. File Schedule 13E-4 on or prior to date of commencement of repurchase offer. File Schedule 13E-3 if going private.	Immediate press publicity. Fifteen-day advance notice to Exchange prior to redemption. Prompt notice to Exchange of any corporate or other action affecting securities in whole or in part.	Fifteen-day advance notice to Exchange prior to redemption. Prompt notice of corporate action that will result in any of these.	Usually advertisement is required. Written notice to security holders. News release may be useful.
Rights to subscribe	Registration under the Securities Act of 1933. Prefiling notice covered by SEC Rule 135. Notice to NASD or exchanges 10 days before record date required under Securities Exchange Act antifraud provisions.	See NYSE requirements. Preliminary discussion necessary. Immediate publicity. Important to work out time schedule with Exchange before any action taken. Notice to shareholders in advance of proposed record date.	See Amex requirements. Preliminary discussion necessary. Immediate publicity. Important to work out time schedule with Exchange before any action taken. Notice to shareholders in advance of proposed record date. Subscription period must extend at least 14 days after mailing date.	Immediate publicity and mailing to stockholders to give all adequate time "to record their interest and to exercise their rights," according to NYSE.
Segment reporting: (Line of business reporting)	Required in Forms S-1, 10, 10-K, S-7, S-8 and Schedule 14A. Segment reporting is described in the newly adopted Regulation S-K. Not for quarterly reports.	No requirement. However, "recommended" for inclusion in annual reports.	Same as NYSE.	May be material and require immediate disclosure if there are widely disproportionate and unexpected differences in income from various operations relative to their sales.

Reporting Required For	Securities and Exchange Commission	New York Stock Exchange	American Stock Exchange	Generally Recommended Publicity Practice All Companies
Stockholder proposals	Written notice to management if proponent intends to personally present proposals at a meeting. Proposal must be submitted at least 90 days before management's solicitation begins for annual meeting. ("Reasonable" time for other meetings.) Final date for receipt of shareholder proposal for next annual meeting must be disclosed in proxy materials. To exclude proposal, management must notify shareholder of its intention, send shareholder copy of management's statement and file five copies of it, the proposal and any supporting statement with the SEC not later than 50 days before filing proxy material.	No requirement.	No requirement.	See "Proxy material."
Stock split, stock dividend or other change in capitalization	10-Q required for increase or decrease if exceeds 5 percent of amount of securities of the class previously outstanding. Important: check with legal counsel. Notice to NASD or exchanges 10 days before record date under Securities Exchange Act antifraud provisions.	Immediate public disclosure and Exchange notification. Issuance of new shares requires prior listing approval. "Telephone Alert" procedure should be followed. See Exchange rules for distinguishing stock splits and stock dividends.	Same as NYSE.	Immediate publicity as soon as proposal becomes known to "outsiders" whether formally voted or not.

Reporting Required For	Securities and Exchange Commission	New York Stock Exchange	American Stock Exchange	Generally Recommended Publicity Practice All Companies
Tender offer	Conduct and published remarks of all parties governed by Sections 13 (d), 13 (e), 14 (d) and 14 (e) of the '34 Act and regulations thereunder. Note: Current Schedule 14D-1 increases disclosure required of tender offerers. Subject company required to disclose its position, and its reasons, toward tender offer within 10 days of commencement of offer. File Schedule 14D-9 for any solicitation or recommendation to security holders. SEC likely to further review entire area during '80-'81.	Consult Exchange Stock List Department in advance. Immediate publicity and notice to Exchange.	Consult Exchange Securities Division in advance. Immediate publicity and notice to Exchange.	Massive publicity effort required; should not be attempted without thorough familiarity with current rules and constant consultation with counsel. Neither raider nor target should comment publicly until necessary SEC filings have been made. Note new trap for raider: direct conflict between State and Federal law on timing start of offer.
Treasury stock: Increase or decrease	Check Form 10-Q, items 5 and 6 for possible application. Note: Special rules apply during tender battle.	Notice within 10 days after close of fiscal quarter in which any transaction takes place. Prompt notice of any purchase above prevailing market price.	Same as NYSE. Companies required to notify Exchange on purchases above market price.	Normally no immediate publicity. Reason for action is normally given in annual or quarterly publication before or after event. However, see remarks under "Float," where applicable.
Withdrawal or substitution of assets securing registered securities	10-Q unless made pursuant to terms of an indenture qualified under Trust Indenture Act of 1939.	Immediate notice to Exchange.	Immediate notice to Exchange. Timely disclosure if materially significant for investors.	Depends on terms of indenture.

APPENDIX C

COPYFITTING

You need to fit copy accurately: (1) To determine how much space a given amount of copy will take when set in type; and (2) to determine how much copy to write to fill a predetermined space.

Occasionally both circumstances are important. If an editor has prepared copy and a layout showing space where copy is to go, some adjustment will usually be necessary. The copy will have to be cut (or lengthened) to fit the space or the layout will have to be redesigned to allow more (or less) space for copy, or both.

In either case the principles of copyfitting are the same.

SIZING COPY

To fit copy, an editor must know the type specifications. Among the things that must be determined are:

1. The type face, type size, and amount of leading
2. A "characters per pica" count for the type face
3. The column width of the copy after being set in type
4. The total number of characters in the original copy

The total number of characters (letters and spaces) in the original copy can be precisely counted (in short copy) or estimated (in long copy). Precise counting is rarely used if the copy exceeds one typewritten page.

To estimate the number of characters in typewritten copy, first determine the number of spaces per line. (There are 10 spaces to the inch with pica typewriters; 12 with elite type.) If lines are typed unevenly, you will have to determine an average line length. One way to do this is to draw a straight line down the right margin so that half the lines go beyond your line and half don't reach it. Then measure the number of spaces from the left hand margin to the line you've drawn.

Once the average number of spaces (characters) per line is determined, simply count the total number of lines in the copy and multiply by the number of characters per line. For example, if each typewritten line contains 65 characters, and the copy has 50 lines, the total number of characters is 65 × 50 or 3250.

Partial lines should be counted as full lines, since space will appear at the end of paragraphs.

Once you've determined the total number of characters, you must determine the specifications of the type to be used. The *type face* is simply the name of the style of type you are using—Times Roman, for example. The *type size* is measured in *points*—it takes about 72 points to make 1 inch. Type size in most general publications ranges from 8 point to 12 point.

Leading refers to the amount of space between lines of type. Sometimes type is set solid, that, is, without leading. Often, to improve legibility, the type is leaded 1 or 2 points. This simply means that 1 or 2 points of space is added between each line of type.

Copy space on a layout is usually measured in *picas*—there are 6 picas to the inch. One pica of copy depth is equal to 12 points. Thus one line of 12-point type takes up 1 pica of copy space.

If the type is set solid—no leading—100 lines of 12-point type take up 100 picas, about 16⅔ inches. The general formula for determining copy depth, then, is:

$$\frac{\text{lines of type} \times \text{point size (plus leading)}}{12} = \text{copy depth in picas}$$

Thus, if you used 10-point type with 1-point leading, 100 lines of type would be:

$$\frac{100 \times (10 + 1)}{12} = 91.7 = 92 \text{ picas}$$

Notice that if 10-point type is used, and is leaded 2 points, the number of lines of type is equal to the copy depth in picas.

The number of lines of type can be determined only after the width of each line is known. In other words, how many characters will each line contain?

Type books commonly give a "characters per pica" count for different type faces and sizes. Ten-point Helvetica, for example, has a characters-per-pica count of 2.4. If your copy space is 10 picas wide, then, the number of characters per line will be 24.

SAMPLE COPYFITTING PROBLEMS

Suppose you want to set the original copy—calculated at 3,250 characters—in 10-point Helvetica. The width of a column of type will be 14 picas. How many lines of copy will you have?

Step One: Characters per pica times line width in picas gives characters per line:
2.4 × 14 = 33.6

Step Two: Total characters divided by characters per line gives number of lines:
$$\frac{3250}{33.6} = 96.4 = 97 \text{ lines}$$

Given 97 lines of 10-point type, and 1-point leading, what will the depth of the copy be when set in type?

Step One: Point size (plus leading) times number of lines gives depth in points:
$$(10 + 1) \times 97 = 1067$$

Step Two: Depth in points divided by 12 gives depth in picas.
$$\frac{1067}{12} = 89 \text{ picas}$$

If the copy had been 10-point leaded 2 instead of 1, the copy depth would have equaled the number of lines—97.

Suppose the layout is flexible. You have copy with 3,250 characters. Type face is 10-point Helvetica leaded 2. You want the length of copy when set in type to be 49 lines. How wide will the column of copy have to be?

Step One: Total number of characters divided by number of lines gives characters per line:
$$\frac{3250}{49} = 66.3$$

Step Two: Characters per line divided by characters per pica gives picas per line:
$$\frac{66.3}{2.4} = 27.6 = 28$$

The column width will have to be 28 picas. Finally, you are given a layout with columns 21 picas wide, and you have a depth of 120 picas. Copy must be written to fill the space. If you set your typewriter to provide a 60-space line, how many typewritten lines will be needed to fill the space. (Assume type will be 10-point Helvetica leaded 2 points).

Step One: Characters per pica times line width in picas gives characters per line:
$$2.4 \times 21 = 50.4$$

Step Two: Characters per line times number of lines gives total characters:
$$50.4 \times 120 = 6048 \text{ characters}$$
(number of lines equals depth in picas because type is set 10 point leaded 2).

Step Three: Typewriter lines equals total characters divided by typewriter characters per line:
$$\frac{6048}{60} = 100.8 = 101 \text{ typewritten lines}$$

APPENDIX D

AP STYLE GUIDELINES

Below are summarized some of the basic requirements of newspaper style. News releases intended for general distribution to newspapers should follow these rules. For questions not covered here, writers should refer to the Associated Press or United Press International stylebooks.

ABBREVIATIONS

In general, abbreviate organizations on second reference only if the abbreviation will be easily understood. Use all caps and no periods: NFL, AMA.

Abbreviate Gov., Dr., Rep., Sen., when used before a name.

Abbreviate Ave., Blvd., St., when used with numbered addresses: 1234 Fifth Ave., but the shop on Fifth Avenue.

Abbreviate months Jan., Feb., Aug., Sept., Oct., Nov., and Dec., when used with dates. Spell out other months. Spell out all months when not used with a specific date. Jan. 22, 1972; January 1972; April 22, 1972.

Abbreviate states when given with cities: San Diego, Calif.; a town in California. Use standard abbreviations (W. Va., Fla., Mass., etc.) *not* post office abbreviations. Do *not* abbreviate Texas, Alaska, Hawaii, Idaho, Iowa, Maine, Ohio and Utah.

For times, use figures and a.m. or p.m.: 9 a.m., 2 p.m. Do not use figures for noon and midnight.

Abbreviate Inc. and Jr. but without commas: Texaco Inc.; Joe Smith Jr.

CAPITALIZATION

In general, follow standard capitalization rules, but check stylebook on specific matters. Titles coming before names are generally capitalized; titles after names are lower case. Capitalize the generic part of proper names: Tarrant County. But Tarrant and Dallas counties.

NUMBERS

In general, spell out one through nine, use figures for 10 and above. For percentages, always use figures: 2 percent; 23 percent; 0.9 percent. For speeds, use figures: 3 mph; 55 mph. For temperatures, use figures except for zero: 5 degrees; 68 degrees. For decades, use figures: the 1960s or the '60s. For money use figures: $4; $500,000; $1,000. For large amounts use figures up to two decimal places: $1.65 million; $300 billion; 225 million Americans.

Use commas to separate thousands: 1,253; 4,789. Spell out numbers beginning a sentence except for years: 1976 was a very good year. Two hundred years has passed since the Declaration of Independence. Spell out casual expressions: Thanks a million; I wish I had a thousand dollars.

PUNCTUATION

Periods and commas *always* go inside quotation marks: He said he was "incredulous." Her best songs are "Fooled by a Feeling," "Years," and "Darlin'." He said, "My favorite is 'Fooled by a Feeling.'"

Other marks are placed according to the sense of the sentence: He asked, "Did you say 'Fooled by a Feeling'?" "What's in it for me?" What song comes after "Fooled by a Feeling"? He responded by saying "I don't know"; I then asked somebody else.

Do not use a comma in conjunction with other marks: "What do you want?" he asked. (NOT "What do you want?," he asked.)

SPELLING

Follow AP/UPI spelling on the following words. Some of them are commonly misspelled; some are exceptions to the spelling given by some dictionaries.

adviser	Dr Pepper	sacrilegious
barbiturate	employee	supersede
canceled	fluorescent	totaled
canceling	impostor	totaling
catalog	judgment	traveled
cataloged	memento	traveling
cigarette	minuscule	weird
dialogue	percent	X-ray
dietitian	questionnaire	OK
disc jockey	restaurateur	

INDEX

Abbreviations, style guideline, 356
Abstract. *See* Synopsis
Accuracy:
   importance of, in brochure, 259–260
   importance of, in news release, 114
   vs. clarity, in annual reports, 222–225
Acting, as step in persuasion process, 18
Action memo, 284
Active voice, use, in broadcast style, 145
Address, form of, in letter, 298
Advertising, defined, 4
Advertising copy, writing, 151–198
   broadcast, 154–178
   as persuasion, 151–154
   in print media, 179–189
Advertising Council, 188
Advocacy advertising, 188–189
Agenda setting, 24
Ambiguity, avoiding, as purpose for grammar, 70–71
Amplifying the lead, in news release, 100–101
Analogy, use:
   to clarify writing, 65
   in writing magazine articles, 246
Analyzing, role in public relations, 3–4
Anecdotes, using, in writing magazine articles, 246
Angle, finding, for magazine article, 241–242
Animation, in television advertising, 155
Announcement release, 106
Announcer format, 155
Annual reports, 222–238
   clarity vs. accuracy in, 222–225
   examples, 230–231, 232–233, 234
   planning, 225–227
   writing, 227–229, 235–237

Appendix, for report or proposal, 301
Applicability, in report or proposal, 301–302
Appositives, comma usage with, 80
AP stylebook. *See* Associated Press stylebook
The Art of Readable Writing, 70
Asimov, Isaac, 63
Associated Press Broadcast stylebook, phonetic guidelines in, 144
Associated Press stylebook, 74, 75, 77, 79, 105, 356
As vs. *like*, use, 69–70
Attending, as step in persuasion process, 17–18
Attitude formation, model of, 13–15
Attitudes, compared to opinions, 13
Audience:
   determining, for annual report, 226–227
   as element in communication, 24–25
   knowing, before writing, 47, 200–201
Audio copy, place on television script page, 137, 156
Available information, role in attitude formation, 14

Background, in position paper, 276
Backgrounders, 265–267, 274–275, 277–280
   defined, 266
   documentation, 274–275
   examples, 279–280
   format, 277–278
   research, 267
   writing, 267, 274
Background research, before writing magazine article, 242–243

Bad-news release, 109
Barzun, Jacques, 31, 35
Bernays, Edward L., 4, 5, 12, 90
Bernstein, Theodore, 71, 71n, 75
Bibliographies, as research source, 31
Billboard advertising, 185
   example, 186
Body, for report or proposal, 300–301
Boise Cascade, 188
Booklet, defined, 251
Both sides of story, importance of giving, 21
Brevity, importance of:
   in broadcast advertising, 155
   in broadcast style, 136
Broadcast advertising, preparing, 154–178
   commercials, 156–157, 158–164, 166–172
   public service announcements, 157, 165, 173–178
Broadcast writing, 120–150
   crises, 126–127
   mini-docs, 128, 134–135
   news conferences, 126
   news releases, 127–128, 129–133
   special events fact sheet, 120–126
   style, 135–149
   talk shows, 128
Brochures, 258–264
   defined, 251
   designing layout and writing copy to fit, 262–264
   example, 260–261
   purpose, 258–259
   writing, 259–261
Brock, Luther, 69
Bulletin memo, 283

Capitalization, style guideline, 356
Cardozo, Benjamin, 223
Cardstacking, 276

INDEX

The Careful Writer, 71, 75
Carpenter, Liz, 78
Chall, Jeanne, 334
Channels of communication, choosing, 8–9. *See also* Medium
Character counting, 263, 353–354
Chiles, Eddie, 189
Churchill, Winston, 73
Church newsletter, 252
Circular, defined, 251
Clarity:
  importance of, in broadcast style, 136
  vs. accuracy, in annual reports, 222–225
  writing for, 46–55
Classified display newspaper advertising, 179
Classified newspaper advertising, 184
Clio Awards, 188
Cloze procedure, 336
Club newsletter, 252
Cognitive design of persuasion, 15–16
Colleges, advertising for, 188
Colored paper, editors' dislike of, 115
Column notes, news release in, 109, 112, 113
Commas, punctuation rules with, 79
Commercials, preparing, 156–157, 158–164, 166–172
  examples, 158–164, 166–172
  radio scripts, 157
  television scripts, 156–157
Common Cause, 252
Commonly confused words, 74
Communication:
  channels of, choosing, 8–9
  elements of, 19–25
  as goal and purpose of writing, 46, 69
  as goal of public relations, 5, 10
Comprehending, as step in persuasion process, 18
Computerized news release, example, 116–117
Concept, determining, for brochure, 259
Conclusion:
  importance of explicit, in persuasion, 22
  writing, for speech, 203
Consequence, evaluating magazine article topics by, 241
Consistency, in good punctuation, 78

Content, in annual report, 227–235
  executive's letter, 227–228, 230–231
  narrative, 228–229, 232–233
Contractions:
  use, in broadcast style, 145
  use, for naturalness in writing, 52
Conversational style:
  how to achieve, 52
  importance of in broadcasting, 136
Copy depth, determining, 354
Copyfitting, 262–264, 353–355
Corporate employee newsletters, 252
Corporate reporting requirements, 338–352
Counseling, role in public relations, 3–4
Cover letter, for report or proposal, 300
"Created news" release, 107
Credibility, importance of in communication, 19–20
Crises, handling, 126–127
Customer interview, in advertising, 155

Dale, Edgar, 334
Dale-Chall readability formula, 335–336
Danielson-Bryan readability formula, 337
Data vs. *datum,* use, 71, 71n, 75
Date, indicating, in broadcast style, 145
"Dead fish and live babies" syndrome, 248
De Beers, 188
Definition vs. description, use, 62–63
Demographics:
  defined, 7
  importance of to advertising, 152, 153
Description:
  use, instead of definition, for simple writing, 62–63
  use, in writing magazine article, 248
Designing brochure and newsletter, 262–264
Designs for Persuasive Communication, 15
Designs of persuasion, 15–16
  cognitive, 15–16
  motivational, 16

  personality, 16
  social, 16
  stimulus-response, 15
Development, use, in writing magazine article, 245
Dictionary of American-English Usage, 75
Direct response and direct mail advertising, 185, 187
"Discrepancy effects," 25
Display newspaper advertising, 179–180
  examples, 180–183
Division of labor in public relations, 4
Documentation, in backgrounder, 274–275
Donut format, 155
Dramatization, in writing magazine article, 247

Effect, as element in communication, 25
Einstein, Albert, 57
"Elegant variation," 53
The Elements of Style, 72, 75
Emotion, appeal to, importance of in advertising, 152
Emotional process, persuasion as, 15
Emotional vs. factual arguments, using, 22
Employee publications. *See* Magazines
Essay memo, 284
Euphony, achieving in writing, 54
Examples, using, in writing magazine article, 246
Executive's letter, in annual report, 227–228
  example, 230–231
Expertise, relation to credibility, 20
External publics, 7

Fabun, Don, 248
Facts, importance of in advertising, 152
Facts on File, 32
Factual vs. emotional arguments, using, 22
Familiar, using to explain unfamiliar, 65–67
Fan club newsletters, 252
Fear techniques, using, 22
Feature release, 109
Files of institutions, as research source, 32

INDEX

Finding Facts, 31
First World Assembly of Public Relations Associations, 3
First World Forum of Public Relations, 3
Flesch, Rudolf, 48, 51, 54, 57, 58, 70, 72, 236, 334
Flesch readability formula, 334–335, 336
Flyer, defined, 251
Fog count, 154
Fog index (Gunning), 224, 335
Follett, Wilson, 71n, 75
Formal letter, defined, 282
Form and style of news release, 104–106, 112, 114
Format, for backgrounder and position paper, 277–278
  examples, 279–280
Form of address, in letter, 298
Fowler, H. W., 71n, 75
Freedom of Information Act, 32
Front matter, for report or proposal, 299–300

Gestalt, relation to Cloze procedure, 336
Gestures, planning, for speech, 204
Gladden, Don, 189
Good news, giving first, 21
Government offices, as research source, 32
Graff, Henry F., 31, 35
Gramm, Phil, 256
Grammar, 69–75
  to avoid ambiguity, 70–71
  myths of, 72–73
  using usage manuals, 73–75
Gray, William, 334
Greeley, Horace, 90
Gropp, Marvin M., 152
Guest column, news release in, 109, 112, 113
Gunning, Robert, 48, 49, 51, 69, 70, 104, 222, 223, 224, 236, 237, 334
Gunning's readability formula, 335, 336

The Harper Dictionary of Contemporary Usage, 71n, 75
Hierarchy of needs (Maslow), 16, 17
Historical setting, role in attitude formation, 14
House ad:
  defined, 151
  preparing, 189

"How Source Affects Response to Public Service Advertising," 165
Human interest, achieving in writing, 54
Human interest formula (Flesch), 335
Humanization, in writing magazine article, 247
Humor technique, 155
Hyphens, use, in broadcast writing, 144

The Iconoclast, 32
Identification of individual, avoiding, in broadcast style, 136
Identity advertising, 187–189
  examples, 190–198
Illustration, in writing magazine articles, 245–246
Image advertising, 187–189
  examples, 190–198
Implementing a script, 205–206
Informal letter, defined, 282
Informative memo, 284
"Inoculation" effect, 21
Institutional advertising, 187–189
  examples, 190–198
Interest:
  evaluating magazine article topics by, 241
  writing for, 46–55
Internal publics, 7
Interviewing:
  as primary research technique, 32–33
  before writing annual report narrative, 229
  before writing magazine article, 243
Introduction to speech, writing, 203, 203–204
Inverted sentence structure, avoiding, in broadcast style, 136

Jargon:
  avoiding, in writing, 60–62
  how to use if necessary, in broadcast style, 145
Jingle, use in advertising, 155
Johnson, Lady Bird, 78
"Journalese," avoiding, in broadcast writing, 136
Journalism Quarterly, 165

Keats, John, 70
Kiplinger Report, 258
Klare, George, 334

Language patterns of audience, importance of to speech writer, 200–201
Lasswell, Harold, elements of communication, 19–25
Layouts, designing, for newsletters and brochures, 262–264
Lead:
  amplifying, in news release, 100–101
  in broadcast style, 145
  writing, for magazine article, 244–245
  writing, for news release, 91, 100
Leading, defined, 354
Leaflet, defined, 251
Learning process, persuasion as, 15
Leary, Bernice, 334
Lee, Ivy, 89
Length, appropriate:
  for letter, 298, 299
  for news release, 104
Lerbinger, Otto, 15, 19, 106
Lesly, Philip, 89
Letter of transmittal, for report or proposal, 300
Letters and memos, 281–299
  differences, 282–283
  letters, 285, 295–299
  memos, 283–285, 286–294
  similarities, 281–282
Letter to editor, news release in, 109, 112, 113
Library, as research source, 31
Library of Congress, as research source, 32
Like vs. *as*, use, 69–70
Liking for source, effect on persuasion, 20
Literal sense of public relations, 2
Live action, in television advertising, 155
Local angle, importance of, in news release, 100
Lyndon Baines Johnson Library, 31

McGuire, William, 17, 19n, 20, 22
McLuhan, Marshall, 23
Magazine article, writing, 244–248, 249
  anecdotes, 246
  checklist, 249
  description, 248

INDEX

development, 245
dramatization, 247
humanization, 247
lead, 244–245
quotations, 246–247
verification and illustration, 245–246
Magazine Publishers Association, 152, 154
Magazines:
advertising in, 184–185
employee publications, 248–249
research before writing, 242–243
as research source, 31–32
topics for articles, 240–242
writing articles for, 244–248, 249
Mailer, Norman, 70
Main idea, making clear, in writing, 64–65
Marlow, James, 101
Marstellar, Inc., 188
Maslow, Abraham, 16, 17
The Mass Media, 6
Mass media, defined, 9
Matching visuals to words, in script, 206
Material, researching, 28–29
Media, defined, 9. *See also* Medium
mass, 9
specialized, 9
Medium:
choosing, for news release, 114–115
credibility ranking of types, 24
as element in communication, 23–24
face to face vs. mass, 23
knowing, before writing, 47–48
researching before choosing, 29
spoken vs. written, 23
writing for specific, 153–154
Memos and letters, 281–299
differences, 282–283
letters, 285, 295–299
memos, 283–285, 286–294
similarities, 281–282
Message:
as element in communication, 20–22
knowing before writing, 47
research as help in writing, 29
Me vs. *myself*, use, 72
"Miles an hour," in broadcast style, 145
"Miles per hour," in broadcast style, 145
Mini-docs, preparing, 128, 135
example, 134
Mini-documentary. *See* Mini-docs

Modern American Usage, 75
Modern English Usage, 71n, 75
The Modern Researcher, 31
Money-maker, newsletter as a, 252, 256–258
Motivational design of persuasion, 16
Myself vs. *me*, use, 72
Myths of grammar, 72–73

Names and titles, use, in broadcast style, 145
Narrative, in annual report, 228–229
example, 232–233
National Investor Relations Institute, 223
Naturalness, achieving, in writing, 52
News:
defined, 89
finding, 89–90
getting it into print, 90–91
News conference, handling, 126
Newsletters, 251–258, 262–264
defined, 251
examples, 253–257
purposes, 251–252, 256–258
writing, designing, and fitting, 262–264
Newspaper Foundation, 154
Newspapers, advertising in, 179–184
classified, 184
display, 179–183
examples, 180–183
News releases, 88–118, 127–133
examples, 92–99, 102–103, 108, 110–111, 116–117, 129–133
preparing and delivering, 112, 114–115, 127–128
recognizing and finding news for, 88–91
when to send, 115
writing, 91, 100–101, 104–107, 109, 112
Newsworthiness, determining, 90–91
New York Times Index, 31, 202
Nicholson, Margaret, 75
None is, use, 71, 72
Nonrestrictive clauses, use of comma with, 79
Numbers:
style guideline, 357
use, in broadcast writing, 145

Objective, finding, for advertising copy, 153
Objectivity, relation to credibility, 20
O'Dwyer's Newsletter, 258
One step at a time, in simple writing, 63–64
On Writing Well, 46
Opinion formation and change, 13–15
Opinion Research Corporation, 229
Organizing:
a speech, 203
stored research, 30
Outdoor and transit advertising, 185
example, 186
Oxford English Dictionary, 72

Pamphlet, defined, 251
Paring of speech, 202
Parker, Captain John, 51
Passive voice, using, in writing, 53
Pavlov, 15
Periodicals. *See* Magazines
Personality design of persuasion, 16
Personality processes and predispositions, role in attitude formation, 14
Persuasion, 12–26
advertising as, 151–154
in communication, 19–25
nature of, 15–19
opinion formation and change, 13–15
in a speech, 202
steps in process, 17–19
Phonetics, using, in broadcast writing, 143–144
Pica, defined, 354
Plain English, using in writing, 60–63
avoiding jargon, 60–62
describing vs. defining, 62–63
Planning a script, 205
Points, defined, 354
Politicians and elected officials, newsletters of, 252
example, 256–257
Position, stating, in position paper, 276–277
considering audience, 277
considering both sides, 276–277
Positioning, defined, 152
Position papers, 265–266, 268–273, 275–278
background, 276

INDEX

Position papers (continued)
  defined, 266, 275
  example, 268-273
  format, 277-278
  position, 276-277
  recommendations, 277
  stating the issue, 275
Power, perceived, effect on persuasion, 20
Power process, persuasion as, 15
Predicting, role in public relations, 3-4
Presentation, as step in persuasion process, 17
Presenting of stored research, 30
Primary sources of research, 32-34, 36-39
  interviewing, 32-33
  questionnaires, 33-34, 36-39
PR News, 258
Professional sense of public relations, 2
Pronouns, use, in broadcast style, 145
Pronunciation clues, use, in broadcast writing, 143-144
  AP style, 144
Proposals and reports, 282, 283, 299-302
  differences, 283
  organization, 299-301
  readability and applicability, 301-302
  similarities, 282
pr reporter, 258
PSAs. See Public service announcements
Psychographics:
  defined, 8
  importance of to advertising, 152, 153
Public, defined, 5
  varieties of, 6-7
Publicity, defined, 4
Public records, as source of research, 32
Public relations, defined, 2-5
Public Relations Society of America, 4
Public service announcements:
  defined, 151
  examples, 173-178
  preparing, 157, 165, 173-178
  radio scripts, 165
  television scripts, 165
Punctuation:
  style guideline, 357
  in writing, 78-80

Purpose of annual report, determining, 225-226

Questionnaire:
  use in research, and example, 33-34, 36-39
  use in writing annual report, and example, 229, 235, 236
Quotation marks, punctuation with, 78-79
Quotations, using:
  in broadcast style, 144
  in magazine article, 246-247
  in news release, 101

Radio, writing for. See Broadcast writing
Radio advertising. See Broadcast advertising
Radio scripts for commercials, preparing, 157
  examples, 169-172
Readability:
  achieving, in writing, 48-51
  formulas, 51, 334-337
  in report or proposal, 301-302
Reader interest, evaluating magazine article topics by, 241
Readers' Guide to Periodical Literature, 32, 201, 242
Recommendations, in position paper, 277
Reference groups, 152
References, for report or proposal, 301
Reference works, as research source, 31
Repetition, importance of, 25
Reports and proposals, 282, 283, 299-302
  differences, 283
  organization, 299-301
  readability and applicability, 301-302
  similarities, 282
Research, using:
  before speech-writing, 201-202
  before writing advertising, 154
  before writing backgrounder, 267
  before writing magazine article, 242-243
  general techniques, 28-40
Response release, 107
  example, 108

Restrictive clauses:
  use of comma with, 79
  which vs. *that*, 70
Retaining the new position, as step in persuasion process, 18
Reusing of stored research, 30
Rivers, William L., 6, 31, 246
Rotoscope, in television advertising, 155
Routing a memo, 284-285

Sales promotion advertising, 187
Scripts, preparing, 204-206
  compared to speech, 205
  examples, 208-209, 210-217
  implementing, 205-206
  matching script and visuals, 206
  planning, 205
Secondary research sources, 31-32
Sentence-ending prepositions, 73
Sentence length, importance to readability, 49-50, 334
Sheet, defined, 185
Simplifying the complex, in writing, 57-68
  explaining familiar with unfamiliar, 65-67
  explaining one step at a time, 63-64
  knowing subject, 58-60
  making central points clear, 64-65
  using plain English, 60-63
Skepticism, importance to research, 35, 40
Slant. See Angle
"Sleeper" effect, 25
Slice of life technique, 155
Slug line, 143
Smith, M. Brewster, 13
Social design of persuasion, 16
Social environment, role in attitude formation, 14
Source, as element in communication, 19-20
Sources for researchers, 30-35, 36-39
  primary, 32-34, 36-39
  secondary, 31-32
Special events, handling, 120-126
  actual coverage, 121, 126
  advance preparation, 120-121
  example, 122-125
Specialized media, defined, 9
Speech, preparing a, 200-204
  compared to script, 205
  organization, 203

INDEX

paring, 202
persuading, 202
planning, 201–202
style, 203–204
Spelling:
 importance of good, 76–78
 style guideline, 357–358
Split infinitives, 72–73
Sports newsletter, 258
Spot news release, 107
Stating the issue, in position paper, 275
Statistical Abstract of the United States, 32
Stimulus-response design of persuasion, 15
Stone, I. W., 32
Storage and retrieval of research results, 29–30
Storyboard, drafting, 157
 examples, 166–168
Strunk, William, 75
Style:
 elements of, in writing, 48–55
 for annual report, 236–237
 for broadcast advertising, 155
 for broadcast writing, 135–149
 for news release, 104–106
 for speech, 203–204
Style year, 337
Subject, knowing your, importance to simple writing, 58–60
Subject-verb agreement, 71
Summary memo, 284
"Swiss cheese" approach, with PSAs, 173
Synopsis, for report or proposal, 300

Talk shows, preparing for, 128
Target audiences:
 defined, 7
 selecting, 7–8
Taylor, Wilson, 336
The Technique of Clear Writing, 336
Techniques, in broadcast advertising, 155–156
Television, writing for. *See* Broadcast writing
Television advertising. *See* Broadcast advertising
Television Information Office, 154
Television scripts for commercials, preparing, 156–157
 examples, 158–164, 166–168
Tel-Med, 258
Testing advertising copy, 154
That vs. *which*, use, 70
Theme, choosing:
 for annual report, 235
 for speech, 203
Thesaurus, using, 54
"30," use, in broadcast writing, 143
Time of day, indicating, in broadcast style, 145
Titles, use, in broadcast style, 145
Topics, for magazine articles, 240–242
 angle, finding, 241–242
 evaluating, 241
 finding, 240–241
Tract, defined, 251
Trade associations, advertising for, 188
TV. *See* Television
"24 sheets" billboard, 185
"Two-step flow" theory of mass communication, 24
Type face, defined, 354
Type size, defined, 354

Unfamiliar, explaining with the familiar, 65–67

United Press International stylebook, 71n, 75, 77, 105, 356
Universities, advertising for, 188
UPI stylebook. *See* United Press International stylebook
Updating of stored research, 30
Usage manuals, using, 73–75

Variety, achieving in writing, 52–54
Verification, importance of:
 in research, 34–35
 in writing magazine articles, 245–246
Video instructions, place on television script page, 137, 156
Voice-over, defined, 165

Wall Street Journal, 247
Webster's New World Dictionary of the American Language, 105
Webster's Third New International, 105
Western Company, 189
What Makes a Book Readable, 334
Which vs. *that*, use, 70
White, E. B., 72, 75
Wire stories, style, 148
Wood, Alden, Sr., 51
Word length, importance to readability, 50–51, 334
Words commonly confused, 74
Words Into Type, 74, 80
Writer's Hotline, 74
Wylie, Frank, 4

Yielding, as step in persuasion process, 18

Zinsser, William, 46, 58, 222, 244

CREDITS

Illustration 3-2, pp. 36-39. Reprinted by permission of the American Heart Association, Austin, TX.

Chapter 3, pp. 41-42. Reprinted by permission of the Dallas Times Herald, Dallas, TX.

Illustration 5-1, p. 66. Reprinted by permission of the Texas Electric Service Company, Fort Worth, TX.

Chapter 5, pp. 66-67. © 1979 by The New York Times Company. Reprinted by permission.

Illustration 7-6, p. 113. Reprinted by permission of Fort Worth Star-Telegram, Fort Worth, TX.

Illustration 8-2, pp. 129-133, illustration 8-4, pp. 137-143. Reprinted by permission of National Trust for Historic Preservation, Washington, D. C.

Chapter 8, p. 144; illustration 8-5, pp. 146-147; illustration 8-6, p. 148. Reprinted by permission of The Associated Press, New York, NY.

Illustration 8-7, p. 149. Reprinted by permission of The Wall Street Journal, New York, NY.

Illustration 9-1, pp. 158-162. Reprinted by permission of Jerre R. Todd & Associates, Fort Worth, TX.

Illustration 9-1, pp. 163-164. Reprinted by permission of Jim Haynes, KCBN, Inc., Dallas, TX.

Illustration 9-3, p. 168. Reprinted by permission of General Electric Company, Fairfield, CN.

Illustration 9-4, pp. 169-170. Reprinted by permission of Champlin Petroleum Company, Fort Worth, TX, and Weekley & Associates, Fort Worth, TX.

Illustration 9-4, pp. 171, 172. Reprinted by permission of Jim Haynes, KCBN, Inc., Dallas, TX.

Illustration 9-6, pp. 180-183. Reprinted by permission of Jim Haynes, KCBN, Inc., Dallas, TX.

Illustration 9-7, p. 186. Reprinted by permission of Philip Poole Associates, Fort Worth, TX.

Illustration 9-8, p. 190. Reprinted by permission of Tenneco, Inc., Houston, TX.

Illustration 9-8, p. 191. Reprinted by permission of American Quasar Petroleum Company.

Illustration 9-8, pp. 192-193. Reprinted by permission of Chemical Manufacturers Association.

Illustration 9-8, p. 194. Reprinted by permission of The Advertising Council, Inc., New York, NY.

Illustration 9-8, p. 195. Reprinted by permission of Mobil Corporation, New York, NY.

Illustration 9-8, p. 197. © 1980 by The New York Times Company. Reprinted by permission.

Illustration 9-8, p. 198. Reprinted by permission of Exxon Corporation, New York, NY.

Illustration 10-1, pp. 208-209. Reprinted by permission of McKone & Company, Fort Worth, TX.

Illustration 10-2, pp. 210-217. Reprinted by permission of Michael O'Shea, Dallas, TX.

Illustration 11-1, pp. 230-231. Reprinted by permission of Exxon Corporation, New York, NY.

Illustration 11-2, pp. 232-234; illustration 11-3, p. 236; illustration 11-4, p. 237. Reprinted by permission of World Industries, Inc., Lancaster, PA.

Illustration 13-1, p. 253. Reprinted by permission of Browder & Associates, Fort Worth, TX.

Illustration 13-2, p. 254. Reprinted by permission of Witherspoon & Associates, Fort Worth, TX.

Illustration 13-3, p. 255. Reprinted by permission of First National Bank of Fort Worth, Fort Worth, TX.

Illustration 13-5, pp. 260-261. Reprinted by permission of the American Heart Association, Austin, TX.

Illustration 14-2, pp. 279-280. Reprinted by permission of the Texas Electric Service Company, Fort Worth, TX.

Illustration 15-2, p. 295. Reprinted by permission of the North Texas Commission, Arlington, TX.

Illustration 15-3, pp. 296-297. Reprinted by permission of Cox's, Fort Worth, TX.

Corporate Reporting Requirements, pp. 338-352. Prepared by Robert W. Taft, Sr., Vice President, Financial Relations Division, Hill & Knowlton, New York, NY. Reprinted by permission.